PENGUIN  CLASSICS

METAPHYSICS

ARISTOTLE was born at Stageira, in the dominion of the kings of Macedonia, in 384 BC. For twenty years he studied at Athens in the Academy of Plato, on whose death in 347 he left, and, some time later, became tutor of the young Alexander the Great. When Alexander succeeded to the throne of Macedonia in 335, Aristotle returned to Athens and established his school and research institute, the Lyceum, to which his great erudition attracted a large number of scholars. After Alexander's death in 323, anti-Macedonian feeling drove Aristotle out of Athens, and he fled to Chalcis in Euboea, where he died in 322. His writings, which were of extraordinary range, profoundly affected the whole course of ancient and medieval philosophy, and they are still eagerly studied and debated by philosophers today. Very many of them have survived and among the most famous are the *Ethics* and the *Politics*.

HUGH LAWSON-TANCRED was born in 1955 and educated at Eton and Balliol College, Oxford. He is currently a Departmental Fellow in the Department of Philosophy at Birkbeck College in the University of London. He has published extensively on Aristotle and Plato and is engaged in research in the philosophy of linguistics and cognitive science. He also translates widely from the Slavonic and Scandinavian languages. His translations of Aristotle's *The Art of Rhetoric* and *De Anima* are also published in Penguin Classics. He is married with a daughter and a son and lives in north London and Somerset.

ARISTOTLE
Metaphysics

Translated with an introduction by
HUGH LAWSON-TANCRED

PENGUIN BOOKS

PENGUIN BOOKS

Published by the Penguin Group
Penguin Books Ltd, 27 Wrights Lane, London w8 5tz, England
Penguin Putnam Inc., 375 Hudson Street, New York, New York 10014, USA
Penguin Books Australia Ltd, Ringwood, Victoria, Australia
Penguin Books Canada Ltd, 10 Alcorn Avenue, Toronto, Ontario, Canada m4v 3b2
Penguin Books (NZ) Ltd, 182–190 Wairau Road, Auckland 10, New Zealand

Penguin Books Ltd, Registered Offices: Harmondsworth, Middlesex, England

This translation first published 1998
3 5 7 9 10 8 6 4

Set in 10/12.5 pt Monotype Bembo
Typeset by Rowland Phototypesetting Ltd, Bury St Edmunds, Suffolk
Printed in England by Clays Ltd, St Ives plc

PARENTIBUS OPTIMIS

CONTENTS

PREFACE

There are, no doubt, some books of which it can be justly claimed that they will both prove invaluable for the new student and be a source of stimulation for experienced readers. This is not such a book. Indeed, I have doubts about the extent to which such a work can be produced on the subject, at any rate, of Aristotelian metaphysics.

Forced, therefore, into choosing between an exoteric or an esoteric translation of the *Metaphysics*, I have complied with the constraints of time and of the limitations of my own competence in seeking to address myself *orbi* rather than *urbi*. The result, I hope, will be a useful, if humble, rung on the Wittgensteinian ladder up which anyone seeking to become acquainted with Aristotle's central ruminations on the substance of the world must climb.

Three brief acknowledgements. I would like to express my gratitude to the Philosophy Department of Birkbeck College, to whom I am indebted for an extraordinary amount of philosophical stimulation and encouragement over the last ten years. During the course of making this translation, I became a husband and a father. This experience has caused me to wonder whether Aristotle may exaggerate the importance of what persists through any change. An older debt of similar nature is acknowledged by the Dedication.

H. C. L.-T.

Queens Park
June 1998

INTRODUCTION

1. Substance

What is the purpose of studying metaphysics, and what is the purpose of studying the *Metaphysics*? It has been argued in the twentieth century (and before) with great force, elegance and coherence that there is no point in studying either, and indeed that the temptation to take seriously the latter and perhaps also the former can only be a source of deep philosophical perplexity. On the other hand, in previous philosophical epochs metaphysics was routinely regarded as the pinnacle of philosophical speculation and the *Metaphysics* was effectively taken to be its founding charter. There have been many great thinkers for whom the most important question in philosophy has been what response we should make to the claims of metaphysicians in general and of Aristotle in particular.

Of course, we cannot tell the value of metaphysics until we have agreed what it is, nor that of the *Metaphysics* until its central doctrines are at least provisionally familiar. In this introduction I shall say a little about the ambitions and limitations of metaphysical thinking and then try to show why Aristotle's treatise should be considered a paradigm of such thinking, whatever attitude we come to take to its central claims. I also broach two other topics. The first concerns the peculiar nature of the *Metaphysics* as a composition (some would say a compilation). The general architecture of the work is fraught with problems, and there are intriguing and important issues about just how the text that we have before us came into being. The second topic I discuss is the nature and purpose of the present translation.

Many philosophers, conspicuously including Aristotle, as we shall see, have held the view that the understanding of anything either depends on or is profoundly facilitated by obtaining the correct definition of it at the start of one's investigation. If this is right, then it seems certain that we cannot reach understanding of philosophy itself, and certainly not of metaphysics. Many attempts have been made to put into a nutshell the core project of the metaphysician, but severally and collectively they serve only to show that the subject is too elusive and strange to be pinned down in any very manageable way. The nature of metaphysics can only be indicated, if at all, by suggestion rather than stipulation. And perhaps the best way to suggest its nature is to contrast it with other forms of inquiry, and especially with science. The nature of science itself is hardly perspicuous, but it will perhaps be agreed that science attempts to clarify the structure and processes of our world through the patient observation of its sensible phenomena and the cautious or bold construction of hypotheses that are in some way answerable to such observations. The conclusions of science are provisional, their confirmation holistically sensitive to the repercussions of events across the whole range of our experience. This sensitivity of the conclusions of science seems ambiguous and has always been taken in two ways, either as an indication that the scientist is responding to a pattern outside himself to which he must constantly adjust his assumptions or as a reason for deep scepticism about the capacity of the whole enterprise to deliver a convincing picture of the world.

If the latter attitude is adapted to the evolving image that science offers, then this can either be the occasion of a more comprehensive scepticism which holds that there are, quite generally, severe restrictions on the understanding that we can have in any way of our predicament or lead to the desire to seek some more secure, and therefore fundamental, form of knowledge about the world which will not be thus vulnerable to the fluctuations of theoretical fashion. This desire is the point of departure for metaphysics. What the metaphysician is after is a comprehensive account of how the world is that is somehow immune to the uncertainties overshadowing all our reflections on the course and content of our experience. The metaphysician wants to understand the world once and for all.

But how is such understanding to be obtained? Well, two ways in which the world may be available to non-scientific comprehension are that advocated by the religious believer (who may well also be disposed to acknowledge absolute moral values) and that of the mystic (who may also be unusually sensitive to aesthetic experience). The believer standardly lays claim to an understanding of the world that is based on the revelations of a higher Person, and the mystic will insist that certain episodes or aspects of his or her experience are endowed with a value and significance that gives him or her the authority to make broad pronouncements on the arrangement of the world. Neither of these approaches is necessarily incompatible with the project of metaphysics, but neither are they constitutive of it. They both purport to provide the kind of knowledge that the metaphysician wants, but they go about it in ways that are not his.

What is distinctive of metaphysics is that it is, like science, a rational project. What this means is that the metaphysician purports to give grounds for his large conclusions that are not founded either on the appeal to divine authority or on a claim to experience of a privileged kind. The metaphysician aspires, and pretends, to reach his conclusions by logical arguments commencing from assumptions which would be readily accepted by any reasonable person. From the pig's ear of our experience he fashions the silk purse of his vision of the cosmos.

Kant, for instance, starts from the truism that our experience contains particular phenomena between which our minds see general patterns and concludes that the world that we know is the product of the interaction of occult faculties which are constitutive of our subjectivity and that the world in itself is utterly beyond our scrutiny. Russell notes that many sentences of ordinary language are compositions of simpler sentences, with independent meanings of their own, and concludes that the world must ultimately be made up of atomic units whose mutual disconnection is not a chance of nature but a logical necessity. Plato remarks that the descriptions that we give of objects in our world are usually in some way relative to the context of presentation and he passes from this to the conclusion that reality consists of a world of eternal and unchanging entities, of which the world we know is merely a pale reflection. And so on. Always the process is the same: the input is simple, even banal, features of our daily dealings with the world, the output an extraordinary and dramatic reassessment of the fundamental structure of that world.

The metaphysician, then, is open to the objection that, even if we concede the desirability of the sort of knowledge that he seeks, his pretensions to deliver such knowledge are preposterous. After all, someone with no philosophical commitments might think, it is not at all obvious that the claims of a religious believer or a mystic cannot be true, for all the diversity and contrariety of such claims. But it seems excessively implausible that mere rumination on some of the more elementary features of our quotidian experience could lead to a profound revision of our conception of the universe.

It is at this point that consideration of the nature of metaphysics intersects with that of its value. The gap between the premises of metaphysical arguments and their conclusions is indeed characteristically stupendous, and the probability that those conclusions are in any sense right or in any way illuminating is no doubt infinitesimal. It is indeed very plausible to suppose that the critics are right to object that something fundamental is wrong with the entire project, that the urge to metaphysics is a chimera bred of the failure to discern the workings of our conceptual scheme or our language. The history of philosophy is the history of the shift of confidence away from the possibility of direct insights into the world, first towards that of insights into the mind of the knowing subject and latterly towards that of insights into the logical structure of language.

Such objections have dominated the philosophical stage of the century that is shortly to end. Yet it is a remarkable fact that at the end of it sympathy for the project of metaphysics is as great as perhaps it has ever been. The great metaphysicians of the past, none more than Aristotle, are studied with minute care and the connections between their thinking and that of contemporary philosophers are matters of intense discussion. This is indeed remarkable, but we need not look far for an explanation. It lies in the fact that the great metaphysical systems contain deep and fascinating philosophical *arguments*, the value of which in no way depends on their logical validity, still less on the correctness of their premises. Anselm's celebrated ontological argument for the existence of God, once dismissed as a monstrous humbug, is now subjected to rigorous dissection. Descartes' often ridiculed claim that 'I think, therefore I am' still baffles the intellectual heirs of Frege and Wittgenstein. The history of metaphysics is a history of magnificent failures, and it is their magnificence that we now remember and revere, their failure that is buried with their bones.

Let us now turn to Aristotle. Even if we allow that there is value in the study of metaphysics irrespective of the status of its conclusions, why Aristotle? Why a thinker who has been dead for 2,300 years and who has frequently been stigmatized, even demonized, as an impediment to the natural growth of human knowledge and understanding? This is really a historical question and to answer it one must give a little of the historical background to Aristotle's achievement.

By the time that Aristotle started to think about philosophy, the subject was already nearly two hundred years old. It had begun with the attempts of various remarkable and apparently isolated thinkers in Ionia, the Aegean coast of modern Turkey, to generalize about the commonalities that underlie the changing appearance of physical things. If things as apparently diverse as a cloud and a plant have water in common, then maybe, they reasoned, there is something that all the entities we encounter have in common, something which is therefore the stuff of the world. This search for a world stuff dominated the first century of the development of philosophy, but in the middle of the fifth century BC, as the Athenian Empire threatened to swallow up the whole of the Greek world, the course of philosophical speculation was dramatically and permanently changed by three men, Heraclitus of Ephesus, Parmenides of Elea and Socrates of Athens.

Heraclitus and Parmenides probably never met and may well have been ignorant of each other's existence. Yet taken together their work constitutes the first serious threat to the common-sense notion that the world is broadly speaking as we take it to be, the doctrine that philosophers label naïve realism. Heraclitus pointed tentatively towards the sceptical notion that, since we cannot absolutely trust our senses all the time, we can never really trust them any of the time. Things that appear to be solid and more or less permanent are in fact constantly undergoing gradual change, always slowly *becoming* something else, never merely *being* something fixed and set. Thus, whereas we think that we are surrounded by a world of things, we are in fact immersed in a ceaseless flux, with no underlying structure or nature that we might hope to grasp. These thoughts were radical and no doubt not well understood for at least one generation. They seem to have been mainly negative in impact, but this has been contested, and the fragmentary state of the remains of Heraclitus is unlikely ever to permit us to decide the question with confidence.

However, whereas Heraclitus was the first to make the serious suggestion that we cannot merely read the character of the world off its surface, Parmenides is conspicuous for having pioneered the project of acquiring an understanding of the world that makes no use whatever of the less than wholly reassuring senses. Parmenides argued that we could reach certain conclusions as to how the world not merely is, but must be, just by reflecting on certain features of our own thinking about the world and about the fundamental logical rules that seem to apply to all talk about objects. What Parmenides suggested was that ordinary talk about the things around us is vitiated by a deep contradiction. We say of things, in the normal way, that they are, say, large but not, say, green. But how can something both be and not be, any more than it can both walk and not walk? No doubt this question seems naïve, even childish, and to be susceptible of being easily explained away as a confusion of a fairly elementary kind. And indeed no doubt Parmenides' question is, in a way, confused, but the confusion is far from elementary, and the ruthless seriousness with which Parmenides took it was to have a profound effect. For Parmenides advanced, in a perfect example of metaphysical thinking, from the humble origins of his argument to the extraordinary conclusion that the world is not in fact made up of a large variety of things but of one thing only, which exhausts the whole of being. This is the doctrine known as Monism. It is of course absurd, but the thought that it rests on – that anything that is cannot in any way also not be – is far from absurd and retains its fascination for all the logical cold water that has been poured on it.

If you accept, with Heraclitus, that the apparent solidity of the objects of this world is an illusion and, with Parmenides, that just by thinking about the way in which things can be and not be we can reach reliable conclusions, which will not go away, about the reality of our world, then you are ready to start doing serious metaphysics, to start wondering about how the world must be, at base, beyond the irrelevant clutter of the immediate details of the all too present surface. But from where will you take your departure? What feature of our general experience or reflection seems to point towards the illumination to be derived from abstract inquiry?

One possible answer to these questions is that the point of the world is that it has a point. What is really important, on this line of thought, is not that the world is or is not made up of water or superstrings or that there can or cannot be simultaneous contradictory predications of things. What is important is that the world seems to have a purpose, a meaning and even a design. It is an ordered structure, a cosmos, and it may even manifest the intentions of a Creator. We may wince at the vulgarity of suggesting that the purpose of physics is to know the mind of God, but this could be taken merely as a sober and literal statement of the objective of many great thinkers both in antiquity and in the modern era. Perhaps the first of these was Anaxagoras of Clazomenae.

Even less of the writings of Anaxagoras has survived than of most of the early philosophers, but we know that he wrote a book in which he suggested that the force that brought the world into its present more or less ordered state was nothing other than Mind and that the fundamental purpose of philosophy is to understand how Mind thus forged the world from the primordial chaos. We also know that one of the first to fall under the spell of this idea was the young Socrates, who read the book in Athens some time in the 430s. He became convinced that the purpose of thinking about the world is indeed to see its point, but before he could set about the construction of some new metaphysical system his attention moved to the related question of what the point is of our own lives – the problem of ethics.

The most familiar story in the history of philosophy is that of how Socrates, after distinguished service to his country as a heavily armed foot soldier, came to be deeply concerned by the apparent collapse of what are now called traditional values in the Athens of the late fifth century, began to embark on discussions with leaders of opinion in which no stone was left unturned in the pursuit of a secure basis on which to re-establish the morality of the city, gradually infuriated too many people with his well-intended but devastating criticisms of the received wisdom and paid with his life for his impertinence in the vindictive backlash that followed the disastrous end to the Peloponnesian

War and the loss of the Athenian Empire and, for a brief time, the democracy. It is also well known that in the last two decades of his life, the period of his greatest creativity, he came to be surrounded by an eager coterie of acolytes, fascinated by his ruthless technique of cross-examination and his unflinching determination to follow the consequences of an argument. It is also well known that one of these acolytes was Plato.

Plato built the metaphysical system from which Socrates was distracted by his more directly ethical concerns. At some point, possibly during his ten years of travel in the aftermath of the execution of Socrates, possibly while establishing in Athens after his return that institution which was intended to vindicate his mentor's name and to develop and propagate his thought, Plato achieved a remarkable synthesis. He combined a Heraclitean distrust of the world of the senses with a Parmenidean faith in the capacities of pure reason and the Socratic conviction that whatever is is right. The result was the Theory of Forms. The Theory of Forms is a theory that can be extracted from the masterpieces of Plato's middle period, especially the great dialogues the *Meno*, the *Phaedo*, the *Republic*, the *Symposium* and the *Phaedrus*. The Theory doubtless emerged through paths that were tortuous and perplexed and which we cannot hope to retrace, and it may well have been taken seriously by its author for only a relatively short section of his philosophical career; perhaps it was never taken really seriously by him at all. The Theory holds that the objects of our familiar world, including our own bodies, have no real existence at all. They are merely strange pseudo-existent reflections of the true realities, eternally existing and unchanging entities which lie behind and, in some way, ground all the features and properties of the world that we know. These Forms, as we call them, are perpetually unchanging and indeed wholly outside the world of space and time. They are completely inaccessible to sensory apprehension of any kind, but we can through the use of our intellect achieve a measure of communion with them. The purpose of all philosophy and science is to exhibit the working of the Forms, and this is also the core of morality and the happy life, since it is in knowledge of the Forms that knowledge of how to act consists.

The Theory of Forms is now so encrusted with the long history of reactions and abreactions to it that it is impossible for us to re-experience in imagination the impact that it must at first have had. Widely dismissed by the many as alarming evidence of insanity in its author, it must have been embraced by the few with that intellectual passion that is felt only by those whose conviction is sharpened by the exhilaration of doctrinal isolation. By the mid 360s, when Plato's Academy was probably some twenty years old, that institution must have been full of fervent converts to the contemplative reverence of a supersensible perfection. It was into this institution that the seventeen-year-old Aristotle was plunged.

There is no prospect of there being any end to the debate about how the young Aristotle reacted to Platonism. Discussion has raged across the twentieth century, and at the end of it two views continue to provide the central focus. The first is that Aristotle became himself for a time a convinced adherent of this new secular religion, and that gradually thereafter his faith lapsed until he came to cherish the immediate and particular in a way that he could not have done without his idealistic aberration. The other is that Aristotle immediately and very strongly reacted against Platonism, that he at once set about the task of showing that the reality of the world cannot rest on such remote entities as the Forms, that we must make sense of the idea that what lies around us is indeed the foundation of the world. It might be thought that such dissidence would not be tolerated in the Academy, where, after all, Aristotle remained for more than twenty years, but it is at least clear that this is wrong: the author of the intellectual tyranny of the *Republic* was a passionate defender of doctrinal pluralism in the administration of his own school.

The pattern of the development of Aristotle's thought, then, remains hotly controversial even in its broadest outlines, but no serious student would dispute that Aristotle's agenda is to a large extent that of Plato. It is impossible to understand Aristotle's philosophical project without realizing that he thought that it was of central importance to get clear about the Theory of Forms or the philosophical stance that it embodies, and it is, I think, impossible to read Aristotle with sympathy and profit without sharing some of his fascination with the thought that the fundamental structure of the world is ideal, not natural.

That Aristotle is a critic of idealism, albeit in many ways a sympathetic one, is clear, but it is no less important to see that he is as severe a critic of unreconstructed materialism. We are, perhaps, so adjusted to thinking of materialism as a relative latecomer in the history of ideas (if we mean by materialism the philosophical view that the world is made up of matter and force and absolutely nothing else) that it is easy for us to overlook the fact that in Aristotle's intellectual context materialism was a potent factor. So natural is it for us to see the development of philosophy as leading to Athenian rationalism and its aftermath that we forget that in the Aegean world the task of explaining the world continued to be focused on the elucidation of its material constituents. The attempt to inventorize the material of the world, which was, as we have seen, in many ways the point of departure for philosophy as a whole, was not abandoned, as it might have been, in the face of the logical challenge from Ephesus and Elea. Rather than wither, materialism evolved into new and more sophisticated forms.

The form of materialism with which Aristotle was most familiar, and which loomed largest on the philosophical stage that he knew, was that of atomism. This remarkable doctrine seems to have been first launched by Leucippus of Abdera, on the Northern Aegean coast, not far from Aristotle's birthplace of Stagirus, and then greatly developed and extended by his disciple Democritus, of the same city. Our knowledge of the theory is filtered through the writings of later adherents, notably the versification by the extraordinary Roman poet T. Lucretius Carus of the version of the theory espoused by the Hellenistic thinker Epicurus. Whereas we can be reasonably confident that Lucretius does not deviate far in doctrine from his Greek master, it is less easy to say how close Epicurus is to the details of Democritus' atomism. The central idea of the theory, however, is clear. It is a response to the challenge of Parmenides. Parmenides objected that we cannot say of anything that it both is and is not. Very well, then, says Democritus, let us divide the world into what is and what is not. We call the former matter and the latter void. Still, we can reconstruct the diversity of the contents of the world by supposing that matter takes the form of tiny particles of undifferentiated content but widely differing shape, which are susceptible of indefinite combination into the ordered structures that we observe. On this basis, we can explain order as the product of statistical regularity, without needing to bring in any such dubious agency as Anaxagoras' Mind.

There is no doubt that Democritus' atomism was widely appreciated and admired among thinkers of the fourth century BC. It was, of course, flagrantly at odds with any kind of Platonism, and so far as we can tell most philosophers tended to orientate themselves very clearly towards one or other of these apparently exclusive alternatives. What is distinctive about Aristotle is that, no doubt by a combination of reasons of temperament and circumstance, he attempted a kind of synthesis of, or compromise between, the two positions. In this respect, he can perhaps be compared with the more recent and thus familiar case of Kant, who similarly saw himself as achieving a historic reconciliation between the insights of empiricism and rationalism.

The tension between Platonic idealism and Democritean materialism set the stage for the development of Aristotle's thought, but we cannot hope now to reconstruct with confidence the precise plot of the drama. It seems likely that Aristotle's ideas were forming during the first thirty, perhaps even forty, years of his life and that he inclined at various times now towards the materialist, now towards the idealist perspective, before reaching his final remarkable synthesis (or syntheses, as we shall see). It is unlikely that we will ever know for certain more than this, but my own feeling is that Aristotle's development up to the time at which he left the Academy after the death of Plato in 347 BC went approximately as follows.

His early years were dominated by the intellectual climate of the Northern Aegean in general and by his father's profession in particular. As we have already seen, the Aegean basin, and perhaps especially its northern littoral, had always tended to produce thinkers of a relatively hard-headed and materialistic outlook. It tended to be in the West that philosophers dreamed of an ideal order transcending the mundanities of our imperfect world and in the East that the spirit of mechanistic explanation even of animate phenomena was most pervasive. This involved to a particular extent the profession of Aristotle's father, Nicomachus, which was that of medicine.

The history of Greek medicine is that of an institution of caste-like and exclusive character, which nevertheless was prepared to tolerate radical innovation and a critical attitude to accepted practices that would have been praised by Sir Karl Popper. The medical profession in Ancient Greece was a profession that one joined not by a formal qualification but by birth. All doctors claimed to be descendants of the legendary, or mythical, Asclepius, and membership of this descent-group was, it seems, not only a necessary but also, in the normal way, a sufficient cause for membership of the profession. Thus Aristotle would from his earliest awareness have known what his destined profession was to be. He would no doubt soon have sensed the prestige attached to itinerant Asclepiad doctors and the cult of secrecy that tended to surround their art. But he would also, we may assume, have known of the bold and speculative writings that had been produced by the membership of the medical guild, writings which have come traditionally to be attached to the name of Hippocrates of Ceos. He may well have been brought up to think that speculation on the inner workings of natural processes, far from being an affront to religious susceptibilities, was actually a pious recognition of the wishes of Asclepius for his successors and heirs.

In assessing the influence on Aristotle of Nicomachus and the medical profession, we must take into account that his father died when Aristotle was merely ten years old. Whereas this probably weakened his direct connection with practising doctors and perhaps his own predetermination for a medical career, it may well have given a special place in his feelings to the naturalistic perspective that was at the heart of Greek medicine. His education between the ages of ten and seventeen was of the conventional Hellenizing kind favoured by the states that stood within the penumbra of the Greek world proper. This would no doubt have given him a reverence of a different kind for Athens and everything associated with it, which would have had some influence on his state of mind when he was dispatched by his father's former employer, the King of Macedon, to study in Plato's Academy.

Entering the Academy in the late 360s, he would have encountered idealist metaphysics in full cry and it is certainly possible that he fell immediately under its spell. It has often been pointed out that in the period of his stay in the Academy he wrote several works for popular consumption of an overtly Platonizing nature. It is unlikely that these were merely exercises or routine pieces of institutional propaganda. He seems to have lavished on them his rhetorical gifts, which had no doubt been sharpened by his tutors in Macedon, and the fragments that have survived suggest a powerful emotional identification with the aspirations of the Theory of Forms, as well as mastery of the arguments on which the Theory was held to rest. He did not – and this is crucial to the greatness of his own system – merely dismiss the perspective of idealism with the animus that scientifically minded philosophers have often felt against it.

Nevertheless, it seems likely that, perhaps by the 340s, when he had been in the Academy for some ten years, he was coming to see that a reconciliation of some kind had to be effected between the science of nature, especially as it related to living things, for which it is clear that he felt an extraordinary attraction, and the more abstract reflections that seemed to point away from the reality of the world of the senses towards a quite different ultimate structure of the world. It is the fact that he achieved this reconciliation with such mastery, and in a way so palatable to common sense and to perennial philosophical intuitions, that has made his system, for all its obscurities and even occasional absurdities, the intellectual foundation for the received metaphysics of the Western world.

It is best, I think, to see Aristotle's philosophy as being dominated by the following three questions. What is being and what are the things that are? How can the things that are undergo the changes that we see all around us in nature? How can the world be understood? It is, of course, true that his thinking covers a vast range of other major topics in the formal, empirical and philosophical domains, but he would have regarded these other topics as being dependent on, and in some way secondary to, the ones that I have given, in a way that was not reciprocal. It is, in any case, these three questions that dominate his metaphysical theory. But if we wish to understand how he answers these questions in his mature metaphysics, contained in the central books of the *Metaphysics*, we must first look briefly at two other major works, the *Categories* and the *Physics*, which constitute preliminary stages of his metaphysical view, whether earlier stages in its evolution or preparatory contributions to its presentation.

In the *Categories*, Aristotle sets out the range of the things that are,

itemizing the inventory of being. This is the philosophical study of
ontology, the attempt to say what things have being. The task is, of
course, not that of listing all the things that are in the world, a patently
futile and impossible endeavour. Rather it is that of saying what sorts
of things have being and what sorts of things do not. Does, for instance,
a physical object have being, a sound, a colour, a belief, a number, a
flame, a memory, an event? A central ambition of the ontologist is to
give an answer for every sensible question of this kind and, for those
that he does not consider sensible, to show why they are not sensible.
But the ontologist may not be content even when he has given his
catalogue of *onta*, of things having being. He may also hold the at first
sight rather obscure belief that the things that have being have being
in different ways, and he may further hold that there is a kind of
structure and hierarchy in the different ways in which things can have
being. And if he does this, he may well attach especial significance to
those things that have being in the way that seems to be in some sense
at the foundation of this structure.

Now all these descriptions of the ontologist's project apply to Aristotle, both in the *Categories* and in the *Metaphysics*. Aristotle thinks that
there is indeed a diversity of things that have being and that this diversity
does indeed form a hierarchy. And he pays special attention to the
foundational element of that hierarchy. In the *Categories*, he argues that
there are ten kinds of things that have being. The number ten is
suspiciously neat in such a context (one of Aristotle's colleagues in the
Academy is said to have written a hymn to it), and the details of
Aristotle's list are not particularly illuminating. What is crucial for
Aristotle is the contrast between the first of his categories of things that
are and the nine others. For he holds that the first category, substance,
is indeed fundamental to the being of all the others, which are thus
non-reciprocally dependent on it. To see why he thinks this, we need
consider only one of his other categories, that of quality, the second
category.

Aristotle holds that substances are things that have qualities or,
conversely, qualities are things that belong to substance. If, for instance,
the man Socrates is a substance and being musical is a quality, then
Socrates may have the quality of being musical or the quality of being

musical may belong to Socrates. Both Socrates and the quality of being musical are things that have being, but they have being in radically different ways. The former has being as a substance, the latter as a quality; and this means that the former is more fundamental and, as Aristotle puts it, prior to the latter. Why is this so? Aristotle's answer is that the being of the quality depends on that of the substance but the being of the substance does not depend on that of the quality. The thought is that Socrates need not have had the quality of musicality, but the quality of musicality would have to have some bearer for it to have any being at all. To this it can be rejoined that Socrates, presumably, must have some qualities, and it is far from obvious that Aristotle can have any ultimately persuasive response to this objection to his picture of the ontological dependency of qualities on substances.

For present purposes, however, we can leave aside the issue of the dependency hierarchy between the categories and consider more directly what Aristotle thinks, in the *Categories*, that substance is. After all, to hold that the bearer of properties is in some sense more fundamental than the properties that it bears, though constitutive of the notion of substance, remains merely schematic until we are told what things are in fact the bearers of properties. After all, we might, as in the example of the last paragraph, want to say that particular men like Socrates are substances, or we might want to say that quite different sorts of things, such as perhaps Platonic Forms, are the substances to which everything else belongs. In the *Categories*, Aristotle subdivides the category of substance itself (and makes a similar subdivision of all the other categories as well). He holds that some substances are particular, like Socrates or Red Rum, while others are general, such as the species of man and horse, or the genus of animal. But if there is thus a plurality of substances, we can in turn ask which of them is more fundamental. A Platonist would say that the most general of them, the genus of animal, was closest to being substance, but Aristotle takes precisely the opposite view, holding that it is particular individuals that are fundamental, with the other, classificatory substances being dependent on them, in that if there were nothing for them to classify they would have no being at all.

Thus the metaphysical scheme of the *Categories* is robustly particularist. It is particular things, conspicuously particular animals, that have the most fundamental being of all, and everything else has being in a way that then depends on them. The common-sense intuitions of the non-philosopher are, after all, vindicated against the insidious challenges of rationalism. But in Aristotle's writings, whether we treat them as the sediment of a process of intellectual development or the skilfully graded presentation of a unified position, we cannot rest with such straightforward substantialism. The reason is that the favoured entities of the *Categories*, particular substances, are vulnerable to attack from another direction, from their patent susceptibility to change.

In the *Physics*, Aristotle deals with the conceptual problem of change, the second of the three key questions that we have seen he confronts. His solution was so successful that it takes an effort of imagination for us to perceive the severity of the problem. But it is necessary to try to do so if one is to see why Aristotle thought that it was so pressingly urgent a task and why he was prepared to threaten the metaphysical scheme of the *Categories* in order to be able to carry it out. The fact was that naturalistic philosophers, sympathetic to taking change seriously and making science out of the study of it, had not been able to find a fully satisfactory and convincing refutation of the arguments of Parmenides and his followers to show that change was in fact merely illusory. These arguments were variations on a core argument which went as follows. Suppose that Socrates changes from not being musical one day to being musical the next. We can comment on this as being a case of the musical Socrates' coming into being. But then we have to defend the conceptual coherence of saying that something has come into being. But there seem to be only two ways in which something could come into being, either, that is, from something that already exists or from nothing at all. But if the coming into being was from something that already exists, then it would have to be from the very same thing previously existing as has supposedly come into being (on pain of the same objection arising in a different form), and in that case there would simply not be a case of something coming into being here at all. On the other hand, it is self-evidently absurd to suggest that anything could come into being from absolutely nothing at all. Thus the notion of coming into being, and with it of all change, is fundamentally incoherent.

Aristotle's solution to this difficulty is to show that the way in which we should look on such changes is in terms of there being something that persists through the change and acquires some feature that it did not have before. Thus in a way the end product, in our case the musical Socrates, did not exist previously and in a way it did. This solution might seem to work well enough when a composite thing, such as the musical Socrates, comes into being, but what about the case when Socrates himself is born? Here it cannot be that Socrates has acquired some property, since before his birth (or, if you prefer, his conception) he did not have being at all. What happens when a substance comes into being?

The answer to which Aristotle resorts is that this latter case too is a case of something composite being rearranged. Even in the case of the generation of a substance, there is something that persists and something that is added to it (or taken away from it). There is something, to put it a little crudely, of which Socrates himself is a modification, just as the musical Socrates is a modification of Socrates himself. That something, says Aristotle, is matter, which had previously been distributed around Socrates' environment and has now had the form of Socrates imposed on it. This matter thus in some sense underlies the very substance of Socrates himself. This is the doctrine that all particular individual entities around us are, in a radical metaphysical way, composites. It is fundamental to their being that they are fusions of two quite different ingredients, form and matter. This position is sometimes known as hylemorphism (from the Greek words for matter and form).

Hylemorphism is a brilliantly bold solution to the problem of substantial generation, but it produces a crisis in Aristotle's metaphysics, as set out in the *Categories*. For it is a central implication of the hylemorphic account of change that matter underlies the particular substances in which it is involved. But then if matter underlies substance, how can substance be metaphysically fundamental? How can it fail to be the case that the world is ultimately founded on matter? And if we assume that the matter from which Socrates is made is itself composite, as Aristotle standardly does, then the matter underlying Socrates must in turn be underlain by some more fundamental matter, and so on downwards until we reach a basic kind of matter, which, presumably, will be without any form at all. We reach what has become traditionally known as mere, or primary, matter. Surely, the account of being and the account of change, the answers to the first two questions, have shown that wholly formless matter is the ultimate foundation of the whole structure of reality. But this cannot be right. No doubt there are many reasons for recoiling from this possibility, but there is one that was especially important, I believe, for Aristotle, and this was that the consequence thus derived from the answers provided for his first two questions would rule out the very possibility of answering his third. If the world is ultimately made just of formless matter, then it must, ultimately, be unintelligible. To accept this consequence would be a counsel of despair for any Greek philosopher.

It was to deal with this absolutely central question that Aristotle wrote the *Metaphysics*. It had to be shown that the hylemorphic conception of substance, under which alone the reality of change could be defended, did not mean that the world in itself is ultimately quite beyond our understanding. The metaphysical and the conceptual foundation of the world had to be made one. Few books have been written with such an ambitious brief.

In marking out the resolution of the problem of substance as the central task of the *Metaphysics*, I do not wish to deny that there are many other topics of fundamental philosophical importance that are covered in the work, including the general nature of being, the scope and methods of philosophy, the foundations of philosophical logic, the doctrine of potentiality and actuality, Aristotelian theology and the nature of number. All these other areas are, however, viewed from the perspective of substance, and their conclusions do not undermine the claim that it is substance that is the hub of Aristotle's entire philosophical system. The whole project of philosophy, Aristotle believed and the *Metaphysics* presupposes, depends on the clarification of the notion of substance. It is above all books Zeta and Eta that are devoted to this central task, and in this introduction I confine myself to suggesting a way of seeing how they resolve it. I attempt in the bibliography to direct the reader towards points of entry into the vast literature that has developed around Aristotle's views of each of the other major topics of the *Metaphysics*.

It is, then, in book Zeta that the problem of refining the notion of substance is first directly addressed. Aristotle's difficulty is that substance has to achieve the seemingly impossible combination of being the bottom line of the hierarchy of being and the root of the intelligibility of the world, in terms of which all else is understood. It is this second requirement that rules out taking substance to be the mere matter that would seem ultimately to underlie the changeability of nature according to the teaching of the *Physics*. In Zeta, Aristotle broaches the problem by posing two interconnected questions: what it is to be a substance and what things are substances. He naturally takes the answer to the second of these questions to depend on that to the first, and, although chapter 2 lists the candidate answers to the second question that have been favoured by philosophers and by lay opinion (this list is reviewed in chapter 16), it is to the answering of the first, crucial question that Zeta is overwhelmingly devoted.

In chapter 3, Aristotle lists his four candidates for substancehood, his four criteria of substantiality. The list (not in Aristotle's order) is: the subject or substrate, the what-it-was-to-be-that or essence of the thing whose substance is sought, the universal under which the thing falls and the genus or kind to which the thing belongs. In the structure of the discussion, the remainder of chapter 3 deals succinctly with the first criterion, the bulk of the whole book (chapters 4–12) covers in a tortuous manner the second criterion, and chapters 13–15/16 are devoted to the discussion of the universal (under which that of the genus must be taken to be subsumed). Chapter 17 looks at substance from the new perspective of cause, from which, however, the central conclusions of Zeta will be upheld rather than undermined. The conclusion of chapter 3 is one that we have already reached, that the ultimate subject, pure matter, is not a plausible candidate for substantiality, at least not in the fullest sense. (There is a major traditional issue as to whether Aristotle accepts that pure matter has being at all, but even if he does it is clear that he does not see it as providing a conception of substance that meets his requirements.)

In chapter 4, we begin the discussion of the claims of the what-it-was-to-be-that-thing of a thing to be its substance. It can be said at the start that it is this criterion of substantiality that Aristotle will favour and the discussion of it is the core of the entire *Metaphysics*, having an importance within that work comparable to the Transcendental Deduction of the Categories in Kant's *Critique of Pure Reason*. The claim that the what-it-was-to-be-that-thing of something is its substance is a classic piece of metaphysical reasoning. It is deeply obscure and it is wholly natural to dismiss it, as many have done, as a piece of meaningless and scholastic mumbo-jumbo, a mere exercise in juggling with a barbarous and oppressive terminology. And yet it retains a fascination, such that all attempts to kill it off seem only to lead to its recrudescence. But let us begin with its obscurity. What, if anything, does the phrase the 'what-it-was-to-be-that-thing' of something mean? This is a translation of an equally puzzling expression in Aristotle's Greek, which could be still more literally translated just as 'what it was to be'. It is as unnatural in Greek as it is in English to use a phrase in this way in the grammatical role of a noun. Such a usage would be unthinkable in Plato, and it is a mark of the extraordinary growth in the technical repertoire of philosophy that Aristotle makes such free employment of it, albeit in a work intended for specialist consumption. The expression has been extensively analysed, but the key to its meaning seems to lie in the puzzling past tense embedded in it. This has affinities in expressions from Aristotle's philosophy of nature, and it suggests the idea of what something was all along going to, destined to, become. Although Aristotle would have been aghast at almost everything written by the German Romantic philosopher Friedrich Nietzsche, his only objection to that thinker's celebrated injunction to 'become what you are' would be that it is superfluous. It is the destiny of everything to become what it is, and it is that which it was thus all along destined to be that it most really is. The medieval philosophers coined the term *essentia* to pick out this key idea, and its value has secured its survival into the vernaculars of modern Europe.

So Aristotle's central claim in the *Metaphysics* is that a thing's substance is its essence. This at least gives us something in English to work with, but it is still profoundly unclear what it can amount to. How can this equation of substance and essence be anything other than sophistry? How can it have real philosophical content at all, let alone be a revolutionary insight? We can hardly imagine T-shirts emblazoned with the slogan 'Substance is Essence', as an alternative to 'Property is Theft' or 'I think, therefore I am'.

This is the problem that is resolved, though in baffling style, in chapter 4 of Zeta. The upshot of chapter 4 is that what it means to say that substance is essence is just this, that what is ontologically fundamental as that on whose being the being of everything else depends is also conceptually prior, as that in terms of which everything else is to be explained. It is the equation of substance and essence that solves the problem at the heart of Aristotle's entire system by reintegrating the being of the world with our need to comprehend it. But why should the essence of something be regarded as what is most intelligible about it? Surely, we might think that the surface properties of things are familiar and reasonably manageable but their essences are recondite and obscure, hidden from the ordinary view and available only to the more penetrating scrutiny of science. Surely it was a triumph of centuries of scholarly labour to discover that the essence of water is H_2O.

Well, Aristotle's reason for holding that essence is, as he puts it, prior in thought, more intelligible, that is, than anything else, rests on a distinction that he draws (though it is not specifically present in Zeta 4) between what is intelligible to us and what is intelligible in itself. The case of water and H_2O is indeed not one that Aristotle would be at home with, but we can use it to make his point. Aristotle would say that the surface properties of water, its wetness and coldness and so forth, are intelligible to us, in that we do not have to make much of an effort to understand them, they come naturally to us. The essential structure of water as that combination of hydrogen and oxygen that we label H_2O is, by contrast, intelligible in itself, not because it is easy and natural for us to understand it but because when, after much labour, we do come so to understand it we understand it in a far more real and profound way than we had previously understood its mere surface characteristics. The essence H_2O is really intelligible, whereas the wetness of water is merely familiar. The understanding of the scientist is the benchmark against which that of all others is to be measured.

But even if we accept that scientific understanding, if we can but get it, is understanding in the fullest sense, why should we think that it is the essence of something that is thus the object of scientific understanding? Aristotle's answer is clear. The essence of a thing is that which is most intelligible about it because it is the essence of the thing that is caught in the definition of it. Thus the notion of definition comes in turn to play a crucial part in Aristotle's position. In chapters 4–6 Aristotle seeks to show that it is only the essence of something that can be defined. His arguments are profoundly difficult, not least because of textual uncertainties, but a central consideration seems to be that for something to be definable it must have a certain kind of unity, it must be, in some deep way, a single thing and not a combination of more than one thing. And Aristotle argues that it is only essences that are definable in this way. This great stress on the notion of unity as a criterion for definability will expose Aristotle to the objection that a definition itself is inherently a combination – water, for instance, must be defined as hydrogen *and* oxygen in a ratio of 2:1 – and it is this difficulty that he deals with in the extraordinary discussion in chapters 10–12. But for the moment we can concentrate on the claim of chapter 4 that essences and essences alone are definable unities. From this it follows that to be a substance is to be an essence and nothing but an essence, to be a pure essence, something, that is, with only essential features.

Thus Aristotle has arrived at an answer to the first of the two questions of Zeta. He has shown what it is to be a substance. He now has three remaining tasks, that of clarifying the many remaining obscurities in the answer that he has given, that of rejecting the remaining candidate criteria of substantiality, the universal and the genus, and that of answering his second question of what things, then, are substances. It is the last of these tasks that he addresses in the discussion in chapter 4. He announces an extraordinary answer. On the essence criterion of substantiality, it turns out that the substances that underpin the world are no longer the particular individuals of the *Categories* but *the species to which they belong*. It is not now Socrates and Red Rum that are fundamental, but the species of man and of horse. This is indeed a radical shift. Whereas before Aristotle seemed to be defending a notion of thinghood which was deeply in tune with common sense, he seems now to have moved to a conception which is wholly at odds with it, under which the fundamental building blocks of the world, on whose

matter + form → substance = species

thisness

separab ility

being that of everything else depends, are now entire species of animals. It is important to see the magnitude of this change. There are many possible objections to it, to be sure, but the most fundamental charge that Aristotle must rebut is that, in moving to the claim that it is species that are substances, the doctrine, as I shall call it, of special substance, Aristotle has effectively relapsed into Platonism; that his view is not to be distinguished, in the final analysis, from the doctrine of universal substance that Aristotle himself took to be the heart of the Theory of Forms.

Aristotle will seek to show that the doctrine of special substance is not to be equated with that of universal substance, and does not suffer from its fatal flaws, in the section of Zeta in which he attacks universal substance. We will look at his argument in due course. But even at this stage it should be mentioned that Aristotle thinks that species have two crucial features that they share with particulars and do not share with universals. These features are those which Aristotle calls *thisness* and *separability*. The meaning and relevance of these two features has been much discussed. Separability is a term that Aristotle uses in a wide variety of ways in his system, but in this context it seems to be less central to Aristotle's point than the notion of thisness. Thisness is something that a thing has by dint of being determinate in a particular kind of way. There just are some things that one can point to and refer to as this, without thereby exposing oneself to the question 'This what?' It is clear, for Aristotle, that individual horses and men have this feature. Particularity is a kind of thisness. If I point to Socrates and say 'this one', my reference is clear. But particularity does not exhaust thisness. A thing can be a this without being a particular. A thing can be a this by being a species of particulars. If we are deciding, say, on the purchase of a pet dog, I can point to a breed in the catalogue and say, 'I like this one.' Here again my reference is clear. I am not indicating a predilection for the particular dog of the illustration, but for the no less determinate species to which it belongs. Species too have thisness. And genera do not. I cannot point to an animal and, by saying 'this one', refer to the genus of animals as against that of plants. The thisness criterion clearly brackets species with particulars and not with universals.

Species, then, are entities unitary in a certain way, whose essences exhaust their natures, in other words substances. This is a remarkable, if unstable, position. It is remarkable because it assigns a fundamental metaphysical role to a certain subset of natural kinds. It steers a middle way between the ascription of a profound ontological significance to the commonplace entities of our experience and the Platonic insistence that reality must lie in a transcendent realm of purely intelligible entities. It is unstable for two reasons. First, it is far from clear that species can be defended against the objections that Aristotle himself brings against Platonic universal substance, and, secondly, the roles played by the concepts of unity and of definition in the account of essence may well turn out to be incompatible. Aristotle will confront these two difficulties in the later chapters of Zeta, but, in the text that we read before we come to those chapters, we find a three-chapter section which has in many ways the feel of being an insertion at some point in the history of the text. In this section, Aristotle appears to be equating the species to which an entity belongs with the form that is an ingredient in the composite nature of that entity. And if form is to be equated with species (they are often referred to by the same word in Greek), then form is also to be equated with substance. And since form has played a crucial part in the hylemorphic account of change and in Aristotle's natural philosophy in general, the discussion of substance is yet more fully tied into the other features of Aristotle's system. (It is always important, of course, to be as clear as possible about the distinction between Aristotelian 'immanent' form, which can only, or at any rate only normally, exist in conjunction with matter, and Platonic 'separable' Form, which can only have dealings with matter through the weak relationship of the participation in it of things with the latter in them. To mark the distinction, I follow the conventional practice of capitalizing the Platonic but not the Aristotelian conception of Form/form.)

Chapters 10–12 offer a subtle defence of the claim that a definition, and thus the object of a definition, has an intrinsic unity, something that we have seen to be required by Aristotle's whole position on substance. The problem that Aristotle confronts is that a definition seems necessarily to be something involving parts. To define A just is to say that A is (by definition) B with features C, D . . . In the case with which Aristotle works, that of definition by genus and differentia, a species is defined in terms of its genus and its differentia (that feature that distinguishes it from all other species in the same genus). Thus the species man may be defined as featherless, two-footed (differentia) animal (genus). There are, to be sure, problems enough in connection with the notion of differentia in general, but they need not concern us in the present context. The problem is that of how A can be a unity if it is really B and C, how man can be a unity if it is really animal and, say, two-footed. The details of Aristotle's solution to this difficulty are far from being beyond dispute, but its general thrust seems to rest on the distinction between two kinds of parts that something may have. A thing can have parts which are prior (in understanding) and/or parts that are posterior (in understanding). A part that is prior in understanding is a part the understanding of which must precede understanding of that entity as a whole. Thus Aristotle says that the letters of a syllable are prior parts of it, since one cannot understand a syllable, say ae, without first understanding its constituent parts, a and e. By contrast, a part that is posterior in understanding is a part that can only be understood when the thing of which it is a part is already understood. Aristotle's example is a section of a circle. One cannot understand what a section of a circle is unless one already understands a circle. Given this distinction, Aristotle can now make two further claims. The first is that the parts of a definition are posterior to the definition as a whole, the second is that having posterior parts does not compromise something's unity in the way that having prior ones does. If these two further claims are allowed, then he can feel that he has met the objection that his fundamental entities are radically divided.

The discussion of the unity of the definition has been hailed as the first sustained discussion in the discipline of philosophical logic, and interpretation is cloaked in controversy. It is impossible to discuss it in any depth in the present introduction, nor is the account that I have given any more than the crudest of initial summaries. It may well be that the unity of definition is not something that can be defended in the way that Aristotle requires and that it is in fact the Achilles' heel of his system, but one can only admire the candour with which Aristotle recognizes the problem and the energy and ingenuity with which he takes it on.

He is no less ingenious in his confrontation of the objection that special substance must itself be a kind of universal substance and thus in effect constitute a relapse, on Aristotle's part, into Platonism. The objection can be formulated straightforwardly enough as follows. Aristotle says that a species is a substance, but a species inherently has several members (one-member species, though perfectly possible, are the exception and clearly not necessary). But anything that has several members must be universal – that is just what it is to be a universal, to be constituted of, or apply to, a range of separate things. So Aristotle must be saying that substance is universal, *pace* the teaching of the *Categories*, and be a Platonist after all. Aristotle's response to this has to be reconstructed from his text, and the most promising attempt to reconstruct it has him claiming that the key second stage of the argument is mistaken. The second stage says that anything under which several things fall, or may fall, is a universal, but the counter-claim is that this is not so. Something is not a universal just if several things fall under it but only if it is also predicated of several things. A species is something under which several things fall, but it is not predicated of several things. Therefore, it is not a universal. What can this mean? The idea is that B can only be predicated of A if I can have discriminatory understanding of A, can pick A out from all other objects in the world, without already knowing that it is B. If I cannot know what B is without knowing that it is A, then I cannot predicatively say that B is A. A predication, on this view, cannot be analytic. And then it can be said that anything that is a member of a species is something that can indeed only be discriminatingly picked out on the basis of the knowledge that it is a member of that species. And so it can turn out that species is substance without being universal.

This is, of course, only one way of interpreting the treatment of the universal objection to special substance that Aristotle provides in the later chapters of Zeta. Once again, it may well turn out that the objection is insuperable, so that Aristotle's position, even in its own terms, is self-contradictory. But once again the extraordinary wealth of debate that has flourished around his contentions is testimony to the suggestive power of his insights. It seems that Aristotle has raised an issue that cannot be ignored by anyone who is prepared to take seriously the notion that both particular and universal items can have being. And even for nominalists about universals, the notion that there is an important distinction between being a universal and being universally predicable is a pregnant topic for discussion.

The upshot of this slightest of introductions to Zeta 3–16 is that by the end of that passage Aristotle has reached, and defended, an entirely new metaphysical position. We can still see him as trying to achieve an intermediate position between what he sees as the extremes of material-ism and Platonism, as he was in the *Categories*. But whereas in the *Categories* it was particular individuals in whom being primarily resided, that honour is now given to the species to which they belong. This position is, as we have seen, exposed, but if it can be maintained there are great advantages that can flow from it. It represents a successful resolution of the three questions that we saw at the start to be of fundamental importance for Aristotle, and especially deals with the difficulties created by the hylemorphic doctrine of change, and in addition, through the connection between the notions of species and of form, it connects Aristotle's metaphysics in the strongest possible way with his philosophy of nature and in particular his teleological account of the general operation of the natural world. The doctrine of special substance is one of the most trenchant and striking of all the positions adopted by the metaphysical system builders of philosophical history.

And yet, for all its attractions, there is reason to think that the doctrine had been abandoned even before the work that makes up the *Metaphysics* had been completed. For it seems clearly to be the case that book Eta tries to move back to a position more or less like that of the *Categories*, only suitably updated, in which the role of substance is again played by composite particulars rather than species. The conclusion reached in chapter 6 of Eta is that composite particulars are not, after all, underlain by matter persisting through change in a way that is incompatible with their being the fundamental realities. Thus Aristotle has returned to the safer ground of the *Categories*, but to do so he must meet the objection to particular substances based on the hylemorphic account of change which was, as we have seen, the original reason for abandoning the *Categories* position. It is far from clear, as always, that Aristotle can successfully do this, but the most promising construal of his attempt to do so is that offered by M. L. Gill. She takes Aristotle to be arguing that there is still something in a composite entity that has persisted through the change that has brought that entity into being, so that the Parmenidean dilemma does not arise, but that that persistent thing has in the composite only potential being. This means that that part of the composite, having, in the composite, only potential being (though actual being when not in it), cannot be more fundamental than the composite that has being in actuality. So particulars are once again freed to be both composite and substantial. This is a highly ingenious reconstruction of Aristotle's new position, though it may well be too generous to him, and it also has the merit of highlighting the connection between the discussion of substance in terms of matter, the particular and the universal and the discussion of substance in terms of actuality and potentiality that begins in book Theta and is extended in important new directions in book Lambda.

It may well be that Aristotle's second position on substance in the *Metaphysics*, that of book Eta, is no more successful than his first, from which it would seem to be a kind of retreat. But the vigour and tenacity with which the second position is defended is on a par with that of the first. The notion of the potential persistent is no less fruitful for philosophical discussion than that of the unity of posterior parts or the contrast between universality and universal predicability. All these positions reflect Aristotle's attempt to reconcile his three fundamental desiderata, that the world should be grounded in a certain class of really existing things, that such things should be susceptible of change and that such things should be in principle available for our comprehension. We are at liberty to abandon any one of these three claims. We can take the world not to have a real existence independent of ourselves in anything like Aristotle's sense, we can acquiesce in the concession that change is in a certain way illusory or we can give up the hope of ever coming to know the world in its real nature. Each of these abandonments has been extensively defended by whole schools of philosophers, but each of them is to a greater or lesser extent repugnant to common sense. If we wish, then, to 'save the appearances', we must try to find an answer to each of Aristotle's fundamental questions. And, if we are committed to this project, it is far from clear that we can carry it out any better than Aristotle has done or that there is nothing that we can learn from the ambitious programme at the heart of the *Metaphysics*.

I have attempted to say something about the central strand of argument in the *Metaphysics*. It is very far indeed from being the only position that the text adopts. It is not for nothing that the work has been hailed as the foundation of an entire branch of philosophy, and it could be claimed that there is no major problem of traditional metaphysics that is not to some extent covered in its pages. For all that, however, it is not a mere encyclopedia of metaphysics. It does have a structure, albeit submerged beneath its surface encrustations, and the huge range of issues that it covers is presented, however remotely, from the perspective of substance. We might say that substance is the sun in the solar system of the *Metaphysics* and the other issues the planets, comets, asteroids and meteors.

While it is not possible to look in detail at all the issues in the work, it might be helpful to offer an account of how the presentation of them coheres. In doing this we can also confront and assess the highly plausible claim that the work is in one way or another a compilation, perhaps by Aristotle himself, perhaps by his contemporary assistants, perhaps by his immediate philosophical heirs and perhaps by editors of a much later age, of some of the most important metaphysical writings circulating in the Lyceum at the height of its creative phase.

2. *The Structure and Composition of the* Metaphysics

The *Metaphysics* is, by any account, an unusual book. Not only is its content strange and difficult, but its very structure has often struck its readers as baffling and many questions suggest themselves in connection with the process by which it was brought into being. For all that, I do not believe that the structural coherence of the work is as questionable as has often been made out. The work, when understood on its own terms, can still be followed with no greater difficulty than other Great Texts of Philosophy.

We can begin with the title. Almost everyone who has had much dealing with academic philosophy, and absolutely everyone who has had any dealing with Academic philosophy, will know the celebrated anecdote about how this work received its title, which it was then to bequeath to the whole branch of philosophy that it founds, from some chance entry note made for it in a catalogue in an unknown collection or library. The point of the note, the anecdote variously vouchsafes, was either that the work in some sense continues the agenda of the (perhaps more digestible and therefore no doubt more familiar *Physics*) or, more banally, that a copy simply arrived just after a copy of the *Physics* in some job lot delivery of manuscripts. The anecdote, we may say, has both a type and a token variant.

It is quite impossible to say whether there is any truth in this hoariest of chestnuts. Since it is a matter of conjecture, it is reasonable to make the conjecture that most fits with one's account of the work's emergence. If you think that the work descended to its first editor Andronicus of Rhodes in the first century more or less as a kind of scrapbook, then the anecdote makes sense. If, on the other hand, you feel that the work was put together in something fairly like its present form either by Aristotle himself or during or at least pretty soon after his lifetime, then you will probably be disposed to ascribe a deeper significance to the title than that plausibly licensed by either variant of the anecdote. In any case, all sides to the dispute can at least agree on its supreme inconsequence. It is clear that the work is indeed intended to cover issues that arise *after* the central claims of the *Physics* have been absorbed. However, given that it is also a reaction to Aristotle's earlier naïve substantialism, it is perhaps surprising that the ever fertile ancient doxographical tradition has not furnished us with an alternative version in which the text is dubbed the *Metacategories*.

For readers unfamiliar with Aristotle (and especially for those who are familiar with Plato), it would be as well to add a few remarks on the texture of the work. The text of this treatise, as of all the extant treatises of Aristotle, might be described, with lavish generosity, as grainy. All the extant treatises, the so-called Corpus that we have, were intended for the consumption of specialists. We follow the Greeks in calling such works esoteric, in contrast to those directed to a wider, lay audience, which are exoteric. This distinction was clearly of major importance in both Plato's Academy and Aristotle's Lyceum, and very probably in all the other schools of philosophy, rhetoric, medicine and natural science that flourished at the time. The literary output of school members was no doubt standardly divided into these two kinds of work. Certainly, we know that Aristotle wrote exoteric treatises, and Plato himself may very well have written esoteric ones.

The whole nature of the two kinds of text was determined by their different purposes, more thoroughly, perhaps, than is the case with the comparable distinction today. Exoteric texts were intended above all to capture the imagination and interest of the reader, esoteric ones above all to carry on the business of philosophical research. With reservations for some of the later dialogues, we can assign Plato's extant works exclusively to the former category and those of Aristotle exclusively to the latter. Of course, this has always coloured perception of the two thinkers. The contrast between our acquaintance with the thought of one and of the other can perhaps be compared to that between acquaintance with a city through its thriving harbour or buzzing financial quarter and acquaintance with it through the grandiose boulevards and majestic *prospekts* of its imperial administrative and ceremonial centre. Of course, it is harder to read and enjoy Aristotle at first sight.

The esoteric texts are often described as lecture notes, and there is every reason to think that they were used for that purpose. But the description probably only half describes their role in the school. We have to imagine a world in which writing materials were both scarce and inconvenient – paper was an invention of the Hellenistic Age and remained so rare that an unused side was a luxurious waste of resources until well into the modern era. There was no telephone, fax, e-mail and computer memory, on which the modern academic industry depends. The progress of philosophical research, when it has reached the technical level achieved by both the Academy and the Lyceum, is inevitably to a large extent by accretion, by footnote, reference and apostil as much as by full-blooded treatise and substantive article. The contemporary medium for this process is the academic journal, which was also absent in antiquity. The substitute, I believe, was the school library, whose texts were not static and immutable records of finished bodies of work but more like diaries or *cahiers*, on to which the latest developments and refinements would be encrusted. It is this sort of text that has come down to us under the name of Aristotle.

The provenance lends itself to three peculiarities: ellipse, disorder and interpolation. All three features can be found in rich abundance on almost every page of the *Metaphysics*. So marked are they that it is likely to occur to any reader that the text is a hotchpotch collage of different hands at different times. It is remarkable that this possibility, which has been exhaustively canvassed in the twentieth century, was almost entirely ignored (no doubt partly for institutional reasons) in earlier ages of the study of Aristotle. It is certainly possible to adopt an extreme deconstructionist approach to the text of the *Metaphysics*. On such an account, as presented, for example, by Felix Grayeff in his *Aristotle and His School*, the text was put together during the course of the two decades following Aristotle's death by the collective, but not necessarily harmonious, labours of members of the school in a way that was based on Aristotle's own teachings though it by no means refrained from extending or even revising them. This account gives us, if not quite a social Aristotle, at least an institutional Aristotle. It is, as I say, perfectly on the cards that some such account is more or less right. But, of course, this is far from being proven, and the current tide of opinion is perhaps moving away from the deconstruction of Aristotle. It is impossible to discuss this issue further in the course of this introduction, but I think it is worth pointing out that nobody who is coming to the text for the first time need feel that it is crucial to have a view on the *Entstehungsgeschichte* of the work he or she has in their hands. The *Metaphysics* can be read as though it flows from a single pen – there will be problems enough, even on this assumption, for the new reader.

If, then, we work on the assumption that the treatise is the product of a single architect, we can notice at once that the design is ample and impressive. The fourteen books (corresponding to the amounts of material that it was convenient to fit on a single scroll and so only rather loosely equivalent to modern chapters) are arranged as follows. Three books on the historical background, the method to be followed and the problems to be resolved. Then three books setting out the general nature of the subject, providing a budget of definitions of key terms and dealing with an aspect of the subject which, though important, is secondary to our present interests. Then a core set of four books, in which the doctrine, or doctrines, of substance is, or are, presented, and the two key supporting contrasts of potentiality/actuality and unity/diversity are explored. There then follows a book consisting of recapitulations of material both from earlier books of the *Metaphysics* and from the *Physics* (book Kappa), and finally there are three books that deal with two major corollaries of the central position, one covering Aristotelian theology and two on the philosophy of mathematics in relation to the Theory of Forms.

This arrangement is orderly and convincing: we move from preliminaries to the general presentation of the subject and then to the detailed presentation of the position adopted, followed by a treatment of the major areas on which the position has an impact. It is only book Kappa that spoils this pattern, since there is no discernible purpose to its standing where it does in the text. (There are interesting divergences between Kappa and the texts that it recapitulates, and it is plausible to look on it as a mass of material available for possible replacement of the standing version of various passages. In our time, it would no doubt have been published separately as notebooks or posthumous papers.) The treatise, then, is well ordered in terms of its large-scale structure, and this is the more impressive if one bears in mind that it comes very early in the history of the scientific treatise as a literary form. Indeed, it could be said that with the *Metaphysics* and the *Nicomachean Ethics* the treatise as a genre comes of age.

A minor possible distraction can be briefly dealt with. Whereas the books of other works of ancient philosophy and literature, including the other treatises of Aristotle, are conventionally referred to by Roman numerals, the books of the *Metaphysics* have Greek letters as their conventional titles. The reason for this is that there are two book Alphas, the greater and the lesser, and therefore, since the letters of all the other books do not correspond to their appropriate numerals, they are retained and have come by and large to supplant the numerals. Numerals are, however, still sometimes used. The conversion formula for all letters after Alpha is letter = appropriate numeral + 1! The text is also referred to in terms of the pages of the first full edition of the entire corpus by the nineteenth-century German scholar Immanuel Becker.

I shall now comment very briefly on the content of each of the books. In the bibliography I indicate points of departure for anyone planning a voyage into the interior of the huge literature that now surrounds them.

In book Alpha, Aristotle gives the historical background to his inquiry. His arresting opening sentence, ascribing a natural desire for knowledge to all men, is not intended as a specious piece of anthology fodder but a commonplace remark in empirical zoology. Given that we are thus doomed by nature to seek enlightenment, Aristotle tells us that the highest form in which we can have it is *sophia* (wisdom), the object of *philosophia* (the love of wisdom). And the highest form of philosophia – this we are not quite told in so many words – is the study which is the subject of the present inquiry. This study, which, for convenience, we may call metaphysics, is, like all sciences, a study of causes and principles. It is distinctive in that it is the study of the primary or fundamental principles and causes.

There are in fact four such irreducible principles of fundamental causation, as we have already been told in the *Physics*. All causation, and by the same token all explanation, is in terms either of matter or of form or of the initiation of a process or of purpose. This tetrachotomy was presented dogmatically in the *Physics*. It is now shown, by a historical excursus, to be the inevitable outcome of the serious investigation of nature. The entire previous history of philosophy and science, including Platonism, are interpreted as a process of sleepwalking towards Aristotle's four causes. After the narrative, the final three chapters present a kind of critical response. Needless to say, this way of doing the history of philosophy has not met with universal approval. Since Aristotle is so important a source for the views of others, it matters how objective he is in reporting them. The bibliography signposts the ensuing discussion.

Book Alpha the Lesser is the shortest book of the treatise. Nevertheless it is important in that it points towards the identification of the search for causes, which is proper to natural philosophy, with the search for truth that belongs to metaphysics. Truth, we are told, is a kind of supreme cause of the being of things. The search for causes and the search for truth are not ultimately to be distinguished. This equation is then buttressed by an argument demonstrating that the number of causes is necessarily finite, and the book concludes with some further methodological prescriptions. By the end of it, we have reached a clearer understanding both of what we are looking for and of how we may hope to find it.

Book Beta concludes the preliminary section of the treatise in a remarkable way. It has aptly been said that philosophy cannot be described but only done, and Aristotle shows his sympathy with this view by forgoing all further setting up of his inquiry and plunging directly into the presentation of fifteen central metaphysical problems. It is as though he is replying to our question as to what metaphysics is really about, a question that remains open after the first two books, not by describing it in yet more conflations of terminology but by showing us. We are thrown into the deep end of the metaphysical pool in the hope that this will encourage in us the desire to be taught how to swim. Aristotle's conception of the inquiry could well be said to be problem-driven, and he clearly intends that our bafflement and fascination with the problems set out and ventilated in Beta will generate the motivation that is to sustain us through the long and arduous journey that is to come.

With book Gamma the direct presentation of the inquiry of metaphysics starts, based on the preliminaries of the books Alpha and especially on the problematic of book Beta. Aristotle starts with what has often been taken to be his working definition of metaphysics, as the study of being *qua* being. The little word *qua*, which is the Latin translation of the Greek relative pronoun in the ablative case, has come down into English as a useful abbreviation of some such phrase as 'under the aspect of'. Its use is ubiquitous in Aristotle. It is very clearly illustrated by the present passage, in which the study of being *qua* being is contrasted with the study of being *qua* various other things. In a sense, all science studies being in some way, but the 'departmental' sciences study it under the restriction appropriate to each one of them. It falls to metaphysics to study being, so to speak, in its own right. The study of metaphysics is the study of all the things that are just in regard to those aspects of them which pertain to their being merely by virtue of their having being.

We shall see that the core of metaphysics is rather more restricted, but we are approaching the topic from the outside and we are first given an overview of the whole terrain before we come to concentrate on the strategic commanding heights.

Gamma continues by examining the notion of being and the closely connected notion of unity. It then insists, in the third chapter, that the study of metaphysics cannot be complete without an examination of the fundamental principles of logic. These in turn depend upon one sovereign principle, that of non-contradiction, the principle that nothing can both have and not have the same property in the same regard at the same time. It has often been thought – and Aristotle concedes the plausibility of the thought – that the principle is too fundamental to be treated as anything other than a kind of axiom. It cannot be supported by any argument that does not already depend on it. Aristotle, however, embarks on an extraordinary attempt to defend the principle not by a direct justification but by a kind of *reductio ad absurdum* of anyone who seeks to deny it. Both the form and the upshot of this argument have been extensively discussed, and it remains a classic early contribution to philosophical logic.

Book Delta is Aristotle's glossary both for the present treatise and, to some extent, for his writings as a whole. It is clear on the most cursory inspection that it is not specifically integrated into the text of this particular treatise. Nor are the definitions and discussions that it contains a very secure guide to the use of the terms to which they apply later in the work. However, this in itself is no more evidence that the treatise is a compilation of some later editor than that Aristotle never had the opportunity adequately and definitively to polish his production. (Given the enormous workload that we may presume him to have taken on as the first head of the Lyceum, and the general difficulty of editing and revising texts in the material conditions of antiquity, it seems surprising that this possibility is not more generally allowed than it is.)

Book Epsilon completes the general presentation of metaphysics, by focusing our attention, within the study of being, on that aspect which is fundamental to the rest, and dealing succinctly with a part of the subject, which, though important, is here of subsidiary interest.

Although Epsilon is a short book, it has an important structural role, and a great deal goes on in it. The book begins by identifying the study of being with the study of God, and this identification confirms the value and worth of the subject in the most effective possible way.

We are now reminded again of the multiplicity of being. Things are said to be in many ways, but, as modern scholars have put it, the ways in which they are said to be are focused on one particular way. That way of being, as we have already seen, is substance, and substance is, of course, the central topic of the treatise, to be discussed in the next book, Zeta. Book Epsilon first deals with two less central ways in which things are, with the being of accidental properties and with being as truth (and not-being as falsity). Neither discussion requires extensive treatment, though for different reasons. Accidental being, by virtue of which we might say that Socrates *is*, say, musical without its being the case that Socrates' ceasing to be musical would entail his ceasing to be Socrates, is in every way an inferior way of being for Aristotelian science and is more appropriate to the *Physics*, where it is illuminatingly discussed in connection with the notion of chance. Being as truth is by no means unimportant for Aristotle, but it has already been exhaustively discussed in book Gamma, and Aristotle is anxious not to dull our appetites before we proceed to the very heart of the study of being.

The stage is thus fully set for the entry of the hero, substance. Aristotle begins book Zeta with a very clear statement that the central question in the entire history of philosophy, what being is, is really the question of what substance is. If he has been successful in the arguments of the previous books, this should strike us as a mere summary of an already established position rather than a bold and striking claim. The task of the *Metaphysics* so far has been to show the centrality of substance. It is now time to turn to the examination of the centre itself. I have already tried to indicate how book Zeta arrives at its remarkable conclusion that the substance of something is to be equated with its definable essence and thus with its form and the species to which it belongs. The discussion is formally structured around the four criteria for substantiality but in fact comes to be dominated by the attempt to sustain the brilliant compromise that is the doctrine of special substance. It has sometimes been regretted that the final chapter should seem rather incongruously to embark on a new discussion, but this should rather be welcomed as an indication of the extent to which the reasoning of books Zeta and Eta forms a whole for all the diversity of the conclusions of the two books.

The shift to the particular that we find in Eta is also a shift towards the sensible and the material. It is the individual composites of form and matter that the book will in the end vindicate as primary substances, in a sophisticated return to the position of the *Categories*. It is accordingly appropriate that a considerable amount of the book should be devoted to clarifying the different roles of form and matter within the composite, a subject that inevitably connects with the contrast between actuality and potentiality that is noticeably more prominent in this book than in Zeta and which will form the central topic of the next book, Theta. The position eventually reached in Eta is that particulars can, for all their susceptibility to change, still be substances, because the persisting matter that survives both their coming into, and their going out of, being is only potentially present in them during the period of their life – and thus is not a candidate to be their substance – and the metaphysical buck can stop with the whole composite. This position is one that, of course, depends on a subtle use of the potentiality/actuality distinction, but also one that makes use of the approach to substance that has been explored in Zeta. It seems fair to say that Eta would have been impossible without Zeta or something like it. This, however, makes it all the harder to decide what the relation is between these two clearly closely connected but doctrinally contradictory books. It is obviously possible, to take a developmentalist approach, to hold that Eta simply represents a recantation on the part of Aristotle of what must always have struck him as a rather extraordinary position. It would therefore be true to say that he could not have reached the new account of particular substance without first holding that of special substance, but it would not be true to say that he had to present the doctrine of special substance in order to make palatable his eventual position. Alternatively, from a more 'unitarian' perspective, it could be argued that Aristotle clearly feels that the conclusions of Eta will only be intelligible for someone who has already worked through Zeta. This, of course, could be the case whatever the actual timetable of discovery of the positions defended.

The latter view is, of course, more attractive to anyone who wishes to see the work as a solid construction, an organism rather than a heap.

Light is also thrown on the structure of the treatise by book Theta, which deals with the subject of actuality and potentiality directly. A treatment of this topic is required by the agenda set in Gamma, since one of the ways in which things can be simply by virtue of being is by being either potentially or actually. But we are also owed a detailed treatment in view of the significance that the distinction has come to acquire for the account of substance itself. Thus what might have been a merely taxonomic continuation of the survey of being comes to have an important role in supporting the central concerns of the entire treatise. In chapter 8, Aristotle defends his celebrated thesis that actuality precedes potentiality. This doctrine constitutes a kind of bridge between the general treatment of substance that we have just completed and the treatment of immaterial substance that is to come. Whatever the relationship between Zeta and Eta, it is clear that book Lambda, which presents Aristotle's theology, rests heavily on the conclusions of Theta. The book is also divided between discussing the study of the actualization of a process and that of the actuality, in the sense of fullest being, of a substance. This is a suggestive distinction, but unfortunately not one that Aristotle draws either with great clarity or with great consistency, and it has accordingly been extensively discussed in the literature.

The connection of Iota with the general course of the treatise is perhaps less immediate than that of Theta, but it too deals with a topic which is both on the agenda set in Gamma and of increased significance because of the discussion in Zeta–Eta. Iota deals with the subject of unity, or the one, and diversity. This had been a central topic of philosophy for the Academy and before that for the Pythagoreans, and it was to become so again for the long Neoplatonist era. It is perhaps less important for the Lyceum, but Aristotle has already argued that, just as metaphysics cannot fight shy of the need to examine the principles of logic, so must it also cover the topics of unity and diversity and with them identity and difference. Thus the material in Iota would in any case be relevant to the scope of the treatise, as well as being a clear indication of its largeness of view. But, in addition to that, the subject of unity has become a very important one in the light of the stress laid in Zeta on the need to make sense of the idea that a definition and its object are both irreducible unities in some way, despite the fact that they are clearly composed of parts of another unity. It is true that the contents of Iota are not targeted as directly as they might be on the concept of unity as it relates to the problem of the unity of the definition, but here too one might argue that Aristotle would have sharpened up the relevance of the book had he had time to give it the necessary consideration.

We have already seen that book Kappa is a problem book. Perhaps all that need be added here is that, given the availability of reworkings of important passages from both the *Metaphysics* and the *Physics*, it makes as much sense to locate them where they are as anywhere else in either work. It is reasonably clear that, whereas book Iota concludes that section of the treatise concerned with the central issue of substance in general, book Lambda starts the discussion of two major but in a sense departmental problems about substance, those of divine and of mathematical substance.

Lambda itself is one of the most intensively studied of all the books of the treatise. It is here that Aristotle presents his famous conception of God as an Unmoved First Mover, as an originator of all processes who Himself stands outside all change. The conception has fascinated both theologians and philosophers, but it is worth observing that it grows organically enough from the discussions both of substance and, especially, of actuality in the central books of the treatise. Aristotle's theology is extraordinarily well integrated with both his general metaphysics and his philosophy of nature, and it is thus appropriate that the account of the divine nature should be preceded, as it is, with a compressed guide to the general outlines of Aristotelian science. Lambda can also be read, partly for this reason, relatively independently of the rest of the treatise. It is in many ways a good place to start reading the *Metaphysics*, since in some ways it presents the most remarkable fruits of what has gone before it. Wonder at how Aristotle can have arrived at the conception of God that we find in Lambda has often proved a powerful motivation for readers, initially more interested in theology than metaphysics, to attempt to grapple with the general account of substance.

The last subject that must be covered in a full course of metaphysics is that of the metaphysical status of mathematics. Rationalist philosophers have always pointed to the apparent certainty and solidity of mathematics to support their claim that extra-sensory knowledge is possible, and this association is conspicuously present in Plato's dialogues of all periods. It is not therefore surprising that Aristotle combines his discussion, in books Mu and Nu, of the status of the entities studied in arithmetic with a recast version of the attack on Platonism in book Alpha. The attack on Platonism in both the Alpha and the Mu versions is enormously important in helping us to understand not only Aristotle's objections to the Theory of Forms but also the content of the Theory itself, especially as it was discussed inside the Academy as opposed to the manner in which it was presented to a wider audience in such clearly 'literary' works as the *Symposium* and the *Phaedrus*. Interest in the details of the rather baffling accounts of mathematical entities offered by both Plato and Aristotle has always tended to be rather less intense, though there has been a revival to some extent through the important work of Julia Annas.

From this whistle-stop tour through the work I hope it will have emerged that we have on our hands an impressive and spacious construction and one which sticks to a clearly defined course of exegesis. We have historical background, then methodology and appetite-whetting puzzles, followed by a general account of being, supplemented by a glossary, which then issues in a survey of the range of ways in which things have being that is clearly focused on the central case of substance. With the exception of book Kappa, I believe that there is no part of the treatise whose relevance to the overall design cannot be defended. It is, therefore, prima facie at least as reasonable to suppose the designer was Aristotle as that it was anybody else.

To say this is not to claim that the treatise is in any sense a finished production. Even those sections which clearly contribute to, or support, the central position are fraught with obscurity and apparent contradiction. It is quite clear that this is a work that has been put together from pre-existing materials and that the process of welding has been interrupted at a relatively early stage. In my view, given the position of the work in the history of philosophy and of scientific writing more generally, it would be amazing if a work of unprecedented ambition, complexity and difficulty had proved any easier than it evidently did to bring to birth. If the *Metaphysics* is a building, it is still covered in scaffolding, with gaps in its plaster and decoration and even with key structural elements tottering insecurely on makeshift supports. But, for all that, it is still more like a palace or a cathedral than the workshop or warehouse as which it has so often been treated.

3. *The Translation*

No single translation of, any more than any single commentary on, a major work of Aristotle can aspire to be definitive or even to meet the needs of more than a specific limited range of readers. Work on Aristotle, perhaps more than that on any other philosopher, necessarily falls into layers. It is evident in the case of a commentary that some readers benefit from a presentation which for others is superficial, and it is no less the case with a translation that, in the inevitable trade-off between greater readability and greater literal precision, there will be readers who will derive benefit from either end of the spectrum. Whatever may be thought of the present translation, its purpose is clear. It has been written with one overriding intention, that of making accessible to readers at a relatively early stage of their philosophical development a masterpiece of philosophy which, by reason of its length, complexity, difficulty and stylistic aridity, has often been thought to lie beyond the reach of all but advanced students. If it achieves any measure of success in this objective, its provider will be content.

Indeed, I would like to consider this version to be an introductory, or even preliminary, translation. It will ideally be useful to readers at the start of their acquaintance with the text and then decline in relevance as that acquaintance blossoms into familiarity and perhaps even friendship. The purpose is to help people work their way into the treatise, not to give them at a stroke everything that they need to know about the suggestions and nuances of the Greek. It is a distinctive fact about the tradition of studying Aristotle that for many centuries this study was carried on in three forms, that of the translation, that of the commentary and that of the paraphrase. It is not obviously a good thing that the last of these has declined as an institution of the study of Aristotle (and perhaps the philosophy of remote cultures more generally), although it survives in large numbers of secondary works of exegesis that continue to be produced with no sign of abatement. While I would not like the present translation to be thought of as a paraphrase, I do consider that it serves something of the purpose of the traditional paraphrase in providing the new reader with the opportunity to read reasonably large sections of the text at a time with as much continuity as their nature permits.

I now propose to say a little about what makes it so difficult to read and therefore to translate Aristotle and how I have tried to deal with these difficulties within the scope of the overall objective set out above. I take there to be four main areas of difficulty. The first concerns Aristotle's terminology. Here the difficulties are, in turn, of three kinds. The first is the sheer complexity and richness of the theoretical vocabulary which, together with a certain inconsistency in its use, requires the exercise of considerable control across the entire text. The second problem is that, as we have already seen, Aristotle frequently uses a phrase where we would expect an abstract noun. The third trouble is of rather a different kind. It is simply that almost all the key terms of Aristotle-speak have entered into the abstract vernacular of the modern European languages, including English. In so entering, they have, of course, acquired nuances and connotations which take them a long way from their original meaning, and these associations constitute a kind of minefield through which the translator of Aristotle has to pick a path with care.

The second of the four main difficulties is that Aristotle is no master of syntax. He lived in what is arguably the most golden of all the golden ages of prose, and we know that he himself enjoyed a reputation as a stylist. This, however, was for his esoteric works, of which only fragments have survived. His extant, esoteric treatises are, with the exception of a few well-known passages, flat in sentence construction and without the relief of syntactic contours. This, over a sustained period, can lead to an oppressive sense of monotony, tolerance of which is not well conducive to the enticement of new readers.

The third, related difficulty is that the text is highly elliptical. As is the way with preachers to the converted, Aristotle frequently omits premises and stages of arguments which, from our perspective, by no means deserve to be left tacit. Often, indeed, it is hard to see where one argument ends and another begins, and there are cases of the insertion of one argument into the course of another. In addition to this fondness, which verges on addiction, for the enthymeme, Aristotle is also disdainful of even the routine padding of formal prose. It is evident that he was not paid by the inch for his copy. Something must be done to offset this stylistic anorexia, but any remedy is likely to involve implications and commitments which go to some extent beyond what is absolutely licensed by the text that we have.

The final difficulty is that Aristotle is insouciant about a distinction which has become of paramount importance in modern philosophical writing, that between use and mention. Contemporary philosophy attaches the greatest possible importance to its being absolutely clear at all stages whether the writer is talking about the term 'man', say, or the species man. This, of course, reflects the central role played in modern philosophy by the problems of linguistic reference. For Aristotle such problems are by no means central (though not as little considered as is sometimes argued), and the distinction is correspondingly less momentous. He therefore frequently talks about an entity in a way in which we would talk about the meaning of a term. Many translators bite this bullet and use, for instance, the word 'sense' in translating such passages or, alternatively, make extensive use of quotation marks. In my view, this is unwarranted and gives the translated text a feel quite different from that of the original. In the cases where it has not seemed possible to get round the difficulty by some kind of periphrasis, I have made use of italicization to indicate that a term is not being used in the straightforward manner of merely picking out an object.

I hope that my attempts to resolve these four areas of difficulty have produced a readable English text, though it is certainly possible that I have been pushed by one pressure or another outside the bandwidth of comfortable intelligibility. In any case, I am doubtful that there is a useful *via media*, given the objectives of this translation, between the approach that I have adopted and that of Montgomery Furth in his (1986) version of books Zeta–Iota. Furth, whose purpose is quite different from my own, translates the text into a language he dubs Eek, which is a kind of inter-language between Aristotle's Greek and English. Study of the text in Eek brings the reader as close as possible to the actual structure of Aristotle's words without actually mastering Greek itself. This is, of course, appropriate for established students, but it is hardly right for neophytes. One way of looking on the present version is as a preparation for reading Eek.

After these remarks about the general difficulties of translating the mature philosophical prose of Aristotle, I would like to survey the way I have dealt with certain key elements of the jargon. By and large, I have kept, where possible, to the conventional translations of individual terms, while feeling relatively free to adjust the syntax of the sentences in which they occur. The intention is that it should always be easy for the reader to locate a passage against the background of the secondary debate. However, this has not always been possible – indeed there is in some cases no received translation – and it will perhaps be useful to offer, not a full glossary, but a kind of *catalogue raisonné* of those terms that belong to the core of Aristotle's system.

accident (*sumbebēkos*) – sometimes translated as 'incident', this term indicates features that belong to something not as part of its *per se* nature.

account (*logos*) – it is in connection with Aristotle's language for speaking of things that the difficulties of the use-mention distinction, or its absence, discussed above, are especially acute. I have tried to use the English term 'account' as a blanket term for all Aristotle's Greek expressions involving forms or derivatives of *legein*, the main verb in Greek for speaking or saying. The most important of such derivatives is the ubiquitous abstract noun *logos*. It is not, however, the case that every use of *logos* in the Greek is translated with the English word 'account', since it is sometimes clearly to be translated as 'proportion' or 'ratio' and sometimes as 'reason'.

actuality (*energeia, entelekheia*) – I have translated both these terms with the same English word, although *energeia* has more the sense of the realization of a process, *entelekheia* that of a substance.

being (*einai*) – I have used the conventional English gerund translation of what is an infinitive in Aristotle's Greek, since they are grammatically equivalent.

cause (*aition*) – it is often suggested that this term should be translated into English as something like 'explanatory factor'. It is also the case that it corresponds equally to the English notions of cause and reason. For consistency, I have stayed with the traditional 'cause'.

change/process/movement (*kinēsis*) – the most literal meaning is that of movement, but the term is extremely wide in application and the English term 'process' is the only one that really approaches it in generality. I have used 'process' wherever possible, but I have not attempted a uniform translation at the expense of accuracy in context.

composite (*ex amphoterou*) – standard term for the particular that is, on Aristotle's mature theory, metaphysically made up of the bringing together of form and matter.

element (*stoikheion*) – conventional translation alternatives that I have sometimes used are 'constituent' and 'component'.

form (*eidos/morphē*) – the term *morphē* literally means 'shape', but I have followed what is close to a convention in translating it too as 'form'.

Form (*idea*) – I have referred throughout to Plato's notion of a transcendent, non-immanent Form with capitalization (as also the Theory of Forms).

matter (*hulē*) – occasionally translated as 'material' for stylistic variation.

per se (*kath'heauton*) – I have used the literal Latin translation, from the Scholastic tradition, throughout.

posterior (*husteros*) – could be translated 'derivative' or 'secondary', but both have potentially misleading connotations.

potentiality (*dunamis*) – also sometimes translated as 'power' or 'faculty'.

primary (*prōtos*) – this usually has the sense of 'basic' or 'fundamental' rather than 'primordial'. It does not, unless qualified, suggest temporal priority.

principle (*arkhē*) also means 'beginning', but I have translated as 'principle' wherever possible.

prior (*proteros*) – the complementary term to *husteros* (see *posterior*).

qua (*hēi*) – I have retained the traditional Latin throughout.

separable (*khoristos*) – this term is used extremely widely by Aristotle, with a range of qualifying phrases. It is a form of the verb which can equally easily be taken to suggest either actual separation or the potentiality for it. In the *Metaphysics*, it is primarily used to refer to the supposed transcendence of Platonic Forms.

species (*eidos*) – Aristotle has the same term for both species and (immanent) form, despite the fact that the equation of the two is not a mere statement of equivalence but an important piece of doctrine. Nevertheless, disambiguation is usually relatively easy in each context.

strictly (*kuriōs*) – this is another term that cries out for translation into the modern idiom of sense, but I have eschewed this option, persisting with the somewhat cumbrous use of the adjective and adverb.

substance (*ousia*) – sometimes translated 'reality', but I retain the traditional version for convenience of reference.

thisness (*tode ti*) – a key hallmark of substance for Aristotle, translated as 'haeccitas' by the scholastics. It is also Aristotle's habitual way of referring to the particular as opposed to the universal.

universal (*kath'holou*) – it is striking that Aristotle uses a phrase, not an abstract noun, for both particularity and universality, although the distinction between them is crucial to his thinking.

what-it-was-to-be-that-thing (*ti ēn einai*) – another remarkable phrase, which I have discussed in the first part of the introduction. The conventional translation is 'essence', but I have followed the recent trend to translate in a way that reflects the internal structure of the phrase.

This list is, of course, far from being exhaustive. I have merely tried to indicate my policy on at least some of the key terms of the treatise. I have not made use of subscripts, flagging or textual features other than italics. These undoubtedly have their role, but they inevitably diminish readability and, in the spirit of my overall objective, I have refrained from indulging in them.

The translation, then, is in every way intended to be a *vade mecum* to only the first faltering steps of a journey of discovery into Aristotle. The ideal reader will progress through dissatisfaction with its many shortcomings to a sympathy for the extraordinary difficulty of producing anything that can render tolerable, within the constraints of reasonable fidelity, a sustained reading of this most enigmatically pregnant of texts.

Book Alpha

ALPHA I

The book opens by broaching a topic which is to be of recurring concern throughout the work. What is the nature of philosophy? We can make some progress with this question, Aristotle assumes, if we can determine what it is that is the proper object of philosophical interest. This, in a way, is easy to do – the philosopher can be said boldly to be someone interested in the acquisition of wisdom. However, this does not of course get us much further. We need to know what wisdom is and how, if at all, it can be acquired by our limited human capacities. The first of these two questions is answered in this first chapter and the second throughout the course of the work.

Aristotle approaches the question of the nature of wisdom indirectly, by drawing a contrast between two fundamentally different forms of cognition, which are between them constitutive of our cognitive handling of the world. On the one hand, we have direct experience of particular objects and events, but on the other we are, in certain circumstances, able to derive general propositions from our experience of particulars which go beyond the content of any thoughts just about particulars. The capacity for the latter form of knowledge is something that Aristotle thinks we owe to the possession of an art or science. And this distinction is also crucial for illustrating the nature of wisdom, which turns out to be a special sort of science. It is a peculiarity of the distinction that, whereas experience may often be more helpful in practice than art or science, it is the latter two which are always accorded the greater prestige. This is because it is felt – a general assumption with which Aristotle by no means disagrees – that knowledge of universals is somehow higher or more valuable than that of particular things. And the kind of universal knowledge that is most valuable of all is that connected with the fundamental causes and principles of all things. Since it is agreed that wisdom is the highest science, it must be such things that constitute its domain. Philosophy is thus the search for the most fundamental causes and principles of the most general aspects of the world.

As already suggested, this exercise will be of little practical value, and it will be impossible to determine whether the philosopher has succeeded in his search

3

by seeing whether he is thereby better at any practical, productive or technical task. He will, if he has been successful, rather have achieved a state of intrinsic value. Philosophy is supremely useless and supremely elevating. One mark that can be held to indicate real progress in philosophy or in any abstract study is, however, the ability to teach what one has learned. Aristotle clearly considers that a philosopher who did not teach would be a contradiction in terms. Certainly, there have not been sufficient major philosophers who have refrained from disseminating their views to give the lie to this claim.

[980a] By nature, all men long to know. An indication is their delight in the senses. For these, quite apart from their utility, are intrinsically delightful, and that through the eyes more than the others. For it is not only with a view to action but also when we have no intention to do anything that we choose, so to speak, sight rather than all the others. And the reason for this is that sight is the sense that especially produces cognition in us and reveals many distinguishing features of things.

Now the animals in general are by nature possessed of senses, but of them some do not also have memory, though others do. [980b] And so the latter are more intelligent and capable of learning than those that are not capable of remembering, whereas those that are not able to hear sounds are intelligent without being able to learn (e.g. the bee and any other such kind of animal that there may be). Learning is reserved for those that in addition to memory also have the sense of hearing. For other animals live by their imaginings and recollections, with only a small share of experience, whereas mankind lives also by his skill and calculations. But it is from memory that men derive their experience. For many recollections of the same thing perform the function of a single experience. Indeed, it is thought that experience is more or less similar to knowledge and skill, [981a] and that men acquire knowledge and skill through experience. As Polus so rightly says, experience produces skill, inexperience chance.

Now the circumstances in which a skill arises are that from the many cases of thinking in experience a single general assumption is formed in connection with similar things. For instance, to have the assumption that when Callias is ill with such and such a disease such and such a medicine is appropriate and similarly for Socrates and for many others individually is a matter of experience. But the knowledge that for all such people, defined by species, when ill with such and such a disease, such and such a medicine is beneficial belongs to skill.

However, in regard to practice, experience is not thought to be different at all from skill. In fact, we rather observe those with experience being practically successful than those who, without experience, have a theoretical understanding. This is because experience is the knowledge of particulars and skill that of universals, and practical actions, like all occurrences, are concerned with particulars. For it is not a man that the practising doctor cures, except accidentally, but rather Callias or Socrates or some other of those thus named, to whom being a man is accidental. If, then, one were to have a theoretical account without experience, knowing the universal but being ignorant of the immediate particular, he will often err in his treatment. For it is the particular that must be treated.

And yet we think that knowledge and expertise belong rather to skill than to experience, and we assume that the skilled are wiser than the experienced, in that it is more in connection with knowledge that wisdom is associated with anything. And the reason for this is that the skilled know the cause, whereas the experienced do not. For the experienced know the 'that' but not the 'because', whereas the skilled have a grasp of the 'because', the cause.

That is why in each field designers are thought more prestigious and to have more knowledge than craftsmen and to be wiser, [981b] in that they know the causes for what is being done. The assumption is that it is not being practical that makes them wiser but their possession of an account and their grasp of the causes. And in general the ability to teach is a distinguishing mark between the knowledgeable and the ignorant man, and that is why we think that skill is rather a form of knowledge than experience. For the skilled can, whereas the merely experienced cannot, teach.

Furthermore, we do not think that any of the senses is wisdom, even those that are the most important forms of cognition at the level of particulars. They do not, though, give the reason for anything, e.g. as *why* fire is hot, but merely indicate *that* it is hot. And so it would not

5

be surprising if the first man to discover some skill or other, beyond the common senses, was admired by other men not only because of the utility of some of what he discovered but as being wise and above the herd. For when several skills had been discovered, some having to do with necessity and some with indulgence, it is reasonable that the practitioners of the latter were always more admired than those of the former because of the uselessness of their knowledge. Hence, indeed, it was that when all such arts had been discovered, those arts were discovered which had to do neither with pleasure nor with necessities, and this happened first in those places where men had leisure. That is why it was in Egypt that the mathematical sciences were first developed, for there leisure was available to the priestly caste. And so, as we said above, the man of experience is thought to be wiser than the man who has just any perception of a subject, the craftsman wiser than the man of experience, the designer wiser than the artisan and the theoretical sciences wiser than the productive ones.

[982a] It is clear, then, that wisdom is knowledge having to do with certain principles and causes.

ALPHA 2

Aristotle has indicated that wisdom, the highest science, which is the object of philosophy, is a science of causes and principles. In this second chapter he spells out that the causes and principles studied by philosophy are the most fundamental and valuable. He feels that this characterization of wisdom is supported by the received opinion, always an important consideration for Aristotle, which assigns to the wise man knowledge of universal and inaccessible truths, knowledge of superior exactitude, and the ability to teach others, by dint of having a grasp of the supreme, and supremely useless, principles of the world. The study of philosophy holds out the promise of making sense of the world in a more profound way than through any other science. It has always been accepted, albeit vaguely, that such an understanding of the world is possible, but it is only now that we are on the sure way to acquiring it.

Philosophy, so characterized, has a special relationship with the divine. On the one hand, divinity is clearly a primary principle of the world and so itself falls in the domain of philosophy. Indeed, there are points in the work in which Aristotle seems to come close to equating philosophy with theology. On the other hand, the practice of philosophy, over the course of a lifetime, has an ennobling effect on the philosopher, such that he or she is brought as close as possible to a divine state. We share some fragment of the divine nature, which through philosophy we can nourish and promote.

This conception of philosophy as a liberation from the complexities of our existence is one that Aristotle supports with a few brief, but often quoted, comments on the origins of philosophy in a sense of wonder or amazement at the arrangement of the world. The history of philosophy is the history of the gradual, progressive abstraction of this sense of wonder.

But now, since it is this knowledge that we are seeking, we must consider the following point: of what kind of principles and of what kind of causes is wisdom the knowledge? If, indeed, one were to take the assumptions that we have concerning the wise man, perhaps from this the answer would become more clear. Our assumptions are, then, first: that the wise man knows everything in the appropriate way, not having knowledge of these subjects at the level of particulars. Secondly, that the man who is able to know difficult things and not easy for a man to know, that is the wise man – for sense perception is common to all men and so easy and not wise at all. Thirdly, that the man who is more accurate and more capable of teaching the causes is wiser in connection with every sort of knowledge. Fourthly, that of forms of knowledge that which is chosen for itself and for the sake of knowledge is wisdom more than that which is chosen for its results, and the directive science is wisdom more than that which subserves it. For the wise man should not be instructed but should instruct, and it is not he who should obey another, but rather the less wise should obey him.

These, then, are the kind and number of assumptions that we have about wisdom and the wise. And of these we think that it is necessary that the knowledge of everything belongs especially to the man who has universal knowledge. For this man in a way knows all the subjects, and more or less also the hardest for men to know, those that are most general – for these are furthest removed from the senses. And the most exact of the sciences are those that are connected particularly with primary things. For those which are from fewer things are more exact than those which are said by addition, as arithmetic is more exact than geometry. And it is also the case that theoretical knowledge is more capable of teaching the causes. For it is those who give the causes in connection with each thing that can teach, and knowledge and science for their own sake belong especially to the knowledge of that which is especially known. For the man who chooses to know for its own sake will especially choose the most extreme form of knowledge, and this is the knowledge of the most known thing. [982b] And the things that are most known are the primary things and the causes. For it is through them and from them that the other things are known and not the latter through the underlying things. And the most fundamental of the sciences, more fundamental than that which subserves it, is that which discerns for what end each thing must be done. And this is the good for each thing, and in general the best in all natures. From everything that has been said, then, the name that we are seeking falls to the same science. For this science must be theoretical of the primary principles and causes. And indeed the good and the 'for the sake of what' are one of the causes.

But it is clear that this science is not productive also from the early history of philosophy. For it was because of wonder that men both now and originally began to philosophize. To begin with, they wondered at those puzzles that were to hand, such as about the affections of the moon and events connected with the sun and the stars and about the origins of the universe. And the man who is puzzled and amazed is thought to be ignorant (hence the lover of stories is, in a way, a lover of wisdom, since a story is composed of wonders). And so, if men indeed began to philosophize to escape ignorance, it is clear that they pursued science for the sake of knowledge and not for any utility. And events bear this out. For when more or less all the necessary sciences existed, and also those connected with leisure and lifestyle, this kind of understanding began to be sought after. So it is clear that we seek it for no other use but rather, as we say, as a free man is for himself and not for another, so is this science the only one of the sciences that is free. For it alone exists for its own sake.

And for this reason it is with justice that its acquisition would not be thought to be human. For in many ways the nature of men is enslaved. Thus, according to Simonides:

'Only a god might have this boon . . .',

and a man might not be thought worthy to seek out knowledge itself. [983a] And if indeed the poets have a point and it is a divine thing to be envious, it would accordingly be reasonable that all the outstanding should suffer. But in fact it is not divine to envy, but rather, as in the proverb,

'Many are the lies of seers . . .',

and it is also necessary to think another skill of more worth than this one. For that which is most divine is also most worthy. And such a science would be alone in two ways. For it would be that which a god would most choose, that is the one of the sciences that is divine, if indeed any of them is divine. And this happens to be alone in both of these ways. For god is thought to be among the causes for all things and to be a kind of principle, and also god would have such knowledge either exclusively or mainly. So all sciences are more necessary than this one and none is better.

In a way, however, we must make the acquisition of it the opposite of fundamental inquiries. For, as we said, all men began to philosophize from wonder whether it is really so, as with spontaneous natural wonders, such as those of the changes of the sun or the incommensurability of the diameter (for everybody thinks that this is amazing, if something cannot be measured exactly). But on the contrary, we must produce the best, according to the proverb, just as with these subjects when there has been learning. For a geometer would be surprised by nothing so much as if the diameter were measurable. We have, then, said what the nature is of the science that we are seeking and what the end is at which the search should aim and the whole method.

ALPHA 3

We have now established that philosophy is a study of causes and, indeed, of the most fundamental, primary and valuable causes. However, we have still not been told much about what it is to investigate a cause, let alone a primary cause. This is a topic to which Aristotle has devoted a great deal of thought. His view is that to have any philosophical understanding of causation, it is necessary to accept a certain taxonomy of causes which he has already presented in the Physics. *There are four basic ways in which one thing can cause another. It can be its cause by providing the form that it realizes, by being the matter from which it is made, by being the source of the process that leads to its coming to be or by being that for the sake of which the thing is produced. In any actual case of causal explanation it is vital to distinguish these four kinds of causation. Modern philosophers have often been puzzled at the willingness of Aristotle to talk of four kinds of cause, and it may be simpler to regard Aristotle as attempting to isolate four fundamentally different ways in which things can be explained.*

In any case, he certainly thinks that all explanation, including philosophical explanation, must conform with his scheme, and, very characteristically, he proceeds to show that earlier philosophical practice did in fact observe the distinction of kinds of explanation, and acknowledge the need for them all, although incoherently. This claim is supported by a historical sketch of earlier metaphysical thinking. Philosophers began, naturally enough, by looking for the material cause of the world, with various elements or combinations of elements being the preferred candidates. It became apparent, however, that no understanding of the material constitution of the world could account for the prescience in it of movement and change, and so philosophers began to seek for a causal explanation in terms of the source or sources of processes in the world. This produced problems, not least the crisis precipitated by the Eleatic rejection of change as a whole, but in any case even the finding of the motive cause of the world would not have been felt to be adequate. An explanation was also needed of the intrinsic value of the world. It was Anaxagoras who pioneered the way to such an explanation by suggesting that the arrangement of the world must be the product of a supreme mind. In Aristotle's terms, this is to say that there must be some feature of the world for which it exists.

It is a hallmark of Aristotle's philosophical outlook that he sees his work as continuous with that of his predecessors. Indeed, he sometimes seems to conceive his project as that of effecting a kind of grand synthesis of the diverse strands of earlier scientific and metaphysical speculation. It is for this reason that all the major treatises provide a survey in at least some depth of the previous debate. As this chapter shows, Aristotle is inclusive – even the poets are reviewed, and, on subjects on which the ordinary man has an opinion, his view is also presented. The 'doxographical' survey in the Metaphysics, *however, is distinctive both for its length and for the fact that it detects a large-scale evolution in the discussion of the causes of the world from a simple-minded concentration on the material substrate towards the higher and more elusive causality of form and purpose. Such a sense of development in intellectual history has become familiar enough in the nineteenth and twentieth centuries, but was unusual in antiquity, and on the strength of it Aristotle could be hailed, if not as the father, at least as a remote progenitor of what we call the history of ideas.*

Now since it is clear that we must grasp knowledge of fundamental causes (for we say that each man has knowledge, when we think that he knows the primary cause), and the causes are spoken of in four ways, of which one cause we say to be the substance and the essence (for the 'why' is referred to the extreme term, and the cause and principle is the primary 'why'), and the second is the matter and substrate, and the third is that from which comes the beginning of the change, and the fourth is the opposite cause to this, the 'wherefore' and the good (for this is the end of all coming into being and change), we have sufficiently theorized about them in the *Physics*. [983b] Nevertheless, let us take those who have engaged in the consideration of the things that there are before us and who have philosophized concerning truth. For it is clear that they too mentioned certain principles and causes. And as we go through them, there will be some advantages for our present method – either we will discover some other kind of cause or we will have greater confidence in those that we now state.

Well, of the first philosophers the majority thought that the causes in the form of matter were alone the principles of all things. For that from which all entities come, from which each thing primarily arises and into which it is at the end resolved, the substance remaining but changing as to affections, this they announced to be the element and principle of all entities, and for this reason they thought that nothing either came to be or was destroyed, since this sort of nature was always preserved, so that we do not even say that Socrates either came into being *simpliciter*, when he became fine or musical, nor that he was destroyed when he lost these dispositions, since the substrate remained, Socrates himself, and the same consideration they thought applied to all other things. For they thought that there must be some nature, either one or more than one, from which other things arose while it was conserved.

But the number and form of such a principle they do not all proclaim to be the same. Thales, the introducer of this sort of philosophy, said that it was water (that is why he declared the earth to be sitting on water), perhaps drawing this supposition from seeing that the nourishment of all creatures is moist and that warmth itself arises from this and that it is by this that all creatures live (and the assumption that that from which a thing comes is its principle in all cases). For this reason, indeed, taking this assumption and also because the seeds of all creatures have a moist nature and water is the natural principle for moist things. And there are also some who think that the very ancient thinkers and those long before the present generation and the first to reason about the gods made the same assumptions about nature. For these poets made Ocean and Tethys the parents of creation and said that the oath of the gods was water, which they called Styx. For the assumption was that the most ancient thing was the most worthy, and that an oath was the most worthy thing. [984a] If then this opinion that nature happens to be primordial and ancient is perhaps unclear, yet Thales is said to have made these declarations concerning the primary cause. (For Hippo one would not think right to include with these thinkers because of the triviality of his mind.)

Anaximenes, however, assumed that air was prior to water and was especially a principle of the simple bodies, and Diogenes thought the same, while Hippasus of Metapontum and Heraclitus of Ephesus thought

13

it was fire. Empedocles thought that there were four elements, adding to those mentioned earth as a fourth (for these things always remained and did not come into being except in frequency or rarity, being mixed together and separated into and out of one thing). Anaxagoras of Clazomenae was earlier than he in date but later in his works, and he said that the number of principles was infinite. For he said that more or less all the homoeomerous bodies, such as water and fire, did come to be and perish in this way only, by mixing and discrimination, and that otherwise they did not come into being or perish but remained eternally.

From these thinkers, then, one might think that there is only a single cause, that said in the form of matter. But as they continued in this way, the facts themselves guided them and forced them to seek further. For even if, as much as you like, all coming to be and destruction are from some simple thing or from several, why does this happen and what is the cause? For indeed it cannot be that the substrate itself forces itself to change. I mean that, for instance, neither wood nor bronze is the cause of either of them changing, neither does wood make a bed or bronze a statue, but there is some other cause of the change. And to seek for this is to seek for the second kind of principle, as we would say, that from which comes the beginning of the change.

Those, then, who right from the beginning grasped this method and asserted that the substrate was single did not fall out with one another, but some of those who asserted a single principle, as though defeated by this inquiry, said that the single thing was unchanging and so was the whole of nature, not only in regard to generation and destruction (for this was ancient and agreed by everybody) but also in regard to every other kind of change. [984b] And this is peculiar to them. So of those who asserted that the universe was one none managed to see such a cause except perhaps Parmenides, and he did so only in so far as he supposed that there was not only one but in a way also two causes. Those, however, who said that there were many principles had greater ease in stating it, such as those who said that there was hot and cold or fire and earth. For they used fire as having a kinetic nature, the opposite of earth and water and suchlike things.

After these thinkers and principles like these, as they were not sufficient to generate the nature of entities, once again, by the truth itself, as we have said, they were obliged to seek out the next principle. For of the fact that some entities have and some entities are the good and noble perhaps neither fire nor earth nor any of such things is either likely to be the cause nor did they think that it was. Nor indeed would it be good to hand so great a responsibility over to chance and the automatic. Now one of them said that mind was present in the universe, as in the animals, and that this was the cause of order in nature and the whole arrangement – making the earlier thinkers look absurd. We clearly know then that Anaxagoras embraced this account, but that it was Hermotimus of Clazomenae who earlier gave it as a cause. Those, then, who made this supposition said that the cause of nobility was a principle of entities, and also a cause of the kind from which change comes to entities.

ALPHA 4

Aristotle continues his critical survey of the history of philosophy before Plato, in which philosophers felt obscurely the need to go beyond explanation of the world in purely material terms, but were unable to come up with any very satisfactory accounts of either movement or purpose. Anaxagoras, as already said, and Empedocles came closest to understanding the need for an explanation in terms of purpose, but their explanations were schematic, metaphorical, self-contradictory or in various other ways unsatisfactory. The approach of the Atomists was even less complete. They had difficulty even in accounting for movement and had nothing at all to say about purpose.

Aristotle clearly feels that the value of studying these earlier schools is that one acquires a vivid realization of the poverty of their explanatory assumptions. This will justify the much broader conception of science and philosophy that he will have to offer.

And one might suppose that Hesiod was the first to seek for such a thing, or anyone else who placed love and desire among the entities as their principle – as also did Parmenides. For he too, in describing the creation of the universe, first says:

> 'And he devised Love for all the gods.',

while Hesiod says:

> 'Foremost of all was Chaos, and then next
> 'Broad-fronted Earth . . .
> 'And Love, who ministers to every god.',

on the assumption that among entities there must be some cause which moves and combines things. One ought then in a way to decide among them for who was first, but it is possible to judge later also. But since the opposites of good things are also obviously present in nature – there is not only arrangement and nobility but also disorder and ugliness, [985a] and the bad things are more numerous than the good and the base than the fine, accordingly another philosopher introduced love and strife, each being the cause of each of these groups. For if one were to attend carefully and take in their sense and not on the face of the cryptic remarks of Empedocles, one will find that love is the cause of good things and strife of bad things. And so if one were to say that in a way Empedocles both gave and was the first to give evil and good as principles, perhaps one would put it rightly, if indeed the same good itself is the cause of all good things.

These thinkers, then, were as we have said, and so far, there being two causes of which we have defined in the *Physics*, they seem to have a glimpse of them, that of matter and that from which the motion comes, indistinctly though, and in no way clearly, but in the way that unarmed soldiers do in battles. For indeed they in the peregrinations often strike good blows, but they do not do so from knowledge, and no more do these thinkers seem to have known what they were saying. For they seem to have made more or less no use of these principles except to a small extent. For Anaxagoras uses the mind as a device for the making of the cosmos, and when he puzzles for what reason it is of necessity, then he drags in mind, but in other matters he ascribes cause to anything else rather than to mind, and Empedocles makes even more use than he of the causes, but still insufficiently, nor does he find in these what is agreed. For often indeed for him love divides and strife combines. For when the universe is reduced by strife to its elements, fire and each of the other elements is reduced to a single thing. But whenever again through love they are brought to a single thing, it is necessary that the parts of each thing are again dissolved.

Empedocles, then, among earlier thinkers, was the first to distinguish and introduce this cause, not making the principle of change single but different and opposite, and he was also the first to make the elements said in the form of matter four (he did not indeed treat them as four but as being two only, [985b] fire in itself and the opposites as a single nature, earth, air and water – one can understand this by considering his words). He, then, as we say, in this way gave this number of causes. Leucippus, however, and his companion Democritus said that the elements were the full and the empty, and that of these the full and the solid were what is and the empty was what is not (accordingly he denies that what is exists any more than what is not, any more than the void exists more than body), and he says that these things are the causes of entities as matter. And just as those who make the underlying substance one produce other things by affections of it, positing that the rare and the dense are the principles of the affections, in the same way these thinkers too say that the differences are the causes of the other things. And they say that these are three, shape, order and position. For they say that what is differs in shape, place and manner only; and of these shape is shape, location is arrangement and manner is position. For instance, A differs from N in shape, AN from NA in arrangement and Z from N in position. As regards change, then, whence and in what way entities have it, these thinkers too, like the others, spoke loosely. So about the first two causes, as we say, the earlier thinkers seem to have got so far in their inquiry.

ALPHA 5

Aristotle now turns to considering two schools that do not so obviously fit into his account of earlier philosophy as seeking for his four kinds of explanation, without explicitly realizing that it was doing so. The hallmark of Pythagorean thinking, both originally and in Aristotle's time, was that numbers are the primary constituents of the world. It has always been difficult to be clear about precisely what this means, and our task is not made easier by Aristotle's evident hostility. (One reason for his leaving the Academy was probably the rise in it of a Pythagorean tendency.) In the present chapter, he vacillates between regarding the key role given by the Pythagoreans to numbers as an attempt to state the material cause of the world and treating it as an inchoate first approach to the search for a formal cause.

As for Parmenides and his followers, Aristotle does allow that Parmenides at least saw the need for a formal explanation of the world, even though this led him into adopting absurd views on the explanation of movement and change. He also criticizes Parmenides for moving away from his own central insight and thus arriving at an inherently confused position. This discussion has fuelled the heated debate about the 'way of illusion' which seems to have been a pluralistic addition to Parmenides' philosophical monism.

Among these thinkers and before them the so-called Pythagoreans, in their interest in mathematics, were the first to bring these in and, being involved in them, they thought that the principles of mathematical entities were the principles of all entities. And since of mathematical entities numbers are by nature primary, and among these they seemed to observe many similarities with entities and things coming into being, rather than in fire and earth and water, so that such and such an affection of numbers is justice and such and such soul and mind and another time and with each of the other things likewise, so to speak, and also seeing the affections of harmonies in numbers and ratios. Since then all other things seemed to be assimilable to numbers in their nature, and the numbers were primary of the whole of nature, **[986a]** they assumed that the elements of the numbers were the elements of things as a whole, and they thought that the whole heaven was a harmony and a number. And all features of numbers and harmonies that were in common with the affections and parts of the heaven and the whole cosmic order, these they brought together and applied. And if anything was missing they added it on, so that the whole matter should be complete for them. I mean such as, since the decad is thought to be complete and to embrace the whole nature of numbers, they also said that the bodies in the heavens were ten, and since there are only observed to be nine they made the anti-earth the tenth. We have treated of all this more accurately elsewhere. But the reason why we are going through this here is that we may understand with these thinkers too what they supposed the principles to be and how their views fit in with the causes that we have announced.

Well, even these thinkers seem to hold that number is a principle both as matter for the things that are and as affections and dispositions, and that the elements of number are the odd and the even, and that of these the one is limited and the other unlimited, and that one is from both these (since it is both even and odd), and that number comes from the one, and that, as we have said, the whole heaven is numbers. Now other members of this same group say that the principles in the sense of elements are ten:

limited	unlimited
even	odd
one	many
right	left
male	female
still	moving
straight	bent
light	darkness
good	bad
square	oblong

And this is what Alcmaeon of Croton also seems to have supposed, and either he from them or they from him took over this account. For Alcmaeon was a young man in Pythagoras' old age, and his system was pretty much like theirs. For he said that most human factors are two, giving the oppositions not in a defined way like the Pythagoreans but chance ones, such as white and black, sweet and bitter, good and bad, large and small. He then indistinctly speculated about the others, while the Pythagoreans were explicit about the number and nature [**986b**] of the oppositions. From both these two groups, then, we can understand this much, that the opposites are principles of entities. But the number and nature of them differs from the two groups. How, then, can we bring this into connection with the causes that we have mentioned, this is not made clear by them, but they seem to be giving their elements as principles in the form of matter. For they say that substance is constituted and filled by them as indwelling.

So the ancient thinkers, and those that postulated a plurality of elements, their intentions can be sufficiently clearly discerned from these considerations. But there are some who made declarations about the universe as a single nature, but not in the same way did they declare either in regard to fineness or to the arrangement by nature. So to our present consideration of causes in no way does their account of them fit (for it is not that like some of the philosophers of nature they supposed reality to be one and yet they generated it out of the matter of one, but these spoke in a different way; for the former group added movement, thus creating the universe, while the latter said that it was unchanged). Not but what this much fits in with our present consideration. For Parmenides seemed to be thinking of what is one in account, Melissus of what is one in matter (that is why one says that it is limited and the other that it is unlimited). But Xenophanes, who was the first of these monists (for Parmenides is said to have been his pupil), was in no way clear, nor did he seem to grasp either of these natures. He merely looked up at the whole sky and pronounced that god was one. These men, then, as we said, can be fitted into our present inquiry, although two of them are a little unsophisticated, Melissus and Xenophanes. Parmenides, however, seemed to be speaking with a little more understanding. For he did not think that that which is not could in any way exist in addition to that which is, and so he thought that of necessity that which is is one and nothing else (we have dealt with this more exactly in the *Physics*), but being constrained to follow the evidence, he supposed that what is one in account is several in sensation, and he again supposed that the causes and the principles were two, hot and cold, meaning by this fire and earth. **[987a]** And of these he made the hot that which is, the cold that which is not.

From what has been said, then, and from the consideration of the sages that have been assembled here we have gathered this much. The first thinkers assumed that the principle was bodily (for water and fire and such things are bodies), and they divided into those that thought there was a single body and those that thought there were several, but both groups treated them as causes in the form of matter, whereas some later thinkers thought that there was this cause and in addition to this the source of movement, and this was thought by some to be one and by others to be two. Up, then, to the Italian school and apart from them the others spoke rather unclearly about these things, except in so far as they used two causes, as we have said, and of these some made the second single and some double, that from which comes movement. But the Pythagoreans said that there were two principles in the same way, and they added only what is special to them, that the limited and the unlimited they did not think to be some other natures, such as fire and earth and some other such, but the unlimited itself and the one itself they thought to be substance for their categories, and that is why they thought that number is the substance of all things. On these subjects, then, they made declarations in these ways, and about what is they began to speak and make definitions, but they operated rather too straightforwardly. For they made superficial definitions, and whatever had the mentioned definition, this they thought to be the substance of the thing, just as if someone were to think that the double and the dyad were the same because the double belongs primarily to dyads. But perhaps it is not the same thing to be a double and to be a dyad. But if not, the one will be many, as they also found out. These then are the conclusions that we can find in the earlier thinkers.

ALPHA 6

Aristotle now attempts to integrate Plato into his survey, very much from his own perspective, of earlier thought. He gives an account of the origin of Plato's thought from the fusion of rejection of the sensible world in the spirit of Heraclitus and confidence in the method of definition championed by Socrates to achieve certain objects of knowledge. He expounds with some sympathy Plato's account of the role of the Forms as the ultimate objects of definition and the building blocks of reality as well as the connection that Plato suggests between the supra-sensible forms and the perceptible objects of ordinary experience.

These aspects of the Theory of Forms are familiar from the surviving writings of Plato, especially the Republic, *but Aristotle also discusses ideas which are not explicitly presented in any of the dialogues. These concern the great-small and the One which the doctrine of the Academy seems to have held to underlie even the Forms in some mysterious way. Aristotle feels entitled to conclude that Plato not only initiated the serious pursuit of formal explanation but also had an (unusual) account to give of material causation through the strange concept of the great-small. It is very hard to assess the account here given of Plato's 'secret doctrines', but Aristotle does bring out very effectively how Plato's Theory of Forms sets a requirement on philosophical explanation of the world which had to be integrated into a proper understanding of philosophy and science. This assumption is fundamental to his own system.*

After the philosophies that we have mentioned, the system of Plato appeared, following these in many respects, but having features of its own apart from the Italian philosophy. For as a young man Plato was originally an associate of Cratylus and Heraclitean opinions, to the effect that all perceptible things were in a permanent state of flux and that there was no knowledge of them, and these things he also later on maintained. [987b] But when Socrates started to think about ethics and not at all about the whole of nature, but in ethics seeking universals and first seeing the importance of definitions, by accepting him as such he thought that this could apply also to other things and not to the objects of perception. For a general definition was impossible of any of the sensible things, which were constantly changing. He then called such entities Forms, and he said that all sensible things were spoken of in accordance with them. For the homonyms existed by participation in the Forms. And participation he took over with a mere change of name. For the Pythagoreans had said that entities existed by imitation of the numbers, whereas Plato said that it was by participation, changing the name. However, they left it to common inquiry to determine what might be the imitation or participation of the Forms.

Again, in addition to sensible objects and Forms, they said that mathematical objects existed between them, differing from the sensibles in that they were eternal and unchanging and from the Forms in that there were many similar ones but only one Form of any kind. And since the Forms are causes for other things, he thought that their elements were the elements of all entities. For he thought that the large and the small were elements as matter, and that the one was so as substance. For the Forms came from these by participation in the one, and the one was substance, and the one should not be considered another thing, and he held a similar position to the Pythagoreans, also as to the view that the numbers are the causes of substance for other things, and also in regard to making the dyad replace the single unlimited and the unlimited come from large and small, this is special to him. And he also supposed numbers in addition to those that are perceived, whereas they said that numbers are things themselves, and they did not posit mathematicals between them. So the introduction of one and the numbers in addition to things, and not in the same way as the Pythagoreans, and also the introduction of the Forms came about for logical reasons (for the previous thinkers had not engaged in dialectic), and the making of the dyad a different nature from the numbers through their being outside the primary things he was able to achieve without great difficulty. [988a] And yet it turns out differently; for it is not reasonable that it should be so. For the Pythagoreans make many things out of matter, whereas the Form only generates on one occasion, and it seems that one table comes from one matter, but the man who brings in the Forms being himself single makes several things. And the male is in the same position in regard to the female. For the one is filled by many vessels, whereas the male fills many things. And yet these things are imitations of those principles. Plato, then, gave definitions as follows about what we are investigating. But it is clear from what we have said that of the two causes he made use of only one, that of the what it is and that of matter (for the Forms are the causes of what it is for other things, and the one for the Forms), and what is the underlying matter by which the Forms are mentioned of sensibles and the one of the Forms, such that it is the dyad, the large and the small, and he also gave the well and the badly as the causes of the elements, each for each, as we say that even some of the earlier thinkers inquired, such as Empedocles and Anaxagoras.

ALPHA 7

Aristotle is now able to draw his survey of earlier thought to a triumphant conclusion, vindicating his claim that every serious attempt at explanation of the world must fit into one of his four approved styles. The majority of philosophers have concentrated on material explanation, though many have seen the need also to explain the origin of movement, change and, more generally, process. There has been still less clarity about the nature of formal and teleological explanation, although the Platonists in particular made most progress in this direction. The fact that the great thinkers of the past did not have a systematic overview of the whole project of philosophy does not mean that their insights are of no value. To be used, however, they must be integrated into the general scheme of explanation that Aristotle is defending. What is in any case completely clear is that there is no significant explanation that has been offered by a major previous philosopher which cannot be brought into one or other of the styles of explanation that Aristotle set out in chapter 3. This means that we can be sure that if we can account for causal explanation – and doing so is vital for the acquisition of wisdom – then there will be no important kind of causal explanation that lies outside the Aristotelian canon. We have erected a ring-fence around the subject matter of philosophy.

In brief and summary style, then, we have gone through which thinkers, and in what ways, happen to have said something about the principles and the truth. And yet we have this much from them, that of those that have spoken of the principles and causes none has mentioned any beyond those that are defined by us in the *Physics*, but rather all seem to be indistinctly grappling after these. For some of them give the principle as matter, differing as to whether there is one or many, and as to whether this is bodily or not bodily (for instance, Plato gives the large and the small, the Italians the unlimited, Empedocles fire, earth, water and air, Anaxagoras the infinity of homoeomeries – all these thinkers are fumbling for this sort of cause, and also those who posit air or fire or water or something that is thicker than fire but lighter than air – for in fact some thinkers have asserted that some such thing is the primary element).

These men, then, grasped only this cause, but some others grasped that from which comes the source of change (for instance, those who posited love and strife and mind and love as the principle). And yet none of them clearly presented the what it was to be and the substance, and in particular those who posit the Forms [988b] speak of it (for the Forms are not as the matter for the sensibles and that which is in the Forms is not thence, in their supposition, the principle of change – for they assert rather that it is a principle of motionlessness and being at rest – but rather they provide the Forms as the essence of other things, and the One for the Forms). But that for which actions, changes and movements occur in a way they mention as a cause, but they do not mention it in this way and as it is. For those that speak of mind and love posit these causes as the good, but not indeed in the sense that it is for the sake of these that any of the entities exist or become, but rather as that the movements come from these. And in just the same way those who assert the One or Being say that such a nature is the cause of substance, but not indeed that for the sake of this a thing either is or becomes, so that in a way they do and in a way they do not say that the good is a cause. For they do not speak *simpliciter* but by accident.

That, then, we have given the right definitions about the causes both as to their numbers and as to their characters, all these thinkers would seem to attest, not being able to posit causes, and in addition to these that the causes must be sought, it is clear, either them all in this way or in one of these ways. And how each of these has spoken and how he stands in connection with the principles, and the subsequent puzzles after this in connection with them, let us now go through.

ALPHA 8

We have been shown that the Aristotelian conception of explanation is implicit in the practice, although not acknowledged in the rhetoric, of earlier philosophy. It is now time to make clear the limitations of the earlier thinkers. Aristotle attacks the physicist monists, the physicist pluralists and the Pythagoreans.

The physicist monists are criticized for their excessive concentration on bodily entities, at the expense of those without body, of having made little sense of motive and formal explanation and of having shown general naïvety in the postulation of causes. The physicist pluralists, especially Empedocles and Anaxagoras, had a more plausible position, but they both encountered difficulties, which were insuperable within their systems, with regard to the explanation of movement and change. As for the Pythagoreans, they also had no real suggestion about how number could be the cause of change, and, in any case, their account of the physical constitution of bodily entities in terms of numbers was irredeemably obscure.

Of those, then, who assert that the universe is one and a single nature, and that this is bodily and has magnitude, it is clear that they are wrong in many respects. For it is only of bodies that they posit the elements and not of the unbodily things. And when they try to give the causes for generation and destruction, and give a comprehensive physical account, they miss the cause of movement. And also by their failure to posit substance as the cause of anything nor the essence, and further by their easily giving as the principle of simple bodies anything rather than earth, not considering how they will bring about mutual generation, I mean of fire and water and earth and air. For these come about by combination or discrimination from each other, and this is very different from their being prior or posterior. For in a way the most elementary thing for all things might seem to be that from which they come first by combination, **[989a]** and this would be the smallest part and lightest

28

of the bodies (hence all those who posit fire as a principle would be speaking especially in conformity with this line of reasoning: and each of the others also agrees such a thing to be an element of bodies. Though none of the monists thinks that earth is an element, obviously through its large-partedness, but each of the three others has found a supporter, for some assert that the element is fire, others water and others air. And yet why do they not also suggest earth, as the majority of men do? For they say that all things are earth, and indeed Hesiod says that earth is the first born of bodies – so ancient and popular does the opinion seem to be.)

So according to this account, neither if one said one of these things except fire, nor if one supposed something that was thicker than air but lighter than water, would one be speaking rightly. But if there is something that is posterior in origin but prior in nature, then this is digested and mixed later in creation, and this would be the opposite of these things, water being prior to air and earth to water. About those, then, who have suggested some single cause of the type that we have described, let so much be said. And the same would apply even to those who posit a plurality of such causes, as Empedocles says that the four bodies are matter. For he must encounter both the same and other special problems. For we see these bodies arising out of each other, so that fire and earth cannot always remain as the same bodies (we have talked about this in the *Physics*), and about the cause of things moving, whether we should posit one or two, we should not think in general that they have spoken either correctly or well. And in general those who think like this will have to abandon alteration. For there will not be a change from the hot to the cold or from the cold to the hot. For why would these opposites be thus affected, and what would be the single nature that became fire and water, that man does not say. And if one supposed Anaxagoras to be saying two elements, one would especially suppose this in accordance with the argument that he himself did not distinguish them but that he followed of necessity those that introduced them. For while it is in general absurd to say that in the beginning all things were mixed, and through their being unmixed they should be first [989b] and through their not being available for chance mixing, and in addition that the affections and the accidents would be separated from substances (for there is mixture and separation of the same things), yet if someone went through articulating what he wanted to say, he would no doubt be shown to be speaking baloney. For when there was nothing separated off, it is clear that it was not possible to say anything true about such substance, by which I mean that one could not say that it was white or black or light or dark or any other colour, but it was of necessity colourless – for it would have some one of these colours. And in the same way by this argument it would be weightless, nor would it have any other of the similarities. For it would not be possible for it to have a quality or a quantity or an essence. For one of the partial forms would belong to it, and this is impossible when all things are mixed. For it would already be discerned, but he says that all things were mixed except mind, and that this alone was unmixed and pure.

From this he has to say that the principles are the one (for this is simple and unmixed) and the other, as we suppose that the indefinite is before it is defined and has some Form, so that he is speaking neither well nor clearly but he intends something similar to those who speak later and those who are rather now appearing. But these too in their remarks on generation and destruction only happen to be right. For it is only about such substance that they seek the principles and causes. But those who conduct their investigation into all the entities, and assume that some entities are sensible and some are insensible, it is clear that about both kinds they make their investigation. So one would spend more time asking them what they say well and what not well about the inquiry that now lies before us.

Well, the so-called Pythagoreans use pretty strange principles and elements for the study of nature (and the reason is that they have not taken them from sensible things; for the mathematicals are entities without change except for those connected with astronomy), and yet they discuss and work about nature as a whole. For they produce the heaven and the parts about it [990a] and they distinguish its affections and works and they bring the principles and causes to the same things, in that they agree with the other students of nature that this entity is perceptible and is embraced by the so-called heaven. But the causes and principles, as we said, they say are sufficient to go through even for the upper entities, and fitting them rather than the discussion of nature. However, in what way there will be change of the limit and unlimited with the odd and the even being the only substrates, they do not at all say, or how it will be possible for there to be generation and destruction or change and modification of the works of the bodies that move around the heaven. And even if one granted that they could make magnitude from these things or even showed this, yet in what way will there be heavy and light among bodies? For on the basis of their premises, they are talking no more about mathematical bodies than about sensible ones. And so about fire or earth or other such bodies they have not spoken at all, since I think that they have nothing to say in connection with sensible bodies. Again, how can one assume that the affections of numbers are causes and number a cause of the things in the heaven and the things coming about both originally and now, but that there is no other number beyond this number from which the cosmos is derived? For if this is their account of space and time, then injustice would have little to do with it and mixing, but let them give a demonstration that each of these is a number, and it will turn out that by this argument there will already be a plurality of composed magnitudes since these affections follow each place, whether this is the same number, that in the heaven, which one should take to be one of each of these, or another besides this one. For Plato says that there is another, and yet even he thinks that these things too are numbers and the causes of these things, but that some of them are intellectual and some of them sensible.

ALPHA 9

Having demolished the other most important philosophical traditions of the past, Aristotle is now in a position to train his fire on Plato. In this extremely important chapter, he voices criticisms of the Theory of Forms which must have been current in the Academy and which were certainly developed in some of Aristotle's earlier writings, notably in the treatise On the Forms.

Aristotle attacks the theory on an extremely broad front, building on and extending the criticisms that Plato himself makes in the Parmenides. *The thrust of the attack can, however, be summarized as follows. The fundamental objection is that the Forms explain nothing. They merely provide a shadow world in parallel to the world of sensible entities. No sense can be made of the idea that sensible entities have their being through participation in the non-sensible Forms. Even if the Forms did have a possible explanatory role, no convincing reasons are offered to persuade us that such separable, detached entities exist. If arguments to this effect could be found, moreover, there would be no reason why they should not support the existence of a Form corresponding to every feature of the sensible world. This might mean that the number of Forms was indeterminate, but in any case would certainly mean that there were Forms corresponding to even the humblest entities, which is clearly against the spirit of the Theory. The account of number and the mathematical entities suffers from similar problems. Finally, the Forms cannot be invoked to explain our possession of knowledge of universals, since the only mechanism by which they could cause such knowledge, that of recollection, is fraught with difficulties.*

Whatever the logical status of the many particular arguments in this chapter, there is no doubt that it embodies the assumptions which were the point of departure for Aristotle's own metaphysics. His whole system is devoted to obtaining the advantages of formal explanation, which he acknowledges that Plato was the first to grasp, without the absurdities attendant upon the postulation of metaphysically detached entities.

Concerning the Pythagoreans let the above suffice for now (for it is enough to have said so much about them). But those who suppose the Forms were the first in their inquiries [990b] to take the causes for these entities and to introduce others equal to these in number, just as if one in wanting to count thought that it was impossible to do so, since there were fewer things, but on making more would be able to count. For the Forms are more or less equal and not less than those things concerning which in seeking the causes they went from these things to those. For the particular is a kind of homonym of the other things of which there is the one over many, both with these things and with eternal things.

Again, in the ways in which we have shown that the Forms exist, by none of them is this made clear. For from some it is not necessary that the syllogism should arise, and from others of which we have not thought there will be syllogism. For by the arguments from the sciences there will be Forms for all the things for which there are sciences, and also by the one over many and the demonstrations, and by thinking there will be something lacking from what is destroyed. For there is a kind of imagination of these. Again the most accurate of the arguments, some make the Forms of the qualities, of which we do not say that there is a genus in itself, whereas others cite the Third Man Argument. And in general the arguments about the Forms remove that which we especially want the Forms to be. For it turns out that the dyad is not prior but number, and the relative is prior to the intrinsic, and all things which some, following the Theory of Forms, have made opposite to the principles.

Again, by the supposition by which we say that Forms exist, they will be the Forms not only of substances but also of many other things (for indeed the thought is single not only in connection with substances but also with the other entities, and the sciences are not only of substances but also of the other things, and very many other similar results occur). But of necessity also the opinions about them, if the Forms are participatory, will necessarily only be the Forms of substances. For it is not by accident that they will participate, but it will be necessary for each thing to participate in the way in which it is described not as subject (I mean, for instance, that if something participates in the double, then it also participates in the eternal, but this by accident; for it is an accident of the double to be eternal), so that the Forms will be substance. So these things indicate substance also in the other case. [991a] Or what will it be to say that things are beyond this, the one over the many? And if there is the same Form for the Forms and the participants, then there will be something in common (for what more should there be in the case of perishable dyads, and of the many things that are eternal, and the dyad will be one and the same, if it is for this and the what). But if it is not the same Form, then they would be homonymous, and it would be the same as if one called both Callias and a statue a man, not observing any commonality of them.

But above all one might raise the problem what the Forms of perceptibles might contribute to the eternal things or to things that come into being and are destroyed. For they are the cause neither of change nor of any modification for them. And indeed they do not contribute in any way either to the science of the others (for these are not substance, for they would be in something), nor to their being, not being present in the participants. For they might be thought to be causes in the way that white mixed with white is, but this account is too easily moved, which first Anaxagoras and then Eudoxus and certain others gave (for it is easy to connect many impossibilities with this sort of doctrine). And indeed it is not even possible from the Forms to say any of the other things. And to say that they are paradigms and that other things participate in them is to say nothing and to give poetic metaphors. For what will be the efficient factor in regard to the Forms? But it is possible that there might be and become something similar and not being likened to it, so that whether or not Socrates existed there might be something similar to Socrates; and this would be the case even if Socrates were eternal. And there will be many paradigms of the same thing, and so also many Forms, as both animal and biped are Forms of man, and also man himself.

And again the Forms would not only be paradigms of the sensibles but also of themselves, such as the genus, as the genus of Forms. So that paradigm and image are the same. [991b] And again it would seem to be impossible that the substance should exist apart from that of which it is the substance; so how would the Forms, being the substances of

34

things, exist apart from them? But in the *Phaedo* it is said that the Forms are the cause both of being and of becoming. And yet with the Forms existing the participants would still not come into being unless there was a mover, and many other problems will arise, such as the house and the finger, of which we do not say that there are Forms. So it is clear that it is possible also for other things both to be and to become for the same sort of reasons as the things which we have just been talking about.

Again, if the Forms are numbers, how will they be causal? Because entities will be other numbers, so that such and such a number is man and such and such a number is Socrates and such and such a number is Callias? How then would these be responsible for those? For it will make no difference even if one group are eternal and the other not. And if there are accounts of numbers in this case, as with symphony, it is clear that there will be some one thing of which they are the account. If then there is this thing, the matter, it is clear that the numbers themselves will be a kind of account of the one to the other. I mean that if Callias is a numerical ratio of fire, earth, water and air, then the Form will also be the number of other substrates. And man himself, whether he is a number or not, will yet be a numerical ratio of some things and not a number and no Form will be for this reason a number. And also one number will come from many numbers, but how is one Form to come from many Forms? And if not from them then from the things in number, such as the myriad, then how will the monads be? For if they share the Form, then many absurdities will follow, but if they do not, then they will neither be like each other nor have much in common. For what difference will it make if they are unaffected? For these claims are neither rational nor in accordance with thought. And also it will be necessary to establish another kind of number, of which arithmetic treats, and all the intermediate things said of things, then how will there be principles? And why will they be beyond the further? And again both the monads in the dyad will be from some previous dyad, [992a] and yet that is impossible.

Again, why will the assumed number be one? And in addition to what we have said, if the monads are different, one should say this, as do those who say that the elements are four or two. For indeed each of these does not say the common element, such as body, but fire and earth, whether there is something in common, body, or not. But the present theory treats the being of the one as that of a homoeomerous thing such as fire or water. But if this is so then the numbers will not be substances, but it is clear that if there is such a thing as the one itself and if this is a principle, then the one will be said in many ways. For otherwise it is impossible.

But if we wish to connect the substances with the principles, then we must posit length from short and long, from some short and large particular, and plane from broad and narrow, and body from deep and shallow. And yet how will either the plane have a mark or the solid a mark and a plane? For the broad and hollow are different kinds and the deep and shallow. So that there would also be no number in them, since the many and few are different from these, and so also none of the upper things will also belong to the lower. And indeed broad is not even a kind of depth – for then body would be a kind of plane. And again what will points be from? This kind Plato fought against as being a geometrical dogma, but he called it the principle of mark – and this he posited in many ways – individual marks. And yet it is necessary that there be some limit of these, so that point is from the same account as mark.

And in general wisdom seeks the cause of the things that appear, and this we guess (for we say nothing of the cause from which comes the beginning of change), but when we think to give its substance we give the substance of other things, so that the latter are the substances of the former, and we are speaking nonsense. For participation, as we said before, is nothing. Nor should we define the substances as we do in the sciences, as all mind and nature do, nor for this cause, which we say to be one of the principles, does it touch the Forms at all, but philosophy has become mathematics for the present thinkers, asserting that they ought to do it for the sake of something else. And indeed one might mathematicize the underlying substance as matter **[992b]** and hold that substances should be more categorized and distinguished and matter from matter, such as the large and the small, in the way in which the students of nature indeed speak of the dry and the moist, saying that these are the primary discriminations of the substrate. For these things are a kind of excess and deficiency. But about movement, if these things are a kind of movement, it is obvious that the Forms will do the moving. If not, whence else will it come? For the entire study of nature will be undermined. But what seems to be easier, to accept that all things are one, will not come about. For all things do not become one by addition but the one itself would if all things were added to it. And not even this unless it were giving the kind of a universal, and in some cases this is impossible. And there will also be no ratio of the sizes without numbers and the planes and solids, so that there is no potentiality that it should either exist or not. For it is impossible that these things should be able to be Forms (for they are not numbers) nor the intermediates (for they are mathematicals) nor perishable things, but again this is revealed as being some fourth further stuff. And in general to seek the elements of entities without discrimination, said in many ways, it is impossible to find them, especially if you look for them in the way in which they are elements. For from what will there be agency or affection for the straight, it is not possible to grasp, but if it is, then it is only possible for substances, so that either to seek or to think that there are elements for all the entities is false.

And how indeed would one understand the elements of all entities? For it is obvious that one could make no progress by knowing them as priorities. For just as one who has learned geometry can anticipate other things too, but he does not know what his science is about nor can he anticipate its future discoveries, so is it also with the other sciences, so that if there is some science of all things, of the kind that some assert, then there would be no possibility of knowing it. And yet all learning comes about through the cognition of either all or some things, both that by demonstration and that by definitions, and it is the same with learning by induction. And indeed even if it happened to be of the same nature, [993a] how is it that it escapes our notice that we possess the most important of the sciences? And again how will one know from what premises it comes and how will it be clear? For this too is puzzling. For one might be in doubt about various suppositions – for some think that za comes from s, d and a, but others say that it is a different sound and not one of those that we know. And again with the things that are perceptible, how will one have cognition of them if one does not have sense? And yet one should have, if the constitutive elements of all things are the same, as diphthongs are from simple vowels.

ALPHA 10

In this brief final chapter, Aristotle once more reasserts his conclusions with regard to the relationship between the earlier philosophy and his own. He draws the discussion to an end by citing a final illustration from the philosophy of Empedocles of the confused character of earlier thinking. At the very end he points to the agenda for the next two books.

That all thinkers seem to have been seeking for the causes that we have enumerated in the *Physics*, and that apart from these we would not be able to mention any other, is clear from what we have said above. But these conclusions are obscure, and in a way they were trying to find these causes and in a way not at all. For the earliest philosophy seemed to be whispering about all things, since it was young and original, since even Empedocles says that bone exists by ratio, whereas this is the essence and substance of the thing. And indeed in the same way it is necessary that flesh and each of the other things is a ratio, or not even one. For this reason both flesh and bone will be and also each of the other things and not through matter, which he mentions, namely fire, earth, water and air. But if someone else mentioned these things then he would have to agree, but he did not speak clearly. Well, we have already made it clear about these things, but as to the things that one might query in regard to the causes themselves, let us go over them again. For perhaps from that we will gain some advantage for our later inquiries.

Book Alpha the Lesser

ALPHA THE LESSER I

In this chapter, Aristotle makes some general comments on the prospects for making progress with philosophical investigations. These are, on the one hand, difficult because of the extent and variety of the field, but on the other they are easy in that human beings have a natural aptitude to philosophize at least to some extent. What is hard is to do philosophy well, just as it is hard for moles to see by daylight. A recipe for progress, at any rate, is collaboration. The best way to pursue the object of philosophy is by systematic inquiry in a well-organized institution. It is a striking feature of the Metaphysics *that it suggests that philosophy is naturally a group activity, not a matter of individual, personal inspiration.*

In the second half of the chapter, Aristotle makes some remarks about truth. Truth, here, is something closer perhaps to the concept of reality. Aristotle thinks that things, especially causes, have greater or lesser truth depending on whether they have more or less being.

The investigation of the truth is in a way difficult and in a way easy. An indication is that no one can worthily reach it nor does everyone completely miss it, [**993b**] but each thinker says something about nature, and individually they make small contributions to it, and from them all together a certain volume arises. So that if the situation was as in the proverb, who could miss the doors? In this way then it is easy, but the difficulty of grasping the whole and not merely a part shows how difficult it is. And perhaps its difficulty exists in two ways, not in the things but in us as responsible for them. For just as bats' eyes are towards daylight, so in our soul is the mind towards those things that are clearest of all. And we should not only be grateful to those in whose opinions we at all share but also to those who have gone astray. For even the latter have contributed something, since they have prepared the condition for us. For if Timotheus had never existed, there would be a lot of lyric poetry that we would not have, and if Phrynis had not existed, then neither would Timotheus. And it is the same with the theorists of nature. For from some of them we have taken over certain doctrines, whereas others were responsible for their existence. And it is also right that the study of the truth is called philosophy. For truth is the aim of theoretical thought as action is of practical thought; and if we consider how things are, the cause is not in itself, but the practical thinkers consider what is relevant to a context. But we do not know the truth without the cause. And this is all the more true in each case in which synonymy arises (as fire is the hottest thing; for it is the cause of heat for other things too), so that it is more true in each case that the earlier thing is the cause. And so it is necessary that the principles of the eternally existing things are most true (for they are not just sometimes true, nor is there any cause of their being, but rather they are such causes for other things), so that as each thing is related to being so is it to truth.

ALPHA THE LESSER 2

The central purpose of this chapter is to meet a possible objection in principle to the idea of understanding the cause of something, which we have seen to be central to understanding the truth of things and thus to acquiring wisdom, the goal of philosophy. The possible objection is that any case of causation will involve an infinite series of causes. Aristotle considers that this objection, if it were to be sustained, would destroy his conception of philosophy, and he accordingly devotes a large number of arguments to rebutting it.

The main argument is that in any series of causes the intermediate causes between the start and end of the series must both cause and themselves be caused. There must therefore always be some first cause which is not itself caused. This sort of argument against infinite causal series is developed at greater length in book Lambda. Moreover, just as a causal series must have a beginning, so must it also have an end. Any process has a natural and well-defined endpoint. The idea of infinite causal series is equally absurd for final and formal as for motive causation, since it would destroy in the one case the notion of a goal and in the other the very possibility of thought and knowledge about objects. The same consideration rules out the possibility, against which Aristotle has already argued, that there could be an infinite variety of causes.

[994a] But that there is some principle and that the causes of the entities are not infinite either in perspective or in form is clear. For neither the derivation from matter nor relative terms can sustain an infinite regress (for instance, flesh is from earth, earth from fire, fire from air and at this point it stops), nor that of the source of change (for instance, a man is moved by the air and this by the sun and the sun by strife and of this there is no limit). And similarly it is impossible that the for the sake of what should sustain an infinite regress, such that walking is for the sake of health and this is for the sake of happiness and happiness for the sake of something else, and thus one thing is always for something else. And

it is the same with essence. For of middle things, of which there is an extreme and prior, it is necessary that the prior is the cause of the things that come after it. For if we had to say which of the three is the cause, we would say the first. For it would certainly not be the last, for it is the last of nothing. But neither would we say the middle term, for it is of one thing (and it makes no difference if it is one or many, nor whether infinite or limited). But of the things that are unlimited in this way and in general of the unlimited all the parts are mediate in the same way as up to now; so that if there is no primary thing, then in general there is no cause.

And indeed we cannot even have the regress in the downward direction, with the upper having the principle, so that water comes from fire, and earth from this, and in the same way something will always be generated. For one thing comes from another in two ways, either as a man comes by change from a child or as air comes from water. For in the former way we say that the created arises from the creator or the complete from the completer (for there is always a medium, as the creation of being and not being), and so is the being to the becoming and not becoming. For the learner is the becoming knower, and this is a case of what is said, that the knower comes from the learner. But the second kind of change comes about with the destruction of the second thing. And so these changes are not bent back on to others, nor does a child come from a man (for the producer does not come about in production **[994b]** but that which exists after the production; in this way the day comes from dawn, in that it is after it, and so the dawn does not come from the day). But the other kind of change does bend back. But for either kind it is impossible to have an infinite regress. For of mediate entities there must be an end, while the mutual ones bend back. For the destruction of one is the generation of the other.

At the same time it is impossible that the primary existent, being eternal, should be destroyed. For since the upper creation is not limited, it is necessary that, since it is not itself eternal, it be generated from some non-destroyed primary thing. And since that for the sake of which is an end, it would be the sort of thing that would not be for other things, but rather other things for it, so that if there were to be some

46

such final thing, there will not be a regress, but if there is no such thing, there will not be that for the sake of which, but those who posit the infinite will, without realizing it, have removed the nature of the good (and yet no one would have done anything with the intention to act if that meant a regress). Nor would there be mind among the entities. For the thing that has mind is always acting for the sake of something, and this is a limit. For the end is a limit. And indeed the essence cannot either be taken to another definition increasing by the account. For there will always rather be something ahead of it, and that which is second does not exist, and of that of which there is not a prior there is also no sequential. And this theory also gets rid of knowledge, for we cannot know before we reach the atoms. Nor does cognition exist, for how is it possible to have cognition of such limitless things? For it is not the same as with marks, which are not established by division, but we cannot know that which does not stand (which is why you cannot count an infinity of points), but it is also necessary to know the matter in something that is changing. And it is not possible for any infinite thing to exist; otherwise, infinity would not be infinite. And indeed if the forms of causes were limitless in number, not even so would cognition be possible. For we are thought to know when we have cognition of the causes. And the infinite by addition it is not possible to go through in finite time.

ALPHA THE LESSER 3

In this short chapter Aristotle makes some pet points about method. Different types of study require different methodological approaches, but methodical preferences will also depend on the inclinations of the students. What is important is that the method for conducting any study is mastered before the study is attempted – it is not possible to learn the method and pursue the study at the same time. The best of all methods of study is that of mathematics, but this can only be used for things that do not undergo processes of change. For natural things, which do move and change, a less rigorous method than mathematics must be employed.

And our lectures on ethics are in accordance with this. For let us be prepared to speak in our accustomed manner, and the things in addition to these do not seem the same **[995a]** but because of their unfamiliarity they are less well known and stranger. For the well known is familiar. And the power of familiarity is shown by customs, in which mythical and childish factors because of habit have the same influence as knowledge about them. And some people will not accept a speech unless it is made in mathematical style, and others only if it does not use examples, and others demand that a poet be dragged in as a witness. And some say all things accurately, while others are offended by exactitude either because they cannot grasp it or because of its brevity. For accuracy has a feature like this, so that, as with agreements, so in arguments it strikes some people as illiberal. And so one must be educated as to how each thing should be demonstrated, as it is absurd at the same time to seek a science and the style of a science, though not even the latter is easy to attain. And we should not seek mathematical exactitude in all things, but only for things that do not have matter. That is why this manner is not that of the natural scientist, since, I suppose, all nature has matter. And so we must first inquire what nature is, for we will thus make it clear what the subject matter of physics is.

Book Beta

Book Beta is a collection of metaphysical problems. These fifteen puzzles are developed in the course of the book, but no attempt is made to resolve them. The point of the book is to provide not answers but questions. The characteristic structure of the problems is that of a plausible seeming thesis and an equally plausible but contradictory antithesis. Usually, the thesis and antithesis are taken one from the extreme naturalists or Atomists, the other from the Idealists, Pythagoreans and Platonists. The purpose of the whole exercise is to illustrate the poverty of both these extreme positions, so as to prepare the way for the exposition of Aristotle's own solution in the bulk of the work, which will in many respects be a compromise between materialism and idealism. The first chapter contains a list of the problems, which, however, does not exactly correspond to the order in which they are in fact presented in chapters 2 to 6, and some advisory remarks on how to read the problems.

Puzzle 1

Is there a single science of the four causes or several such sciences? Thesis: there cannot be a single such science, because the four kinds of causation are not contraries and it is only contraries that make up the domain of a single science. Antithesis: if there are several such sciences, then there can be no way of deciding which science is to be identified with First Philosophy.

Puzzle 2

Does the same science cover the study of the basic principles of logic and the study of substance? Thesis: the same science cannot study both, because the principles of logic are common to all disciplines and cannot in any case be demonstrated, because they are self-evident and demonstration depends on them.

Antithesis: on the other hand, if the science of logical axioms is different from that of substance, it is necessary to decide which has priority, a decision which must favour the universal logical principles, so that it will be they, not substance, that is the proper study of philosophy.

Puzzle 3

Is there one or several sciences for these sensible and supra-sensible substances? Thesis: if there are two sciences, one for sensible and one for supra-sensible substances, we cannot then give a principled decision as to which science is First Philosophy. Antithesis: if there is a single science for both substances, how can it fail to turn out that there is really only one science of all things, whether sensible or supra-sensible?

Puzzle 4

Is the science which studies substance the same as that which also studies the properties of substance? Thesis: if it is the same, then, since the science of the properties must be demonstrative, so must the science of substance itself, but substance is not something that can be demonstrated, but only defined. Antithesis: if it is not the same, the science that deals with the properties of substance but not with substance itself will not be a science, because a science must deal with a subject and its properties.

Puzzle 5

Are there only sensible substances or also supra-sensible substances, and if the latter, are they only Platonic Forms or also the mathematical entities? Thesis: both Platonic Forms and mathematical entities are absurd. Platonic Forms merely echo the sensible world without explaining it, and the mathematical entities, if they existed, would have to be paralleled by similar intermediate entities in the other sciences, and this would lead to an infinite regress in all cases. Antithesis: the mathematical sciences are evidently not based on sensible entities, so there must be mathematical entities in their case. However, it is not possible to consider such entities to be immanent in sensible entities themselves, on pain of having two entities with contrary properties in the same place at the same time.

Puzzle 6

Are the principles of entities the material elements of which they are composed or the genera to which they belong? Thesis: there are many examples of principles being taken to be the elements of which something is composed. For instance, the principles of words are their physical elements and the principles in geometry are those propositions on which demonstration is based. Natural objects too are said by philosophers to have as their principles the natural elements of which they are made, and it is thought that we know, for instance, artefacts when we know their material components. Antithesis: but the principles are also taken to be the genera, because things are known by definitions of which the genera are principles and also through their species, for which the genera are also principles. This perspective is, of course, supported by the teaching of Plato.

Puzzle 7

If the genera are principles, is it the primary or the ultimate genera that are principles? Thesis: the primary genera cannot be principles, because on this basis the principles would have to be the supreme genera of being and unity, which are not really genera at all. Also, all intermediate genera would have to count as principles, so that the principles of anything would have to be infinite in number. Thus the principles could only be the ultimate principles. Antithesis: but if the ultimate genera are principles, then the principle of a thing will not be external to it at all. But principles must be external to what they are principles of, and so what is most a principle must be most external, so that it should be the primary, not the ultimate, genera that are principles.

Puzzle 8

Is there something over and above particular individuals? Thesis: if there is nothing but an infinity of particulars, then science is impossible. It would also in such circumstances be impossible for there to be anything that was immune to process, but, since things subject to process depend on at least one thing that is not subject to process, this would mean that things subject to process did not exist either. Antithesis: but if there is something over and above particulars, must there or must there not be one such thing for each sensible particular? This question cannot be given a principled answer, but in any case there is a dilemma. If there is only one universal object, then everything will share the same form, whereas if there are several there will be many identical forms of substance.

Puzzle 9

Do principles have formal or numerical unity? Thesis: if principles have only formal and not numerical unity, then no entities can have numerical unity either, not even one and being, and also science, which depends on something which is numerical as well as formally a unity uniting particulars, will be impossible. Antithesis: but if the unity of principles is numerical, then there will again be as many entities as there are principles, so that there will turn out to be far too few particular entities.

Puzzle 10

Are the principles of perishable and of imperishable things the same or different? Thesis: if they are the same, how can some of the things of which they are principles be imperishable while others are perishable? Antithesis: if, on the other hand, they are different, there is a dilemma about the principles of perishable things. Are these principles themselves perishable? If they are, then either they will have to have further principles of principles, which is absurd, or all perishable things will at some point cease to be produced. But if they are not, we have the problem that from the same imperishable principles both imperishable and perishable things are derived.

Puzzle 11

Are one and being per se *substances or are they predicable of other things? Thesis: if one and being are not substances, then neither will the other universals be, nor will number be a* per se *substance. Antithesis: if one and being are substances, then everything will have to be one and being, and Parmenides will be right. Also number will be impossible because number requires a plurality of units, which is incompatible with one being a substance. Multiplicity cannot be derived from a necessarily single thing.*

Puzzle 12

Are numbers, bodies, surfaces and points substances or not? Thesis: what else could be? Affections, relations, movements, etc., cannot be substances because they are predicable, nor can the elements and their affections be determinate substances. So only body can be substance, and body is determined by surface, which is in turn determined by line and this by point. So if what determines something is its substance, points would seem to be substances most of all, and it was on this basis that the Platonists and Pythagoreans suggested that numbers were basic substances. Antithesis: on the other hand, if points, lines and surfaces are more substantial than bodies, they cannot be in sensible bodies, whereas in fact it is usually thought that points, lines and surfaces are not substances but divisions of bodies, being present not actually but potentially in them.

Puzzle 13

Is it necessary to allow Forms in addition to sensible entities and the 'intermediate' entities? Thesis: the intermediate entities are not numerically determinate, so that their principles are also not numerically determinate, but it must be the case that their principles are both formally and numerically determinate. Only the admission of Forms can ensure this. Antithesis: but this leads to the difficulty introduced in puzzle 9.

Puzzle 14

Do the principles have being in potentiality or in actuality? Thesis: if they have being in actuality, there must be something prior to the principles, namely their potentiality, since potentiality precedes actuality. Antithesis: but if the principles have being in potentiality, everything which is could not be, since what is not yet also has being in potentiality.

Puzzle 15

Are the principles universal or particular? Thesis: if they are universals they cannot be substances, on pain of Platonism. Antithesis: but if they are particulars, they cannot fall in the domain of a science, which always studies universals. There would then, absurdly, have to be principles of principles for science to study.

BETA I

It is necessary with regard to the science that we are seeking that we should first address those puzzles that first arise. And these are those which others have supposed to be different about these same things, and also anything in addition to these that we may happen to have left out. For those who wish to make good progress must start well; for subsequent progress depends on the resolution of the first puzzles, and one cannot solve these without knowing the difficulty and the confusion of our minds shows this to be the case with the matter. For in the way in which it is puzzled, in that way it undergoes something like what happens to prisoners. For it is impossible for either of them to move forward. So we must first set out all the difficulties, both for these reasons and also because those who inquire without first setting out the difficulties are like those who do not know in which direction they should walk, and in addition do not even know whether they would recognize that which they are looking for. **[995b]** For the end is not clear to these, but it is for those who have begun with the puzzles. And also from the point of view of judging that man must be better off who has heard, as it were, all the rival and opposed positions.

Now the first puzzle is that which we raised in our preliminary remarks, whether it belongs to one or to many sciences to consider the principles. And whether it is for the science only to see the primary principles of the substances or whether all thinkers should, in the way in which we can say that one thing is both the same and not the same, on the basis of what they have shown also make demonstrations about the subsequent points. And also, if it concerns substance, whether it is about one or many, and if there are many then whether they have affinities or rather we should call some of them wisdoms and some by some other name. And this is another thing that it is necessary to seek, whether we should say that only the sensible substances exist or others

57

also in addition to these, and whether in a single way or various kinds of substances, as with those who posit the forms and the mathematical entities mediate between them and the sensibles. Concerning these things, then, as we say, we must consider, and also whether the theory is only about substances or also about the intrinsically accidental properties of substances, and also we must think about sameness and difference and similarity and dissimilarity and opposition and about prior and posterior and all other such things about which dialecticians try to consider basing their inquiry solely on the received opinions, to whom it does belong to consider all things.

And also the intrinsic properties of these things and not only what each of these things is but also whether one thing is the opposite of another. And whether the principles and genera and elements exist or rather the things into which each is divided; and if the genera, then whether they are those called final and first for the individuals, such as whether animal or man is a principle and exists rather than the individual. But we must especially inquire and investigate whether there is any cause beyond matter in itself or not, and whether this is separable or not and whether it is one or many in number, and whether there is anything beyond the whole (by which I mean when something is predicated of the matter) or nothing, or in some cases yes and in some cases no, and of what kind such of the entities are. [996a] And also whether the principles are defined by number or by form, both those in accounts and those in subjects. And whether they are the same or different for both perishable and imperishable substances and whether they are all imperishable or those of perishable substances are perishable.

And also that which has the greatest difficulty of all, whether the one and the existent, as the Pythagoreans and Plato said, is not something else but a substance of the entities, or not, but something else is the substrate, in the way that Empedocles says that it is love and some other says fire or water or air. And whether the principles are general or like particulars and whether in potentiality or actuality, and whether in other ways or by movement. For these things might also provide considerable puzzlement. And also whether the numbers and lengths and shapes and points are kinds of substances or not, and whether the substances would be separated from the sensibles or indwelling in them. For about all these things it is not only hard to reach the truth but not even easy to come up with a sensible account.

BETA 2

Let us deal first, then, with the problems that we first mentioned, whether it belongs to one or to many sciences to consider all the kinds of causes. For how could a single science grasp them, given that the principles are not opposites? And also many entities do not have all features. For in what way can there be a principle of change in things that are unchanged or the nature of good, if indeed everything that might be good in itself and through its own nature is an end and in this way a cause in that it is for the sake of it that other things both come into being and exist? And the end and the for the sake of which are the end of some action, and all actions involve movement. So it would be impossible for this principle to be in the things that are not moved nor for anything to be a good in itself. And that is why nothing in mathematics is shown in this way, nor is there any proof which rests on something's being better or worse, and in fact nobody makes mention of any such things at all, so that for this reason some of the sophists such as Aristippus have rejected them entirely. For in the other skills, even the banausic ones, such as building and cobbling, since all things are said to be better or worse done, but no one gives such an account of mathematics concerning good and bad states.

[996b] But indeed if there are several sciences of the causes and different ones for different principles, which of these should we assert to be the one that we are looking for, or who should we say to be especially knowledgeable of the affair that we are investigating of those which have them? For it is possible for the same man to know all the ways of the causes, such as, for a house, that from which is the movement is the skill and the builder, and that for which is the function, and the matter is earth and stones, and the form is the account. From the things, then, that we have long ago defined which should we call wisdom or should we do so of them all? For to the extent that a science is more directive and hegemonic and to the extent that it is not right for the

other sciences to contradict it any more than slaves might, the science of the end and of the good is of this kind (for it is for this that the others exist), but to the extent that it has been defined to be of the primary causes and of the most knowable thing, that sort of science would be the science of substance. For though they often know the same thing, we say rather that he who knows the essence really knows the thing as to what it is and by knowing what it is not, and of these one more than another, and especially the man who knows the what it is and not how much or of what kind or what it naturally does or undergoes. And in all other subjects we think that that man knows on each occasion and we think that he has knowledge when we know what the thing is (e.g. what is squaring – the discovery of the median – and so with the others), whereas about its coming into being and its doings and about all its alteration we think that we have knowledge when we know the source of its movement. And this is the opposite and set against the end, so that it would seem to belong to another science to survey each of these two causes.

And indeed in connection with demonstrative principles, whether they belong to one science or to many, there is controversy (and by demonstrative I mean those common opinions from which they demonstrate everything else), for instance it is necessary that everything be either asserted or denied, and that it is impossible for something both to be and not to be, and all other such premises, whether there is one single science of these and of substances or another, and if there should be one, how we should describe that which we are currently seeking. Well, it is not reasonable that there should be one. For how could one claim any resemblance between this science and, say, geometry? If then it is the same with absolutely any science, then it cannot be so for all of them, **[997a]** just as it does not belong to the others nor to that which scrutinizes substance to have knowledge about these. And again in what way will it be a science of them? For what each of these things happens to be we already know (indeed other skills make use of them as already known), for it is necessary that a demonstration must have some fundamental premises. So that the result is that there is one single kind of all these things, since all the demonstrative sciences use the axioms.

And indeed if there is a different science for these and for substances, which of them is prior and master? For the axioms are rather the more general and the principles of all things. If this does not belong to the philosopher, who else will have the job of considering truth and falsity in their case? And in general is there some one single science of all substances or many? And if there is not one, of what sort of substance should we suppose that one to be? It is not reasonable that there should be one for all substances. For then there would also be one science that would be demonstrative about all accidents, if all demonstrative science considers some substrate and the things happening to it from the received opinions. And it surely belongs to the same science to consider the accidental properties of what is its subject from the same opinions. For there is a single science of the what and of the whence, either the same or some other, so that either these same ones or some one of them will also consider the accidents.

And also whether the theory is only concerned with substances or also with their accidents. I mean, for instance, if the solid is a kind of substance and also the line and the plane, whether it belongs to the same science to know all these things and the accidents for each kind about which mathematics makes demonstrations, or to some other. For if it is for the same one, then the science of substance would also be demonstrative, but there does not seem to be a demonstration of the what it is; but if it belongs to some other science, which science will it be that considers the accidents for a substance? For this would be very hard to deliver.

Or should we say that there are only the sensible substances or others also besides these? And do there happen to be manifold or only single kinds of entities, **[997b]** such as with those who posit the forms and the intermediates, concerning which we assert the mathematical sciences to be? As we say, then, the forms are said to be causes and substances in themselves in the first book about them. But in many ways they present difficulties, none less than the absurdity of saying that there are some natures in addition to those in the heaven, and to say that there are these same ones for the sensibles except that some are eternal and some perishable. For we say that there is the form of man and also of horse and health, but nothing else, making the same sort of mistake as

62

those who say that there are gods but that they are in the form of men. For they are doing nothing else than positing eternal men, and these thinkers are not positing forms but eternal sensibles. And if one posits, in addition to the sensibles and the forms, the mediate entities, then there will be many absurdities. For it is obvious how lines will be in regard to themselves and to the perceptible ones and so with each of the other kinds, so that, given that astrology is the single science of these things, there will be some heaven in addition to the sensible heaven and sun and moon and all the other things in the heaven. And yet how should one believe in such things? For it is not even reasonable that they should be unmoved, but since they are moved it is completely impossible. And the same goes for those things studied by optics and mathematical harmonics. For it is impossible that these should exist in addition to the sensibles for the same reasons. For if there are mediate sensibles and sensations, it is obvious that there will also be mediate animals between them and the perishable ones, and one might have the problem about which entities one should seek in such sciences. For if geometry will discern the geodesics in this way only, in that one is of the things that we perceive while the other is of those that we do not, it is obvious that in addition to medicine there will be some other science and with all the others the same, between medicine itself and the medicine of everyday experience. And yet how is that possible? For there would then also be certain healthy things between the healthy itself and the perceived healthies. And yet this is not true either, that the geodesic is of perceived and perishable magnitudes. For it would have been destroyed when they are. And similar astrology would turn out not to be about the perceived sizes and the observed heaven. For perceived lines [998a] are not of the same kind as the geometer pronounces (for none of the sensibles is in this way straight or curved; for the circle does not touch the ruler at a point, as Protagoras said in his criticism of the geometers), nor are the movements and rotations of the heaven such as those with which astrology deals, nor do the signs have the same natures as the stars. But there are some who say that there are these so-called intermediate entities between the forms and the sensibles, but not separate from the sensibles but in them. And the absurd consequences of this it would take a long argument to reveal, and it is sufficient to consider such things. For it would not be reasonable to say this much only on this case, but it is clear that the forms would also have to be in the sensibles (for they both have the same account), so that there would also have to be two bodies in the same place, and the forms could not be changeless if they were in changing things. And anyway why should one suppose that there are such things but that they are in the sensibles? For the same absurdities will follow as above – there will be a heaven in addition to the heaven, except that it will not be separate but in the same place, which is still more impossible.

Concerned with these matters there is great uncertainty as to which positions are likely to be conducive to truth, and in connection with the principles whether it is right to suppose that the kinds are the elements and principles or rather the primary things from which each thing is, as the elements and principles of voice are thought to be the things from which primary voices are made, but not the common thing voice. And we say that those things are elements of diagrams, of which the demonstrations are present in the demonstrations of either all or most other things. Even of bodies the pluralists think that there are elements and so do the monists, as Empedocles says that fire and water and so forth are the elements from which entities are constructed, but he does not mention these things as types of entity. And in addition to these if anyone else wanted to conjecture a nature, such as that of a bed, [998b] saying from what parts it was constructed and how put together, then he will know its nature.

On these grounds the principles would not be the kinds of entities, and if we know each thing by definitions, and the principles are the kinds of definitions, it is necessary that the kinds are the principles of defined things. And if it is possible to grasp the science of entities and also to grasp the science of the forms by which they say that things exist, then the kinds will be the principles of the forms. And it seems that some also of those who say that the elements of entities are the one or the being or the great and the small are using them as creations. But in neither way can we speak of the principles. For the account of substance is one, and another will be that of definition by kind and that which gives the constituents. In addition, even if the kinds are as much principles as you like, should we think that the primary kinds are principles or the ultimate ones categorized of individuals? For this too is controversial. For if it is always the universals that are rather principles, it is clear that they will be the highest of the kinds, for these are said of all things. There will then be as many principles of entities as there are primary kinds, so that one and being will be principles and substances. For these things are said of the largest number of things. But it is not possible that there be one kind of things either the one or the being; for it is necessary that the differentiae of each kind both are and are each single, and it is impossible either to predicate the species of the genus with their own differentiae or the genus without its own species, so that if the one or being were a kind, then neither being nor the one would be a differentia. But if there are no kinds, then there will not be any principles either, if the kinds are principles. And the mediates included with the differentiae will be kinds down to the individuals (whereas in fact some are thought to be and some are not). And furthermore the differentiae are still more principles than the kinds. And if these are principles, then there will be an infinity of principles, so to speak, especially if one were to make the primary kind a principle.

[999a] But indeed even if the one is more like a principle, and the one is undivided, then the whole universe will be undivided either in quantity or in form, so that the one would be more like the last predicable. For man is not the kind of certain men. And in things for which the prior and posterior arise, it is not possible that in this case there should be anything beyond them (e.g. if the dyad is the first of numbers, then there will be no number beyond the forms of numbers, and similarly no shapes beyond the form of shape, and if it is not of these, then it is unlikely that there will be principles of other entities except for the forms; for of them they especially seem to be kinds). But in individuals there is no prior and posterior, but wherever there is better and worse, there always the better is prior, so that of these too there would not be a genus. From all this it rather appears that the things predicated of individuals are rather the principles than the kinds. But again it is not easy to say how we should take these to be the principles. For the principle and cause should exist beside the thing of which they are and should be separable from them, and why should one assume this of individual properties, except in that they are universally predicated and for all things? But if this is the reason, we should consider more universal things rather to be principles – so that the principles would be the primary kinds.

BETA 4

There is a puzzle connected with these, which is the hardest and yet most necessary to consider of all, and concerning it we have so far given no account. For either there is nothing else besides individuals, the individuals are limitless, then how is it possible to have science of an infinity? For in so far as it is one and the same thing, and in so far as it has some general property, to that extent is it possible to know all things.

But if indeed this is necessary and there must be something in addition to the individuals, then these will either be the ultimates or the primaries, and we have just shown that this is impossible. And if there is as much as you like something other than the whole (whenever something is predicated of matter), if there is something, should it be something beyond everything else, or be beyond some things but not beyond others or beyond nothing? **[999b]** If, then, there is nothing beyond the individuals, then there would be nothing intelligible, but all things would be sensible and there would be science of nothing, unless one were to say that perception was science. And also there would be nothing that was eternal and unmoved (for all sensibles are perishable and in motion). But if there is nothing eternal, then there cannot be generation. For there must be something that is generated and something from which it is generated and the last of this series must be ungenerated, if it comes to an end and it is impossible that there should be generation from what is not. And since there is generation and change, there must also be limit (for no movement is unlimited and of all movement there is an end, and that which cannot become cannot be created, and the becoming must have been when it first became). And again if matter exists through being ungenerated, then it is all the more reasonable that substance can be, whenever matter is generated. For if the one is not then neither will the other be, and there will be nothing at all. But if this is impossible, then there must be something besides the whole, the shape, namely, and the form.

And again if someone should suppose this, then this will produce puzzles in some cases and in some cases not. For it is clear that it cannot be so in all cases; for we would not suppose that there might be some house in addition to particular houses. Furthermore is there one substance for all things, such as for all men? But this is absurd, for all those things are one of which the substance is one. But can they be many and different? This too is unreasonable. But how will the matter for each of these things come about and is the whole both these things?

And one might also raise the following problem about the principles: if they are one in form, then there will be nothing one in number, not even the one itself and being. And indeed it will be possible to know in a way, if there is not the one over many. But if each of the principles is one in number and not as with the sensibles but for the others (as with such and such a syllable being one in form then the principles will be one in form: for these are several in number), but if this is not so and the principles of the entities are one in number, then nothing else will exist apart from the elements. For it makes no difference whether we speak of the particular or the one in number. For by the one in number we mean the particular, and by the general we mean what is above them. [1000a] So that if the elements of voice were defined in number, then it would be necessary that all the lines were as numerous as the elements, there not being two or more the same.

But a no less grave puzzle remains both for the present theorists and for the previous ones, whether there are the same principles for the perishable as for imperishable substances or different ones. Now if there are the same, how is it that some things are perishable and others imperishable and for what cause? Now those of the school of Hesiod and all those who, as theologians, only considered what is plausible in this connection, and made little of us (for by making the gods the principles and making creation from the gods, they say that those who do not eat the nectar and ambrosia are born mortal, clearly mentioning names that are known to them, and yet we have ourselves spoken about such a provision of causes. For if they addressed them for the sake of pleasure, then nectar and ambrosia are not at all the cause of their being,

68

and if they are the cause of their being, then how could they be eternal
if they need food?) – but about those who have invented clever
mythologies it is not worthwhile to take a serious look. But of those
who speak by demonstration, we are entitled to demand an answer to
the question why indeed things coming from the same source are in
some cases eternal in nature and in others are destroyed. But since they
neither give a reason nor is it reasonable that it should be so, it is clear
that there are not the same principles nor causes for them. And indeed
the one to whom one might most reasonably ascribe this opinion,
Empedocles, even he suffered the same thing. For he supposed a certain
principle that was responsible for destruction in strife, but he seemed
no less to generate this from the one. For everything else is from this,
except God. Indeed, he says:

> 'From which all things that were and are,
> Trees flourished forth and men and women both,
> And ominous birds and water-nourished fish,
> And indeed long-yeared gods . . .'

And it is clear even without these lines. [**1000b**] For if they were not
present in affairs, then all things would be one, as he puts it. For when
they came together, then

> 'Lastmost was strife . . .'

And so it happens for him that the most blessed god is the least wise of
them all. For he does not know all things. For he does not have strife,
and cognition is of like by like.

> 'For earth by earth', he says, 'we see, water by water,
> And noble air by air and love by love
> And strife by bitter strife . . .'

But from where the ratio comes, this clear, it comes about that for him
strife is no more the cause of destruction than being is. And in the same
way neither is love the cause of being, for by drawing things to the one
it destroys other things. And at the same time he gives no cause for this
change except that they are so constituted:

'But when great strife was swollen in its limbs,
To honour them in fullest time it came
Which spins about its centre like an oath.'

The assumption is that it changes out of necessity. But he reveals not cause for the necessity. And yet this is as much as he says in agreement; for he does not make some things perishable and other things imperishable, but all things perishable except the elements. But the present puzzle is why some things are perishable and some not, if they are from the same principles.

That, then, there are not the same principles, so much let it be said. But if the principles are different, then one puzzle is whether they will themselves be perishable or imperishable. Now if they are perishable, then it is clear that they too must come from other principles (for everything is destroyed to that from which it comes), so that it turns out that some other principles are prior to the principles, and this is impossible, both if it ends and if there is a regress. And then how will the perishable things be, if their principles are removed? But if they are imperishable, how is it that from imperishable things perishable things should come, but from other principles imperishable things? For this does not make sense, but it is either impossible or requires extensive discussion. And again no one has tried to suggest other ones, but they say that there are the same principles for all things. [**1001a**] And the first puzzle they brush aside, as though assuming that it is trivial.

And also most hard to consider but most necessary for knowledge is the question whether being and the one are substances of entities, with each of them not being some other thing while the one is the one and being, or whether we have to ask what the one is and being with some other nature as substrate. For some think that nature is in one way, some in the other. Well, Plato and the Pythagoreans think that the one and being are not different in nature but the same, since substance is the same to be one and to be being. But the students of nature, such as Empedocles, make the whole point more familiar by saying what the one is. For he would seem to be saying that love is some such thing (for it is the cause of everything's being one), whereas others cite fire or air as the one and being, from which come the things that are and the things that become. And in the same way those who posit a plurality of elements. For it is necessary that these should also say that the one and being are as many as they assert there to be principles. And the result is that if one supposes there to be some substance the one and being, then there will not be any of the other things (for these are the most general of all things, but if there is not one itself or being itself, then there is hardly likely to be one of the others, except for the individuals that have been mentioned). But if there is something that is both the one and being, then it is necessary that its substance be the one and being, for it will not be some other thing predicated of it, but these very things.

But indeed if unity itself and being itself exist, then there is a great puzzle how there will be anything apart from them, by which I mean how entities will be more than one. For there is no other to being, so that, as Parmenides said, it is necessary that all things are one and that this is being. But on either way of taking it is difficult. [1001b] For if the one is not a substance or if the one itself exists, it is impossible that number should be a substance. But if it should not be, we have said above why not, and if it is, then the same puzzle arises in connection with being. For from what other unity will this other unity arise? For it is necessary that it is not one or many things of which each is one. Again if the one itself cannot be divided, then, by Zeno's reasoning, nothing would exist. For that which neither by adding nor by subtracting makes either larger or smaller, one does not say that this is one of the entities, on the obvious assumption that an entity must have magnitude. And if it must have magnitude then it must be bodily — for that is something that is in all ways. And other things do in a way make something larger by their addition, but in a way they do not, such as the plane and the line, but the point and the monad not at all. But since Zeno reasoned wrongly and it is possible to have something that is indivisible, so must we answer this paradox. For such a thing being added will not make something bigger. But how from such a thing or from many such things will magnitude arise? For it is the same as saying that the line is a collection of points. And indeed if one so supposed it so that it would be generated, as some say, from the one itself and something else that is not one in number, then no less must we inquire

71

why and how it is sometimes a number and sometimes a magnitude which is generated, if indeed the not one is oddness and has the same nature. For it cannot be as out of one and the same or as out of some number that magnitude would also arise, as is clear.

BETA 5

The next puzzle after this one is whether numbers and bodies and planes and points are kind of substance or not. For if, on the one hand, they are not, then it escapes us what the being is and what are the substances of entities. For affections and processes and relations and dispositions and ratios are not thought to indicate the substance of anything (for they are all said of some subject, and none of them is a this-such). But the things that might particularly be thought to designate substance, water and earth and fire and air, from which composite bodies are composed, [1002a] of these warmths and coldnesses and suchlike are the affections, not substances, and the body that undergoes them is the only thing that persists, being a kind of entity and a kind of substance. But indeed body would be less of a substance than surface, and this than line, and this than the monad and the point. For it is by these that body is defined, and it is thought that they can exist without body, whereas it is not possible that the body can exist without them. That is why both the majority and the earlier thinkers thought that entity and substance were body and that the other things were affections of it, so that the principles of bodies would also be the principles of entities, while those more recent or wiser thought that they were numbers.

So, as we said, if these things are not substance, there is in general no substance and no entity, for it is certainly not appropriate to call the affections of these entities. But now if this is agreed, that lengths and points are rather substances than bodies, yet we still do not see of what sort of bodies these should be (for it is impossible that they should be among the perceptibles), and so there would turn out to be no substance. And it also seems that all these things are divisions of bodies, in width, depth and length. And in addition, there is similarly present in the solid some sort of shape or none; so that if the Hermes is not in the stone, then neither is the half cube in the cube in the way that is defined. And so neither would the surface be (for if it is of any kind, then this would also be the one that marked off the half), and the same goes for points, lines and monads, so that if body is substance most of all, and some more than others, but that not even the latter are substances, it escapes us what the being is and what is the substance of the entities.

For in addition to what has been said, it also turns out that our account of creation and destruction does not make sense. For it is thought that substance, if it is not prior in actuality, or should not be posterior, suffers these things from being created and being destroyed. But it is not possible that points and lines and surfaces should be either created or destroyed, sometimes being and sometimes not. For whenever bodies are touched or divided, [**1002b**] then either a single one touched or two divided arise. So that it is not agreed to be destroyed, and when they are divided ones that did not previously exist now do (for the individual point could not be divided into two), and if they do get created and destroyed, from what would they be created? And the situation over time is the same as that in the present, since this too cannot come into existence and cease to be, but always seems to be something else, not being some substance. And it is also clear that this applies to points, lines and planes. The argument is the same. For they are all in the same way either divisions or boundaries.

BETA 6

And we might in general pose the puzzle why we should also seek certain other things beyond the perceptibles and the intermediaries, such as the posited Forms. For if it is because the mathematicals differ from the latter in some other way, and that the many are of the same form, this makes no difference, so that their principles will not be defined in number (just as the numerical principles of our lines will not be circumscribed altogether, but will be in form, if one should not take a given syllable or vowel. And of these they will also be numerically circumscribed – and the same will go for the case of the intermediaries. For there too co-specifics are limitless.), so that if there are not in addition to the perceptibles and the mathematicals certain other entities which some call forms, there will be no numerically single substance, nor will the principles of entities be of a certain number but only in form.

If, then, this is necessary, then it is necessary for this reason to posit the forms. For if those who have supported them have not argued well, this is still what they want, and it is necessary that they should say this, that each of the forms is a kind of substance and nothing accidental. But if indeed we suppose the forms to exist and that the principles are one in number but not in form, we will be articulating impossibilities as necessary consequences. And next to these there is the question whether the elements exist potentially or in some other way. For if they do so in some other way, then there will be something else prior to the principles [1003a] (for the potentiality is prior to that type of cause, and it is not necessary that all the potential should be in that way). But if the elements do exist potentially, then it is possible that none of the entities exists. For that which does not yet exist is also a potential existent. For that which is not comes into being, and nothing comes into being of the things that cannot be.

These, then, are the puzzles with which we must deal in connection with the principles, and also whether they are general or, as we claim, particular. For if they are general, they will not be substances (for none of the common things signifies a this-such but an of such a kind, whereas substance is a this-such. But if some this-such is to exist and the universal category be excluded, then Socrates will be many things, both himself and man and an animal, if each one of these indicates a this-such and a unity.) If, then, the principles are general, this turns out, but if they are not universal but as particulars, then they will not be knowable. For knowledge is always of generalities. So other principles which are universally predicated will be prior to the principles, if there is to be knowledge of them.

Book Gamma

GAMMA I

Aristotle is now in a position to give what is presumably his definitive statement of what philosophy and especially metaphysics is. There must be, he tells us, a science of being just qua *being, which will be different from all other, departmental sciences, which deal with some limited part of being. The study of being* qua *being turns out to be the same thing as the study of the primary causes and principles, which has previously been said to be the task of philosophy, because the primary causes and principles are the causes and principles of being* qua *being.*

There is a kind of science whose remit is being *qua* being and the things pertaining to that which is *per se*. This science is not the same as any of the departmental disciplines. For none of these latter engages in this *general* speculation about that which is *qua* that which is. Rather, they delimit some section of what is and study its accidental features (a prime example is mathematics). We, however, are investigating principles and fundamental causes, and these must evidently pertain *per se* to a kind of nature. Now the traditional search for the *elements* of the things that there are is in fact the search for these very *principles*. So the elements, too, of that which is must pertain to it not accidentally but *qua* thing that is. And by the same token this inquiry also comprises the investigation of the primary *causes* of that which is *qua* that which is.

GAMMA 2

We have now learnt that First Philosophy is the study of the causes and principles of being qua *being. However, this will not help us greatly until we have a clear understanding of what being is. This is perplexed by the fact that there is a great variety of accounts of being, but fortunately there is a common link between them in that all accounts of being are given with reference to a 'focal' account, which is the account of being as substance. We can, therefore, still more precisely define the task of philosophy as the study of the causes and principles of substance. At the same time, although this is the central task of philosophy, it does not exhaust the business of philosophy, which is interested in the other accounts of being, though seen from the perspective of the account of being as substance.*

Being is also very closely associated with unity and the one. So it also comes within the remit of the philosopher to study unity and its various related items, such as number, identity, similarity, etc. Also, as we are later told, philosophy will interest itself in plurality, the contrary of unity, since all sciences study contraries, and so consider difference, dissimilarity, etc.

Aristotle also draws a distinction here between the philosophy which has to do with primary, supra-sensible substance and that which has to do with secondary, sensible substance. The former is First, the latter Second Philosophy. It is not clear how exactly this distinction is to be squared with the account of philosophy as the study of being qua *being. In the bulk of the* Metaphysics, *and especially in books Zeta and Eta, the distinction between primary and secondary substance does not seem to play a crucial part. Rather, Aristotle is concerned to get clear about the difficult notion of substance itself and, in a sense, the causes and principles of substance, pretty much as announced at the start of the present chapter.*

Now that which is is indeed spoken of in many ways. But it is spoken of with regard to one thing and a single kind of nature. It is *not* spoken of by homonymy.

Its position is similar to that with health. Everything that is healthy is spoken of *with regard to* health. So, one thing is said to be healthy by dint of preserving health, another by dint of producing it, another by being a sign of it, another by being capable of having it. [**1003b**] Also with the medical. A thing is said to be medical *with regard to* the art of medicine. One thing is said to be medical by dint of having the art of medicine, another by being naturally adjusted to it, another by being a function of it. And this, of course, will not exhaust the examples of things spoken of with regard to something in this way.

It is in just this way that that which is, although spoken of in many ways, is nevertheless always spoken of with regard to a single principle. So, some things are called things that are because they are substances, other things are called things that are because they are affections of a substance. Also, some things are so called because they are a way into substance, or because they are destructions or deprivations or qualities of a substance, or productive or generative of a substance or of the things that are spoken of with regard to substance, or a negation either of a substance or of one of these latter (and hence we say even that that which is not *is* what is not).

OK. For everything that is healthy there is one single science. Surely, this should be the case in a parallel way with the other things spoken of in this way. For the domain of a single science is not set only by things spoken of in a single respect but also by things spoken of with regard to a single nature. Indeed, there is a way in which these latter are also spoken of in a single respect. It, therefore, does indeed belong, if this is right, to some *single* science to study the things that are *qua* things that are.

Now it is a quite general feature of science that its overriding concern is with its primary object, that on which the rest of its domain depends and because of which the things in that domain are called what they are. So, if, in the case of things that are, the primary object is *substance*, then we can state the fundamental duty of the philosopher: *it is to gain possession of the principles and causes of substances*.

Now, every single genus has its own single perceptual range and its own single proprietary science. Grammar, for instance, is a single science covering all spoken sounds. Therefore there must be some one science single in kind that considers how many forms there are of that which is *qua* that which is and the forms of those forms.

Now consider this possibility. That which is and the one are the same thing. They are a single nature by dint of their always accompanying one another, as do principle and cause. There will still be no single account by which they are both disclosed. (We could, in fact, equally easily imagine for these purposes that they did have the same account. Far from weakening the position, this would actually strengthen it.) It is, indeed, surely plausible that one man and a man in existence and a man *simpliciter* are the same thing. Nothing is added by the extension of the expression to 'He is one man' and 'He is one man that is'. It is also clear that these items are not separated either in their coming to be or in their destruction, and the same goes for 'one thing'. So it is quite clear that in this sort of case the addition of words does not change the reference, and that the one is not something else alongside that which is and that the substance of each thing is non-accidentally a single thing, and the same goes for that which a certain kind of thing is. So there must be as many forms of that which is as there are of the one. And the what-it-is of such things, i.e. the same and the similar and the rest of that sort, fall under the same science single in kind. And the opposites are all, in effect, derived from this principle, [**1004a**] as we have sufficiently established in the *Enumeration of Opposites*.

There are, too, as many departments of philosophy as there are substances, which requires that among the latter there must be a primary and subsequent. And given that the immediate divisions of that which is are genera, there will be one science for each genus. Thus the philosopher has the same sort of project as those known as mathematicians. Mathematics too has departments, with a primary and secondary science and a series of studies thereafter.

The study, too, of each pair of opposites is the province of a single science. Now the opposite of the one is plurality.

[Footnote: a single science studies the negation and privation of a thing because it studies in both ways the single thing that is negated or in privation. There are two ways of negating. Either we can say that a thing does not obtain (*simpliciter*), or we can say that it does not pertain to a certain kind. The second way of negating involves the addition of the differentia to the single thing and not just the negating factor, since the negation of a thing in this way marks an absence. By contrast, in the case of privation, some underlying nature also arises, *whose* privation it is said to be.]

As we were saying, plurality is the opposite of the one. So the science we have specified must also cognize the opposites of the things that we have mentioned, the other, the dissimilar and the unequal and such other things as are spoken of either in relation to one of these or in relation to plurality and the one. And opposition itself is one such thing. For opposition is a kind of differentia, and the differentia is an otherness. Since, then, the one is said in many ways, these things too will also have been said in many ways, and yet it belongs to a single science to take cognizance of them all. It does not suffice for them each to fall to different sciences just that they are spoken of in many ways. For that it is also necessary that the accounts have neither single-aspect nor single-reference connection.

In any case, everything is connected to the primary (so all things said to be one are connected to the primary one; ditto for the same, the other and the opposites). So once we have distinguished in how many ways a thing is spoken of, we must demonstrate in what way it is spoken with regard to that which is primary in each relevant category. And some things will turn out to be thus related by dint of comprising the primary, others by dint of producing it and others in other similar ways.

The conclusion of all this is very clear. There must be some one science that gives an account of all these items and that also gives an account of substance (substance, in fact, was one of the puzzles that we looked at). And the philosopher should be able to engage in the study of all these items. [1004b] For who, except the philosopher, is going to ask whether Socrates and Socrates seated *is the same thing*? Who is going to ask whether one is opposite to one? Or indeed what the opposite is and in how many ways it is spoken of? And the same goes for all the rest of such items. They are all *per se* properties of that which is one *qua* that which is one and of that which is *qua* that which is, not *qua* numbers or lines or fire. Of course it is the task of philosophy to get to know both their essence and their accidents. The shortcoming of current examinations of these topics is not their failure to be philosophy, but the priority of substance, on which the current philosophical consensus has no view. There are affections peculiar to number *qua* number (e.g. oddness and evenness, commensurability and equality, excess and deficiency), which pertain to the numbers both *per se* and in mutual relation. And there are similar lists for the solid, the unchanging, the changing, the weightless and the weighted. And in just the same way there are peculiarities of that which is just *qua* that which is. And it is the truth about these that the philosopher is after.

A pointer to this is the fact that dialecticians and sophists *prennent l'allure des philosophes*. Sophistry is but philosophy in appearance only, and the scope of dialectic is every item, which all have in common only that they are things that are. And in fact it is quite clear that this breadth of dialectic debate is motivated by the fact that all things that are are proprietary to philosophy. Sophistry, dialectic, philosophy. They all have the same genus as their domain. But philosophy differs from dialectic in the manner of its powers, and from sophistry in the choice of life that it involves. Dialectic experiments with the topics on which philosophy gives knowledge, whereas sophistry bears the appearance of philosophy, but not the reality.

Now, one of the two columns of opposites is always the privation column. And all the items in both columns are derived from that which is and that which is not, from one and plurality (e.g. stasis is derived from one and movement from plurality). But it is also true that almost everybody agrees that the things that are and substance are composed of opposites. At least, everybody claims that the principles are opposite. Some have it that they are odd and even, some that they are hot and cold, some limit and limitless, some love and strife. It needs no demonstration that all the others are also derived from one and plurality (let us not linger over the derivation), [1005a] and even principles proposed by other schools fall naturally into these kinds. So this is yet another way of showing that there is a single science for that which is *qua* that which is. For all things are either opposites or derived from opposites, and the principles of the opposites are one and plurality. And the opposites, whether spoken of in single-aspect style or not, are the province of a single science (the latter is no doubt more plausible). And yet even if the one is spoken of in many ways, the others will be spoken of with regard to the primary and so also with the opposites. (And this even if that which is and the one is not general and the same in all cases or separable. It is, in fact, probable that they are not and that some are single-aspect while others form a series.) And given all this, it is also hardly surprising if it is not incumbent on the geometer to study what the opposite is, or what the complete, or one, or the same, or other (save *ex hypothesi*).

Some firm conclusions can be drawn. A single science has as its domain that which is *qua* that which is, and also its properties *qua* that which is. This science concerns itself with both substances and their properties, all those we have mentioned and also prior and posterior, genus and species, whole and part and all other such.

GAMMA 3

Aristotle has now shown that philosophy is concerned primarily with substance, but also with the other accounts of being and with unity and plurality and their related items. He now adds to this list that philosophy is also the study of the fundamental principles of demonstration and logic. In making this addition, he is resolving the dilemma posed by puzzle 2 of book Beta (page 51). The reason why it falls to philosophy to study the fundamental principles of logic is that these principles are not concerned with some specific departments of being, such as the departmental sciences study, but with being as a whole, the province of philosophy. It is true that non-philosophers, especially natural scientists, have taken an interest in the past in the foundations of logic, but, in so doing, they have been wearing the hat not of the scientist but of the philosopher. In any case, being is wider than nature, so that the natural scientists would not be competent to study something that applies to all of it.

The rest of book Gamma is, accordingly, devoted to the defence of the fundamental principles of demonstration. Aristotle evidently feels that it will not be possible to be certain about the conclusions later to be drawn about substance, unless the principles of demonstration itself have first been vindicated. He begins in this chapter by declaring that the most fundamental principle of all is the principle of non-contradiction, about which it is not even possible for us to be deluded. The principle states that it is impossible for the same thing to have and not to have the same feature at a single time, and it is the principle upon which all the other principles of demonstration ultimately rest.

Here is another issue to be decided. Is there one science both for the so-called axioms of mathematics and for substance, or different ones for each? In fact, the answer is clear. A single science, that of the philosopher, also covers the axioms of mathematics. Mathematical axioms, too, apply to all the things that there are, after all, and not separately to some genus of things demarcated off from the others.

They are also available to every departmental science, since they are of that which is *qua* that which is and of every genus of that which is. But the use made of them by each departmental science is only to the extent that is sufficient for its purposes, i.e. just in regard to the genus for which that science produces its demonstrations. There is, then, no question but that mathematical axioms apply to all things just *qua* things that are (they constitute indeed the commonality of things that are). So the science that gets to grips with that which is *qua* that which is will also be the science of mathematical axioms. Hence the fact that no departmental science takes a view on the truth or falsity of these axioms. Geometry does not, neither does arithmetic. Some natural scientists *do*, but that's OK since they (and only they) conceive themselves as studying nature as a whole and thus the domain of that which is. However, there is a science higher than natural science. For in truth nature is but one genus of that which is. It is a science whose subject matter is universal and which is exclusively concerned with primary substance. And it is also concerned with the axioms of mathematics. Natural science is a kind of philosophy, [**1005b**] but it is not First Philosophy.

Fitful discussion proceeds about the way in which the truth of the axioms of mathematics should be taken. This debate reflects the poverty of current logical training. Knowledge of mathematical axioms should be a propaedeutic to philosophy, not something you pick up while doing it.

What is quite clear is that philosophy, whose domain is the whole of substance, in regard to its essential nature, must also examine the principles of logic. The specialist in each genus ought to be able to give the securest principles of his domain. So the 'specialist' in the thing that is *qua* the things that are should be able to give the securest principles of this domain, i.e. of everything. And this 'specialist' is the philosopher. And the securest principle of all is that about which error is impossible. And this sort of principle must also be that which is most completely known, since it is about the unknown that error occurs, and it must also be non-hypothetical. Anyone studying anything of the things that are must grasp this principle. And to say that is to say that it is not a mere 'hypothesis'. And if a principle is such that anyone who is to know anything must grasp it, then the approach to any subject matter presupposes mastery of that principle. It brooks, then, no discussion that this sort of principle is the most secure of all principles.

The question is – which principle is this? It is, we are now in a position to say, the principle that:

P: It is impossible for the same thing at the same time both to be-in and not to be-in the same thing in the same respect.

(This will bear some logical sharpening, but let that pass for now.)

Here, indeed, we have our securest of all principles, which entirely fits the standards that we have set for it. No one can believe that the same thing both is and is-not. On one interpretation, this is the point that Heraclitus was making. (What of course is *not* impossible is that one can say one thing and believe another.)

It is, then, not possible for opposites to be-in the same subject at the same time (again with the usual logical provisos). But also the opinion opposite to an opinion is the negation of it. And this makes clear why it is impossible for the same person to believe that the same thing both is and is-not at the same time. For if one were to fall into such error, it would amount to the simultaneous holding of opposite beliefs with regard to that object. And that is why this principle is the ultimate root of all demonstration – it is its very nature to be the principle of all other axioms.

GAMMA 4

Aristotle now begins his remarkable defence of the principle of non-contradiction. It might be felt that so fundamental a principle cannot be defended but must simply be accepted as the foundation of all reasoning, but Aristotle, while allowing that it cannot be demonstrated in any normal sense, since a demonstration would have to proceed from some still more fundamental principle and this would generate an infinite regress, nevertheless offers a demonstration by refutation. The idea is that if anyone denies the principle from whatever direction, he can be refuted and the totality of such refutations amounts to an indirect demonstration of the principle. What is required is, in fact, not even that the opponent explicitly denies the principle but merely that he says anything at all. If he refuses even this, he rules himself out from having anything to say about the foundations of logic or indeed anything else. But if he does say anything, he is committed to what he says being true and not false, in line with the very principle which he is supposed to be denying. Aristotle hammers the point home with an extraordinary array of arguments.

For all that, it is certainly the case, as we have been saying, that there are some philosophers [**1006a**] who hold both that it is possible for the same thing to be and not to be and that it is possible for us to entertain beliefs to that effect. These claims are used as premises, furthermore, by many natural scientists. Nevertheless, as far as we are concerned, the present argument has shown that the same thing *cannot* at the same time both be and not be, and indeed we have gone on to show that this is the securest of all principles. Amazingly there are even philosophers who try to *prove* this. This reveals their innocence of logical training. A major point of such training is to be able to recognize which subject matters require proof and which do not. After all, it must be true, quite generally, that not everything can be proven, on pain of an infinite regress (which would in any case undermine the proof). And if there are to be some premises for which it is not appropriate to require proof, these philosophers would be quite unable to give reasons for any other principle to be more of this kind.

However, the impossibility of the denial of our principle *can* in fact be proven. It can be done by the *elenchus* (provided only, of course, that the disputant advances some kind of proposition. Should he choose not to, there is something comical about seeking to refute, and just in that respect, a position that has absolutely no content of any kind. It would be like taking issue with a vegetable.) Now we must carefully distinguish between demonstration by means of an *elenchus* and demonstration *tout court*. If, in this case, one attempted a straightforward demonstration, one would be presupposing, at the start, the very principle to be defended. If, however, the other party advances a comparable first principle, this problem does not arise – one can simply deploy the *elenchus* rather than assay a demonstration. And the way to start to deal with anything like this is not to demand a statement either that something is or that it does not. This might well be taken to be begging the original question. Rather it is to require that he say something with content both for himself and for anybody else (a necessary minimum for any statement). If he will not do this, then his position admits of no rational defence against internal challenges or those of anybody else. If once, however, he does make this first meaningful statement, there is something definite enough to get to grips with and the proof can proceed. But the whole process has not been initiated by the conductor of the proof but by its victim, since it is by the elimination of his initial statement that he comes to accept the correct account. (Also anyone who accepts the challenge will *eo ipso* have agreed that there is something true independently of proof.) As a result of all this, it will not turn out to be the case that everything is such that it is in a certain way and also is not in that same way.

Here, then, is how our proof proceeds:

1. *First assumption:* we take it to be self-evident that the locution 'to be' and the locution 'not to be' both have a definite meaning. This, I think, rules out at least the possibility that everything both is in a certain way and is not in that way.

Elucidation: suppose the locution 'man' has a definite meaning. (Let us say that this is 'biped animal'.) Then what is meant by 'having a definite meaning' is just this: if some arbitrary item is a man, and if there is something that you have to be in order to be a man, then this will be what it is to be a man for that item.

[Footnote: in fact it makes no difference even if one allows there to be several meanings to these locutions, provided that the number is definite. For a different locution could be assigned to each account. In the [1006b] present case, if we denied that 'man' was univocal and that for one of its several meanings the proprietary account was 'biped animal', it would still be perfectly possible for there to be a (definite) plurality of other meanings, just by the assignment of a proprietary locution for each account. Were, on the other hand, these assignments not to be made and the number of meanings to be infinite, then we would not in effect be dealing with a possible ingredient in a proposition. For *this kind* of non-univocality is meaninglessness, and if locutions have no meaning mutual communication is eliminated (as also, to tell the truth, is internal consistency of thought. A man cannot think unless he thinks of some single thing, and if such thought is possible for him, what is to stop the assignment of a locution to this object of his thought?)]

Well, given all that, we may as well revert to our original supposition, that the locution has a meaning and that it has only one meaning. This rules out the possibility that by 'to be a man' whatever 'not to be a man' is is meant, provided 'man' not only has meaning in regard to a single thing but has *the* meaning *of* a single thing. (NB. It is not meaning *in regard to* a single thing that we consider to be having *a single meaning*. Were we to make that equation, 'the musical', 'the white' and 'man' might all have meant a single thing – a semantic shortcut (by dint of their synonymy) to monism.)

We can say, further, that it will only be possible for the same thing to be and not to be by dint of a homonymy (e.g. what we call 'man' others would call 'not man'). But our present question is not whether it is possible for the same thing to be and not to be in regard to the locution, but whether it is possible in regard to the object. But if 'man' and 'not man' do not mean something different, it cannot be denied that 'not to be a man' will mean the same as 'to be a man', and this will mean that 'to be a man' will just *be* 'not to be a man', since they will be a single thing. That is what it is to be a single thing, after all. It is to be like 'raiment' and 'cloak', assuming that their proprietary account is one. And if to be a man and not to be a man are a single thing, then 'to be a man' and 'not to be a man' have a single meaning.

However, a proof has been offered of their not meaning a single thing. And so it is necessary that, if it is right to say of anything that it is a man, that thing must be a biped animal (what 'man' meant), and if this is necessary, then it is not possible for the same thing at the same time not to be a biped animal (that is the force of saying that something is necessary; it is to deny the possibility that it not be the case). So we have our proof: *it is not possible to say truly at the same time that the same thing both is and is not a man.*

Exactly the same reasoning can be used on 'not to be a man'. [**1007a**] 'To be a man' and 'not to be a man' mean different things, on the assumption only that, say, to be white and to be a man are different. After all, the former pair are much more directly opposed, which would bring with it their meaning different things. If, in face of this, the tack is taken that 'the white' and 'man' *do* mean a single thing, the same thing indeed, we will simply redeploy the argument given above, that this leads to monism (for everything, not just opposites). Assuming this cannot be right, the argument goes through as described. All that was necessary was to get an answer to the first question.

Another dodge might be as follows. We put the question without qualifications, but our opponent, in replying, adds the contradictories. But this just means that he is *not*, in fact, replying to the question at all. For on these assumptions, there is nothing to stop 'man', 'white' and endlessly many other things being the same. No, we must insist that to the question whether it is true that a given object is or is not a man an answer that means a single thing must be returned. We cannot accept the addition of, say, 'it is *also* white and large'. It is, indeed, impossible to go through all such accidental properties of the object, and we are quite entitled to insist that our opponent add all or none. And it follows in exactly parallel style that even if the same thing is in a thousand ways both man and not man, it is still not acceptable, as part of a reply to the question whether or not it is a man, to add that it is also simultaneously not man, unless the respondent is prepared to add all the other accidental properties too, which the entity either is or is not. To attempt this last project would be to drop off the map of philosophical debate.

A more general complaint can also be raised. It is that the adoption of this theory carries with it the elimination of substance and essence. In effect, it commits you to saying that all properties are accidents and that there is nothing which it is to be to be a man or an animal. For suppose that there is something which it is to be to be a man, this will not be to be a non-man or not to be a man (I take it that these are the negations). After all, there was a single thing that 'man' meant, to wit the substance of a certain thing. And to have the substance of a certain thing as meaning is to have the meaning that nothing else than that is what it is to be that thing. If, however, in the present case to be a man just is either to be a non-man or not to be a man, then it *will* be something else other than what it is to be a man. And that is why this position ends up saddled with the consequence that there cannot be a proprietary account of this kind of anything. Hence all properties are accidents, given that it is in terms of a proprietary account that we draw the distinction between substance and accident (so the white is an accidental property of a man in as much as the man (a) is white but (b) is not what it is to be white).

But this is a disastrous result. If all predication is accidental, there will be no primary subject, assuming that in all cases an accidental property indicates a category-item *pertaining to some subject*. The absence of such a subject produces, straight off, an infinite regress. But such a regress is also impossible. [1007b] There cannot be concatenation even of more than two accidents. Argument: (a) an accident is not an accident of an accident (except in that they are both accidents of the same subject – in the sense that white is (accidentally) musical and musical (accidentally) white in that they are both accidental properties of a man); (b) when Socrates is musical, this is not because both Socrates and musical are accidental properties of something else. So there are these two ways in which things are said to be accidental properties. Now (i), things said to be accidental properties in the way that white is said to be

93

accidental to Socrates (b-accidental) cannot extend upwards to infinity, by dint of there being an accidental property of Socrates–white and so on. No *single thing* will emerge from such a pillar of predicates.

But also (ii) there will be no further (a-)accidental property just of the white (say, the musical). There is no reason for saying that the musical is (a-)accidental to the white any more than that the white is (a-)accidental to the musical. And even if this is denied, we fall back on the distinction between this a–accidentality and b-accidentality (e.g. musical to Socrates). For all b-accidents being an accident of an accident is ruled out. It is only for a-accidents that it is possible. And this precludes its being the case that every property is predicated accidentally.

The point is this. Even on these assumptions, there must be something that indicates substance. But once this is conceded, we have a proof that the simultaneous predication of contradictories is impossible.

OK. If all contradictories are simultaneously true of the same thing, we can take it as settled that we get monism. A trireme, a wall and a man will be the same thing, if for anything at all it is possible both to assert and to deny any given claim. Anyone who signs up for Protagoreanism has to bite this bullet. It suffices, after all, for someone to *think* that the man in question is not a trireme for it to be indisputable that he is not a trireme. But this just means that he *is* a trireme, if the negation is as true as the assertion. In fact, we get not just Protagoreanism but Anaxagoreanism (the doctrine of 'all things at once') – nothing really exists as a single thing. The best interpretation is that the present view is really about the indeterminate. They are deluded in thinking that they are talking about what is – in fact they are talking about what is not. (Anything that is in potentiality and not in entelechy is the indeterminate.) The result is that they are committed to the joint assertion and denial of every property of every subject, on pain of the absurd consequence that, for each subject, the negation of the subject itself is available but not the negation of something else which is not a property of it! (Let me clarify this from the present example. If it *is* true to say of a man that he is not a man, then it is evidently also true to say of him either that he is or that he is not a trireme. So if the assertion can be made, then so too can the negation, whereas if the assertion cannot be made, then at least the negation corresponding to it will be available to a greater extent than the negation of the thing itself. So if the negation of the thing itself *is* available (as our opponents claim), then so too will be that of the thing (man)'s being a trireme. [**1008a**] And if the negation of this can be made, so too can its assertion.)

Well. This is what happens if you adopt this crazy view. *And* you also lose the exclusive dichotomy of assertion and negation. If it is true that something is both a man and not a man, it will also, of course, be true that it is neither a man nor not a man. There are two negations of the two assertions, and if the first of the assertions is treated as a compound of two, then the second too would be a single (opposite) compound.

Also, either this is true of all subjects, and everything both is-white and is-not-white and both is and is-not (and so *pari passu* for all other assertions and negations) or it is not, but rather true of some but not of others. Now if (a) it is not true for all assertions, then those for which it is not true will have to be conceded to us, while if (b) it is true for all, then either (i) wherever assertion is true so will negation be and wherever negation is true so will assertion be or (ii) wherever assertion is true so will negation be, but it will not be the case that wherever negation is true so will assertion be. Now in (b)(ii), it would turn out that there is something which brutely is not, and the corresponding belief will be a secure one. But if a belief that something is *not* the case is secure and perspicuous to the mind, then the opposite positive assertion would be still more perspicuous.

However, if (b)(i) is right, then, necessarily, either you get a true statement by disjoining the terms (so one says that a thing is white *and also* that it is not white), or you do not. And if (α) you do not get true statements by disjoining the terms, then it follows both that the position under attack has shifted and that nothing exists (and then the question is how non-existents could do things like speaking and walking). On top of that, all things will be one (see above), and man, god, trireme and stone will be the same thing, as also will their contradictories. After all, assuming contradictories operate in the same way for all subjects, there can be no difference between subject and subject in this respect (if there were a difference, then *that* would be something true and a special property). But if (β) it *is* possible to get true statements by disjoining the terms, then the consequence we have claimed goes through and is crowned by the further consequences that all men speak the truth and that all men are in error and that the holder of the view is himself acknowledging that he is himself wrong.

Nor does this prevent its also being the case that the debate is about nothing at all. Our opponent is still saying nothing. He speaks in neither one way nor another, but speaks in both ways at the same time. And, of course, at the same time he is negating both these and insisting that he is speaking neither in one way nor in the other! (If he does not do this, then he is stuck with something definite one way or the other.)

If, furthermore, it is the case that whenever the assertion is true the negation is false, then it will not be possible both to assert and to negate the same thing truly at the same time. (Perhaps, however, the opponent might make the rejoinder that [1008b] whether this is so was all along the real question.)

Can it, also, be that anyone who believes that something must either be or not be in some given way is embroiled in falsehood, whereas anyone who thinks that it is both has the truth? For if such a person does have the truth, what would be the content of the claim that the nature of the things that are is of this kind? And if he does not have it, but at least has it to a greater extent than the holder of the former belief, then even so there would be some definite way in which the things that are are. And this would be true and not also at the same time not true. If, however, the holders of any view all speak both truth and falsity in exactly the same way, it will not be possible for anyone in these circumstances either to give utterance or to say anything of content; for such a person is at the same time saying that such and such is the case and that it is not. And if he has not serious belief anyway but is merely equivalently both entertaining and not entertaining a thought, in what respect would he be at an advantage over mere plant life?

All this makes it especially clear that nobody is really in these circumstances, neither any of those who advance this argument nor anybody else. Why after all, if someone thinks that he should walk to Megara, does he actually do so rather than merely twiddle his toes? Why does he not just get up first thing and walk into a well or, if he finds one, over a cliff? In fact, he seems rather careful about cliffs and wells. He, for his part, does not seem to think that falling into or over one is no more bad than it is good. On the contrary, he is of the settled opinion that one outcome of the cliff/well-episode is better than the other. But his dogmatism will immediately embroil him in holding that one item is a man *and that some other thing is not a man*, that one thing is pleasant *and that some other thing is not pleasant*. Anyone who (a) thinks that it is preferable in some circumstances to drink water and to see a man and (b) attempts to do these things is not someone framing his strategies and beliefs on the basis of comprehensive global indifferentism. And yet that is just what their basis should be, if indeed both man and not-man are the same thing in the same way. In fact, however, as we have laboured to proclaim, you do not come across all that many people of whom it is not true that they carefully avoid some possibilities while showing the most extravagant insouciance towards others. So it would seem that there is at least one area where the disposition is pretty universal to suppose that things are one way or the other, the area of bottom-line good or bad. And if you say that they do not know but merely have opinions, so much the worse. They should be all the more concerned that their opinions are true, just as someone who is ailing is likely to be more concerned about his health than someone in the pink of it. (Beside the knower, the opiner is in a poor way as far as truth is concerned.)

One final argument. OK. Let us suppose, as much as you like, that things are always both thus and so and not thus and so. Still are the greater and the lesser present in the nature of the things that are. After all, we would not say that two and three are even to the same extent. And the man who mistakes a tetrad for a pentad is not as erroneous as he who takes it for a chiliad. But then, if they are not equally erroneous, this can only mean that one has less, and so one more, of the truth. But now, [**1009a**] if to have more of something is to be closer to the thing of which you have more, then there will indeed be a kind of truth closer to which is the one who has more of it. And even if that is not the case, there is at any rate something here more like the truth, more grounded – and that is enough. With that we have dispensed with that indifferentism which would block us from arriving at any definition in our thoughts.

GAMMA 5

The demonstration continues, becoming more specifically directed against particular opponents of the principle. The most important of these is Protagoras, whose relativism entails the rejection of the principle. Aristotle also distinguishes between objections to the principle based on genuine reflection on natural phenomena and objections based on purely 'eristic' or gratuitous arguments. The latter are actually harder to refute, since it is necessary to descend to the level of the opponent.

The bulk of the chapter is taken up with arguments against those who suppose that the principle is in some way undermined by the fact that with sensible entities contrary features appear to be both based on the same subject, and also with arguments which in some other way question the principle on the basis of the observation of nature. Aristotle reviews a wide range of earlier thinkers, including Homer, before concentrating his fire on Protagoras himself and his followers.

The same opinion is the basis of the position of Protagoras. His position and that just examined must stand or fall together. For (1) if all opinions held and all appearances are true, then they must all be at the same time both true and false (it will often happen, after all, that two men hold opposite opinions, such that they think that those who do not believe as they do have lapsed into error, and this can only mean that the same thing is both true and not true). But also (2) on this assumption all opinions held must be *true* (the right-believers and the wrong-believers believe opposite things, so that, if the things that are are as supposed on this view, they must both believe truths).

There can then be no dispute but that both positions stem from the same basic mind-set. But this does not mean that they are all to be dealt with in the same way. Some need persuasion, some compulsion. Some philosophers have taken up this sort of position out of sheer perplexity. Their ignorance can easily be alleviated (the treatment applies not to their argument as such but to their mind-set). Others, however, adopt the position for vexatious purposes. For this the treatment is refutation of the actual words spoken, using the very same terms as the opponents.

If we consider those motivated by genuine perplexity, we find that they were driven to this view by considering the sensible object. One way of being driven to the view is by observing that opposites arise from the same sensible thing and concluding that statements and their negations (or contraries) must simultaneously be true. The argument is that that which is not cannot come into being, so the sensible object in question must have antecedently existed as both the things that it is. Hence Anaxagoras' mixture of all in all and Democritus' variation on the same theme (for him the full and the empty are similarly present in all parts and these correspond respectively to what is and what is not).

The way to deal with anyone basing his opinion on this sort of consideration is as follows. They should be told that in a way they are right and in a way wrong. That which is is spoken of in two ways, so that there is a way in which it is possible for something to come to be from that which is not and a way in which it is not possible. By the same token, the same thing can be both a thing that is and a thing that is not, only not in the same respect. In potentiality, a single thing can be simultaneous opposites. In actuality, however, it cannot. On top of this, we invite them to accept that there is a certain other substance pertaining to the things that are, a substance characterized neither by movement, nor by destruction nor by coming into being in any way.

Another way [**1009b**] of getting to the truth = appearance doctrine from observation of sensibles is this. You start by insisting that the judgement of truth is not an appropriate matter for majorities and minorities. Then you allow that when two men taste the same thing one will (very often) find it sweet and the other bitter. Suppose, then, that all men were sick or deranged, save one or two who were healthy and of right mind. It would then be the latter two who would be thought to be sick and deranged and the former not!

In the same vein, many animals have sensory impressions quite at odds with ours, and about the same objects. Nay, the selfsame individual can be at odds with himself as to whether he takes the same matters of appearance to be true at all times. But there can be no principled way of deciding which of these various impressions is true and which false. It seems that none of them is any better placed than the others – they are all in the same boat. Hence the dichotomous conclusion of Democritus. Either there is no truth or it is concealed from us.

The underlying assumption of this whole approach is as follows. Discernment is identified with perception and perception with the alteration of the sensory organ. That is why they say that what appears in sensation must be what is true. That is the reasoning that led Empedocles and Democritus and, let's face it, all the rest of them into these erroneous doctrines.

Empedocles certainly signs up for the view that any state change is a cognitive change:

> 'For from what stands before him is the thought
> Of man increased . . .'

Somewhere else he has:

> 'So far as into other states they came,
> New thoughts presented wisdom to their minds.'

Parmenides, for his part, has the same ring to him:

> 'For as at each time lie the jointed limbs,
> So is the mind of man configured.
> No other organ is it but the limbs
> That thinks for every man, for every one.
> And thought is what is more . . .'

An apophthegm is also to be found among the *obiter dicta* of Anaxagoras. He pointed out to those of the company that, as far as they were concerned, things would be just as they thought. And, for Heaven's sake, let's not forget Homer, who, we are told, espoused this same line. Does he not, after all, have Hector, of all people, in his recovery of consciousness after Ajax has floored him, lie there '*thinking other thoughts*'? What can this mean except that those whose thinking processes have been radically disrupted are, for all that, still thinking – only their thoughts are not the same? But then, surely, if both states involve kinds of thought, things in existence must also both be so and not be so. For if those very people who have gazed most on the truth as it is revealed to us, those who have devoted their lives to the search for truth, those who love the truth, if this is what they think, or at any rate officially say, about the truth, how can that be anything other than a counsel of despair for anyone trying to start to do philosophy? If anything like these views is right, the 'search for truth' is a wild-goose chase.

Let us, then, diagnose this error. [1010a] The thinkers in question were after the truth about the things that are. But they supposed the things that are to be restricted to the sensibles. But in these there is a large presence of the indeterminate and of that which is in the way explained above. Hence their position is far from absurd, but also far from true (felicitously to adapt the dictum of Epicharmus on Xenophanes). Another line of thought was that they observed that all nature around us undergoes change and held that one cannot speak the truth about that which is undergoing change. So *a fortiori* nothing true could be said about what was changing at all points in all ways. It was from the seed-bed of such thinking that there flowered the most extreme of the views we went through above. This is the position of those who appropriated the legacy of Heraclitus, notably of Cratylus. His mature position was that speech of any kind was radically inappropriate and that expression should be restricted exclusively to the movement of the finger. He was appalled that Heraclitus had claimed that you could not step *twice* into the same river. In his, Cratylus', opinion it was already going far too far to admit stepping into the *same* river *once*.

We, however, shall adopt the following line with all this. OK. There is a kind of point in saying that what changes, when it is actually changing, *is not*. And yet, *en fin des comptes*, this conclusion can be resisted. For the property-bearer that is discarding a property retains some part of that which it is discarding, and similarly of that which comes into being there must already have been something. Quite generally, for every case in which a thing is destroyed, there will be in that case something that is and for every case in which something comes into being there must necessarily be something from which it is produced and something by which it is produced. And it is also necessary that an infinite regress not be generated.

Even, however, if we refrain from this sort of solution, we must still distinguish changing in quantity from changing in quality. Nothing, let us allow, persists quantitatively, whereas it is by its persistent form that each thing is known.

Anyway, a rap on the knuckles is surely earned by anyone who, perceiving things to be thus in what is in any case the statistical exception even of sensibles, extrapolates to the entire universe. Our little corner of the observable universe is unique in its constant exposure to birth and decay. It is an entirely negligible component of the universe as a whole. The verdict of a fair judge would be that our part can be let off because of the good behaviour of the rest rather than vice versa. And why should we not also use against these opponents the same line that we originally took. It must be demonstrated to them that there is a kind of unchanging nature. This is a belief that they must acquire. (Anyway, if you say that all things simultaneously both are and are not, you should say rather that everything is at rest than that everything is in motion. There is no possible destination of change, what with everything already being a property of everything else.)

On the truth question, then, [**1010b**] we reject the doctrine that whatever appears is true. We have several reasons for doing this. The first is that, even if (special) sensation is veridical, appearance production is not the same thing as sensation. Next, can *this* really be the issue – whether magnitudes are equally great and colours of the same character as they appear at a distance or as they appear near by, and whether they are as they appear to those who are healthy and to those who are ill, and whether things are relatively heavy as they so appear to the weak or to the strong, and whether those things are true that appear to those asleep or to those awake? Clearly, at any rate, they do not take it to be the issue. None of them, I suppose, would, if while in Libya he dreamt that he was in Athens, set off in the morning for the Odeon. And as far as the future is concerned, a point made by Plato is that the opinion of the doctor and that of the lay person are by no means on the same footing, with regard, shall we say, to whether someone will recover or not.

Next, consider the senses themselves. A sense does not enjoy the same cognitive autonomy with regard to a non-proprietory or merely related object as with regard to its proper object; rather, sight, not taste has jurisdiction over colour, and taste, not sight, over flavour. And it is never the case that each of these senses asserts of the same thing at the same time that it both is and is not F. Indeed, not even at different times is there disagreement between them about the affection itself, but only about that to which it applies. What I mean is that the same wine, say, might be deemed, under appropriate changes either in its state or in that of the body of the drinker, to be now sweet now not sweet. But the sweetness at the time when it was sweet does not change (ever), and the sense remains always right about that, and its sweetness is the same as that of anything that will become sweet in the future. And yet it is just this that all these arguments undermine, with their claim that since nothing has a substance there is nothing that is of necessity. (Since the necessary does not admit of being both F and not F, there being something of necessity is incompatible with its being both F and not F.)

In general if the only thing that is is the sensible object, the absence of ensouled beings would mean the existence of nothing, given that no sensation would be taking place. But while the claim that in such circumstances there would be no sense objects and no sensations is very likely true (for they are both things that happen to some perceiver), it is an absurdity to argue that the underlying things that give rise to the sensation do not exist unless the sensation exists. In sensation, the subject is not presented with the sensation itself, but there is rather something else over and above the sensation which is necessarily prior to the sensation. For that which produces change is by nature prior to that which undergoes it, [1011a] a fact not diminished by their being treated as correlative terms.

But this brings us to the real rub for this position.

GAMMA 6

The polemic against the followers of Protagoras continues, as does the different treatment of serious and eristic objections. The main lines of Aristotle's argument against Protagoras are as follows. If anyone claims that whatever appears is, he must accept that everything is relative. Even if he does this, he will have to acknowledge that things do not appear absolutely but only relative to particular observers, times, etc. When this is fully accepted, even the equation of appearance and being does not pose a threat to the principle. If the opponent continues, eristically, to reject this he will either have to accept that everything is relative, which is in fact absurd, or allow that there is something true or false irrespective of what anybody thinks. Moreover, the very structure of thinking about something requires that there be a thing thought about as well as a thing thinking.

Now among both the serious and the frivolous proponents of these views there are those who are fond of the following conundrum. Who is to identify the healthy man or, more generally, the standard-setting cognizer of each topic? All questions of this kind are like the question whether we are currently asleep or awake. They all have the same dialectical force, to require an explanation of everything. What they are after is a foundation, to be apodeictically grasped, and their behaviour makes it clear that they do not yet think that they have found it. Anyway, what is wrong with them is what we have just said: they want an account of things for which there is no account. The starting point of a proof is not a proof.

Well, anyone troubled by these difficulties can be readily convinced by these arguments (which, in truth, are not hard to grasp), whereas those who seek nothing but compulsion in argument are asking for the moon. They claim the right to be contradictory, and the claim is itself contradictory. In any case, if all things are not relational and there are some things that are what they are *per se*, then it will not be the case that all appearances are true. After all, what appears appears *to* some subject, and anyone who says that all appearances are true is making all things thus relational. Hence anyone who is looking for a knock-down argument here and also is willing to be subjected to scrutiny has to fence himself by shifting from the claim that all appearances are true *simpliciter* to the claim that all appearances are true relative to a subject, time, sense and context. Any other attempt to defend the position will lead immediately to contradiction. For something can seem honey to the sight but not to the taste, or, given that we have two eyes, things may not seem the same to the sight of them both, in the event of their being dissimilar.

For to those who assert the truth of appearances for the reasons given above . . . and for this reason all things to be equally true and false. For neither do all subjects share the same appearances nor does the same subject at all times. In fact the same subject often experiences opposite appearances at the same time (as touch says that there are two things in a crossing of fingers and sight one). But there is nothing that appears differently to the same sense and in the same respect and in the same way and at the same time. So at least this claim would be true. So perhaps eristic, [**1011b**] as opposed to sincere, defenders of this position must for this reason shift to the claim not that a given thing is true but that it is true for some subject. And of course, as pointed out earlier, they will have to make all things relational and relational to opinion and sensation, so that nothing will either come into being or exist if there is nothing to have an opinion about it. If, however, things have come to be or will be, it is clear that all things cannot be relational to opinion. Moreover, if something is one, then it is so either in relation to some one thing or in relation to a definite number of things; or if the same thing is both half and equal that does not mean that the equal is relational to the double. If, then, in relation to that which is thinking about it, a man and that which is thought to be a man are the same, then it will turn out not to be the one doing the thinking but the one that is the object of thought that is the man. And if each entity is relational on a subject, then the subject itself will be relational, and to a formal infinity.

Our discussion has reached three conclusions. (1) The most secure of all beliefs is that mutually contradictory statements cannot be jointly true. (2) We have shown what happens to you if you deny (1). (3) We have diagnosed the motivation of philosophers for denying (1). But, if we accept that contradictions cannot be jointly true of the same thing, it is also clear that nothing can jointly have opposite properties. For one of a pair of contraries is as much a privation as a contrary, and a privation of a substance, and privation is negation with regard to some determinate genus. So if it is impossible both to assert and to deny truly at the same time, then it is also impossible for opposite properties to pertain simultaneously, unless the two properties pertain in different ways or one qualifiedly and the other *simpliciter*.

GAMMA 7

Aristotle passes on to the defence of the principle of excluded middle, which is closely connected to the principle of non-contradiction. The principle of excluded middle states that between two contradictory propositions there can be no third proposition. Aristotle employs seven arguments in defence of the principle, with the same strategy of distinguishing between serious and eristic objections and of demanding from the opponent only the making of at least one proposition. In the last part of the chapter, Aristotle castigates both Heraclitus for making everything true and Anaxagoras for making everything false with his doctrine of the primordial mixture.

Now it is also the case that there can be nothing intermediate to an assertion and a denial. We must either assert or deny any single predicate of any single subject. The quickest way to show this is by defining truth and falsity. Well, falsity is the assertion that that which is is not or that that which is not is and truth is the assertion that that which is is and that that which is not is not. Thus anyone who asserts anything to be or not to be is either telling the truth or telling a falsehood. On the other hand, neither that which is is said either not to be or to be nor is that which is not.

And if there were an intermediate of contradictory statements, then it would either be like grey between black and white or like the non-man-non-horse between man and horse. Suppose the latter. In that case, it could not change into either one or the other of what it stands between (for change to good is from not-good and to the latter from good), whereas in fact it appears always to do so. In fact change can only be to opposites and intermediaries. If, then, we suppose that it is a real intermediary, there would still be something like the coming to be of white not from not-white, [1012a] and this is in fact never observed. Again, thinking either asserts or negates every object of

107

thinking or of intuition – this much is clear from the definition – whenever it engages in either truth or falsity. And when in its assertion or negation it connects the terms in a certain way it is saying what is true and when it does so in another way it is saying what is false.

In any case, all opposites, unless merely gratuitously proposed, must have an intermediary. Hence one might be saying something that is neither true nor false, and there might be something that neither is nor is not and there might be some change that is neither a coming into being nor a destruction. Also for whatever genera negation of an attribute implies assertion of its opposite, there will also turn out to be an intermediary even here, so that in number, for instance, there might be some number that is neither odd nor not odd. Which would be, given the definition, odd.

Also, an infinite regress looms. And we will have to raise the stock of entities not just by half but by more. For it will be in turn possible to negate the intermediate in terms of either assertion or denial, and yet it will be something, given that its substance is different from that of the others. And if someone is asked whether something is white and replies that it is not, he has not denied anything other than its so being, and this not so being is a negation.

Some philosophers have fallen into this opinion in the same way that they have into other paradoxes. They are confronted by an eristical argument, find it impossible to refute and end up by giving in to it and accepting its conclusion! This explains the confusion of some, while that of others is to be ascribed to the search for an explanation of everything. In either case, the basis of the cure is definition. Now a definition arises from the necessity that words have some meaning; for the definition is the account of which the word is the sign. Thus, while the remark of Heraclitus that all things are and are not effectively renders all assertions true, that of Anaxagoras that there is an intermediary between assertion and negation makes all assertions false. For if things are mixed, then the mixture will, for instance, be neither good nor not good and it will be impossible to say anything true of it.

GAMMA 8

Aristotle concludes a book devoted to logic by rejecting two claims which both amount to a rejection of the principle of non-contradiction. First, he deals with those who claim either that everything is true or that everything is false. Each of these claims is in fact self-destructive: if everything is true, then so is the denial that everything is true, and if everything is false, then so is the claim that everything is false. Secondly, he also refutes those who claim either that everything is at rest or that everything is in motion. That everything is not at rest is shown by the fact that the very proponent of the claim himself came into existence at some time in the past. That everything is not in motion is shown by the fact that for anything to be in motion there must be something which is not in motion and also by the fact that there are some things that are eternal. In fact, in Aristotle's view, to be defended at greater length in book Lambda, there is something permanently in motion, something permanently moving and the primary cause of motion which is itself permanently motionless.

Given all these distinctions, it becomes clear that things said in a unitary way cannot apply to all things. For instance, some say that nothing is true (they claim that there is nothing to stop all statements being like the claim that the diameter of the square is commensurate with its side) and others claim that everything is true. The positions are pretty much the same as that of Heraclitus, since anyone who says that all things are true and all things are false is also separately asserting each of the two conjuncts, [1012b] so that if they are indeed impossible then so must the conjunction be. In any case there are some contradictions that clearly cannot be jointly true – nor indeed all false. Yet this would seem rather to be a possibility on the present assumptions.

But in the face of all these reasonings the position to be adopted is that already outlined above. We should require not that something is or is not but that something has meaning, so that the argument should proceed from a definition, through a grasp of the meaning of truth and falsity. If truth be nothing other than the assertion of what it is falsity to negate, then it is impossible that all things can be false, since one half of the pair of contradictories must be true. Indeed these arguments themselves fall victim to the very difficulty about which their defenders are always canting. They effectively destroy themselves. For if anyone says that all things are true then he is making even the negation of his own claim true, so that his own statement in turn is not true (that is, after all, what its negation asserts), while if anyone says that all things are false, then he is making his own claim to be false. And if the first claimant excepts the contradiction of his claim on the grounds that it alone is not true and the second excepts his own claim as not being false, nevertheless they still require an infinite number of statements to be true and false, since the statement that says that the true statement is true is true and so on *ad infinitum*.

(It is, by the way, similarly clear that all those who say that all things are at rest or that all are in motion are also wrong. For if all things are at rest, then the same statements will always be true and false, but it is clear that they change. Indeed, the speaker himself was not at some time in the past and will not be again at some time in the future. But if all things are in motion, then nothing will be true. So all things will be false. But it has been shown that this is impossible. Also that which is must change, since change is from something to something. Also it cannot be that all things are sometimes at rest or in motion, but nothing always. For there is something that always moves the things in motion, and the First Mover is itself unmoved.)

Book Delta

BOOK DELTA

Book Delta concludes the preliminary sections of the Metaphysics, *so that the investigation of being can commence immediately at the start of book Epsilon. Of the previous books, Alpha (and Alpha the Lesser) has provided a historical survey of earlier metaphysics, Beta has set a range of problems to give the flavour of the difficulties that a comprehensive metaphysical position should be able to handle and Gamma has given an overview of the method and range of philosophy. Delta is intended to complete our preparation by equipping us with a kind of philosophical dictionary providing the conceptual apparatus needed to follow the discussion of being and especially of substance.*

To some extent the book succeeds in this. It comprises definitions of some thirty terms. Some of these terms are arguably more appropriate to physical science than to metaphysics, and there are other terms, such as those for account and definition, which might well have been included. It is also the case that the dictionary entries vary greatly in length for different items. The longest entries amount to philosophical essays on the concepts they cover, while the shortest are hardly more than notes. There is also considerable variation in the range of uses considered for different terms. In addition to this, it is not completely clear whether the dictionary is intended to indicate the usage of these terms in contemporary language or to prescribe new and specialized uses of them for the purpose of doing Aristotelian metaphysics.

Nevertheless, the book does indeed contain invaluable material for clarifying Aristotle's arguments and any discussion of the use of major terms which are covered in it must begin by examining the discussion here. I do not provide introductions to the separate articles, since their structure is apparent.

1. *Principle/start*

(i) That in something from which a process might first arise. For instance, a line or road has a start at either end, though each in a contrary direction.

(ii) That from which each thing might best be produced. [**1013a**] For instance, even in the acquisition of understanding, it is sometimes right to make a **start** not from the primary item, i.e. the **principle** proper of the object of study, but from whatever point of entry is most conducive to progress.

(iii) That from which, as an intrinsic part, something is primarily produced. Examples: keel of a ship/foundation of a house. Also with animals the heart, brain or other parts are variously supposed to be of this kind.

(iv) That from which, not as an intrinsic part, something is primarily produced and that from which it is natural for a process or change to originate. Examples: a child coming from its mother and father or a punch-up arising out of a slanging match.

(v) That by whose choice processes and changes are initiated. For instance, political **principles**. Also juntas, monarchies and dictatorships are said to be **princedoms**, and one speaks of the **principles** of the arts, especially the architectonic ones.

(vi) That by which a thing is primarily cognizable. This too is called the **principle** of the thing, as demonstrations **start** with suppositions.

And for each account of **principle/start** there is an account of cause, unsurprisingly in that all causes are **principles**.

The common feature, then, of all **principles/starts** is to be the primary origin (of being, production or cognition). And some **principles/starts** are intrinsic, others external. So both a nature and an element are a **principle**, as also thinking and choice, substance and the final cause – there are many cases where the **principle** both of cognition and of process is the good or beautiful.

II. *Cause*

(i) An intrinsic feature from which something is produced. Examples: the bronze is the **cause** of the statue, the silver of the salver. Also the kinds of such things are **causes** of them in this way.

(ii) The form and template, which is the account of the what–it–was–to–be–that–thing. Also the kinds of form are **causes** in this way. Example: the proportion of 1 to 2 and, at a more general level, number are the **cause** of the octave. Also the intrinsic parts of the account.

(iii) The source of the primary principle of change or stasis. For example, the man who deliberates is the **cause** of action, and the father is the **cause** of the child. In general, the producer is the **cause** of the product and the changer of the thing changing.

(iv) **Cause** as end. The end of something is what that thing is for. For example, the end of taking a constitutional is to be healthy. 'Why', we might ask, 'is this chap walking about the place?' 'It is in order', replies the expert, 'to be healthy', and in so saying he reckons to have put his finger on a **cause** of the behaviour.

　　Causes in this way are also all things which lie on the way to the end, when some other agent has initiated the process. For instance, to reach health you may have to go through dieting, [**1013b**] purgation, medication or surgery, all of which are for the end of health (though they differ from one another in involving in some cases instruments, in other procedures).

The above is a pretty comprehensive survey of the accounts of **cause**. And there are two consequences of the plurality of accounts of **cause**. First, there are many **causes** of the same thing, and this is not in an accidental way. For instance, the **causes** of the statue include both the art of sculpture and the bronze, and they **cause** the statue not *qua* something else but *qua* statue. They do not, of course, **cause** it in the same way – the bronze is the material **cause** and the art the source of the process. Secondly, reciprocal **causation** occurs. Exercise is the **cause** of fitness, but fitness is also the **cause** of exercise. Of course, the ways differ: fitness is the end, exercise the source of process.

Another consequence is that the same thing is a **cause** of contraries. It very often happens that if something by its presence **causes** something we take its absence to be the **cause** of the contrary. Since the skipper by his presence is the **cause** of survival, we take his absence to be the **cause** of the shipwreck. Both presence and privation, of course, are **causes** as sources of process.

All the **causes** we have here mentioned are subsumed under four conspicuous manners. Letters, for instance, are **causes** of syllables, material of artefacts, fire and earth and all such things of bodies, parts of the whole and premises of the conclusion, all being **causes** as that from which. But some of them are **cause** as the substrate, e.g. the parts, some as the essence (the whole, composition and form). Sperm, meanwhile, the doctor, the deliberator and, more generally, the doer are all **causes** as sources of change or stasis. The other **causes** are **causes** as the end and advantage of other things. For that-for-the-sake-of-which is prone to be the best, to be the end for other things, and, for present purposes, we can overlook the distinction between advantage and apparent advantage.

This is, as we have said, a pretty fair, and comprehensive, summary of the species of **cause**. Now there are, of course, a great many variations of **cause**, and yet, on summary, these too are not that many. There is indeed a plurality of accounts of **cause**, and even where **causes** are of the same kind there is priority and posteriority among them. Thus the **causes** of health comprise both *doctor* and *expert*, those of the octave both *the proportion of 2 to 1* and *number*. Also, in all cases the comprehending classifications of a **cause** are **causes**.

Then again there are the accidental **causes** and the comprehending classifications of these. For instance, in a way it is the sculptor that is the **cause** of the statue and in a way Polycleitus, in as much as it is an accidental feature of the sculptor that he is Polycleitus. [**1014a**] And so too the comprehending classifications. *Man*, for instance, is the cause of the statue or more generally *animal*, since Polycleitus is a man and *man* is an *animal*.

There is also greater and lesser proximity among accidental **causes**. For instance, *white man* and *musical man* could more remotely be said to be **causes** of the statue. And of all things said to be **causes** either properly or accidentally some are said to be so as potential **causes**, some as actual. Either the builder or the builder-building is the **cause** of building. And the same goes for the effects of **causation** – the effect might be this statue or a statue or an image and this bronze or bronze or, more generally, matter. Ditto accidental effects. Also both accidental and proper **causes** can be conjoined: not either Polycleitus or the sculptor, but Polycleitus the sculptor.

Yet even these variations only amount to six in number, albeit there are two accounts of each. They can be **causes** either as the particular or as the kind or as the accidental or as the kind of the accidental and in conjunction or *simpliciter*. And they can all be taken either as actualized or as potential. The difference between these latter is this. The actualized **cause**, especially the particular, is/is not at the same time as the effect. This particular healer is at the same time as this particular recipient of healing, and this particular builder is at the same time as this particular object of building. But this is not always so with potential **causes**. The house is not, for instance, necessarily destroyed at the same time as its builder.

III. *Element*

(i) The primary intrinsic component of something, not being formally divisible into some other species of thing. The **elements** of speech, for instance, are the components of speech and the products of its final analysis, not being themselves further divisible into other speech **elements** differing in species from themselves. Were they to be further divided, their parts would be, like parts of water and water, of the same species, in contrast with the parts of the syllable.

And by the same token the **elements** of bodies are said by their proponents to be the products of the final analysis of bodies, not them-selves being further divisible into other **elements** differing in species. Whether such things be one or many, they are said to be **elements**.

Similar too are the **elements** of geometrical proofs and of demon-strations in general. Primary demonstrations, present in a large number of demonstrations, [**1014b**] are said to be the **elements** of demonstrations, of this kind being primary syllogisms, with their three terms and their middle term.

(ii) Taking the term **element** from this usage some also apply it to anything which, being single and small, is used for many purposes, so that what is small and simple and indivisible is also said to be an **element**. And this is why the most universal things are **elements**, in that each of them, being single and simple, is present in many things, either in all instances or in the largest possible number. And there have also been those who hold that unity and the point are principles.

Also, since what are called the kinds are universal and indivisible (there being no account of them), they too are said by some to be **elements**, more so indeed than the differentia, since the kind is more universal. For whenever the differentia pertains, so too does the kind, whereas the kind can pertain in some cases without the differentia doing so.

The common feature of these uses is that the **element** of each thing is its primary intrinsic component.

IV. *Nature*

(i) The production of things growing. This aspect is suggested by the affinity between **nature** and native.

(ii) The intrinsic component of something growing from which its growth primarily proceeds.

(iii) The intrinsic source of the primary process for each growing thing, just *qua* the growing thing that it is.

And a thing is said to grow if it undergoes increase from some external supply through contact, this either by assimilation or, as in the case of the foetus, by **natural** addition. Assimilation is different from contact in that in the case of contact there is no need for anything else to be present over and above the contact, whereas in cases of assimilation there is something that is one and the same in both items and this makes them assimilate rather than merely be in contact and be a unity in terms of continuity and quantity, though not in terms of quality.

(iv) The primary material from which some one of the things having **natural** being is either composed or produced. Such stuff is pretty unstructured and insusceptible to change from its own potentiality. In this way, bronze is said to be the **nature** of a bronze statue and of bronze utensils, wood of wooden ones. And this also applies to the other cases, for which anything made from such material the primary matter is conserved through the production.

It is also in this way that people say that the elements of things having **natural** being are their **nature**. The suggestions range from fire, earth, air and water to something else similar, some selection of them or the whole lot.

(v) The substance of things with **natural** being. One view, for instance, is that **nature** is primary composition. [**1015a**] Or Empedocles has it that:

> 'There is no thing with being has a nature,
> Only the ceaseless mingling and discernment
> Of what is mingled – nature is but a word
> Of human framing . . .'

That is also why for things with **natural** being or production, when that from which they have **natural** being or production already exists but they do not yet have their form/shape, we do not say that they have their **nature**. And something composed of both matter and form has **natural** being, such as the animals and their parts. Thus primary material is **nature** (and in two ways, either relatively primary or primary *simpliciter*: bronze is relatively primary for bronze artefacts, but what is primary *simpliciter* might for instance be water, on the assumption that all smeltable things are water), but so too is form and substance, and substance/form is also the end of the production.

(vi) All substance (by extension from the above case), in as much as **nature** too is a sort of substance.

The discussion should have established that primary **nature**, in the fundamental account, is the substance of those things with a principle of process within themselves *qua* themselves. Matter is then said to be **nature** by dint of its being receptive of the above, and it is because they are processes from it that productions and growth are said to be **natural**. And it is such **nature** that is the principle of process for things having **natural** being, in some way dwelling in such things either potentially or actually.

v. *Necessary*

(i) A causal contributor without which it is impossible for something to live. Examples: respiration and nutrition for an animal, which cannot have being without them.

(ii) Preconditions of its being possible for good either to be or to be produced, or for evil being removed or eliminated. Examples: taking the medicine is **necessary** for not being ill, and a voyage to Aegina may be **necessary** to collect some money.

(iii) The enforced and force. Whatever, in the face of drive and choice, conduces to impediment and prevention. For the enforced is said to be **necessary** and hence, as Euenus reminds us, also unpleasant:

'Everything needful is always a bore.'

And force too is a kind of **necessity**. Cp. Sophocles:

'Force is the sheer necessity that drives me . . .'

And **necessity** is thought (quite rightly) to be something ineluctable – is it not, after all, contrary to the process associated with choice and calculation?

(iv) When something does not admit of being otherwise, we say that it is necessarily as it is. Indeed it is from this use of **necessary** that all the other accounts of the **necessary** are derived in one way or another. For an action or affection is said to be **necessary** by enforcement, **[1015b]** when the action cannot take place according to impulse because of some operative enforcement. And the rationale for this is that **necessity** is what makes it impossible for something to be other than it is. And the same goes for the preconditions of living and of the good. For whenever it is impossible for, on the one hand, the good and, on the other, living to have being in default of certain preconditions, those preconditions are **necessary** and the cause here is a sort of **necessity**.

Demonstration is also something **necessary**, because a demonstration cannot go otherwise than it does, assuming that it is demonstration *simpliciter*. And the cause of this lies with the primary premises, assuming that it is impossible for what the argument proceeds from to be otherwise than they are.

For some things, the cause of their being **necessary** is something other than themselves, whereas for others there is no such external cause, but rather they are themselves the **necessary** causes of other things being the case. So it is the simple that is primarily and fundamentally **necessary**. For this cannot be in a plurality of states, so that it cannot be in one state and another either (this would already involve it in a plurality of states).

If, then, there are any things that are eternal and immune to process, then there is nothing among them that is enforced or against nature.

VI. *One*

(i) **One** by accident.

(ii) **One** *per se*.

(i) Examples: *Coriscus and musicality, musical Coriscus* (asserting the **unity** of *Coriscus and musicality* is tautologous with asserting the **unity** of *musical Coriscus*), *musicality and justice* and *musical and just Coriscus*.

These are all said to be **one** by accident. In the case of *justice and musicality*, they are accidents of a single substance, in that of *musicality and Coriscus*, **one** is an accident of the other. Similarly, in a way, with the **one**ness of *musical Coriscus* and *Coriscus*. **One** of the two parts of **one** of these two conjuncts, viz. *musical*, is an accident of the other conjunct, viz. *Coriscus*. And *musical Coriscus* is **one** with *just Coriscus* because a part of each of the two terms is an accident of the same thing.

And it is pretty much the same if the accident is predicated of a kind or of **one** of the universal words, if, say, it was said that *man* is the same as *musical man*. This could either be because *musicality* is an accident of *man*, which is a single substance, or because both are accidents of some particular, e.g. Coriscus. Of course, they could not both pertain to Coriscus in the same way; rather *man* presumably would pertain to him as his genus and as intrinsic to his substance, whereas *musicality* would pertain to him as a state or affection of his substance.

OK, so much for the way in which things are said to be **one** by accident.

(ii) Of things said to be **one** *per se*, some are so said by dint of being continuous. [**1016a**] A faggot is **one** through its binding, timbers by their glue. A line too, if continuous and even if bent, is said to be **one**, and ditto all bodily parts, such as a leg or arm. And of this group it is rather things continuous by nature than by art that are **one**. And something is said to be continuous if it has *per se* a single process and cannot be otherwise. And a process is single if it is indivisible, the indivisibility being temporal.

And things are *per se* continuous unless they are **one** merely by contact. If you were so to arrange some pieces of wood that they were in contact, I do not suppose that you would be disposed to say that they were **one** piece of wood/body/any other continuous thing. So quite generally continuous things are said to be **one**, even if they are bent, and still more those that do not have bends. So the shin or thigh is more **one** than the leg, since the process of the leg does not have to be single. Also the straight line is more **one** than the bent line. In fact, if a line is bent and has an angle, we say that it is and is not **one**, since it is possible for its process to be both not simultaneous and simultaneous, whereas the process of the straight line is in all cases simultaneous: there is no part of it with magnitude that is in stasis while another part is in process, as is the case with the bent line.

And there is another way in which things are said to be **one**, and this is that their substrate is not differentiated in species. And there is no such differentiation when the species is perceptibly indivisible. And the substrate here is either the primary or the latest relative to the end. On the **one** hand, wine is said to be **one** and water is said to be **one**, *qua* indivisible in species, but, on the other, all sauces (e.g. olive oil, wine) and all smeltable things are said to be **one** on the grounds that the ultimate substrate of them all is the same – they are all either water or air.

Things are also said to be **one** if their genus is **one**, though differentiated by opposite differentiae. The reason here too why they are all said to be **one** is that the genus underlying the differentiae is **one** (so horse, dog and man are **one** in that they are all animals), and this is in fact quite like the way it is with things whose matter is **one**. Sometimes, then, this is the basis for saying that these things are **one**, but sometimes it is that the higher genus is said to be the same (if they are lowest species of their kind). For instance, the isosceles and the equilateral are **one** and the same figure in that they are both triangles – but they are not, of course, the same triangles.

And things are also said to be **one** if the account that states the what–it–was–to–be–that–thing for **one** of them is indivisible from an account that reveals another of them (*per se*, of course, every account is divisible). In this way even things that are increased or diminished are **one**, because the account of them is **one**, as with the account of the form for plane figures.

More generally, [**1016b**] if there are things such that the thought that thinks the what–it–was–to–be–that–thing for those things is indivisible and cannot separate those things in time, place or account, these most of all are **one** and especially those that are substances. For, generally speaking, things that do not involve division are said to be **one** just to the extent that they do not involve it, so that, for instance, if things do not involve division *qua* man, then they are **one** man, and if not *qua* animal, then they are **one** animal, and if not *qua* magnitude, then they are **one** magnitude.

So most things are said to be **one** by dint of their either doing, or involving, or undergoing or being related to something else that is **one**, but those things that are primarily said to be **one** are those whose substance is **one**, in continuity, form or account. Indeed, in counting, we treat as plural either those things that are not continuous or whose form is not **one** or the account of which is not **one**.

Now it is true that we say of anything that is a continuous quantity that it is **one**, but also in a way we do not, unless it be a kind of whole, unless, that is, it has a single form. Suppose, for instance, we see the parts of a shoe lying higgeldy-piggeldy about. We would not say that they were **one** in the same way, only in fact in terms of continuity. If, on the other hand, we saw them so arranged as to be a shoe and possessed of a single form, then we would at this point say that they were **one**. Which is also why the circle is most fully **one** of all lines, because it is a complete whole.

Now the what-it-was-to-be-that-thing of **one** is a principle of the what-it-was-to-be-that-thing for some number (the primary measure is the principle, since the primary measure is that by which we primarily have cognition of each kind). And so the **one** is the principle of cognizability for each thing. And yet the **one** is not the same for all the kinds. In **one** case, for instance, it is the quarter-**tone**, in another the vowel or consonant. And the **one** for weight and the **one** for process are different. In all cases, however, the **one** is indivisible either in quantity or in form.

And something indivisible in quantity, if indivisible in all directions and without position, is said to be a unit, whereas if divisible in all directions and with position, it is said to be a point. Something divisible in **one** direction is said to be a line, and something divisible in two directions is said to be a plane, and anything that is divisible in all three directions in quantity is said to be a body. To put it the other way round, what is divisible in two directions is a plane, what in **one** direction is a line and what is not divisible at all in quantity is a point or a unit, a point if with, and a unit if without, position.

Also, some things are numerically **one**, some formally, some generically and some by analogy. Those things are numerically **one** whose matter is **one**; those things are formally **one** whose account is **one**; those things are generically **one** to which the same pattern of predication applies, and those things are **one** by analogy which are related as some further thing is to some yet further **one**. And the posterior unities always accompany the prior **ones**, so that any things that are numerically are also formally **one**, whereas not all things that are formally **one** are numerically **one**. And any things that are formally **one** are also generically **one**, [**1017a**] whereas not all things that are generically **one** are formally **one** but are **one** by analogy, even though not all those things that are **one** by analogy are generically **one**.

And of course accounts of plurality are ranged over against those of **unity**. Some are based on non-continuity, some on the possession of formally divisible matter, whether primary or final, and some on the obtaining of a plurality of accounts stating the what-it-was-to-be-that-thing.

VII. *Being*

(i) Accidental **being**.

(ii) *Per se* **being**.

(i) Accidental **being**. Examples: we say that a just man **is** musical, that a man **is** musical and that a musician **is** a man. This is exactly similar to saying that the musician builds, in that the builder has the accidental feature of **being** a musician or, if you prefer, the musician has the accidental feature of **being** a builder. In this context to say that a **is** b indicates that b **is** an accidental feature of a.

And this goes also for our cases of **being**. For when we say that a man **is** musical or a musician **is** a man, or that a white man **is** a musician or that the latter **is** white, what we are saying in the last two cases is that the same thing has both accidental features, whereas what we are saying in the first two cases is that something that **is** has an accidental feature, and to say that *the musical* **is** a man is to say that musicality **is** an accidental feature of a man. Indeed, in this way it is also said that the not-white has **being**, because the thing of which it **is** an accidental feature has **being**.

So if a is said to **be** b, this is said either because both a and b **are** features of the same thing that has **being**, or because b **is** an accidental feature of a and a has **being**, or because a has **being** and b of which it is itself predicated **is** an accidental feature of it.

As for *per se* **being**, those things are said to have it which are revealed by the patterns of predication. There are as many ways of indicating **being** as there are fundamental ways of saying something. And since some predicates indicate a what-it-is, some a quality, some a quantity, some a relation, some action or affection, some location and some time, for each of these **being** indicates the same thing. There is no difference between saying that a man **is** getting better and that a man gets better, or between saying that a man **is** walking or cutting and walks or cuts, and so on.

(iii) Another use of **being** and **is** is to say that something **is** true, and another use of **not-being** is to say that something **is** not true but false, similarly both for assertion and denial. For instance, to assert that Socrates **is** musical is to assert that it **is** true that Socrates **is** musical, and to assert that Socrates **is** not-white is to assert that it **is** true that Socrates **is** not-white. Conversely, to assert that the diagonal **is** not commensurable is to assert that it **is** false that the diagonal **is** commensurable.

(iv) **Being** and that which **is** [**1017b**] indicate both (a) what **is** potentially and (b) what **is** actually, among the cases that we have reviewed. For we say both that what potentially, and that what actually, sees **is** seeing, and in the same vein we say both that what can use its knowledge **is** knowledgeable and what is actually using it. And we say that both what **is** already in stasis and what can **be** in stasis **is** in stasis.

And it is the same with substances. We say that the Hermes **is** in the stone and that the half-line **is** in the line and we say that corn **is** corn even when it **is** not ripe. It is, of course, a quite different question when something **is**, and when it **is** not yet, potential.

VIII. *Substance*

(i) The simple bodies. Examples: earth, fire, water, etc. Also bodies more generally and the compounds of them, animals, divinities and their parts. All these things are said to be **substance** because, far from their being predicated of some subject, the other things are predicated of them.

(ii) In another way, something which, being intrinsic to one of the sort of things that are not predicated of another, is the cause of being for it, as the soul is for the animal.

(iii) The intrinsic parts of such things, which delimit them and indicate their thisness, parts on the elimination of which the whole is eliminated, as the body is eliminated by the elimination of the plane, on some views, and the plane by the elimination of the line. More generally, some hold that number is like this (the claim is that if it is eliminated then nothing has being and that it delimits all things).

(iv) The what-it-was-to-be-that-thing, whose account is a definition, is also said to be the **substance** of the particular.

The upshot is that there are two ways of giving an account of **substance**, as the ultimate subject, which is never predicated of something else, and as something which is a this-something and is also separable. And the shape/form of the particular is like this.

IX. *Identity*

(i) Accidental **identity**. Examples: whiteness and musicality are the **same** because they are accidental features of the **same** thing, and man and musicality are the **same** because the latter is an accidental feature of the former. Also the musical is a man because it is an accidental feature of the man. Each of the two simples is the **same** as the combination and vice versa: the man and the musical are both said to be the **same** as the musical man, and the musical man is said to be the **same** as they.

That indeed is why there is no universal assertion of these **identities**. It is not, of course, true to say that every man is the **same** thing as the musical. This is because universals pertain *per se*, whereas accidentals do not. [**1018a**] In the case of particulars, however, the assertion is made *simpliciter*. Socrates and musical Socrates are indeed held to be the **same** thing, and, since Socrates is not predicable of a plurality of subjects, we do not speak of all Socrates-es as we do speak of all men.

(ii) *Per se* **identity**. There are as many cases of this as there are of *per se* unity. Those things are said to be the **same** whose matter is either

127

formally or numerically one and also those things whose substance is one, so that it is clear that **identity** is a kind of unity of being either for a plurality or for a single thing treated as a plurality, as in the case where we say that something is the **same** as itself and thereby treat it as two.

As for **otherness**, things are said to have it if their forms, matter or substantial account are not one. In general, the accounts of **otherness** are correspondingly opposed to those of **identity**.

Difference

(i) Things that are **other** while being the **same** something, and not only numerically but either formally or generically or by analogy.

(ii) Things of which the genus is **other**, also contraries and things having **otherness** in their substance.

And things are said to be **similar** if they have the **same** affections in every respect, also if they have more **identical** than **other** affections, also things whose quality is one. Also one thing having more or more fundamental affections **identical** than **other** with something else, of those affections (from among the contraries) in regard to which things can undergo alteration.

And cases of **dissimilarity** are correspondingly opposed to those of **similarity**.

x. Opposite

Contradiction, contraries, relational terms, privation and condition and the end-points from and to which cases of production and destruction occur. Also features that cannot be simultaneously present in something that can have them both. These are said to be **opposites**, either themselves or their counterparts. Grey, for instance, and white are not to be found pertaining simultaneously to the same thing, and this is because their components are **opposites**.

Contrary

(i) Things differing in genus which cannot simultaneously pertain to the same thing.
(ii) The most widely differentiated things in the same genus.
(iii) The most widely differentiated features pertaining to the same recipient.
(iv) The most widely differentiated items in the domain of the same faculty.
(v) Things between which the difference is greatest either *simpliciter*, or generically or formally.

And other things are said to be **contrary**, in some cases because they possess such items as the above, in some cases because they are receptive of them, in some cases because they are productive of, or affected by, them, or are in the course of producing, or being affected by, them, or are connected with such things either as losses of them or as early acquisitions or as conditions or privations of them. And, of course, since there are a plurality of accounts of one and of being, it must be the case that the other things whose accounts are related to them, including the same, the other and the **contrary**, have an otherness corresponding to each category.

Formally other

Things in the same genus not subordinate one to another, and things in the same genus with a differentiation, [**1018b**] and things with a contrariety in their substance. Contraries are also **other** than each other within a form, either all of them or those whose account is primary, and also those things whose accounts in the lowest form of the kind are **other** (for example, man and horse are indivisible in kind and yet their accounts are **other**), and things having being in the same substance but also possessed of a differentiation.

And the accounts of **formally the same** are ranged correspondingly against these.

XI. *Prior and posterior*

(i) On the assumption that there is some primary item and principle in each genus, certain things by dint of their being more proximate to some principle, as defined either *simpliciter* and by its nature, or with relation to something or in some location, or by some particular group. For instance, some things are **prior** in place, by being nearer either to some place defined in nature (such as the midpoint or the extreme) or to an arbitrary point. And what is further removed is **posterior**. Others are **prior** in time, by being, in some cases, further removed from the present time, as with past events (the Trojan War being thus **prior** to the Persian War as being further removed from the present), and, in others, by being nearer to the present, as with future events (the Nemean Games are **prior** to the Pythian Games as being nearer to the present, which we take to be the principle and primary item). Other things are **prior** in process, in that what is nearer to the primary source of process is **prior**, as a child is **prior** to a man (the primary source of process, by the way, is a principle *simpliciter*). Other things are **prior** in respect of potentiality (whatever has an excess of potentiality, and is thus more potent, is **prior**, such being whatever it is with whose choice it is necessary for the other, **posterior**, thing to comply, so that whether the **posterior** thing does or does not undergo the process depends on whether the **prior** thing initiates it, with the choice here being the principle). Still other things are **prior** in arrangement, such things, that is, as arranged relative to some defined item in accordance with some prescription. Examples: the second chorus member is **prior** in this way to the third, and the second lowest string is **prior** to the lowest, the principle being, in the former case, the chorus leader and, in the latter, the middle string.

(ii) Also, in a different way, the cognitively **prior**, treated as being also **prior** *simpliciter*. And among such things, those that are **prior** in account are so on another basis from those that are perceptibly **prior**. For in account it is universals that are **prior**, whereas it is particulars that are perceptibly **prior**. In account, too, the accident is **prior** to the whole, as for instance *musical* is **prior** to *musical man*, in that the whole account will not have being without the part (for all that it is not possible for musicality to have being without there being someone who is musical). **[1019a]**

(iii) Affections of **prior** things. Example: straightness is **prior** to smoothness, since the former is a *per se* affection of a line, the latter of a surface.

(iv) Also, **prior** and **posterior** by nature and substance, viz. **prior** things that can have being without **posterior** things, without the **posterior** being able to have being without the **prior**, to adopt Plato's distinction.

Given the plurality of accounts of being, it is primarily the subject – and hence the substance – that is **prior**, and thereafter things are **prior** in different ways in respect of potentiality and of entelechy. Some things, that is to say, are **prior** in potentiality, others in entelechy. For instance, the half line is potentially **prior** to the whole line, the part to the whole and the matter of something to its substance, whereas in entelechy they are **posterior**, in that only on the breaking of the connection will they have being in entelechy.

So in a way all things that are said to be **prior** and **posterior** are said so to be on the basis of this last account, given that some things can have being without others in respect of production, as the whole without its parts, others in respect of destruction, as the part without the whole. And this carries over to all cases.

XII. *Potentiality*

(i) The principle of process and change, either in another thing or in the same thing *qua* other. The art, for instance, of building is not present in what is built, whereas with the art of medicine, it may, since it is a **potentiality**, be present in the person being healed, but not *qua* a person being healed.

So what is a principle of change or process in this way is said to be a **potentiality**, whether in something else or in the thing itself *qua* something else.

(ii) Also, a principle of change or process through the agency of something else or of the thing itself *qua* something else. After all, it is by dint of the principle by which something affected is affected in some way that we say that the thing affected has a **potentiality** for being affected, and this sometimes merely if it is affected at all, sometimes not with regard to its each and every affection but only if it is affected for the better.

(iii) The **potentiality** for performing the given function well or in an intentionally guided manner. For instance, on occasion one says of those who can just about walk or talk but not do so well that they do not have the **potentiality** to talk or walk.

(iv) Ditto for affection.

(v) Those states in virtue of which things are immune to affection *simpliciter*, or incapable of change or not easily to be changed for the worse. For things are broken, compressed, bent and, in a word, destroyed not by dint of having a **potentiality** but by dint of not having one and by missing out on something. And of such things those are immune to affection which are affected but slightly, if at all, through a **potentiality** and by dint of their having the **potentiality** and being in a certain condition.

Given that there is this plurality of accounts of **potentiality**, in one way the account of the **potential** will correspondingly be of something that has a principle of process and change (given that what can induce stasis is also a sort of **potential**) in something else or in the same thing *qua* something else. [**1019b**] Another account has it that a thing is **potential** if something else has a **potentiality** of this stripe over it, and another is that it is **potential** if it has the **potentiality** to change into something of whatever sort, whether for worse or for better. Indeed even what is destroyed is held to be **potentially** destructible, since it would not have been destroyed if it had no **potential** for it. In fact, however, what is destroyed has a certain disposition, a cause and principle of an affection of this sort, this being held sometimes because it is thought to have some state and sometimes because it is thought to have been deprived of it. If, then, a privation is in a way a state, then everything would be deemed to be **potential** by dint of having a certain state, and, if not, then by homonymy, with the result that things are **potential** both by dint of having a certain state and a principle and by having the privation of this – assuming one can be said to *have* a privation. Yet another account is that something is **potential** by dint of the fact that neither any other thing nor itself *qua* other thing has a **potentiality** to destroy it.

Now, also all these cases are examples of **potentiality** either by dint of the fact that the event in question might or might not turn out to happen or by dint of the fact that it might do so either well or badly. Even in inanimates, in fact, there is present a **potentiality** of this sort. Think of the case of musical instruments. One says that one lyre gives voice and another does not, just if it does not do so in a euphonious way.

And **non-potentiality** is a privation of a **potentiality** and of the principle of the sort that has been stated. And this can either be general or when something is naturally constituted to have the **potentiality** or indeed when it should, by its constitution, already have the **potentiality**. There are, I take it, differences between the account of the **non-potentiality** for fathering of a boy, a man and a eunuch!

And ranged against each of the two sorts of **potentiality** there is a corresponding **non-potentiality**, both, that is, to the mere source of process and to the source of good process.

This is one way in which things are said to be **non-potential**, but there is another way in which things are said to be both **potential** and **non-potential**. Thus the **non-potential** is that whose contrary is true of necessity. For instance, it is **non-potential** for the diagonal to be commensurate, because to say that it is is a falsehood, of which not only is the contrary true but it is necessary that the diagonal be incommensurate. So it is not just false but necessarily false to say that it is commensurate.

And the contrary of this, the **potential**, occurs when it is not necessary that its contrary be false. For example, it is **potential** that a man should be seated, since it is not false of necessity that he is not seated.

So in one way, as we have said, the **potential** indicates what is not necessarily false, in another way what is true and in another still what admits of being true.

And the **potentiality** in geometry is spoken of metaphorically.

Now things that are **potential** in this way are not so by dint of a **potentiality**. Those **potential** things, however, whose account is based on a **potentiality**, have in all cases accounts that relate to the single primary **potentiality**, [**1020a**] viz. a principle of change in something else or in the same thing *qua* something else. Other things, then, are said to be **potential** by dint, in some cases, of having something else with this sort of **potentiality** over them, in other cases, by dint of not having such and, in other cases, by dint of having it in one way rather than another. And the same goes for **non-potential** things.

So the basic definition of the primary **potentiality** would be *a principle of change in something else or in the same thing* qua *something else.*

XIII. *Quantity*

What is divisible into intrinsic parts each of which has by constitution a sort of unity and thisness.

A plurality is a denumerable **quantity**, and a magnitude is a measurable **quantity**. What is said to be a plurality is what is potentially divisible into things that are not continuous, whereas what is said to be a magnitude is what is potentially divisible into things that are continuous. And the sort of magnitude which has continuity in one direction is length, in two directions breadth and in three directions depth. And a delimited plurality is number, a delimited plurality is line, a delimited breadth is surface and a delimited depth is body.

And some things are said to be **quantities** *per se*, some to be **quantities** accidentally. For instance, the line is a *per se* **quantity**, whereas musicality is a **quantity** accidentally. And some of the things that are *per se* **quantities** are **quantities** by substance. The line is a **quantity** in this way, given that a sort of **quantity** is involved in the account stating its what-it-was-to-be-that-thing. Others are affections and states of a substance of this sort, such as much and little, long and short, broad and narrow, deep and shallow, etc. Great and small too, and greater and smaller, under both an intrinsic and a mutual account, are *per se* affections of **quantity**. And these words are also applied by metaphor to other cases.

As for things that are said to be **quantities** accidentally, the account of some of them is like that in which it has been said that musicality and whiteness are **quantities** in that there is some **quantity** to which they pertain, and the account of others is like that in which process and time are said to be **quantities** (which are also said to be sorts of **quantities** and continuous by dint of the fact that the things of which they are affections are indivisible – and in this I am speaking not of what undergoes the process but of that interval through which the process occurs, since it is because this is a **quantity** that the process too is a **quantity** and it is because the process is a **quantity** that the time is a **quantity**).

XIV. *Quality*

(i) The differentia of the substance. Examples: man is an animal of a certain **quality** in that he is bipedal, and horse is an animal of a certain **quality** in that it is quadripedal, and circle is a figure of a certain **quality** in that it has no angles, and this is because the substantial differentia is a **quality**.

(ii) Also, [**1020b**] as in the case of things immune to process and the mathematicals. Numbers, for instance, have certain **qualities**, such as composite, multi-directional numbers of which the plane and the solid are imitations, numbers, that is, with two or three factorials. More generally, whatever, over and above quantity, pertains to the substance of number. And of course the substance of a number is that number times one, the substance of, say, six being not two times six or three times six but one times six. Six *is* one times six.

(iii) All things that are affections of substances undergoing process. Examples: heat and cold, whiteness and blackness, heaviness and lightness, etc. It is in terms of these that bodies, when they undergo a change, are said to be altered.

(iv) Regarding virtue and vice and evil and good more generally.

There seem, then, to be more or less two styles of account of **quality**, and one of these is the more fundamental. Primary **quality** is the differentia of the substance (in fact **quality** even in the case of numbers is a part of this – it too is a differentia of substances, although either of substances that are immune to process or of substances *qua* immune to process).

And the other **qualities** are modifications of things subject to process *qua* subject to process and the differentiations of processes. And virtue and vice are a part of these affections, indicating as they do the differentiations of the process and of the actualization, by dint of which the things undergoing process either act or are acted on in a good or ill way. For something that has the potentiality to undergo process or be actualized in a certain way is good, while something that has the potentiality to do so in the contrary way is wicked. And it is especially in animate things that good and evil indicate a **quality**, and above all in the case of those possessed of rational choice.

xv. *Relation*

(i) As the double stands to the half and the threefold to the third; more generally, in the way that anything that is many times something stands to that thing divided many times and in which what has an excess stands to that over which it has an excess.
(ii) As what heats stands to what is heated, what cuts to what is cut and, more generally, what produces to what is acted on.
(iii) As what is measurable stands to the measure, what is knowable to knowledge and what is perceptible to perception.

Now examples of (i) are in a numerical **relation**, either *simpliciter* or in some defined way, to numbers themselves or to the number one. Examples: the double is a defined number relative to the number one, whereas the multiple is indeed numerically related to the number one but not in a defined way, not, that is, in such and such or such and such a way. Then again what is one and a half times a big as something to that thing is in a defined numerical **relation** to a number, [**1021a**] and what is 1.x times something else is in an undefined numerical **relation** to that thing, just as the multiple is towards the number one.

As for the **relation** of what has an excess to that over which it has an excess, this is not numerically defined at all. After all, number is commensurate, and number is not said of what is not commensurate, whereas what has an excess is, relative to that over which it has an excess, something and something else, the something else not being defined and being equally easily able to be equal or not to be equal to that over which there is an excess.

So the accounts of all the **relations** at which we have so far looked are numerical, and such **relations** are affections of number. And so too, for that matter, are the equal, the similar and the same in another way. Their accounts are, after all, based on the number one. Things are the same, for instance, if their substance is one, similar if their quality is one and equal if their quantity is one. And the number one is the principle and measure of number, and so all the accounts that we have studied of **relations** are based on number, though not in the same way.

Things of group (ii), which are active and undergo affection, are and do so by dint of an active and affective potentiality and of the actualizations of these potentialities. Thus what has the potentiality to effect heating stands in a **relation** to what has a potentiality for being heated in as much as it has the potentiality to heat it, whereas what is actually heating stands in a **relation** to what is actually being heated – and what is actually cutting stands in a **relation** to what is being cut – in as much as it is actually heating/cutting it.

There are, on the other hand, no actualizations of numerical **relations**, except in the way that has been indicated. There are no actualizations for them in terms of process.

And some potentiality **relations** have accounts based on references to tenses. For instance, what has made something stands in a **relation** to what has been made by it and what will make something stands in a **relation** to what will be made by it. In fact, it is in just this way that a father is said to be the father of his son, in as much as the father is what has made something and the son is what has been made in a particular way. And there are also some potentiality **relations** that have accounts based on a privation of a potentiality, such as the non-potential and things with similar accounts such as the invisible.

All things, then, with **relational** accounts, whether numerical or potential, are **relations** by dint of the fact that the account of something else is involved in what they are, not that what they are is involved in the account of something else.

And things of group (iii), which are what can be measured, what can be known and what can be thought, are said to be **relations** by dint of the fact that the account of something else is related to them. For that something is something that can be thought indicates that there can be thinking of it, but the thinking is not **relational** to that which it thinks. To say that it was would involve saying the same thing twice. And in the same way, sight is the sight of something, not the sight of what it is the sight of (for all that that may be patently true). [**1021b**] It is **relational** to colour or some other such item. (On the other way of putting it, the same thing will have been said twice, to wit that *sight* is of that of which it is *sight*.)

And things with a *per se* **relational** account are, in some cases, said in this way to be **relational** and, in other cases, if their genera are of this sort. Medicine, for instance, is a **relational** thing because its genus, knowledge, is thought to be **relational**. And there are also certain features by dint of having which a thing is said to be **relational**, such as equality, because the equal is, and similarity, because the similar is.

And other things are accidentally **relational**. Examples: a man may be **relational** in that it is an accidental feature of him that he is double something, and double is a **relation**, or whiteness may be **relational** if the same thing has the accidental features of being double and being white.

XVI. *Complete*

(i) Something outside which it is not possible to come across even a single one of its parts. Example: the **complete** period of an event is the period such that it is not possible outside it to come across some time that is a part of it.
(ii) Something which, in point of excellence and rightness, cannot be excelled in its kind. Examples: a doctor and a flute player are **complete**

when they are in no way deficient in point of the form of their proprietary excellence. And in fact we transfer the word to bad things and say that someone is a **complete** sycophant or a **complete** thief. Not surprisingly, given that we go so far as to say that such people are good, speaking of a good thief and a good sycophant.

And excellence is a sort of **completion**. After all, a particular is **complete** and every substance is **complete**, just in case in point of the form of its proprietary excellence it is not deficient in any part of its natural magnitude.

(iii) Also, if a thing's end is a feature of it, and if that end is serious, that thing is said to be **complete**. For it is by dint of possessing their ends that things are **complete**. And so, because the end is an extreme, we transfer the word to base things as well and say that something has been **completely** ruined or **completely** destroyed, when there is no deficiency in the destruction and the harm, which, rather, is at the extreme. And this is why death is also, metaphorically, said to be an end, since it, like an end, is an extreme. (But, of course, what something is ultimately for is also an end.)

This then is the range of ways in which things can have *per se* an account in terms of **completion**: some because in point of rightness they are not deficient in any way and do not admit of being exceeded or of having any part of themselves outside themselves, some, more generally, by not admitting of being exceeded in the genus in question and by not having any part of themselves outside themselves. [**1022a**] And other cases are based on the two above and are **complete** by either making or having a thing of that sort, or by being adapted to such a thing or by having an account that is in some way related to those things that are primarily said to be **complete**.

XVII. *Limit*

(i) The extreme point of a particular, the first point outside which no part of the thing can be found and inside which all parts of the thing can be found.

(ii) Whatever is the form of a magnitude or of something that has magnitude.

(iii) The end of the particular. And this sort of thing is what the process and action of the particular is *to*, not what they are *from* (in fact, sometimes it is both, both that from which and that to which).

(iv) The final cause, substance and what-it-was-to-be-that-thing of the particular, in as much as this is the cognitive **limit** of the particular. And if it is a cognitive **limit**, it must also be a **limit** of the object.

This shows that there are as many accounts of **limit** as there are of principle, or indeed more, since the principle is a sort of **limit** whereas not every **limit** is a principle.

XVIII. *Respect*

A range of accounts.

(i) The form and substance of the particular thing. Example: that in **respect** of which the good man is good is The Good Itself.

(ii) The primary subject in which it is natural for something to be produced, in the way that it is natural for colour to be produced in a surface. (Thus in the primary account the **respect** is the form, but in a secondary account it is in a way the matter and primary subject of the particular.)

(iii) More generally, there are as many accounts of the **respect** as there are of the cause. It is equally easy to speak to that in **respect** of which someone came and of that for which someone came or to ask in **respect** of what someone has calculated or miscalculated and by what cause he has (mis)calculated.

(iv) **Respect** in terms of position, in **respect** of which someone is standing or walking. All such situations indicate position and location.

In the light of this, it is necessary that the *per se* (in **respect** of itself) also have a plurality of accounts, as follows:

(i) The what-it-was-to-be-that-thing of the particular. Example: Callias is *per se* Callias and what-it-was-to-be-Callias.

(ii) Whatever pertains to a thing's what-is-it?, so that, for example, Callias is *per se* an animal, given that *animal* is included in the account of Callias and that Callias is a sort of animal.

(iii) a pertains *per se* to b, if b has received a into its primary self or into some part of itself. Examples: the surface is white *per se*, and a man is alive *per se* in view of the fact that the soul, in which life is primarily situated, is a sort of part of a man.

(iv) Something of which nothing else is a cause. Man, for instance, has a plurality of causes, it is true, such as *animal* and *bipedal*, and yet a man is *per se man*.

(v) All things that pertain to something on its own and *qua* that thing on its own. Hence:

(vi) The separable *per se*.

XIX. *Disposition*

The arrangement of something [**1022b**] with parts in terms either of its place, or of its potentiality or of its form. Some sort of position has to be involved, as indeed the very word **dis***position* suggests.

XX. *Having/habit (state)*

(i) A sort of actualization of what **has** and what is **had**, just as with a sort of action or process. When, for instance, a makes and b is made, there is between a and b a making, and in the same way, when there is something which **has** a piece of clothing and a piece of clothing that is **had**, there is between the **haver** and the **had** a **having**.

One obvious corollary is that this **having** cannot itself be **had** on pain of an infinite regress if one can indeed **have** the **having** of the **had**!

(ii) In another way, a disposition, in respect of which what is disposed is disposed well or badly, and this either *per se* or with respect to something else. It is in this way that health is a **habit (state)** in that it is a disposition of this sort.

(iii) Whatever is a part of such a disposition, so that the excellence of a thing's parts is also a sort of **habit (state)** of it.

XXI. *Affection*

(i) A quality in respect of which something admits of alteration, such as white and black, sweet and sour, heaviness and lightness, etc.

(ii) Actualizations of the above, i.e. when the alteration is actually occurring.

(iii) And above all harmful alterations and processes, conspicuously where harm is combined with pain.

(iv) Significant magnitudes of disasters.

XXII. *Privation*

(i) When something does not have one of the things that it is natural for things to have, even if it would not be natural for the something in question to have it. Example: a plant is said to be **deprived** of eyes.

(ii) When something that would naturally have a feature, either in itself or in its genus, does not in fact have it. For instance, a blind man and a mole, which are both **deprived** of sight, are so in a different way, the man relative to the features of a man and the mole relative to the features of the genus.

(iii) When something that would naturally have a feature does not in fact have it at the very time when it would be natural for it to have it. Blindness, for instance, is a sort of **privation**, but the blind man is not someone who does not have sight at each and every age but only someone who does not have sight at the age at which it would be natural for him to have sight. And, in the same vein, something is said to be blind in any of the following circumstances: it is without sight in the medium in which it is natural for it to have sight; it is without sight in the bodily part in which it is natural for it to have sight; it is without sight relative to what would naturally be an object of its seeing; it is without sight in some way in which it is natural for it to have sight.

(iv) Forceful removal of something.

In fact there are as many accounts of **privation** as there are negatives using the in-/un-/a-/non- prefixes. Something is, for instance, said to be unequal if, although naturally constituted to have equality, it does not have it. And something is said to be invisible either by dint of its not having colour at all or by its having colour only poorly, or non-footed by dint either of not having feet at all or of having only weak feet. And something can be said to be non-F by dint of having F only to a small extent (e.g. non-cored), i.e. one way of having it poorly. [1023a] And also by dint of having F with difficulty or unsatisfactorily. (For instance, what cannot be cut is so not only by dint of not being able to be cut at all but also by dint of only being able to be cut with difficulty or unsatisfactorily.)

Also by dint of not having the feature in any way. In this way, we do not say that the one-eyed man is blind but only he who does not have sight in either eye. And it is because of this account of **privation** that it is not the case that everyone is either good or bad, either just or unjust, but that there is, rather, an intermediate state.

XXIII. *To have/possess*

A range of accounts.

(i) To act in regard to something on the basis of one's own nature or on the basis of one's own urge. Examples: a fever is said to **possess** a man, tyrants to **possess** their cities and those who are dressed to **have** clothes on.

(ii) If something is a recipient of x and x is in it, it **has** x. Examples: the bronze **has** the form of the statue and the body **has** a disease.

(iii) A container **has** what it contains. For if something is in a container it is said to be had by it. Examples: we say that the vessel **has** the liquid in it, that the city **has** men in it and that the ship **has** sailors in it. And it is also in this way that the whole **has** the parts in it.

(iv) Whatever restrains something from some process or action based on its own urge is said to **have** it in the way that pillars are said to **have** the weights thrust on them or that the poets tell us that Atlas **has** the sky in his hands on the assumption (shared indeed by some of the natural philosophers) that it would otherwise collapse on to the earth. And it is also in this way that the container is said to **have** in it what it contains, in that otherwise they would disperse, each under its own urge.

And there are as many, and corresponding, accounts of to be in something as there are of to **have/possess** something.

XXIV. *To be from something*

(i) What something is *from* as its matter. And this in two ways, with respect, that is, either to the primary genus or to the last form. Thus there is a way in which all smeltable things are *from* water, but there is also a way in which the statue is *from* bronze.

(ii) As *from* the primary principle that has initiated a process. Consider: Q. What is the fight *from*? A. *From* a slanging-match, since this is the original principle of the fight.

(iii) As *from* the composite of matter and form, in the way that the parts are *from* the whole, the line is *from* the *Iliad* and the stones are *from* the house. For it is the shape that is the end, and something is only complete (and therefore whole) if it has an end.

(iv) As the form is *from* a part of it, in the way that *man* is *from* bipedal and the syllable is *from* the letter. (Because this is different *from* the way that the statue is *from* bronze: the composite substance is *from* the perceptible matter, [**1023b**] whereas the form is *from* the formal matter.)

(v) Also, if one of these accounts applies in part. Examples: the child is *from* his mother and his father and plants are *from* the earth in as much as they are *from* a certain part of them.

(vi) To follow something in time. So night is *from* day and stormy *from* good weather in that the former follow the latter. And such accounts are, in some cases, such as those we have just given, based on the possession of mutual interchange, and, in others, only on chronological sequence. One says, for instance, that the voyage was made *from* the equinox because it was made after the equinox and that the Thargelia are *from* the Dionysia, since the former follow the latter.

XXV. *Part*

(i) What a quantity can be divided into in no matter what way. For anything subtracted from a quantity *qua* quantity is always said to be a **part** of it. For example, there is a way in which two can be said to be a **part** of three.

(ii) Only those of the above that give a measurement. And so, as we have said, there is a way in which two is said to be **part** of three, but there is also a way in which it is not.

(iii) What a form can be divided into irrespective of quantity are also said to be **parts** of it. That is why they say that the species are **parts** of the genus.

(iv) What the whole is divided into or of what it is composed, either, that is, the form or what has the form. For example, in the case of a bronze sphere or a bronze cube, both the bronze (this is the matter in which the form resides) and the angle of inclination are a **part** of the whole.

(v) The contents of the account that displays the particular are also **parts** of the whole. It is in this way that the genus is also said to be a **part** of the species, as well as there being the other way in which the species is said to be a **part** of the genus.

XXVI. *Whole*

(i) Something from which there is not absent any of the things of which it is said to be a **whole** by nature.

(ii) What contains its contents in such a way that they are a sort of unity. And this in two ways, either as being each individual particular or as being the unity derived from them.

For what is universal and whose account is general on the basis that it is a sort of **whole** is universal in that it contains many things in its domain of particular predication and that they are each individually a single thing, e.g. man, horse and god, since they are each individually living things. And the continuous and delimited is also a **whole**, just in case it is a sort of unity from several items, especially when they are only potentially present but, if not, also when they are actually present. And of this group it is those that are **wholes** by nature rather than those that are **wholes** by artifice that are most fully **wholes**. This is like what we said in the case of unity, and indeed **whole**ness is a kind of unity.

(iii) In the case of a quantity that has a beginning, a middle and an end, [**1024a**] there are those instances in which the order does not create a differentia, which are said to be sums, and those in which it does, which are said to be **wholes**. Those for which both are possible are both **wholes** and sums, and of this sort are those whose nature, but not whose shape, remains the same after the rearrangement, such as wax or a cloak. These are said both to be **wholes** and to be sums, since their order does and does not create a differentia. Water, by contrast, and all liquids and also number are said to be a sum – nobody talks about **whole** number and **whole** water except metaphorically. And if something, *qua* a unity, is said to be a sum, then *qua* divided it is said to be an all, this number *qua* unity and all these units *qua* divided.

XXVII. *Mutilated*

A feature of quantities which must be divisible into parts as well as being wholes.

Thus two, for instance, is not **mutilated** when one of the two ones is subtracted – in no cases is the extent of the mutilation equal to what is left – and this goes for number in general. This is because another requirement is that the substance be left: if a cup is **mutilated**, it must still be a cup, but a number will not be the same after mutilation.

It can also not be the case that all things with dissimilar parts can be

mutilated, since in a way number has dissimilar parts as well (such as, say, two and three). What can be said in general is that none of those things whose order does not produce a differentia, such as water and fire, can be **mutilated**. Things that can be **mutilated** must be those things that have an order by virtue of their substance.

They must also be continuous. The scale in music, for instance, consists of dissimilar parts and has an order but is not something that can be **mutilated**. And even in the case of things that are wholes, not even these can be **mutilated** by the privation of just any part. On the contrary, the parts removed in a mutilation have to be neither those fundamental to the substance nor parts located in any arbitrary position. If, for instance, a hole is bored in a cup, the cup is not, by this token, **mutilated**, whereas it would be if the handle or some protuberance were removed, and a man is **mutilated** not if he has some flesh or his spleen removed but only if some protuberance is removed such that when removed in its entirety it cannot grow back. Bald men, accordingly, have not been **mutilated**.

XXVIII. *Kind*

(i) Applied if there is continuous generation of things having the same form. Examples: the phrase 'as long as human **kind** survives' amounts to 'as long as there is continuous generation of men'.

(ii) Said with reference to the primary source of the process leading to a thing's being. It is in this way that we speak of the Hellene **kind** or the Ionian, the primary originator of the former being Hellen and of the latter Ion. And it is those who are from an originator rather than those from some matter that are said to be a **kind**. Indeed **kinds** are sometimes named from the female, such as the Descendants of Pyrrha.

(iii) **[1024b]** In the way in which *plane* is the genus of figures in the plane and *solid* is the genus of solids. For every figure is either a plane with abc features or a solid with xyz features. So it is *plane* and *solid* which underlie these differentiae.

(iv) The primary ingredient in accounts, which is in the account of the

what-is-it?, since this is a genus of which we say that the differentiae
are the qualities.

So the range of accounts of **kind** are as follows:

(i) With reference to continuous generation of the same form.
(ii) With reference to the primary source of process which is of the
same form.
(iii) As matter. For anything that has a differentia and quality is a
substrate, which we are saying to be matter.

Things are said to be other in **kind** if their primary substrate is other
and if they are not to be resolved one into the other or both into the
same thing. Thus form and matter are other in **kind**. Also things whose
account is based on another pattern of predication of being, given that
some of the things that have being indicate a what-is-it?, some a sort
of quality, some others of the categories as previously distinguished.
And these too are not to be resolved either into one another or into
some single thing.

XXIX. *False*

(i) Used of a **false** thing. On the one hand, either because it has not
been assembled or because it would be impossible for it to be
assembled. Examples: the claim the diagonal is commensurable or
the claim that you are seated. For of these one is always, the other
sometimes, **false**. And it is in this way that these things do not have
being.

On the other hand, all things as do have being but are by nature
such that they appear either not to be of the sort of which they are
or to be things that do not have being. Examples: a sketch or dreams.
These certainly are something but not those things that they induce
us to imagine.

Things, then, are said in this way to be **false** either by dint of their
not themselves having being or by dint of the fact that the appearance
induced by them is of something that does not have being.

(ii) A **false** account, *qua* **false**, is an account of things that do not have being. Accordingly, every account is **false** of something other than that of which it is a true account. The account, for instance, of a circle is **false** of a triangle.

And in a way there is but one account of the particular, that of the what-it-was-to-be-that-thing, whereas in another way there are many. This is because the particular itself and the particular as under some affection (e.g. Socrates and the musical Socrates) are in a way the same. And a **false** account is not an account of anything *simpliciter*. This, in fact, is why the view of Antisthenes is simplistic. He held that nothing is to be spoken of except under its proprietary account, there being one such for each object. The conclusion drawn was that it was impossible to have a contradiction, almost indeed that it was impossible to speak **falsely**. However, it is possible to speak of the particular not only under its own account but also under that of something else. Now, of course, this can by all means be a case of **falsehood**, but there is also a way in which such a statement can be true. For instance, eight can be said to be a double number under the account of two.

(iii) Also, a man, if he is adept at, and prone to, such accounts, [**1025a**] not for some other reason but for the **falsity** itself. Also the man who is disposed to induce such accounts in others, which is like the way in which we say that things are **false** if they induce a **false** appearance. Hence, indeed, the deceptiveness of the argument in the Hippias to the effect that the same man is both **false** and true. This argument makes two assumptions: (a) that the man who is able to speak **false** is **false** (and this, of course, is the man of knowledge and good sense) and (b) that the man who willingly does wicked things is the better man. But this second assumption is **falsely** derived by induction, for instance from the fact that the man who willingly limps (i.e., in the context, who imitates a limp) is better off than the man who does so unwillingly, given that, if the man was willingly lame (and not just pretending), he would presumably be worse off in this way, as also would the corresponding man in the moral case.

XXX. *Accident*

(i) What pertains to something and what it is true to assert of it, but neither necessarily nor for the most part. Example: someone is digging a trench for a plant and finds treasure. This finding of the treasure is an **accident** for the man who digs the trench. It is not the case that finding treasure necessarily comes from or after digging a trench, nor would one for the most part in doing some planting find treasure.

Another example: a musician happens to be white. This does not happen either of necessity or for the most part, and so we say that it is an **accident**.

So, given that things have features, and that some features belong to certain things in certain places and at certain times, anything that is a feature, but not of something because it is that thing or because the time is now or the place is here, will be an **accident**. This also has the consequence that there is indeed no defined cause for the **accidental**, but only a chance (and therefore indefinite) cause. It was an **accident**, for instance, for someone to go to Aegina, just in case he did not set out to get there but was driven there by a storm or kidnapped by pirates. The **accident** has been produced or has being not *qua* itself but *qua* something else. It was the storm, that is, that was the cause of his coming to a place for which he did not set out.

(ii) Also, and differently, everything that is a feature of a particular *per se* but without being in its substance, as, for instance, it is a feature of the triangle that its angles are equal to two right angles. This sort of **accident** can be eternal, although none of the other sorts is. (We deal with this elsewhere.)

Book Epsilon

Book Eighth

EPSILON I

We are now almost ready to pass to the consideration of substance itself, but in book Epsilon Aristotle still wishes to add a few more distinctions to the picture that he has built up of the activity of philosophy. In this chapter he stresses again that philosophy is concerned with the whole of being and not just some part of it, as is each of the departmental sciences. He also makes the important new point that another difference between philosophy and the departmental sciences is that the former, but not the latter, is interested in the intrinsic properties of the subject of the science itself and not just in demonstrating its accidental features. Furthermore, the departmental sciences take for granted the existence of their domains, whereas it is part of the task of philosophy to prove the existence of its.

Aristotle also takes up the distinction between the practical, productive and theoretical sciences and further subdivides the last of these into physics, which is concerned with separately existing entities which naturally have both matter and movement, mathematics, which is concerned with non-separable entities which do not have movement, and the third and highest theoretical science which is concerned with things that are separable but immune to movement and process. This science is called theology, but it is also to be identified with First Philosophy. The apparent contradiction between claiming that philosophy is the universal science of being and that it is the science of the highest kind of being and substance is removed when it is understood that the highest substance is the cause and principle of being as a whole and thus the proper object of philosophy even on the earlier account.

It is the principles and causes of the things that are [**1025b**] that we are seeking, and clearly it is their principles and causes *just as* things that are. Now there is, to be sure, something that is the cause of health and of fitness, and there are principles, elements and causes of mathematical entities. And quite generally any science which, in whole or in part, involves reasoning or inference, is concerned with causes and principles, be they more precise or more primordial. On the other hand, all these other sciences, being devoted to a certain sort of thing that is and a certain genus, set to work on that delimited domain. They do not at all consider that which is *simpliciter* or *just as* that which is. Nor does any such science offer an account of what it is to be a thing in their domain. Rather, they start this, displaying it, in some cases, to the senses and, in others, taking it as a hypothesis, and go on to offer more or less rigorous demonstrations of the *per se* attributes of their proprietary genera. This sort of procedure is inductive and it is as plain as a pikestaff that it does not amount to a demonstration of essence or of what it is to be a thing. The style of disclosing the entity is some other, at any rate not this. It is in keeping with this that the sciences do not occupy themselves with the question whether or not their proprietary genus exists. The question whether something exists requires the same mode of thinking as the demonstration of an essence.

Now, it so happens, as a matter of fact, that the proprietary domain of the science of nature too is a certain genus of that which is. (This science takes as its domain that kind of substance which has within it the principle of its own undergoing some process or not.) And this is as much as to say that this science is neither practical nor productive. For the principle of anything that is produced lies in that which produces it, mind, as it may be, or skill or some potentiality, and the principle of anything that is done lies in that which does it, the faculty of choice (that which is done and that which is chosen are the same thing). If, then, all rational activity can be divided into the practical, the productive and the theoretical, the science of nature would be a kind of theoretical activity, but theoretical of the kind of entity that can undergo change and with substance according, indeed, to its basic definition, only not separable from matter.

It is, however, vital not to overlook the question of what it is to be a thing and the definitional account of how it is what it is. If we leave these out, scientific inquiry is mere shadow boxing. We can, then, distinguish things which, being susceptible of definition, there is something which it is to be into two types, snub-type entities and concave-type entities. The difference is as follows. Snub-type entities are immersed in matter (the snub is [by definition] a concave *nose*), whereas concave-types, like concavity itself, do not as such involve perceptible matter. Now all natural entities are, quite uniformly, given snub-type definitions. [**1026a**] Consider a few examples: nose, eye, face, flesh, bone, animal in general, and leaf, root, bark, plant in general. In each case the definition must refer to change, so that in each case they must have matter. It is, then, clear how we are to investigate and define essences for the purposes of the science of nature. It is also clear why some types of soul fall within the domain of natural science, those types, that is, that essentially involve matter.

OK, natural science is theoretical, case concluded. What about mathematics? Theoretical too. Ah, but does its domain consist of entities removed from all change and standing apart? Too early to say. (A distinct question, to which a positive answer can indeed be given, is whether some mathematical arguments *treat* these entities *as* unchanged and separate.) Suppose, however, that there is something that is eternal, unchanging and apart. Does this putative Entity form the domain of a theoretical science? Yes, of course, but *not* that either of natural science or of mathematics, but of a science more fundamental than them both. The domain of natural science is things that are in a way separate but which are eminently subject to change, and at least part of the domain of mathematics is things that are not subject to change but also not separable, in the sense of being separable from matter. But First Science deals with things that are separable and are remote from change.

All the causes must be eternal, of course, but eternity must pertain more specially still to the causes of First Science, operating, as they do, to produce those effects of Divinity that are manifest even to us. Let us, then, say that there are three forms of contemplative philosophy – mathematics, natural science and theology. For who can doubt that, if there is Divinity anywhere in the universe, then it is in the nature studied by First Science that It is to be found. And it is also for the Supreme Science to study the Supreme Genus. And contemplative study is to be chosen above all other sciences, but it is this First Science of Theology that we must prefer to all other kinds even of contemplation.

I suppose someone will raise the quibble, is the domain of First Philosophy, then, universal or concerned with some single genus and nature? Actually, you can answer this question both ways even for mathematics; geometry and astrology have single-nature domains, whereas general mathematics is universal. Anyway, our answer is this. Either (a) there is no other substance beyond those furnished by nature, in which case the science of nature is the First Science, or (b) there is some Substance that is without change, and, if (b) is true, then that Substance is prior to all others and the science of it is First Philosophy – *and such a science is universal just because it is first.* And *here* we will have the science to study that which is just as that which is, both in its essence and in the properties which, just as a thing that is, it has.

EPSILON 2

We are now, at last, in a position to commence the study of being, but Aristotle again reminds us that there are at least four basic accounts of being, accidental being, being as truth, the category of being or substance and being in actuality and potentiality. Aristotle's interest is going to be above all in substance, as has already been made clear, and also in questions of actuality and potentiality. He now wishes to eliminate the first two kinds of account of being from the inquiry. In fact, being as truth has already been dealt with in book Gamma. Here in Epsilon he concentrates on accidental being, although he will have more to say on being as truth in the last chapter.

He begins by defining accidental being. Entities can be divided into those that have being always and of necessity, those that have being for the most part and those that only have being sometimes. It is the last sort of entities that we call accidental and their causation is crucially material. This is one reason for their inferiority, and another is that they fall outside the scope of science, which studies only such things as have being either always and of necessity or for the most part.

Now the locution 'the thing that is', unencumbered with qualifications, is used in an important variety of ways. We have seen that one such way is with regard to that which is accidentally, while another is the use as the true (that which is not is, on this usage, the false). And then there is the whole table of categories (substance, quality, quantity, place, time, etc.), [1026b] and finally there is that which is potentially and that which is actually.

Given all these ways of using the locution, we can begin by saying that there can be no theoretical treatment of that which is accidentally. This is clearly borne out by the fact that no science, be it practical, productive or theoretical, takes cognizance of the accidental. Take production. If one produces a building, one does not produce all the accidental properties that come into being with the building. (In fact, there is an infinity of the latter. It happens very often that a building produced provides pleasure for some, harm for others and convenience for still others, so that the building can be described as different from every other thing that is. But the architect has not produced any of these accidental properties.) It is exactly the same with geometry, whose devotees do not contemplate the accidental properties of figures, nor bother with whatever difference there might be between, say, a triangle and a triangle with angles equal to two right angles.

There is no real surprise about all this. For an accidental expression is, in effect, an expression without a definition. We can, in this light, sympathize with Plato's classification of sophistry as dealing with that which is not. For more or less all sophistic arguments concern accidental properties, such as whether the musical and the literate are the same or different, or whether Coriscus is the same or different from the musical Coriscus, or whether everything that is, but is not eternal, has come to be, from which it can be concluded that if someone is musical and become literate then he must also have been literate and become musical! This is but a sample of a veritable galingale of such sophisms. All this goes to show that the accidental is very close to that which is not. But this can, in any case, be shown by the fact that there is generation and destruction for things that are in one of the other ways, but not for things that are accidentally. The discussion of the accidental, however, to the limited extent that such is possible, is not to be dismissed out of hand. We must go on to state its nature and the cause of its being. In doing so, perhaps, we will at the same time be explaining why it is no subject of a science.

Well, the things that are include things that are always (and of necessity) in the same condition (we are not referring to enforced necessity but to the necessity ascribed on the basis that it cannot be otherwise) and things that are not of necessity or indeed for ever, but rather for the most part . . . Now it is the latter that is the principle and cause of being for the accidental. For whatever would be neither always nor for the most part would be classified as accidental. Suppose, for instance, that in the season of the Cynosure arctic cold were to prevail, this we would regard as an accident, whereas, if there were a sweltering heatwave, we would not. And this is because the latter, unlike the former, is always or for the most part the case. It is also an accident that a man is white (for men are not always or for the most part white), but it is not an accident that he is an animal. And it is an accident that the builder heals, [1027a] since it is not the nature of the builder but of the doctor to produce health, whereas it is an accident if the builder is also a doctor. Similarly, the delicatessen, bent only on titillation of the palate, might achieve a miracle cure, but not *just in its capacity as* a delicatessen. We would call it an accident – it sort of produces the health, but not really.

The other things that are have corresponding productive capacities (sometimes), but for accidents there is no skill or dedicated capacity. For when things are, or are generated, accidentally, their cause is also accidental. If, then, not everything either is or is generated always or of necessity, but most things are for the most part, then there must be that which is accidentally. For instance, the white man is neither always nor for the most part musical, so that when he becomes musical this will be an accident (if not, everything would be of necessity). It is, then, matter, capable of being other than it is for the most part, that is the cause of the accidental.

As for the principle, it must be the following question: is there nothing which is neither always nor for the most part, or is this impossible? If we take it that there must be some such thing(s), then these will be the subjects of chance and accidental. Is it, then, the case that there is that which is for the most part but that that which is always is not a property of anything? Or, conversely, are there some things that are eternal? Well, let's put that question off for now. What we *have* seen is that there is no science of the accidental. For all science is either of that which is always or of that which is for the most part. Indeed, how otherwise would understanding, let alone teaching, be possible? A scientific subject has to be defined as arising either always or for the most part (e.g. it is true for the most part that suspension of honey is beneficial for fever patients). But anything that falls outside this will be unpredictable – as also will its non-occurrence be. We cannot, for instance, describe it as not happening on the day of the new moon, since even what happens on the day of the new moon is either something that always happens or something that happens for the most part, whereas the accidental must be different from these.

This concludes the discussion of the accidental. We have seen:

· what it is,
· from what cause it comes, and
· that there is no science of it.

EPSILON 3

The notion of accidental being entails that of accidental causation, and Aristotle explores this in the present chapter. He shows that with accidental causal chains there is some link which is in a way fortuitous, in that its occurrence is not required of necessity. It is an important question, dealt with extensively in the Physics *though not here, whether such fortuitous causation is or is not ultimately reducible to the kinds of causation that Aristotle officially admits.*

Clearly there are principles and causes that are such as to be generated and destroyed without their generation or destruction in fact occurring. If this were not the case, everything would be of necessity, assuming that for each thing that is generated and destroyed there must be a non-accidental cause. We can put the question whether such a thing will exist or not; to which the answer will be yes, if a certain other thing is generated, and, if not, no. And the generation of this other thing will in turn be dependent on that of a third. From this it is clear that if time is of limited duration and a fixed amount is constantly being deducted from it, [**1027b**] the procedure will always lead to the present moment. Thus, a given person will, if he goes out, meet a violent end; and he will do this, viz. go out, if he is thirsty; and he will be thirsty, if xyz. Such a series will always lead either to what is occurring at the moment or to some one of the past events. For instance, he will go out if he is thirsty and he will be thirsty if he eats something hot. And, of course, he is either doing so or not, so that it is a necessary matter either that he will or that he will not die.

And even if you leap back to past events, the same still holds. For this very past event is present in something at the start of the reasoning. So everything that is to be will be of necessity, e.g. that a living animal will eventually die. And this is because of something that has already happened, such as, perhaps, that opposites are combined in the same individual. It is, however, not yet determined whether the animal is to die by disease or violence, but whichever is the outcome will occur conditionally on some other event. The process is therefore clearly to an initial principle, from which there is no further progression to something else. This principle will be that of an outcome of chance, and there will be no further thing which is the cause of *its* coming to be. But of what quality are the principle and cause at the start of such an induction, whether material, final or efficient, is a question of importance and difficulty.

EPSILON 4

Aristotle now deals summarily with being as truth. Being as truth or falsity is a matter of associations made in the mind. If the mind associates things that are associated in the world, then it has a truth, if not, a falsity. This means that this kind of being is merely an affection of the mind and not something in the world.

Thus both accidental being and being as truth fall outside the direct remit of philosophy, the one as being indeterminate and random, the other as being mental not real. This leaves philosophy free to examine being that is both determinate and real, i.e. substance, which is to be the topic of the next two, central books.

We may now leave the subject of that which is accidentally, now that a satisfactory account has been given of it.

Now that which is as being true (and that which is not as being false) have to do with composition and division, and the conjunction of them has to do with the two poles of a contradiction. (For truth involves assertion in the case of a combination and denial in the case of a separation, while falsity is the contradiction of this arrangement.) And as to how thinking of things conjointly or separately occurs, this requires another discussion, and by this I am meaning the togetherness and apartness that is not connected with a sequence but with a single presentation.

For it is not in states of affairs that truth and falsity arise – certainly, the good is not the true and the bad the false straight off – but in thinking. And for things that are simple and for essences, truth and falsity do not arise even in thinking.

In the light of all this, it is for a later discussion to consider what account should be given of that which is and is not in this way. But since it is in thoughts and not in states of affairs that composition and division occurs, and since that which is in this way is a different thing that is from those things that are in the standard-setting way (for the thought process either compounds or divides off the essence of a thing, or its possession of a quality or a quantity or some one of the other categories), we can pass on from that which is as being true just as much as we can from that which is accidentally. The cause of that which is accidentally lacks a definition, while the cause of that which is as being true is something that happens to a thought process. They are thus both connected with the remaining genus of that which is [1028a] and do not reveal some nature of that which is as obtaining independently.

Let us, then, leave these two and turn to the consideration of the causes and principles of that which is proper, just as that which is. [It became clear in the discussion of the many ways in which each thing is said that that which is is said in many ways.]

Book Zeta

Book Four

We are now at last ready to begin the actual business of philosophy, which has so laboriously been circumscribed in the previous books. The task of philosophy is to get to understand being. We have seen that this is a huge task, since there are many different accounts of being. However, we have already seen that among these accounts some are more important than others. In the previous book we eliminated accidental being and being as truth, focusing attention on being as in the categories. The first chapter of book Zeta now once again reminds us of the priority that applies to the categories. We are given a résumé of the position adopted by the earlier work on the relations of the categories, more particularly on the relation of all the other categories to the category of substance. The Metaphysics will, as we will see, differ profoundly in doctrine from the Categories, but there is no change at all in the emphasis that both works put on the centrality of the category of substance. Substance is once again said to be primary, and we are told that it is primary in every respect, in account, in knowledge and in time. This being so, we can safely say that where earlier philosophers have been obsessed with the question what being is, we can now replace this with the question what substance is. Aristotle clearly feels that this sort of replacement of a vague, intuitive wonder with a precisely defined technical research programme is a paradigm of progress in philosophy.

That which is is spoken of in many ways, as we have previously expounded in our discussion of the ways in which things are spoken of. For, on the one hand, it means what something is and an item with *thisness*, and, on the other, a quality or quantity or each of the other items that are predicated in this way.

Now, given that that which is is spoken of in as many ways as this, it is patently the case that the primary thing-that-is is what something is, which picks out the substance. (Whenever we say that a given thing is of a certain kind, we say that it is good or bad, as it may be, but not that it is three feet long or that it is a man, whereas whenever we say what something is, we do not say that it is white or that it is hot or that it is three foot long, but that it is a man or that it is a god.) The other items, then, are said to be things-that-are in so far as, given that something is in a certain way, some of them are quantities, some qualities, some affections and some others such.

Now this gives rise to a real puzzle. Are walking and being healthy and sitting each a thing-that-is or not (and ditto for all other such cases)? For none of them is either something that can exist *per se* or that can be separated from substance; rather is it the case that if there is anything here that is a thing-that-is it is that which is doing the walking, the sitting or the being healthy. It is things that are doing something in this way that it would seem more plausible to consider things-that-are, and for the following reason. There is, in their case, *something defined that underlies* and it is this which is their substance and particular. Its presence is clearly revealed by the very structure of a predication of this type, and_is-good or _sits is not applied other than to such an underlying thing.

Plainly, then, each of these other items owe their being to substance, and so we may say that that which is primarily (i.e. not _is-F but just _is) is substance. In fact, a thing can be said to be primary in a variety of ways, but it is in every way that substance is primary, alike logically, epistemically and temporally. For substance, unlike any of the other predicables, is separable and it also has a primary role in definition (for the definition of anything at all must comprise the definition of its substance). And it is also when we know what a man is or what fire is that we reckon that we know a particular item in the fullest sense, rather than when we merely know its quality, quantity or location – in fact, [**1028b**] our knowledge of these latter is itself dependent on our general grasp of quantity and quality.

From all this we can draw an interesting conclusion, and it is this: from the dawn of philosophy continuously down to, and very much including the present, philosophers have been uninterruptedly engaged with, and uninterruptedly baffled by, the question '*What is that which is?*'. Now this question *just is* the question '*What is substance?*'. It is substance that has been variously asserted to be One or More

Numerous than One, to be Of Finite Number or to be Infinite in Number.

We therefore too have one sovereign, primary and – we may as well say – sole theoretical duty – it is to consider what that which is in this way is.

ZETA 2

Our question then is what substance is, but this can be taken in two ways. On the one hand, we are interested in knowing what substance is in itself. This amounts to knowing what the primary causes and principles of substance are, as announced in book Gamma, and it is to this that the bulk of books Zeta and Eta are devoted. The discussion of the causes and principles of substance which they offer is without question one of the pinnacles of the history of metaphysical reflection. But, on the other hand, we are also interested in the question what items in the world count as substances. This will have profound consequences for our applied metaphysics, our conception of what the meta-physical order of the items of our world is, as well as what the total inventory of such items should be taken to be. Of course, these two questions are con-nected, in that the correct answer to the question about causes and principles is likely to assist us in delimiting the range of substances that there are in the world while also, more inductively, some understanding of the likely range of sub-stances may help us in our speculations as to the causes and principles of substance.

In any case, Aristotle's procedure is to review in this chapter the range of items that have been proposed to play the role of the substance of the world. He then plunges in chapter 3 directly into the question of causes and principles. After this question has been exhaustively discussed, he gives an answer in chapter 16 to the question of the range of substance. He then begins a new discussion of the cause of substance in chapter 17, which is continued in book Eta.

The traditional range of candidate substances given here includes bodies, animals, plants and their parts, the elements, compounds of the elements and their parts, the heavenly bodies, the 'limits of body', surface, line, point and unit, supra-sensible and eternal substances, the Platonic Forms and the mathematical entities, numbers of various kinds and various combinations of these. All the candidates must be given a fair hearing, but it is clear that the real question underlying this list is whether or not we should admit substances which are immune to processes of movement and change, inaccessible to the senses and capable of existence in detachment from the sensible world. Can we construct a metaphysics which does not require such non-natural entities?

Now it would seem that the clearest case where substance is present is that of bodies. Hence our habit of saying that (i) animals and plants and their parts are substances, and also (ii) natural bodies, such as fire, water, earth and every other of that sort, and also (iii) anything that is either a part or a derivative of (either all or some of) these, e.g. the heavens and their parts, the sun, moon and stars. And it is, of course, an issue whether these exhaust the range of substances or whether there are also others, or whether some of those mentioned are substances but not all, or indeed whether none of these is a substance, but some other things are.

Another popular view is that (iv) the boundaries of bodies are substances, e.g. surface, line, point and unit, to a greater extent indeed than the body and solid figure itself.

It is widely held that substance is not present in anything besides perceptible entities, but it is also argued by some that there are more substances than these and that they are eternal in a special way. For instance, (v) Plato's doctrine was that the Forms and mathematicals are two substances and that the third substance is that of perceptible bodies, while (vi) Speusippus introduced still more substances starting from one and suggested principles for each substance, one principle for numbers and another for magnitudes, and also a principle for the soul. Proceeding in this fashion, he arrived at no mean list of substances. On the other hand, it is also argued (vii) that the Forms and numbers have the same nature but that they are the start of a series that stretches across lines and planes to the substance of the heavens and to perceptible entities.

We have, then, the following budget of questions:

(i) what claims are soundly, and what unsoundly, advanced in this area?
(ii) what substances are there?
(iii) are there, or are there not, any substances besides the perceptible ones?

(iv) what is the mode of being of the latter?

(v) is there, or is there not, a kind of substance (besides perceptible substances) that is separable?

(vi) if so, what is its rationale and mode of being?

But there is something that we must do first, before turning to these, and that is give at least a schematic answer to the question: 'What is substance?'

ZETA 3

We now turn to the question of questions, what are the causes of substance? It is customary in modern discussions to take this as the question what is the criterion of substantiality, what does something have to have to be a substance? Aristotle tells us that there are four such candidate criteria that have been put forward: the essence of a thing, the universal that it falls under, the genus to which it belongs and the subject of the properties that it has. The bulk of the discussion, chapters 4–12, is devoted to the consideration of substance as essence, chapters 13–15 consider the universal as substance and the genus, in so far as this is considered at all, and the remainder of chapter 3 considers the subject.

Aristotle begins by remarking that it is widely thought that the subject of properties must be the substance of a thing. It is natural enough to seek to distinguish between the bearer of properties and the properties themselves, giving the former a fundamental role. This was the position clearly adopted in the Categories, *where substance as subject is said to have priority over the other categories of features of substances, in that they were all dependent on substance for their being but not vice versa. There are, to be sure, very many problems connected with this notion of a metaphysical subject, but Aristotle does not directly broach these here. Rather, he adopts a different line and asks how the concept of the subject familiar from the* Categories *is to be squared with the hylomorphic conception of the individual particular which has been developed in the* Physics. *The* Physics *teaches that an individual animal, say, which had been treated as a basic particular in the* Categories, *should now be regarded as a metaphysically composite entity, being a combination of matter and form. But if it is such a composite, with what is the subject to be identified, with the composite as a whole, with its matter or with its form?*

Aristotle addresses this question by taking the concept of a subject to its logical extreme. If we eliminate from something anything which is a property that it has rather than what has the property, we first of all get rid of such things as its colour, weight, etc., and then remove even its basic dimensions. If we go on like this, we must arrive at a subject which has no properties of its own at all. This sort of subject is what Aristotle calls ultimate matter, and it is hotly disputed whether Aristotle acknowledges that such matter exists. What, however, is clear is that Aristotle cannot accept that such ultimate matter is the metaphysical substance of the world. It cannot be substance, because it lacks two characteristics that are crucial to substance, separability and thisness. Thus, either we may say that the discussion has shown that being a subject is not the criterion of substantiality or we must say that the subject criterion needs either to be modified or to be supplemented, in such a way as to ensure that the substance candidate that it yields has the crucial features of separability and thisness.

The discussion of the subject criterion has focused on the notion of thisness, and this prepares us for the discussion of the next candidate substantiality criterion, essence. It has often been pointed out that Aristotle does not seem to have a discussion of form to match that of matter, but, as we shall see, the concepts of form and essence are very closely associated in his thinking, especially in Zeta.

There is no doubt a whole range of ways in which substance is spoken of, and yet four are of special significance. The substance of a particular thing is variously held to be:

(a) that which it was to be that thing,
(b) the universal, and
(c) the genus.

And there is also a fourth item in this list, namely:

(d) the subject.

Now the subject is that of which other entities are said, it itself never being said-of anything else. Consequently, it is important first to achieve a definition of this. [**1029a**] For a strong case can be made for the claim that it is the *primary subject* that is substance to the fullest extent.

What, then, is said to be the primary substance? Well, there is a way in which matter, another way in which shape-form, and a third in which the composite, is assigned this role. (In speaking here of matter I have in mind, say, the bronze of a statue, while by shape-form I mean the geometry of the object's appearance and by the composite the statue itself as a whole entity.) Now this means that, if the form is prior to, and more real than, the matter, then it will, by parity of reasoning, also be prior to the composite.

OK. This amounts to a thumbnail sketch of what substance in fact is. It is that which is not predicated itself and is the subject of the predication of other things. However, we cannot simply leave it at that. The present account *does not go far enough*. For a start, it is in itself obscure, and secondly, on this account as it stands, *it is matter that turns out to be substance*.

That is to say, if matter does not turn out to be substance on the present account, it beats me what else could be. If you extract all other features of the object, what is revealed as being left over? After all, the features of bodies are affections, qualities and capacities and in particular its three spatial dimensions are kinds of quantity and not substances (NB a quantity is not a substance), and it is rather that which is the primary subject of these that is a substance. If, then, we further remove the three spatial dimensions, we find nothing left over, unless just what is delimited by these dimensions is something. But this means that if we adopt this approach it has to turn out that matter stands revealed as the only substance.

Let me be quite clear about what I mean here by substance. I mean an item that is not in itself a something and is also not a quantity nor said to be any of the other things by which that which is is defined. For there is something that is the subject of the predication of each of these others, and being is different for this than for each of the categories (for the others are all predicated of substance, whereas substance is predicated of matter), so that the very last item will not in itself be a something, nor a quantity nor anything in one of the other categories. We will not be able to identify this item even with the denial of these others, since even denials will apply to it only accidentally.

If we start from these assumptions, it has to turn out that it is matter that is substance. And yet this just cannot be so, and this is because surely what we really think to be the most central features of substance, surely, are separability and thisness. And from that perspective, it seems far more plausible to say both that the form and that the composite are substance than that matter is.

Well, OK, but we can eliminate composite (i.e. composite of matter and shape-form) substance on two counts: (a) it is derivative and (b) it does not require elucidation. And in a way matter too is straightforward. What we must scrutinize is the third kind of substance, for this is vexed with perplexities.

Now widespread consensus prevails that some perceptible entities are substances – so let's have a look at them first.

[[It makes sense [1029b] to sneak up on the more intelligible things, after all. This is always the way with understanding – it moves from things less intelligible by nature to things more so. In practical life we start by doing what is good relative to the individual and end up by making what is good generally good relative to the individual, and in just the same way in theorizing we move from that which is intelligible to the individual to making that which is intelligible in general intelligible to the individual. And things intelligible to individuals, things initially intelligible, are often only capable of being understood to a slight degree and contain little or nothing of that which is. But all the same we have to start with things only indifferently understood but understood by the individual and try to achieve a grasp of things that are understood quite generally, progressing in the manner described from our humble starting points.]]

ZETA 4

We turn, then, to the consideration of essence as the criterion of substantiality. But what is essence? It is a concept that has not been formally introduced in either the Categories *or the* Physics. *Aristotle accordingly now gives us a logical exposition of the concept of essence. The essence of something is related to the account that is given of it. But any particular thing will have an account far wider than its essence. For instance, if you happen to be musical, then any account of you will mention your musicality, but this does not mean that musicality is part of your essence. Why not? Aristotle's answer is that musicality is not something that you have* per se.

So the essence of something is what is included in a per se *account of it. There are many objections that can be raised against the whole notion of essence, and against the apparent circularity of this definition of it, but to appreciate Aristotle's line of thought it is necessary to set these aside at least for the time being. What, however, we must see is that the essence of a thing is more restricted than what is included in the* per se *account of it. For instance, it is a* per se *feature of whiteness that it must be whiteness of a surface (it is only surfaces which can be white, or any other colour). But this does not mean that it is essential to whiteness that it be of a surface. We can say that what something is necessarily realized in is not thereby part of its essence.*

So how do we tell just which per se *features of a thing, which parts of its* per se *account, are included in its essence? Aristotle's answer is that the essence of a thing is those* per se *features of it that are mentioned in its definition. But then the question becomes what sort of things can have definitions, and Aristotle insists that things which are in some way compound cannot have a definition and thus an essence.*

Thus Aristotle wants to distinguish one group of items for which the essence is particularly important. It is normal to think that something will have an essence and then perhaps some other non-essential per se *properties and some merely accidental properties as well. But is there anything which only has essential properties? Is there anything the account of which is exhausted by its definition? Yes, says Aristotle, this is the characteristic of the species which are included in the genera of things, especially of living things. Species have no non-essential features – when you have defined a species, you have said all that there is to say about it. This, in Aristotle's opinion, gives species a fundamental importance. He says that it is only species that have an essence, but it is probably best to take them as making the point that because there is no non-essential account of species and because, something that Aristotle is assuming though he ought to prove it, having an essence is in fact the criterion of being a substance, we should conclude that species, whose being is exhausted by their essence, are the substances of the world. This is a clear change of doctrine from the position of the* Categories, *in which the substances, the basic realities, were particular items, notably individual men, horses, cabbages, etc.*

In the second half of the chapter Aristotle modifies his position without significantly undermining it. Whereas he has previously been saying that only things in the category of substance can be defined, he now allows that things in the other categories can also be defined in a secondary way. This should be taken as an indication of his willingness to allow common sense to prevail over dogma, but it does not affect the central conclusion just reached about the nature of substance and its revolutionary identification with species.

We began this discussion by distinguishing the various criteria by which we define substance. One of these we took to be the what-it-was-to-be-that-thing for something and it is time that we took a look at this.

We can begin with a few logical remarks about it. Well, the what-it-was-to-be-that-thing is, for each thing, what it is taken to be *per se*. For example, it is not the case that being for, say, you just is being for the musical man, since it is not *per se* that you are musical.

OK, so being for you is being for you *per se*. But this is not all there is to it. The what-it-was-to-be-that-thing is not the *per se* being of a thing in the way that whiteness belongs *per se* to a surface. This is because it is not the case that being for a surface just is being for something white.

And also, to be sure, it is not the case that it just is being for the compound of the two, the white surface. The reason for this is that it itself *is an additional feature of that being*. So we have a rule for giving an account of something: it is that for an account of a thing to be the account of the what-it-was-to-be-that-thing for it it must be the case that the account, in stating what the thing is, does not contain the very thing itself. To clarify this a little, suppose that to be a white surface is to be a smooth surface. In this case, to be white and to be smooth would indeed be one and the same.

Now let us look at the other categories. Compounds are no less to be found in them. After all each has its subject, a subject for quality, for quantity, for time and place and motion. So the question rather suggests itself whether for each such compound there is an account of what-it-is-to-be-that-thing. Indeed do such compounds – let us work with *a white man* as an example – *have* a what-it-was-to-be-that-thing?

Let us assign the term *anorak* to our exemplary compound. The question then is: 'What is it to be an anorak?'

Now an immediate objection would be that the mere assignation of a term does not make something one of the things that are taken to be *per se*. However, a thing may not qualify to be taken to be *per se* in two ways, of which one involves the problem of addition but the other does not. To take the first case, the item being defined is stated via its own addition to something else. Suppose, for an example, that I had to define *being white*, and, to do so, I stated the account of a white *man*. The other case involves rather the addition of something else to the thing to be accounted for. Staying with our use of *anorak* to be the term for a white man, one would illustrate the second case by just giving a definition of *anorak* as a white thing. Of course, a white man is a white thing, but to be a white man is not just to be white.

But then the question is whether being an anorak is a case of a what-it-was-to-be-that-thing at all. A reason for denying that it is is that a what-it-was-to-be-that-thing is the same sort of thing as a thing with *thisness*. And a thing with thisness is just what we do not get whenever one thing is said-of another. [**1030a**] So, for example, a white man is not something with thisness, assuming that thisness is an exclusive feature of substances.

Now this gives a nice clear conclusion: *a what-it-was-to-be-that-thing only belongs to those things for whom an account just is a definition.*

Now a definition does not arise just when a term means the same thing as an account. This would have the crazy consequence that all accounts would be definitions. After all we can assign a term to any 'account' whatever, so that the *Iliad* would be a definition! No, a definition must be of something primary. And primary things are things said without the predication of one thing of another.

So the only things that will have a what-it-was-to-be-that-thing will be the species of a genus, species and nothing else whatever. (It is, after all, the accepted view that species are not stated in terms of participation of one thing in another or in terms of a modification of something, nor on the basis of any accidental property.)

For each particular thing of every other sort there will, to be sure, be an account of its meaning to be given. If it is a name, the account will state that the G is F – or maybe a more elaborate and precise account will be given instead of such a simple one. But what there will not be is a definition, nor do such things have a what-it-was-to-be-that-thing.

Oh but wait a moment – is not definition and the what it is talked of in a variety of ways? For instance, in one way the what it is indicates the substance, the thing with thisness, but in another way it indicates each of the other categories, quantity, quality, etc. Indeed, just as _is attaches to everything, though not in the same way, but applying primarily to substance and sequentially to the others, so does the what it is apply without qualification to substance and sort of kind of applies to the other categories. After all, we might ask the question 'What is it?' of a quality, so that quality is one of the things with a what it is. But this would not be without qualification. It is like the way in which some philosophers treat that which is not, making the logical point that that which is not is – only, of course, not without qualification, but only that it is a thing that is not. Something similar applies with the being of qualities.

Well, it is important to know how to speak of each thing, but only in strict accordance with the way each thing is. So there is absolutely no difficulty about what we are now saying. In just the way distinguished, the what-it-was-to-be-that-thing will apply primarily and without qualification to substance and secondarily to the other categories (as also with the what it is) not as what-it-was-to-be without qualification but as what-it-was-to-be-of-that-quality or -of-that-quantity.

For we must either say that these other categories have being by homonymy or by addition and subtraction, in the sort of way that we say that what is not known is known. As a matter of fact, the correct way is to speak of them neither by homonymy nor in the same way. It is rather as we use 'medical' by dint of its referring to one and the same thing, but not actually meaning one and the same thing, [**1030b**] and yet not doing so by homonymy. For when a body, a function and an instrument are all said to be medical, this is not by homonymy nor is it with a single meaning, though it is with reference to a single thing. In fact, it does not matter at all in which of the two ways one would want to state these things. What is beyond dispute is that definition and the what-it-was-to-be-that-thing belong primarily and without qualification to substances. Sure, we can also use them in the same sort of way of other things, but this will not be primary usage.

Even, however, if we assume all this, it does not follow that there will be a definition of anything for which the term means the same as an account. Rather, the account must be of the right kind. This will be the case if it is the account of a single thing, and not single by mere continuity (like the *Iliad*) or by conjunction, but rather in all the ways in which a thing is said to be single. And there are as many such ways as there are ways in which that which is is said to be, and that which is means a thing with thisness, a quantity or a quality.

So there will be an account, and even a definition, of white man, *but in a different way from that in which there is an account and definition of whiteness and of substance.*

ZETA 5

Aristotle has established that species can be exhaustively defined and that thus they are substances in the most fundamental way. He is tolerant of the idea that non-substances can be defined in some secondary way. He would regard this as a harmless thing to say. What he is not prepared to countenance is that something combined with its accidental features should be definable as such and thus have an essence. There can be no essence of musical man, for instance. This, of course, is merely a corollary of his insistence that a definition mention no features of a thing that are not per se, as we have seen not to be a per se feature of a man.

What is more problematic however, is the position of per se but non-essential features. Should a thing together with its per se but non-essential features be susceptible of definition? Aristotle has already given a clear negative answer to this in the previous chapter, but he sees that the intuitive temptation to define things with all their per se features is strong, so he argues against it once more. He takes the example of the snub. The snub is a concave nose. Nothing can be a snub unless it is both a nose and concave. Why, then, can we not speak of the definition and essence of snub?

Aristotle's reason for the rejection of the definition of snub throws great light on the intuitive attraction of the essence criterion itself. Aristotle says that if there were a definition of snub it would have to be something like concave nose, but this would mean that the official account contained something which was itself capable of definition in the primary way, namely the nose. But this would mean that if you did not understand the definition of nose, you could be given a definition of the snub which would be unintelligible to you, and this is something that Aristotle considers to be absurd. What this shows is that in insisting that substances be definable exhaustively, Aristotle is really insisting that substances be conceptually or cognitively fundamental.

He reinforces these cognitive arguments by pointing out that if both concavity and snub could be defined and if we can properly talk of a snub nose as well as a concave nose, then in talking of a snub nose we will be talking of a concave-nose nose and so on indefinitely. These two lines of argument both support the claim that for something to have an exhaustive essence it must be independent of the understanding of other things. They must be understood through it, not it through them. At the same time, substances must also comply with the subject criterion in that they must continue to be the bearers of properties, as in the categories. It is not clear that this combination can be coherently sustained, but Aristotle deals with it to some extent in the next chapter by asking whether there is anything which is identical with its essence. His answer to this question will once again point to the central substantiality of species.

Now if you take it that an account involving an addition is not a definition, there is a real question about which of those terms that are not simple but coupled admits of definition, given that such terms must be explained by an addition. I have in mind a case such as the following: we have both nose and concavity and also snubness whose account comes from those two, being a this said to be in a this. Nor is it in any accidental way that either concavity or snubness is an affection of the nose; on the contrary, it is a *per se* feature. If Callias is a white man, then whiteness belongs in a way to Callias, or to man, in as much as Callias, to whom it is accidental here to be a man, is white; but it is not in this way that snubness belongs to the nose. Snubness belongs, rather, to the nose in the same way that maleness belongs to animal and quality to quantity and in the same way that all things belong that are said to belong *per se*. And such things are all those that comprise either the account of, or the term for, that to which they apply and which cannot be separately explained, in the way that whiteness can be explained without man but femaleness cannot be explained without animal. So for things like this, it must either be that none of them has a what-it-was-to-be-that-thing and a definition or, if they do, it must be in a different way, as we have said.

Now there is also another difficulty about this group. If a snub nose and a concave nose are the same thing, then snubness and concavity will turn out to be the same thing. If, however, this is ruled out by the impossibility of stating snubness without bringing in the thing to which it applies *per se* (snubness being concavity *in a nose*), then either it is impossible to state the snub nose at all or in doing so the same thing will be said twice, viz. snub-nose nose (assuming that a snub nose is a concave-nose nose). Hence it would be ludicrous if such items had a what-it-was-to-be-that-thing. Otherwise a regress would be generated, since snub-nose nose will be snub-nose-nose nose, etc.

Proof upon proof that only substance admits of definition. [1031a] Suppose there were definitions in the other categories, they would have to involve addition, as with the 'definition' of the odd. This cannot be given without number, any more than female can be defined without animal (the sort of account by addition that I have in mind is that of accounts, like the present examples, in which the same thing ends up being said twice).

But then, if this is true, there will be no definition of coupled terms either, such as of odd number, though this circumstance is concealed by the casual formulation that such accounts tend to receive. If, on the other hand, there are definitions even of such terms, then either this is in some other way or, as noted above, definition and the what-it-was-to-be-that-thing must be said in many ways, so that in one way there will be neither definition nor a what-it-was-to-be-that-thing for anything except substances and in another way there will be.

Here, then, is what we have now shown:

(a) a definition is an account of a what-it-was-to-be-that-thing, and
(b) a what-it-was-to-be-that-thing either belongs only to substances or belongs to them in the fullest sense, primarily and without qualification.

Aristotle now concludes his central statement of the case that essence is the criterion of substantiality, that essence is what is definable in a thing and that by the essence criterion it is primarily species that are substances. He does this by connecting the essence criterion with the subject criterion examined in chapter 3. That chapter had left it open how the subject criterion was to be used, except that it ruled out its use in such a way as to lead to the ascription of substantiality to ultimate matter. Now Aristotle seeks to bring the two criteria together by insisting that a thing must be identical with its essence.

He begins by explaining that if something does not have an essence in the primary way then it is not identical with its essence in the non-primary way. For instance, there is no essence of white man in the primary way, so that white man is not identical with the essence of white man in the non-primary way. But this merely shows how different the position of such things is from things that are definable in the primary way. Aristotle takes as an example, rather surprisingly, a Platonic Form. If there are such things as Platonic Forms, they must be definable in the primary way and must be identical with their essences. If this were not the case the Good, for instance, would be unintelligible to us, since we understand things through their essence. Why does Aristotle illustrate his point by taking an example which he does not in general accept? The answer must be that the Platonic Forms illustrate particularly clearly what he is claiming. It is just obvious in their case that they must be identical with their essences. But this shows that if there are entities in the natural world which have the Formal property of being exhaustively definable, then they too must be identical with their essences. Such things, of course, are the species, which, taken as a whole, not as a collection of particulars, are identical with their species essence.

Our next question is this: is each thing the same or different from what-it-was-to-be-that-thing?

This question is not without a certain bearing on our investigation concerning substance. It is, after all, widely held that a particular thing is not anything other than its own substance, and the what-it-was-to-be-that-thing is being taken to be the substance of each particular.

Well, in the case of things accidentally predicated, it would be generally agreed that they are different. So, for example, a white man would be different from what it is to be a white man. (If they were the same, then to be a man and to be a white man would also be the same. After all, it is argued, a man and a white man are the same thing, so that to be a white man must also be the same as to be a man. On the other hand, it is perhaps not necessary that things that are accidentally the same should be the same – it is not, for instance, in this way that the extremities become the same. And yet it might be held to turn out that the extremities become accidentally the same, in the same way as to be white and to be musical. However, this is not what is in fact thought.)

But what about things that are said *per se*? Must such a thing be the same as what-it-was-to-be-that-thing? Suppose, for example, that there are certain substances to which neither other substances nor other natures are prior. It is such substances that certain philosophers assert the Forms to be. For if, in the case of the Forms, the Good Itself is to be different from being good and Animal is to be different from being an animal and That Which Is is to be different from being a thing that is, [1031b] then there will be both other substances and other natures and other Forms in addition to those stated and these will be prior and more substantial, assuming that the what-it-was-to-be-that-thing is indeed a substance.

Furthermore, if we do disjoin the two, then there will be no knowledge of Forms and the beings of Forms will not be things that are. (The sort of disjunction I have here in mind is if neither being for a good thing belongs to the Good Itself nor being good belongs to being for a good thing.) This is because, as regards knowledge, we have knowledge of each thing when we grasp the what-it-was-to-be for that thing and, as regards being, the situation is exactly similar with the Good and other things, so that if what it is to be for something good is not something good, then neither will what it is to be for something that is be something that is nor what it is to be for something that is a unity be a unity. However, the cases of what-it-was-to-be-that-thing are similarly either all things or nothing, so that if not even what it is to be for something that is is something that is, then neither will it be for any of the others. And also anything to which what it is to be for something good does not apply is not good.

So, of necessity, the Good and being for something good and Fineness and being for something fine must be a single thing. And so for all things that are not predicated of something else but are *per se* and primary. This feature would in fact be enough, even were they not Forms – perhaps better even if they *were* Forms. (At the same time it has to be admitted that if the Forms are as some philosophers claim, then the subject will not be a substance. For it is necessary that the Forms be substances, only not in virtue of a subject, in which case their being would be by participation.)

On such grounds, then, it can be shown that the particular thing itself and the what-it-was-to-be-that-thing are non-accidentally one and the same, but this can also be shown by the argument that knowledge of some particular thing is constituted by knowledge of the what-it-was-to-be-that-thing, so that there is even a kind of proof by enumeration that both must be one thing.

With, however, the thing that is spoken of as an accidental property (*musical*, *white*, etc.), it would be incorrect to claim that the thing itself and the what-it-was-to-be-that-thing are the same. This is because there is here a double reference. For both that to which white, say, is accidental and the accidental property are white, with the result that in one way the thing and the what-it-was-to-be-that-thing are the same and in another way they are not. For the what-it-was-to-be-that-thing of something white is not the same as the what-it-was-to-be-that-thing of a man or of a white man, but it is the same as that of the property of being white.

The absurdity of denying the identity can be made clear just by the move of giving a name to each what-it-was-to-be-that-thing. For in this case there will be another what-it-was-to-be-that-thing in addition to the original what-it-was-to-be-that-thing. For instance, the what-it-was-to-be-that-thing of horse will have its own what-it-was-to-be-that-thing. But even without this expedient, what is to stop some things just from being, straight off, the what-it-was-to-be-that-thing for them, if we grant that the what-it-was-to-be-that-thing is the substance? Nor indeed is it simply a matter of them being the same – more to the point, the account of each is the same, [1032a] as even the present arguments have shown. For it is not accidental that one and what-it-was-to-be-one are one.

There is also the point that distinguishing them will produce a regress. For the what-it-was-to-be-that-thing of one will be one thing and one the other, so that the same account can be given of these resultants.

Our conclusion is as follows: with things that are primary and spoken of *per se*, the what-it-was-to-be-that-thing and the thing itself are one and the same. Sophistical attempts to unseat this conclusion can patently be thwarted by deploying the same argument as with the issue whether Socrates and what-it-was-to-be-Socrates are the same. The basis for tactical counter-questions is the same and indeed for triumphant refutation of their gambits.

Enough, then, on the ways in which the what-it-was-to-be-that-thing is the same as the thing and the ways in which it is not.

Aristotle has now given his positive answer to the question what it is to be a
substance: it is, primarily, to be a species of a genus. The discussion which has
led to this conclusion, however, was based on the consideration of essence as the
substantiality criterion, which was announced rather abruptly at the start of
chapter 4, when we could be forgiven for having expected some remarks on the
connection between form and substance. It is this gap which is filled in chapters
7–9, which effectively constitute an independent treatise on the core Aristotelian
concept of immanent form. The connection between this treatise and the discussion
of essence and species is not made clear, but Aristotle is asserting the equation
of species and form. To do so is not to assert a tautology, although the same
word is used for both concepts in Greek, but rather to bring together the taxonomic
and physical scientific sides of Aristotle's thought. Thus the treatise on form
supplements and extends the position that we have reached on species substance.

The primary purpose of the treatise is, as we have said, to enforce the
connection between form on the one hand and essence, species and substance on
the other, and the main way in which this is done is by insisting, in chapter 8,
that form is not created. We will consider this in introducing chapter 8, but
Aristotle feels that in order to make this point about form it is necessary to set
up the whole apparatus of form, matter and the composite, illustrating how the
composite particular is produced in the two cases of natural and artificial production.
The doctrine here is basically the same as in the Physics, *but the statement is*
more complete and elaborate than in that work, and it has a general sophistication
which marks it as mature. In the final section of the chapter, Aristotle is stressing
that in the produced composite form is present in a way in which matter is not.
Form persists unchanged through the production, while matter is changed.

Things that are produced differ in that some of them are produced by
nature, some by skill and some by spontaneity. Nevertheless, in all cases
of production there is something that is produced, something by which

it is produced and something from which it is produced. And that which is produced may belong to any of the categories, being either a *this* or some quantity, quality or location.

Now cases of natural production are those in which the production is from nature, and our term for that from which the production is is matter. And in these cases that by which the production occurs is one of the things that exist by nature, while that which is produced is a man, a plant or something else like that. And these are indeed the things that we are especially disposed to call substances. It is not, however, only the productions by nature that have matter but also those by skill. For each of these groups is capable either of existing or not, and this is the effect of the matter in them.

Quite generally, both that from which, and that under which, the production takes places are a nature (for that which is produced (e.g. man, plant) has a nature), and similarly that by which the production occurs is that nature which is spoken of as species-form. This nature is of a single specific form, being the same in a different instance, in the way in which it is man that begets man.

This is a schematic account of the production of things whose production is due to nature.

Now the other sort of productions are called makings. And all makings are either from skill, from ability or from thinking. In fact there can be cases of making owing to spontaneity and to chance in a manner that pretty much mirrors similar cases in things produced from nature. For in that group too productions can occur of the same thing, now from a seed and now without a seed. Consideration of these cases can be deferred for the time being.

Now, things are produced from skill if the form of them is in the mind [**1032b**] (and by form I mean the what-it-was-to-be-that-thing for each thing and the primary substance). Indeed, in a certain way even opposites have the same form. For the substance of the privation is the opposed substance; for instance, health is the substance of disease in as much as it is by the absence of health that disease occurs, and health is also the ratio in the soul and the science thereof. To produce health, that is, you must think as follows: since this present item is health, of necessity, if health is to come about, this item must obtain, say bodily consistency, and if the latter then warmth. The sequence of thoughts always proceeds in this way until a position is reached in which their subject can act on their final claim. And immediately from here on the process is termed a making, the making directed at health. The upshot is that in a way health is produced from health and a building from a building, the building, namely, that has matter from that which does not. For medicine and architecture are respectively the forms of health and a building, and I say that this form without matter is the what-it-was-to-be-that-thing.

A part, then, of productive processes is called thinking and another part is called making. That which is from the principle and form is called thinking and that from the last stage of the thinking process is called making. And in fact each of the intermediate stages in the process is produced in the same way. What I mean is this:

> Suppose that the patient's becoming healthy depends on the achievement of consistency.
>
> Fine, but what is it to achieve consistency?
>
> It is, answer, to do *this* [some demonstration occurs], and *this* will come about if the patient is warmed.
>
> OK again, but what is it to be warmed?
>
> Answer—it is *this* [new demonstration]. And this state is potentially available to the patient. This is something that is directly up to you.

So what does the making, that from which the process of becoming healthy originates, is, if the production is from skill, the form in the mind of the doctor, and, if from spontaneity, from something that is on occasion the principle of production for the productive agency from skill – as in the case of medicine the principle is perhaps from warming and it is this that the agent would directly make, by rubbing.

So bodily warmth is either an element in health or attended by something that is an element in health, either directly or through various stages. And the last stage of this that produces the element is itself in this way an element in health, or of a building (e.g. bricks) and of the other cases. There cannot, then, as they say be production unless something antecedently exists. So clearly some element must of necessity obtain. After all, the matter is an element (it is internal to the thing and becomes what the thing is).

[1033a] But must this also go for the elements in the account of the thing? Answers to the question what bronze circles are reveal an ambivalence about this. We say of the matter that it is bronze and of the form that it is a certain figure, i.e. the genus to which it is primarily assigned. After all, a bronze circle has its matter in its account.

Some things that are produced from something as their matter are, when they are produced, called not that but thattern. So the statue is not called stone but stoney, whereas the healthy man is not known by that from which he is produced. And the reason for this is that he was produced from the privation and the substrate, which we are calling the matter (it is, for instance, both the man and the patient who become healthy), but it is rather from the privation that he is said to be produced, the healthy man from the patient rather than from the man, which is also why the patient is not said to be the healthy man but is said to be a man, whereas the man is said to be healthy.

But with things for which the privation is obscure and without name, such as the lack of any figure at all in bronze or the lack of a building in mere bricks and mortar, it is from these that they are thought to be produced in the way in which the healthy man is thought to be produced from the patient in the other example. Quite consistently, then, we do not, in the case of the patient, say that he is that from which he has been produced, nor, in the present case, that the statue is wood, but rather change the word-form from 'wood' to 'wooden', and similarly 'bronzen' instead of 'bronze' and 'stoney' instead of 'stone'. And conformably with this the building is said to be 'bricked' not 'bricks'. In fact, we should not strictly even say, simply, that the statue comes from wood and the building from bricks, given that production should be from what changes and not from what persists.

Anyway, these remarks account for these locutions.

ZETA 8

Having reminded us of the production of composite particulars through the union of form and matter, Aristotle proceeds to his key point, which is that form itself cannot be produced. In a production, say in the production of a bronze sphere, it is the bronze sphere, the composite particular, that is produced. It is produced by the introduction of the form sphere into the matter bronze. But the form sphere cannot itself be produced, because if it were this would mean that some prior form was introduced into matter to make the form sphere itself, but then the same argument would apply to the prior form, and an infinite regress would be developed. It might be argued that the same point could be made about matter, but Aristotle would reject this on the grounds that form is determinate in a way in which matter is not. Thus, if we accept his premises, his argument shows the special status of form, and, although this is not explicitly argued, the non-created character of form sits well with its being conceptually basic, i.e. pure essence, i.e. species and substance.

Having made the point that form is not created, Aristotle adds to his portrait of composite production an admirably clear and forceful statement of the superiority of his account of such production to that of the Platonists. In Plato's theory, the production of the composite particular is explained as something caused by a separately existing Form, which is wholly external to the composite. Aristotle has many times argued that such a model of production is incoherent, and in this passage he makes very clear his view that an external Formal cause is not needed to explain production. The production of the composite particular is sufficiently explained merely by the entry of the immanent (therefore always embodied) form into new indeterminate matter. This is, no doubt, tangential to the discussion of substance, but it is a peculiarly clear and attractive statement of one of the key contrasts between the Aristotelian and Platonic conception of scientific explanation.

Anything that is produced is produced by something (and by this I mean that from which the origin of the production comes), and it is produced from something (let this be not the privation but the matter – we have already defined in what way we are speaking of this), and it is produced as something (i.e. either a sphere or a circle or whichever it might be of the other figures). And just as the output of the production is not the substrate, bronze, so also is it not the sphere, except accidentally, in so far as the bronze sphere *is* a sphere and it is a bronze sphere that is produced.

To produce a this-thing-here, after all, is to produce a this-thing-here from, generally speaking, the substrate. What I am driving at is that producing a bronze ball is not producing the ball or sphere but rather another thing, which is as this form in something else. For if there is production here, [**1033b**] it must *ex hypothesi* be production *from* something. For instance, a bronze sphere is produced, but this is in such a way that this-thing-here, which is a sphere, is produced from this-thing-here, which is bronze. If, however, this itself is the output of a production, then this production will take place in the same way and this will clearly generate an infinite regress.

What all this shows is that:

(i) the form (shape in object of perception – call it what you will) is not produced,
(ii) there is no production of it, and
(iii) neither does the what-it-was-to-be-that-thing (it is this that is realized in something else, by dint of skill, nature or ability).

However, *that there is a bronze sphere* is an output of production. The production is from bronze and sphere – the form is imported into this stuff and the result is a bronze sphere. But then, quite generally, if *to be in sphere form* is itself the output of a production, then this will be a case of something being produced from something. The rule cannot here be suspended that all outputs of production can be split up, with this component and that component, and I am saying that the one is matter and the other form.

But this would mean that, if we take sphere to be:

(a) a figure at all points equally remote from
(b) its midpoint,

then one of these must be the component in which the other is produced and the other the component which is produced in the other. And the two together will be the output of production, on a parallel with the way the bronze sphere is such an output. But this only goes to show still more clearly that the component that is spoken of as form or substance is not produced, whereas the composite entity that is named after it is an output of production, and that matter is present in every output of production, that such things are both a this and a that.

But then the question is this: is there some sphere *over and above the ones we see around us*, or is there a house *over and above its bricks*? Would that not just be to deny that anything is produced as a this-thing-here? Surely, it is rather the case that the form indicates a such-and-such. It is not a definable this-thing-here, but rather in production a given sort of thing is produced from a this-thing-here and, after production, it is a this-sort-of-thing-here. So a full this-thing-here, a Callias or a Socrates, is in the same boat as the bronze sphere on the table, whereas the man and animal are in the position of *bronze sphere in general*.

But this refutes the claim that the Formal cause (and we have here in mind a certain well-known way of introducing the Forms, in which they are definite things over and above particulars) is in any way relevant to productions and substances. There is no reason in all this for the Forms to be substances in themselves. In fact there are cases in which the producing agent, while indeed the same sort of thing as the output of production, is quite evidently not the same as it, nor one in number but only one in form. Patent examples are furnished by the natural entities (remember 'man begets man'), and the exceptions involve something non-natural occurring, as when a horse produces a mule. (In fact there is nothing very disturbing about such cases: the kind that is common to horse and ass and which most nearly comprises them happens not to have a name, [**1034a**] but can safely be presumed to be both, i.e. the horse-ass or 'mule'.)

So we can do away with the business of Forms Being Established As Templates. After all, if there were such Forms they would surely apply to natural entities, which are the ones that are substances in the fullest way. Rather, all we need is that it is the producer that does the making and, in the matter, is the cause of the form. And the full output, this sort of form in this very flesh and bones is Callias or is Socrates. They differ materially (their matter is different), but they are formally the same (indivisibility of the form).

ZETA 9

This chapter is a kind of appendix to the argument of the previous two, and especially to the general account of composite production in chapter 7. In that chapter, Aristotle had divided productions up into three classes, natural, artificial and spontaneous. He proceeded to discuss natural and artificial production at some length. He now adds some remarks about spontaneous production. It is not clear whether spontaneous production can in fact be successfully married with Aristotle's basic conception of production, and it is the Cinderella of production in his various discussions. In the present chapter, the account of spontaneous production seems to have affinities with the account of chance production in book II of the Physics. *In any case, this is all a digression from our principal interest in substance.*

The chapter ends at least with a clear restatement of the central point that Form is not produced. Aristotle also allows that items in the other categories are also not produced, but he insists that the difference between the other categories and the category of substance in this regard is that substance requires the presence of an actual substance to be realized in the composite produced, whereas in the case of the other categories the category item need only exist previously in potentiality.

The treatise as a whole is clearly somewhat uncomfortable where it sits in Zeta, and it has often been suggested that it is an addition that has not been very effectively integrated into the main text. Something like this is very probably true, but the connection between the doctrines of the treatise and the previous discussion of essence and species is both clear (although not explicitly stated) and important. In addition, the treatise is admirable in its own right as giving a particularly clear statement of the Aristotelian doctrine of immanent form.

Another possible query is the following: how is it that some things, such as health, are produced both by skill and by spontaneity, while others, such as a building, are not? The reason is that for some things the matter that provides a principle for production in the fashioning and producing of something that can be produced by skill, and in which an element of the item in question is present beforehand, is, in some instances, such as to be capable of being set in process by itself and, in others, not. And where it can be so self-initiated, it sometimes can, and sometimes cannot, be set in process in the way appropriate for a production. (There are, of course, lots of things that can be set in process by themselves, but not in some given way, such as, say, dancing.)

Anything, then, whose matter is of the latter kind (e.g. stones), can only be set in the relevant process by something else, even though they can set themselves in another process – fire is another example of this. And this explains why there are some things that would simply not exist in the absence of the possessor of the relevant skill, while other things might well exist in such circumstances, given that they are capable of being set in process by those things which (i) lack the relevant skill, but (ii) can themselves be set in process by other things which lack the relevant skill, or (iii) from some part thereof.

The foregoing also makes it clear that in a way everything is produced either (i) from a bearer of the same name, as in the case of things produced naturally – an example of this among artefacts is a building, which is produced *from* a building to the extent that it is produced *by* thought, in that the skill is the form of the building – or (ii) from a part with the same name or (iii) from the possessor of some such part, ruling out, that is, mere cases of accidental production. For the primary and *per se* cause of production is a part of the output of production. It was, for instance, the warmth in the movement that produced warmth in the body, and such warmth either just is health or is a part of it or is attended either by health itself or by some part of it. And it is in fact by virtue of this that such warmth is said to produce, in that it produces that to which health is attendant and proper. So, just indeed as in the case of demonstrative arguments, the substance is the principle of everything else. (For demonstrative arguments derive from the what-is-it?, and so, in the present case, do instances of production.)

Natural compositions do not differ radically from this. For, on the one hand, the productive effect of the seed is not different from that from skill, given that the seed possesses the form potentially and that

that from which it comes shares its name, in a way, [**1034b**] with the product. In a way, because it is not to be supposed that the name of producer and product will always be exactly the same, on the lines of 'a human being begets a human being', since we can perfectly well say 'a woman is from a man'. (I am bracketing off the abnormal here – a mule does not come from a mule.) And, on the other hand, all natural outputs of production which are, on occasion, the products of spontaneity (as with artefacts) are those whose matter can be set by itself in the very process that the seed initiates, while those whose matter is not like this cannot be produced other than out of conspecifics.

The scope of this argument, to the effect that *form is not a product*, is not confined to the context of substance. Rather the reasoning carries over equally to everything else that is thus primary, viz. quantity, quality and the other categories. It is, after all, the bronze sphere that is the output of a production, not the sphere, nor bronze, and the same must apply to bronze if *it* is an output of production (for there cannot be a case in which the matter and the form do not pre-exist the product), and so too not just for the what-is-it? of substance but also for quality and quantity and the other categories conformably. It is not, you will agree, the quality that is produced but *wood-with-the-quality*, not the quantity but *wood-* or *animal-of-the-quantity*.

The fact is that the cases of the other categories are instructive. They show that it is peculiar to substance that it requires the pre-existence of another substance *being in actuality* which is the agent of production, an animal, say, if an animal is to be the output, whereas it is quite otherwise with a quality or quantity whose productive antecedent need only potentially exist.

ZETA 10

Chapters 10–12 also form a connected discussion, which follows on from the account of essence as substance. The notion of essence is dependent on the notion of definition. The essence of something is just what must be mentioned in the definition of it. The issue of the possibility and value of definitions has been one that has been central to metaphysics, logic and the philosophy of language throughout the history of philosophy, and many objections have been raised to giving definition the central role that it has in the philosophy of Socrates, Plato and Aristotle. Some of these objections were already voiced in Aristotle's time, and in the present discussion he gives his central defence and exposition of the concept of definition. Once again, this discussion has an obvious relevance to the main subject, but it is also of very great importance and interest in its own right.

Chapter 10 contains some of Aristotle's most important insights into the nature of definition, but unfortunately its structure is rather confused. Two questions are considered, whether the parts of a definition must correspond to the parts of the thing defined and whether the whole of a thing is prior to its parts or the parts prior to the whole. These questions turn out to be connected or at least to be answerable in broadly the same way. The point of the first question is that if something has parts, as the objects of definition must have to be definable at all, how can we tell which parts are to be included in the definition and which not? Aristotle answers this by distinguishing between the prior and posterior parts of things. For instance, the sections of a circle are parts of the circle and the letters of the syllable are parts of the syllable, but Aristotle sees a crucial difference between them. It concerns the order in which we come to understand the whole and the parts. In the case of the circle, we understand the circle first and the parts second, in the sense that you can only understand a part of a circle if you already understand a whole circle. With the syllable, however, the reverse is the case. You cannot understand what the syllable as a whole is without already understanding the letters of which it is made up. Aristotle says that the parts of the syllable are prior and the parts of the circle are posterior. In so doing,

200

of course, he also gives an answer to his second question. What the discussion shows again is that the notion of definition is basically connected with that of understanding. The object of a definition must be what is in some way independently and fundamentally intelligible.

The definition is an *account*. Now every account has its parts, and there is an isomorphism between the relation of the account to the entity that it concerns and the relation of a part of the account to a part of the entity. So straight off we have an issue – should the account of the parts be present in the account of the whole or not? Of course there are some instances where the accounts of the parts are clearly so present and some for which, equally obviously, they are not. The account of the circle does not comprise that of its segments, while, by contrast, the account of the letters *is* contained by that of the syllable. But this hardly means that in some way the circle is less divisible into its segments than the syllable into its letters.

And consider this. Suppose parts are prior to the whole. Then, since the acute angle is a part of the right angle and since a finger is part of an animal, this would mean that the acute angle is prior to the right angle and the finger to the man. The received opinion, however, would seem to be that the latter of the two pairs is prior. For (i) it is from these wholes that the accounts of these parts are derived, and (ii) the wholes are prior in respect of mutual independence of being.

But there is another way of looking at it. Suppose there is a plurality of ways in which an account applies to a part. (One way of accounting for a part is as a unit of quantitative measure. This is clearly irrelevant to our present interests. Our concern is exclusively with things that can be parts of a substance.)

And let us make the further suppositions that we have three things on our hands, matter, form and the composite, [**1035a**] and that matter, form and composite *are each a substance*. Then, (i) in a way even the matter will be said to be a *part* of something, but (ii) in another way the matter will not be taken as a part, the parts of the thing being only those comprised by the account of the form. Let's take an example: flesh is not a *part* of concavity (it is rather the matter in which concavity is produced), whereas it is a part of snubness. And, in the same vein, the bronze is a part of the whole composite statue but not a part of the statue as formally specified. And there is a reason for this in that a particular can be spoken of as its form or in respect of the fact that it has a form, whereas in no cases can the material element be referred to *per se*.

And now we have our explanation of the fact that (a) the account of the circle does not comprise that of the segments, while (b) the account of the syllable does comprise that of the letters. It is because the letters are parts of the account of the form and do not constitute matter, while the manner in which the segments are parts is that of the matter on which the form is superimposed. (Well, I concede that they are *closer* to the form than is the bronze when sphericity gets introduced into bronze.) But there is also a way in which not even all letters of the syllable are comprised in the account. These waxen inscriptions that we read, these spoken letters that we hear, for instance, are not so comprised. These letters, though letters, are already to be reckoned as part of the syllable, *as perceptible matter*.

Let us go further. A line is indeed destroyed by being divided into halves. A man is indeed destroyed by being dissipated into bones, sinews and morsels of flesh. But this does not entail that those entities are composed of those items in such a way that they are parts of their substance. The fact is that they are material, being parts of the composite whole but never of the form and the bearer of the account.

This is why these parts are not included in the accounts of the wholes.

OK. For some things the account of the parts of this sort will be comprised by the account of the thing itself, but for other things such an inclusion cannot be permitted on pain of the account's turning out to be of the thing-together-with-its-matter. And this is also why some things have as their component principles the items to which they are resolved on destruction, while other things are not so. Anything which is a conjunction of form and matter, such as the snub or the bronze circle, are resolved on destruction into these things and for them matter is a part, but anything which, far from being conjoined with matter, lacks it utterly, anything whose account is of its form alone, anything like this is either (a) not destructible at all or (b) at any rate not destructible in the here relevant way. So for the first of these two groups of things, the material ingredients are both parts and principles, whereas they are neither for the form. Hence the destruction of the earthenware figure into clay, of the sphere into bronze, of Callias into flesh and bones and also of the circle into its segments. (There is, remember, a certain circle which is conjoint with matter, [**1035b**] given that the same name is applied to the circle specified *simpliciter* and to the particular circle, there being no particular-peculiar name.)

Well, the truth is already out, but let that not stop us going back over the ground to make things yet more radiantly perspicuous. Everything which is a part of the account and such that the account is divided into it is prior, either in all cases or in some. But the account of the right angle is not divided into the account of the acute angle – rather the account of the acute angle is divided into parts of which one is the account of the right angle. For in framing a definition of the acute angle one must bring in the right angle, saying that an acute angle is an angle less than a right angle. And it is just the same with the circle and semicircle. The semicircle is defined via the circle. And, for that matter, the finger is defined via the whole animal: a finger is$_{\text{def}}$ part *of a man* with [. . .] characteristics. So anything that is a part in the material manner and to which destructive resolution as to matter takes place is posterior, but anything that is a part as of the account and of the substance as specified in the account is prior, either in all cases or in some.

In the case of animals, it is the soul (the substance of the living thing) that is the substance as specified in the account, the form and the what-it-was-to-be-that-thing for a body of this kind. (At any rate, I take it that no such body can be (satisfactorily/non-shoddily) defined in isolation from its function and that this will not be performed in the absence of perception.) So the parts of the soul will indeed be prior, either in all cases or in some, to the composite animal, and ditto with the particulars. The body, on the other hand, and its parts will be posterior to the substance that is the soul, and it will be, not the substance, but the composite that is divided into them as into matter. Thus in a way these material parts are prior to the composite and in a way not, in as much as they cannot be in separation from the composite (it is not the finger in any state that you like that is the finger of the animal – as witness the merely homonymous dead finger).

There are, however, some material parts that are *neither prior nor posterior* to the composite. These are the parts that exercise control, notably that part that is the primary seat of the account and substance, be it heart or brain (you can toss a coin between them in the present context).

Man, however, and *horse* and items similarly imposed on the particulars but themselves general are not substances but a kind of composite of the relevant account in the relevant matter, considered universally. By contrast, particulars, Socrates et al., are directly composed from 'mere matter'.

We have, then, on our hands the part of the form (and in speaking of form I have in mind the what-it-was-to-be-that-thing), the part of the composite of the form and the matter and the part of the matter itself. But it is only the parts of the form that are parts of the account, and it is the universal that the account is an account of (given that being-for-a-circle and *circle* are the same thing [**1036a**] and ditto being-for-a-soul and *soul*). But once we have a composite, this circle now lying in front of us, say, or any perceptible or intelligible particular circle (intelligible circles = mathematical ones, perceptible = e.g. bronze/wood), this lot are not susceptible of definition. They are cognized respectively by thought and perception and on moving out of actualization it is a moot point whether they even continue to exist. Reference to, and cognition of, them is always via the universal account, matter being not *per se* an object of cognition. (Matter divides into that which is perceptible and that which is intelligible: the former comprises bronze, wood and all process-apt matter, the latter matter is present in the perceptibles but not *qua* perceptible, e.g. the mathematicals.)

That wraps up the discussion of part and whole and of prior and posterior. To the question whether the right angle, the circle and the animal are things prior to the parts into which they are resolved and of which they are composed it is to be rejoined that the question is simplistic. If the soul too is the animal or is the living thing, or if the soul of the particular animal/living thing is the particular animal/living thing, and if *circle* is being-for-a-circle and *right angle* is being-for-a-right-angle and the substance of the right angle, our position should be that the what is indeed posterior to something, viz. the parts in the account and to those of a particular right angle (this is the right-angle-with-matter, the bronze right angle and the right angle in particular lines), whereas the right-angle-without-matter is posterior to the parts in the account but prior to the parts in the particular right angle. So our questioner cannot be returned a simple answer.

And if, conversely, the soul is something else and not the animal, the position is still the same. Some parts prior, some parts not. Our schema stands.

ZETA II

We have seen how in the previous chapter Aristotle has distinguished between the prior and posterior parts of things and put this distinction to use in answering certain pressing questions about the coherence of the notion of definition. The distinction between the prior and posterior parts of things is tantamount to the distinction between the formal and material parts of things. But in the present chapter, Aristotle considers a possible objection to drawing so sharp a distinction between the formal and material parts of a composite.

He develops the objection as follows. Consider the case of a bronze sphere. In this case, the form sphere could easily have been introduced into some other material, wood, say, or marble. So it is easy and natural to distinguish the formal and material parts of that composite which is a bronze sphere. But there are some cases in which the form is not realized in a variety of matters but always in the same matter. For instance, the form of a man is his soul, and the human soul is always realized in flesh and bones. (Aristotle would rule out the possibility that a robot could be a human being.) In such cases, it seems much more unnatural to insist on the distinction between form and matter, given that a certain matter always accompanies a certain form.

Aristotle's reply begins with a polemic against the Pythagoreans and Platonists who are indeed ready to reject the material parts of such things as particular men. In the Pythagorean view, as in some forms of Platonism, the role of matter is taken by number. Aristotle responds that matter is in fact necessary to produce a difference between the various instantiations of the form. If, for instance, there were really no distinction to be drawn in the case of man between the formal and material parts, then one individual man could not be different from another, which is, of course, absurd. This shows that for all sensible substances (and Aristotle hints that this may also apply to supra-sensible substances), there must be matter as well as form in the particulars.

The chapter ends with what seems to be a concluding summary of the whole discussion of essence. This sits badly with the fact that the very next chapter, chapter 12, deals with a problem that is closely connected with the discussion of essence, the problem of the unity of the definition. This is another indication of the evidence that the whole work shows of having been cobbled together, presumably after Aristotle's death. This issue is discussed at length in the introduction (pages xl–lii).

But what *sort* of parts, you might very reasonably inquire, are of the form and what sort are not of the form, but of the compound?

Until this is cleared up, there will be no defining of the various items, what with definition being of the universal and the form. Any obscurity as to which of the parts are parts as matter and which not will occlude the account of the item too.

Well, some things evidently find themselves superimposed on occasion on items that differ from one another in their form. A circle may be imposed on bronze, on stone and on wood. In this sort of case it is widely accepted to be self-evident that the bronze or stone are excluded by their separability from being any part of the substance of the circle. Not but what a thing's never being observed to be separated from something else is no guarantee that it is not in quite the same position as the above. **[1036b]** (Suppose we only ever saw bronze circles – would that make the bronze a *formal* part of the circle? (I concede it might be hard to eliminate it in one's thinking.))

A very salient example is this: the form of man is always observed in flesh, bones and the familiar parts – are these then also parts of the form/account? Surely not. Surely they are matter, but matter which, by dint of the form of man's being imposed on no other things, is inseparable.

It is not usually contested that cases like this occur; the question is how frequent they are. Indeed, the cases of the circle and the triangle are contentious – it is sometimes claimed that it is somehow wrong to define them in terms of lines and continuity. The account of these latter is in all cases like that of the flesh and bones of the man and of the bronze and stone of the statue. The formal account is thus confined to the numerical expression, the account of the line being the account of two.

If you subscribe to the Theory of Forms, you have a choice. You can either (a) identify the dyad with Line Itself, or (b) call the dyad the form of the line. On view (b), it is conceded that in some cases the form and that-of-which-it-is-the-form are the same (as with the dyad and the form of the dyad), but it is insisted that this is not so with the line. There is, however, a catch. There will turn out to be one form for a plurality of items patently different in form (cf. the problems the Pythagoreans got into). And then we may as well introduce a single Form Itself, with nothing else really being forms. But this just means that Everything Is One.

This much has so far been established: that there is a difficulty about the business of definition and what the root of this difficulty is. One strays from the purpose of definition if one confines oneself to a formal account and simply discards the material element. Some things, it would seem, *just are* a this-in-a-that or such and such items *in such and such a state*. We should not, then, countenance the pet analogy of Socrates the Later between a circle and an animal, which both distracts from the truth and induces the supposition that the man without the parts is just as much on the cards as the circle without the bronze. The analogy, however, does not hold – the animal is a sort of perceptible object and there can be no defining of these which prescinds from processes and thus too none that prescinds from the parts being in the appropriate condition. As witness the fact that it is not the hand-in-absolutely-any-state-you-please that is a part of the man, but the hand with the capacity to discharge its function, viz. the hand that is alive. The lifeless hand, on the other hand (so to speak), is not a part of the man.

This argument, however, will not directly apply to the mathematicals, which are not objects of perception. Why, then, do we not here find accounts that are parts of accounts? Why are the accounts of the semicircles (not, remember, objects of perception) not parts of the account of the circle? Well, the fact is it makes no difference, *since some things that are not objects of perception have matter*. Indeed everything has a sort of matter, [1037a] provided only that it is not a what-it-was-to-be-that-thing and a *per se* Form Itself but a possessor of thisness. So semicircles, as we earlier pointed out, are parts not of the universal, but of particular, circle(s) – recall that some matter is perceptible but some intelligible.

Another point that emerges is that the soul is a primary substance, the body matter and *man* or *animal* the universal composite. Moreover, Socrates and Coriscus are, if we allow the soul of Socrates also to be Socrates, not simple (on the lips of some it is the soul of Socrates and on those of others the composite individual). If, on the other hand, Socrates just is this-particular-soul-and-this-particular-body, then the composition of the particular will mirror that of the universal.

A question that can be deferred, though not for ever, is whether there is some other matter in addition to that of substances of the kinds that we have been examining, whether we should look for some other sort of substance, such as, perhaps, numbers. This is in any case part of our purpose in trying to frame definitions for perceptible substances. After all, it is really up to physics and Second Philosophy to give us a theory of perceptible substances. For the physicist can by no means be content merely with some grasp of the matter of what he studies. On the contrary, his understanding of the substance specified by the account must be, if anything, greater.

Another issue in store concerns the way in which the contents of the account constitute parts of the definitions and what makes it the case that the definition is a single account. (I take it that the object is a single thing, but in what does the object's being a single thing consist, given that, after all, it has parts?)

In this discussion, we have stated:

· what a what–it–was–to–be–that–thing is, universally for all cases, and how it is to be identified *per se* with itself;
· why in some instances the account of the what–it–was–to–be–that–thing contains the parts of the thing defined and in others not; and
· that the parts that are thus present in the account of the substance will not be present as matter (the latter not being parts of that substance but of the composite substance, a substance to which in one way an account applies and in one way not, given that there is no account of it in conjunction with matter (which is indefinable), whereas there is an account to be had of it under specification of the primary substance, so that, for instance, the account of soul is the account of man);

(The key point is that *the substance is the form dwelling in the object* and that from it the substance that is a composite of the form and of matter is said to be a substance. So concavity is a substance, the composite of which and of the nose are the snub nose and snubness, in both of which nose will be present twice, whereas a composite substance, such as snub nose or Callias, will also contain matter.)

· that in some cases the what-it-was-to-be-that-thing and the particular are the same, [1037b] as with primary substances (e.g. if curvature is primary, then curvature and the what-it-was-to-be-curvature), primary substance indicating what is not given by an account of one thing in another as its material substrate;

· that, by contrast, anything that presents itself as matter or in conjunction with matter is not the same as the what-it-was-to-be-that-thing, not even as an accidental unity, like Socrates and something musical, which can be accidentally the same.

ZETA 12

In the last chapter of the extended discussion of essence, definition and form, Aristotle turns to what is perhaps the most serious objection to his doctrine. His claim, remember, is that definable essence is primary substance and that the primary substances are the species of genera. One feature that a primary substance must have on any account is unity. A substance must be a unity in a fundamental way. But the notion of substance as here defended depends, as we have seen, on the notion of definition (via that of essence), and it is far from obvious that a definition can be a unity.

Aristotle both formulates and meets the objection in terms of what he considers to be the fundamental style of definition, definition by division (though he suggests that the explanation can be extended to other cases). A definition by division is the same thing as a definition by genus and differentia. A species, for instance man, is defined as a genus, animal, and a differentia, two-footed. This style of definition is inherited from the Academy and there are many questions about it, with some of which Aristotle has dealt in his logical works. For the present discussion, we can simply bear in mind that a definition of this sort seems ineliminably to involve two things, genus and differentia. How, then, can it be a unity?

Aristotle's answer is sophisticated and resourceful. The genus and the differentia are not really two different things. This is because the differentia is a determinate thing, whereas the genus is not. Thus the genus is in a way subsumed in the differentia as an indeterminate component of it, almost as the matter of the differentia. The unity of the differentia is like that of the composite of form and matter, and this unity explains the unity of the definition itself despite its being apparently composed of different elements.

This answer is ingenious, but there is reason to suspect that Aristotle considered it to be something of a tour de force, since he returns to the problem both in Zeta 16 and in Eta 6. What, at any rate, is clear is that he regards the genus as being indeterminate. The thought is that if I ask what, say, the species horse is, I can be given a definite answer, whereas if I ask what the genus animal is,

I cannot be given an answer except by reference of one kind or another to the species that come under the genus. This conception of the genus will be in evidence in the anti-Platonist chapters which now follow.

Let us now make good the deficiencies of the treatment of definition in the *Analytics*. The problem broached in that work will turn out to be of no little relevance to the examination of substance. The problem that I have in mind is this: what makes it the case that, if we call the account of something a definition, that thing is a unity? Let us, for example, take *two-footed animal* as the account of *man* and let this account be a definition. Why, then, is *man* a single thing and not a plurality, viz. *animal* and *two-footed*?

The contrast with *man* and *white* is instructive. These items are a plurality when the one does not pertain to the other, a unity when one does pertain and the other, *man*, is in some way affected as the substrate, when they become a single thing, a pale man. In the present case, however, there is no pertaining of one item to another, on the assumption (generally made) that differentiae do not pertain to a genus. The reason for this assumption is that, if they did, and given that the differentiae that differentiate a genus are opposites, opposites would be pertaining to the same thing. And even if differentiae do pertain to a genus, the same reasoning will apply whenever there is more than one differentia pertaining to the same species, e.g. apteric bipedal pedestrian. What makes this lot a unity, not a plurality? It cannot be the mere fact of their compresence in a single genus, on pain of collapsing all the differentiae of that genus into a unity.

On the other hand, the elements of a definition had better constitute a unity. After all, a definition is a unitary sort of account and, since it is an account of substance, it must be an account of a single thing, given that, as we have stressed, substance picks out something that is a unity and has thisness.

It makes sense to look first at definitions by division. For the contents of such a definition are just the so-called primary genus and the differentiae, and the other genera are the primary and the differentiae taken in conjunction. An example of a primary genus might be *animal*, with the next genus down being *bipedal animal* and the next after that *apteric bipedal animal* (and the style can be continued for further items).

But surely, [**1038a**] just as it makes in general no difference whether the specification is by many or few differentiae, neither does it whether the specification is by a few or by just two – provided that of the two one is the differentia and the other the genus, as *animal* is the genus and the other the differentia in *bipedal animal*. If, then, the genus *simpliciter* does not exist over and above the specific forms constitutive of it, alternatively if it exists just as matter – in something like the way in which vocalization is a genus and serves as matter, the differentiae of which makes the forms and elements of speech – it is evident what the definition is, the account derived just from the differentiae.

It is in fact also important to obtain in division the differentia of the differentia. For instance, *pedestrian* is a differentia of *animal*, and the differentia of the *pedestrian animal* should be an object of our knowledge *qua* the animal's being pedestrian. It would, then, be quite wrong, on a proper procedure, to subdivide *pedestrian* into *winged* and *wingless* (a feature of current practice, but a mark of its ineptitude), but rather into *cloven-footed* and *whole-footed*, these being the differentiae of foot in as much as being *cloven-footed* is a way of being *pedestrian*. In fact this is how the division ought always to be prosecuted until the level of non-differentiation is reached, at which point there will be as many forms as differentiae of foot, and *pedestrian animals* will also be equal to them in number.

If all this is on the right lines, we have a clear upshot: *the last differentia will be the substance and the definition of the object.* This conclusion is recommended by the consideration that superfluous repetition is to be avoided in definition. (Some such, as it happens, is inevitable – to say *two-footed pedestrian animal* just is to say *animal having feet, having two feet*, and if the latter is in turn subjected to its own proprietary division, the differentia will be mentioned more times, once for each of the differentiae of the whole division.)

Anyway, if differentia arises out of differentia, then one differentia, the last, will be the form and the substance, whereas if division takes place through accidental features, so that *pedestrian* is subdivided into *white* and *black*, then the differentiae will be equinumerous with the cuts. All of which makes it clear that the definition is the account derived from the differentiae, and from the last of these under a correct procedure of division. Another way of showing this would be to reverse this kind of definition, for instance that of *man* to *animal bipedal pedestrian*. There is no need for *pedestrian* after the mention of *bipedal*. But the order cannot be intrinsic to the substance – what sense could be made in this context of earlier and later?

Let's call this a first shot at capturing the character of definitions by division.

ZETA 13

With chapter 13 we reach a profound difficulty in Aristotle's whole mature metaphysics and its interpretation. I have tried to deal with the central problems in the introduction. Here I shall merely remark on the apparent position of the chapter in the economy of book Zeta as a whole.

The task of Zeta is to find a criterion of substantiality, and we are told in Zeta 3 that there are four candidates, the substrate, the essence, the genus and the universal. Chapter 3 then reviews the claim of the substrate, which it appears to dismiss. After that the whole discussion of chapters 4–12 seems to be devoted to the discussion of the essence criterion, which it upholds and takes to show that the forms of species are the basic substances of the world. In a sense therefore, our question seems to have been answered, but it would surely be reasonable to expect some discussion of the other criteria, if only of a polemical nature. In fact, chapters 13, 14 and probably 15 are mainly devoted to an attack on the universal criterion of substantiality, which seems also, not unreasonably, to subsume a dismissal of the genus criterion.

The attack on universal substance is also an attack on Platonism, whose central metaphysical tenet Aristotle takes to be the acceptance of universal substance. This would seem to distinguish his own position clearly and satisfactorily from that of Plato, but it is here that the problem arises. The difficulty is that the account of substance as species and form which Aristotle defends seems to be as vulnerable to objections to universal substance as are the genera and the Platonic Forms. In the Categories, *Aristotle's conception of basic substances makes individual particulars the basic substances on whose being that of everything else depends, and this is indeed a clear contrast with Plato. However, in the* Metaphysics *he appears to have shifted his position, and his new doctrine that species are substances is much less obviously contrasted with Platonism. The problem has been discussed at great length and many scholars have concluded that Aristotle is simply being inconsistent. Others, however, have argued that the way in which species are universal is crucially different from the way in which genera are universal. I defend a version of this position in the introduction and argue that it redeems Aristotle's mature metaphysics from the relapse into Platonism of which it has often been accused.*

[**1038b**] I seem to recall that substance is what we are really interested in, so let's get back to it.

Well, the things that get said to be substance are (i) the substrate, (ii) the what-it-was-to-be-that-thing and (iii) the composite. But also (iv) the universal. OK, so we have gotten through two of these, the what-it-was-to-be-that-thing and the substrate. (Our view, remember, of the latter was that there are two ways of being a substrate, either as a possessor of thisness (as the animal is a substrate for its properties) or as matter is a substrate for the actuality.)

Let us now, therefore, turn our attention to (iv). It is, after all, a view not without support that the universal is a cause in a special way and that it is a principle.

The probability would seem, on the face of it, to approximate to zero that any of those items that are universally predicated could be a substance. Why so? Well, first off, the substance of each thing is something that is peculiar to each thing, not pertaining to anything else, whereas the universal is something common. Indeed, a thing is said to be universal just in virtue of the fact that its nature is to pertain to a plurality of things.

Of which, then, of this range of things would the putative substance be the substance? Either, it would seem, it must be (a) the substance of them all or (b) the substance of none. But (a) we can surely rule out, and the reason why it cannot be the substance of some one is that in that case all the others in the range will then turn out to *be that thing*! For if any two items have a single substance and a single what-it-was-to-be-that-thing, then they are themselves a single thing.

Another objection is that it is said of substance that it is not *said-of* any substrate, whereas a universal is invariably *said-of* some substrate.

Here is a possible line of response. The universal cannot indeed be substance in the way that the what-it-was-to-be-that-thing is, but it is *present in* the what-it-was-to-be-that-thing, in the way that *animal* is present in *man* and *horse*.

But to say this is surely to say that the universal is the subject of some account. Nor does it signify if the account does not cover everything that is in the substance. *That* would not stop it being the substance of something, just as *man* is the substance of the particular man in whom it is present.

But this will lead to the same result as before. The universal (e.g. *animal*) will be the substance of the species to which it peculiarly pertains.

And in any case is it not quite impossible, even outrageous, that a *this* and a substance (even if it can be composed of constituents) should be composed not of substances and the this-thing-here but of a quality? For then what is not a substance but a mere qualification will have priority to a substance and the *this*. This, of course, is out of the question. Neither in account, nor in time, nor in production can the affections have priority over the substance. To be so, they would have also to be separable.

Another objection is that the universal substance on this account will also be present as substance in the individual, Socrates. But this means that it will be the substance of two things, of *man* and of *Socrates*.

The general moral that emerges is this. If *man* and any other item similarly specified is a substance, then *none of the contents of the account of* man *is the substance of anything*, nor can such a content exist in separation from the entities covered by the account nor in anything else. By this I mean that *animal*, for instance, does not exist over and above animals x, y, z, etc., and the same goes for anything else that is a constituent of the account of a species.

I think these arguments show pretty conclusively that none of the things that pertain universally is a substance. And we have also given its due weight [**1039a**] to the fact that none of the things predicated in common picks out a this-thing-here, but rather such-and-such a kind. Once you demur at that, you have no end of difficulties, not least the Third Man.

And here's yet another way of making the point clear. It is not possible that a substance be composed from substances that are present in it *in actuality*. For two things that are actual in this way are never one in actuality. If, however, they are two in potentiality, they will on occasion be one – as instance the fact that a line double some length is (potentially) composed of two halves and that actualization of this potentiality would break the line in two.

So this is another reason why, if substance is single, it will not be composed of indwelling substances, a reason that Democritus showed that he fully understood with his claim that one substance could not be composed from two nor two from one (for him it is the atoms that are substances).

(The same will clearly go for number, on the quite popular assumption, at least, that number is a combination of units. Unless two *is* one, it cannot contain a unit in actuality.)

We have, then, our conclusion, but it is a puzzling one for the following reason. If no substance can be composed either (a) from universals (in that a universal picks out a such-and-such and not a this-thing-here), or (b) of substances present in it in actuality, then all substance turns out to be incomposite. But this means that there can be no account of any substance.

But this is acutely paradoxical. It is agreed on all hands – and has been stated early on by the present author – that substance is either the sole subject of definition or the subject of definition in some privileged way. And now we learn that not even substance can be defined – so nothing can be the subject of definition!!

Well, maybe not. Maybe in one way substance can be defined and in another it cannot. To find out what this riddle means, read on.

ZETA 14

The present chapter continues the attack on universal substance, directing its attention specifically against Platonic Forms. The precise nature of the argument, as well as its connection with the previous chapter and its success, is disputed, but the central ideas seem to be as follows.

If we assume that there are Platonic Forms, in the sense of universal substances, which Aristotle consistently takes Platonic Forms to be, then we must allow that these Forms, assuming that they are to be equated with the genera, must appear as parts in other entities. To take Aristotle's example, the genus animal comprises both the species man and the species horse. In Platonic terms, as here construed, this must mean that both man and horse contain animal, as well as their specific differences. But then the question arises whether the animal that occurs in man is numerically the same as the animal which occurs in horse or not. Aristotle argues that either answer produces absurdities, and, since in his view the question cannot be ducked by anyone who admits Platonic Forms, the argument shows that Platonic Forms are inadmissible.

It is unclear how this argument is supposed not also to apply to the species substance which Zeta has found to be basic, since the same argument occurs in connection with the relation between the general entity (species or genus) and the particular, but the assumption must be that Aristotle is relying on his demonstration of the intrinsic unity of the species, via the demonstration of the unity of definition. In any case, the present argument could be described as provocative rather than convincing.

No further considerations are required to show the fate of the doctrine that the Forms are (separable) substances, when held in conjunction with the view that the form is a construct of genus and differentiae. For if we admit forms, and if the genus *animal* is present in the form *man* and in the form *horse*, then either the genus is one and the same, numerically, in each case or it is different. (It is obviously one and the same in account – in giving an account in each case, it is the same account that one would go through.)

But, then, if there is some Man Himself as a *per se* and separable possessor of thisness, then its constituents, *animal*, say, and *bipedal*, must also pick out a this-thing-here and be separable and substances. But this means that the same must go for *animal* as well.

OK, let's suppose that *animal* is one and the same in *horse* and in *man*, no less than you are identical with yourself, then:

A. How is what is in two separate entities to be, [**1039b**] as supposed, a single thing? How, conversely, is *animal*, so construed, to fail to be separate from itself?

B. If both *bipedal* and *multipedal* pertain to it, we have a textbook impossibility. For opposites will be simultaneously pertaining to the same single thing and a possessor of thisness to boot. And how is the ascription of *bipedal* or *pedestrian* to *animal* to be so construed as to avoid this? Perhaps that they adjacently adjoin or are immixed? Hooey!

Clearly, then, *animal* is different in each form. But then two nasty consequences follow: first, there will be to all intents and purposes an infinity of things whose substance is *animal* (after all, there is nothing accidental about the composition of e.g. *man* from *animal*), and, secondly, there will be a large number of claimants to the title Animal Itself.

This is because (a) the *animal* present in each form is a substance (for it is not something else that is included in the account of *man* and, if it were, that other thing would be a constituent of *man* and his genus), and (b) all the constituents of *man* will be Forms. The genus, then, will not, impossibly, be the Form of one thing and the substance of another, and this means that every single *animal* present in the forms of animal will be Animal Itself!

And we can also inquire after the constituents of each *animal* and after the manner of its composition from Animal Itself. (And anyway how is *animal*, whose very substance is supposed to be *animal*, to exist apart from Animal Itself?)

Finally, if we move to perceptibles, we get all these problems and a whole host more in spades. But all this is poppycock. There are no Forms of perceptibles, *pace* you know who.

ZETA 15

The primary purpose of the present chapter is to continue the attack on Platonism from a different angle. The objection here raised to Platonic Forms is that they are indefinable. This would be, in Aristotle's view, a profound objection, since it would mean that the Forms, which Plato claims to be the foundation of science, would in fact be incapable of playing any role in science at all and also it would exclude Forms from being considered to be substances on the criterion developed in Zeta 4 that it is only definable essences that are substances in the strict sense.

Aristotle's procedure is to rehearse the familiar point that no particular can be defined. This claim is justified in the simplest case, that of ordinary destructible particulars, such as Socrates or this horse, on the insistence that such things are metaphysically compounds of form and matter. The argument is then applied to non-destructible particulars, but no comparable reason is given for their indefinability and no argument is presented against a Platonist who claims that the Forms are not particulars. For good measure the argument is then finally applied to particular items, such as the heavenly bodies, which are sensible but not destructible. It is clear that Aristotle's interest is as much in the conditions of definition as in the attack on Platonism.

So there is a substance that is the composite object and another, quite different substance corresponding to the account of the object. More explicitly, the former is substance by dint of being the account taken in conjunction with the matter, while the latter *is* the account *tout court*.

Now any substance that is specified as a composite is susceptible of (production and) destruction, whereas that of the account is not such as to be capable of undergoing destruction (nor indeed can it be produced – it is not the what-it-is-to-be-*house* that gets produced but the what-it-is-to-be-this-particular-house-right-here). A formal substance, in fact, either has or does not have being without involvement in processes of production and destruction, given that, as we have shown, there is no agency either to produce or to make them.

Hence too particular perceptible substances are excluded from both definition and participation in apodeictic demonstrative reasoning. This is because they have matter in them, the nature of which is to admit both of being and of not being, and this ensures that all such particular substances are susceptible of destruction.

We take it that apodeictic demonstration has to do with necessities and that definition is a scientific procedure. Now patently a piece of scientific knowledge cannot be a piece of scientific knowledge on one occasion and a piece of non-knowledge on another (anything like that is a matter of opinion not of science), and just so is it with apodeictic demonstration and with definition, an object that admits of being in a variety of states being, again, [1040a] an object of opinion and thus incontrovertibly not of definition and demonstrative reasoning.

It is a mark of items susceptible of destruction that their removal from the perceptual field renders them obscure to those that have cognition of them. It is not that the relevant accounts in the mind of the cognizer are disturbed, but still there will be neither definition of, nor demonstrative reasoning from, the objects that have disappeared. So always remember, if someone, bent on a definition, essays a definition of a particular, that you can always get him – there is no defining of particulars.

Nor, for that matter, can one define a Form, any Form. On the Theory, after all, Forms are separable particulars. And account of a Form would perforce consist of *names*, but the stipulation of a *name* cannot amount to a definition, since such a stipulation is not an object of understanding, so that the *names* used must belong to ordinary language. So these *names* will necessarily apply to at least some other object. I mean, suppose I was trying to define you. I would say you are *animal* that is *lean* or *white* or some such, all of which also apply to other things.

I anticipate the following riposte to this: there is nothing to stop all the *names* applying severally to a plurality of referents but jointly to the object of definition alone.

There are a number of things wrong with this. First, the *name*-string will also apply to each of its constituents (e.g. *bipedal animal* will apply to *animal* and to *bipedal*).

(Note: this must always be the case with eternal entities, which are prior parts of the combination, and indeed also separable, assuming that *man* is a separable entity. And either neither such entity is separable or both are. If neither, the genus will not exist over and above the forms, whereas, if it does exist, so too will the differentia. Also both are ontologically prior, so as not to be destroyed along with the combination of them.)

Secondly, if Forms are composed from Forms, and if, as we assume, components have less composition in themselves than what they compose, then such Form-components must themselves have a plurality of predication, as indeed *animal* and *bipedal*, for example, do have, on pain of the Form's failing to be an object of cognition. Such a Form would be one that *could not* be predicated of more than one item. But this is not admitted by the Theory, under which every Form is an object of participation.

So, as has been pointed out, the fact that it is impossible to define particulars is obscured in the case of eternal entities, conspicuously those which, like the sun and the moon, are one of a kind. It is a frequent mistake to ascribe to, say, the sun properties the loss of which would not prevent it from still being the sun, such as *telluricircumambient* or *noctilatent*, which suggests that if it came to a halt or began shining at night it would cease to be the sun! The root error of such folly is the failure to appreciate that *sun* picks out a certain substance. An equally widespread blunder is to ascribe to the sun properties that could also apply to some other entity, so that anything else that came by such properties would turn out to be *sun*!

The fact is that an account is general, [**1040b**] whereas the sun is *ex hypothesi* a particular, like Cleon or Socrates. Why indeed do people not attempt definitions of the Forms of Sun and Moon? If they did, they would only underline the truth of the present contention.

ZETA 16

Aristotle is now able to answer the question raised in chapter 2 about the extent of substances. Now that we know what it is to be a substance, we can arrive at a satisfactory list of what things are substance. Aristotle begins by eliminating the parts of animals, which clearly do not meet his criteria, and then rejects Being and the One, on the grounds that they are not applied to some single thing in the appropriate way.

The most important item to be rejected is, once again, the Platonic Forms, and the second half of the chapter is given over to a final polemic against the doctrine of universal substance, which Aristotle again seems to equate with Platonism. Plato was right, Aristotle allows, to insist that particular sensible entities cannot be basic substances, but the separable Forms that he proposed to take their place as the metaphysical foundation of the world are riddled with problems and must ultimately be rejected. The way is now paved for further consideration of what is involved in the notion of substance that has been reached, and in the last chapter of Zeta this question is approached from the new angle of the causal role of substance.

It is also quite clear that most of the things that are held to be substances are in fact potentialities. Certainly, animal parts are. (None of them can exist in separation and, after separation, their being is always that of matter.) Certainly, earth, fire and air are. (None of them is a unity; rather they resemble a heap until such time as, by subjecting them to concoction, something that is a unity is produced from them.)

A reasonable enough supposition would be that the parts of living things and the parts of the soul in close connection therewith are in fact both substances and potentialities, being as they are both in actuality and in potentiality on occasion, by dint of the fact that they have their principles of motion from something in their joints (which explains why some animals survive dissection). But not so. In fact, they are all in potentiality, at least when constituting a naturally single and continuous structure, not when stuck together by force or by grafting, which produces only freaks.

As for unity and being, the account of the former is not unlike that of the latter, and the substance of a single thing is single. Moreover, if two things have a numerically single substance then they are numerically single. So it is clear that neither unity nor being can be the substance of objects, any more than what-it-was-to-be-an-element or what-it-was-to-be-a-principle can be substances. (Science inquires into what the principle is precisely in order to bring it back to something more apt for cognition.)

No doubt being and unity are a little more plausibly supposed to be substances than principle, element and cause, but for all that they are not substances, any more than anything else that is common to several things. Never forget that a substance pertains to nothing except itself and its possessor, that of which it is the substance. Also, a unity would not be simultaneously in a range of places, whereas a common thing is thus variously present. From which it is clear that no universal exists over and above, and separately from, the particulars.

Theorists of Forms are right to give an account of Them that makes Them Separate, if They are supposed to be substances, but wrong in their claim that it is the One Over Many that is a form. This error stems from their inability to demonstrate which are these alleged imperishable substances existing over and above the perceptible particular substances. Their way out is to make the Forms formally the same as dear old perishable entities, merely adorning these perceptibles with the locution Itself, so as to have Man (Him)self and Horse Itself. And yet I take it that, had we never observed the stars, [1041a] they would none the less for that still have been eternal substances over and above the ones we know. So it may very well be necessary that certain unobserved substances exist as it is, even if we cannot know which they are.

Conclusions: NO UNIVERSAL PREDICABLE A SUBSTANCE ... NO SUBSTANCE COMPOSED OF SUBSTANCES ...

ZETA 17

In the final chapter of Zeta Aristotle appears to be adopting a completely new approach to his central question, what is it to be a substance? The approach here adopted turns on the notion that a substance is a cause. This obscure idea is one that he inherits from Plato, and it is perhaps best made intuitively palatable by being thought of in terms of a particular kind of explanation. Aristotle, in the Physics, distinguishes four kinds of explanation, material, motive, final and formal. The material explanation of a thing adverts to its matter and the motive explanation of an event adverts to whatever initiates it. The final explanation of either an event or a thing specifies its purpose (and Aristotle notoriously seems to apply this style of explanation to natural things as well as to artefacts), and the formal style of explanation shows why something must have some feature simply by dint of being the thing that it is.

In the context of the present chapter, the key idea is that the fact that form is explanatory is a further reason for associating it with substance, since it is reasonable to suppose that substance is the foundation of explanation as well as of being. Thus, although the present chapter does not explicitly make the connection with the arguments establishing form as substance that we find in Zeta 4–12, it is nevertheless in harmony with them and should be seen as corroborating the central doctrine of Zeta, that substance in the primary and strictest sense is immanent form.

Right, it's time to start again completely from fresh with this business of trying to say what and/or what kind of thing substance is. A possible spin-off will be an advance in understanding that kind of substance too which is separated from perceptible substances. And we can kick off with the observation that *substance is a principle and a kind of cause.*

The question why? is always the question why x pertains to y. The question 'Why is a musical man a musical man?' is either to ask why a man (y) is musical (x) or something else. However, to ask why a thing is identical with itself is not to ask a real question in the absence a clear grasp of the fact (perhaps that the moon is in eclipse) or of the object. Of a thing's self-identity, a man's being a man, as it may be, or a musician's being a musician, there is but a single account and a single cause in all cases. A possible challenge would be to the effect that each thing is indivisible from itself and that this constitutes the what-it-was-to-be-one-thing for it. But such an explanation is at once too broad ranging and too concise.

A real question would be why man is such-and-such an animal. This, evidently, is not the same as to ask of someone who is a man what makes it the case that he is a man. Rather the question is of the kind why x pertains to y. (It must, of course, be evident that x does pertain to y, on pain of the question's simply failing to arise at all.) Take the question 'Why does thunder occur?' This amounts to the question 'Why is a noise produced in the clouds?', and this clearly conforms to the model of why x pertains to y. (Same goes for 'Why are these salient objects, bricks and stones *on suppose*, a house?')

Real inquiries thus stand revealed as causal inquiries. (And the cause is, *logice*, the what-it-was-to-be-that-thing.) In some cases this is the beneficiary of something's existence, as, no doubt, with a house/bed, in others it is the process-originator, which is also a kind of cause (such a cause is sought for cases of production and destruction, whereas the former type is sought in connection with being too).

The real question is the most easily obscured when it comes to inquiries about things that are not predicated one of another. One might, for instance, ask 'What is *man*?', [**1041b**] but the simplicity of this formulation would be deceptive and conceal a definition to the effect that *x* is *abc*. The question must be analysed, on pain of generating a bastard which both is and is not a real question.

Moreover, since the existence of the object must be pertinently in place, the question is evidently why it is that the matter is as it is. 'Why', we might be asking, 'are these things a house?', setting up the riposte 'It is because the what-it-was-to-be-a-house is present in them'. Or 'Why', we might be asking, 'is this thing here a man?', or perhaps 'Why is this body here in the state that it's in a man?' And this shows that the cause that is the object of inquiry is that by virtue of which the matter is in the state that it is in. And this cause is the form, and the form the substance.

(What is also clear is that if something is simple there can be neither inquiry into it nor teaching of it. For such items the other manner of investigation is appropriate.)

One thing, too, may be so composed from another that the whole constitutes a single thing, not after the fashion of a heap but after that of the syllable. The syllable, of course, is not just its elements, nor are β and α the same thing as βα, and similarly flesh is not just fire and earth. (This is because on the dissolution of flesh or of the syllable, fire and earth and the elements respectively persist.) So the syllable is something in its own right, not just a heap of vowel and consonant but something different. Similarly, flesh is not just fire and earth, or hot and cold, but a different thing.

Now, this different thing must in its turn either be an element or be composed of elements. But,

A. If it is an element, the same reasoning can be redeployed (viz. flesh will now be composed of this element and of fire and earth and some further different thing) and this will generate an infinite regress; whereas,

B. If it is composed of an element, then it must be composed not merely of one but of several (on pain of its just being that single component element), so that it will again fall victim to the same argument as used with flesh and the syllable.

The further different thing, then, here must be taken to be something, and it cannot be an element but must rather be the cause, in a way, of the fact that one thing is flesh and the other a syllable (and this can be extended to other cases). And so this further different thing is the substance of each thing, in that it is the primary cause of being for it.

Also, not all objects by any means are substances – only those are in fact which are substances as being constituted under, and by, some *nature*. So it would seem to be a reasonable remark that this nature, which is a principle rather than an element, is their substance.

(An element being something into which a thing can be divided and which is present in it materially, as the α and the β are elements of the syllable.)

Book Eta

ETA I

The first two chapters of book Eta continue the programme of book Zeta, and they comprise what purports to be a summary of the whole discussion in Eta 1 and the final statement of conclusions in Eta 2.

The summary offered in Eta 1, however, is to say the least elliptical. The chapter does resume the main themes of Zeta 1−2 and briefly recapitulates the programmatic announcement at the start of Zeta 3, but the actual summary of the discussion is compressed into a very short paragraph, which, in any case, has almost nothing to say about the last four chapters of the book.

Where we might have expected to find helpful summaries of the various positive and negative points made in Zeta, we instead find a slightly inconsistent discussion of the claims of matter to be substance, which were, of course, dismissed in Zeta 3. Now we learn that in a weaker sense matter too can be said to be substance, but this is not taken to undermine in any important way the thrust of Zeta.

The blatant lack of correspondence between the summary in this chapter and the actual course of Zeta is striking even by Aristotle's relaxed standards in this respect. It is naturally grist to the mill for those who argue that the composition of Zeta must have taken place in stages.

Well, we have a considerable amount of material to hand. [**1042a**] Now we must put it all together to achieve a synthesis and so end up with a complete position.

We have, I take it, already expressed what we are after as the causes, principles and elements of substance. And substances can be grouped into those which are universally accepted as such and those which figure only in the proprietary accounts of particular schools. Those generally acknowledged include (i) fire, earth, water and air and the other simple bodies, as also (ii) plants, plant parts, animals and animal parts and, lastly, (iii) the heavens and their parts. By contrast, it is a distinctive

233

philosophical position that Forms and mathematicals are substances.

In a quite different way, it has been the upshot of our arguments that the what-it-was-to-be-that-thing and the substrate are substances. And in yet another way of arguing, it turns out that the genus, more than the species, is a substance and the universal more than the particulars. Of course, the Forms are hardly unconnected with the universal and the genus (the argument that Establishes the One is also that which establishes the other).

Well, the what-it-was-to-be-that-thing is in any case a substance, and, since the account of a what-it-was-to-be-that-thing is a definition, an account has been offered of definition and of *per se* being. But of course the definition is an account and an account has parts. So it behoved us to consider *in re* the parts what kind were parts of the substance and what kind were not and whether they were also the same as the parts of the definition. And, by contrast, neither the universal nor the genus are, in fact, substances. (The jury will remain out for a little on the Forms and mathematicals, which are, of course, advocated in some quarters to be substances over and above the perceptible ones.)

Anyway, back to the non-controversial substances. These are the perceptible substances, and the hallmark of all perceptible substances is the possession of matter.

Now the substrate *is* a substance, but in a variety of ways. It is so, on the one hand, as matter. By matter I mean what (a) is not a possessor of thisness in actuality but (b) is a possessor of thisness in potentiality. On the other hand, the substrate is also, differently, substance as the account and shape. The latter is something which (a) has thisness and (b) can be separated in account. And, in yet a third way, the substrate is a substance as the composite. The distinctive features of the composite are that it can be produced and destroyed and that it can be separated *simpliciter*. (Simple separability is a feature of some, but not all, account-specified substances.)

As for matter, there can be no doubt that it is a substance. Consider all changes between opposites. In all of them there is something that underlies the changes. Take locational change – it involves something that is at p_1 at t_1 and at p_2 at t_2. Or take quantitative change – there is something that is of size x at t_1 and either lesser or greater at t_2. Or qualitative change, in which there is something that is, say, well at t_1 and ill at t_2.

Nor is it otherwise with substantial change. **[1042b]** Here too there is something which is being produced at t_1 and being destroyed at t_2, a substrate as having thisness at t_2 and a substrate by way of privation at t_2. All the other changes are attendant on substantial change, but there are one or two of the other changes that do not bring with them a substantial change. It by no means follows from a thing's having matter for the purposes of locomotion that it must also have it for those of production and destruction. (See the *Physics* for the distinction between *simpliciter* and non-*simpliciter* production.)

ETA 2

In the light of the new discussion of matter in the previous chapter, Aristotle is now in a position to make still clearer the sense in which form is substance, and thus to bring the whole discussion to a conclusion. The distinction between matter and form that is operating in this discussion anticipates the distinction between potentiality and actuality which is the subject of book Theta. In the present discussion the matter of a sensible particular is associated, in Aristotle's usual way, with its potential and the form with its actuality.

More saliently, Aristotle now associates the actual aspects of the being of a composite particular with the species differentia of the genus to which it belongs. Thus the doctrine that form is substance becomes in its final formulation the doctrine that the differentia is substance. It is not entirely clear how this conclusion is to be generalized beyond the case of sensible substances, but it has also become clear progressively through the whole discussion that it is sensible substances, and especially animate beings, in which Aristotle is most interested.

Well, substance as material substrate is non-controversial, and it is this substance which has its being potentially. So the chore we have left is that of saying what the substance is of perceptible things that has its being as an actuality.

It was, it seems, the opinion of Democritus that things are subject to three differentiations. In his system, the (material) substrate persists as a one-and-the-same, but is differentiated either by *rhythm* (aka shape), *slant* (aka position) or *deployment* (aka disposition). However, it is clear that there are in fact a large number of differentiations. For instance, the account of certain things is based on the mode of combination of their matter, with some (e.g. honey-drink) being combined by blending, some (e.g. a besom) by binding, some (e.g. a book) by gluing, some (e.g. a chest) by nailing and some by a combination of combinations. Certain other things are accounted for in terms of their position, such as the threshold and the lintel, which differ only in their location in the design. There are things, too, that are picked out by their timing (as supper and breakfast) and those that are identified merely by their location (which is how we tell one wind from another). And, finally, there are things of which we give an account by making use of some feature that they have as perceptible entities, their hardness, as it might be, or softness, their density and rarity, their aridity or moisture. Sometimes it is a selection of such features that does the job, sometimes all, in all cases by dint either of some surfeit or of some deficiency.

So, of course, for each of these ways of distinguishing there is a corresponding way of saying that something *is*. A threshold *is* a threshold because *this is where it goes*, with the concomitant that the what-it-was-to-be-a-threshold picks out what-it-was-to-fit-in-here, whereas the what-it-was-to-be-ice picks out what-it-was-to-be-solidified-in-a-certain-way. There are, of course, also things for which the what-it-was-to-be-that-thing is defined in terms of all these differentiations, by their being the outcome to some extent of mixture, to some extent of blending, to some extent of fastening, to some extent of solidification, to some extent of the other modes of differentiation. Consider a hand, or a foot, and you will see what I mean.

What this shows is that it is important to understand the kind of differentiation, given that they are the principles of the beings of things. Some things, that is, are marked out by being more or, conversely, less F, by being dense, say, or rare and so forth, which are all instances of the surfeit/deficiency differentiation. (Anything differentiated by its shape (or its smoothness/roughness) is an instance of differentiation by straightness and curvature.) And there are some things for which the what-it-was-to-be-that-thing consists in their being mixed [1043a] and the what-it-was-not-to-be-that-thing in their not being mixed.

All of which serves to underline that, assuming that the substance of each thing is a cause of the what-it-was-to-be-that-thing, it is to these differentiations that we must turn if we are inquiring into the cause of the what-it-was-to-be-that-thing for each of the perceptible things. It is not that any of the differentiations cited *is a substance*, not even in conjunction with matter. Rather for each thing the differentiation is something kind of like substance. In the case of substances it is the

237

actuality itself that gets predicated of the matter, whereas in the case of other definitions it is that which is most nearly the actuality.

This bears some explication. Suppose, for instance, the definiendum is *threshold*. The definition will be *wood/stone in* ⟨. . .⟩ *situation*. (OK, there may be times with this latter definition when we need to rope in the purpose of the building as well.) Suppose the definiendum is *ice*. Then the definition will be *water frozen/solidified in* ⟨. . .⟩ *manner*. Suppose it is *harmony*, and you have ⟨. . .⟩ *mixture of high and low pitch*. You get, I take it, the picture. And what this shows is that for different kinds of matter there will be a different actuality and thus account. In some cases, the actuality will be the combination, in others the mixture and in still others some other one of the differentiations.

So if you want to define *building*, you have three choices. Either (i) you can list the stones, bricks and beams, giving what is potentially a building, viz. the matter of a building. Or (ii) your account can be *enclosed space for the housing of objects or persons* (or something to that sort of effect). In this case what you are giving is the actuality of the building. Alternatively (iii) you can put them both together and give the third, composite substance. Quite a good way of putting the point is to say that the account in terms of differentiation is the account of the form–actuality, whereas that in terms of the constituents of the thing is more the account of the matter.

Such composite definitions are the kind once favoured by Archytas. E.g. definiendum: *no breeze*; definition: *absence of motion in a large volume of air*. Here the air is the matter and the stillness is the actuality and substance. Definiendum: *calm*; definition: *flat sea*. Here the sea is the matter, the flatness the actuality-shape.

Our discussion has made clear both what perceptible substance is and the ways in which it is it. A perceptible substance can be such either as matter, or as shape and actuality or, thirdly, as the composite of matter and actuality.

ETA 3

The discussion has, as we have seen, been brought to a conclusion at the end of Eta 2, and the remaining four chapters constitute a kind of series of appendices to that discussion — which is not to say that they do not broach many new aspects of Aristotle's position. The present chapter deals with three loosely related questions which can be very roughly grouped under the rubric of form and actuality. Eta 4–5 has some further points to make about matter, and Eta 6 returns to the subject of Zeta 12, the unity of the definition, which is in many ways the crucial element in the whole discussion of substance.

The first section of the chapter deals with the problem that the names of things are standardly ambiguous in their indicating either the composite particular or the form of the particular. This problem is mildly vexatious in practice, but it does not raise any profound theoretical difficulties, provided that we keep clearly in mind that it is form which is to be identified with essence and substance. This being so, it is true that in one sense a horse, say, is identical with its substance, though not in another.

The second section of the chapter contains a polemic against those who argue that substance is merely a kind of comprehensive list of the material components of the particular. As against this, Aristotle repeats his position that substance is a formal principle, which can be reduced neither to any one component of the particular nor to the mere list of all of them.

The final section of the chapter contains a rather puzzling discussion of the similarities between substance and number. The key points are that neither number nor substance can be indefinitely divisible, that they cannot remain what they are if they lose some part of themselves, that they are both determinate actualities and determinate natures and that neither of them admit of the more and less.

It is vital to be aware that there are sometimes real cases of uncertainty as to whether some name signifies a compound substance or the actuality and shape of a compound substance. Does, for instance, *building* pick out the compound, viz. *protective structure composed from bricks and stones in* ⟨. . .⟩ *arrangement*, or the formal actuality, *protective structure*? Does *line* signify *longitudinal dyad* or just *dyad*? Does *animal* indicate *embodied soul* or, what is the substance and actuality of a specific body, just *soul*? To be sure, animal could very easily indicate either. It is a name not so much specified by a single account as focused on a single thing.

Anyway, this issue about names matters in some contexts but really has nothing to do with the examination of perceptible substance. [**1043b**] This is because it is the form-actuality to which the what-it-was-to-be-that-thing attaches. So *soul* and what-it-was-to-be-a-soul are the same thing, whereas *man* and what-it-was-to-be-a-man are not the same thing (unless *man* can pick out *soul* too, in which case they are in a way the same and in a way not).

Now it is clear if you look into it that it is not the case that both the letters and their combination are components of the syllable, nor that a building is both its bricks and the combination thereof. This has to be right – the combination/mixture is not *composed of* the things of which it is a combination/mixture. And the point bears generalization: suppose we define *threshold* by its disposition – the disposition is not composed of the threshold but, if anything, the threshold of the disposition.

And in the same spirit *man* does not consist of *animal* and *bipedal*. Rather, if we take these latter to be the material components, there must be some additional entity, neither an element nor composed of an element, but just that very thing the removal of which leads to a purely material account. But if this entity is the cause of being and substance for the object, then it is the account of this that is the account of the substance itself.

As for this substance, it must either (a) be eternal or (b) be (i) perishable without perishing and (ii) produced without being produced. Elsewhere, a proof with expository clarification has been given to the effect that the form is neither made nor produced. What gets made is a this and what gets produced is a composite.

And the question whether, if something is perceptible, its substance is separable is not to be resolved by anything that has been said so far.

(Well, in fact it obviously cannot be in some cases; for instance, there cannot be separable substance for things like *building* and *tool* which cannot exist beyond their instances.) Maybe cases like *building* and *tool* are not even substances anyway. Maybe nothing is a substance that is not a natural composition. It would be perfectly reasonable to hold that it is a nature, and only a nature, that is substance among things that perish.

There is even in this an application of that old chestnut of Antisthenes' acolytes (and other buffoons of the same kidney). Their claim was that a definition of what something is is impossible. Their reason – that a definition is a mega-account. By contrast, on this view, it is possible to explain what something is like. So with *silver*, say, one cannot give a definition of what it is, but one can perfectly well say that it is like tin.

On the same lines as this, there is some substance for which a definition/account is possible, viz. composite substance (whether perceptible or intelligible), whereas the primary components of such substance are indefinable. And the reason for this is that a definitional account indicates an x said of a y, with the y being the matter and the x being the shape-form.

It is also clear that, if there is any way in which substances are numbers, then this is the way in which they are so and not as the numbers of units (though this view has its supporters). After all, definition too is a kind of number, being divisible right down to indivisibles (for a definitional account cannot be infinite), and this is just the sort of thing that a number is. With number, too, if you remove or add some one of the things of which the number is composed, you no longer have the same number on your hands but a different one, even if the subtraction or addition is as small as you like, [**1044a**] and in the same way neither the definition nor the what-it-was-to-be-that-thing will persist through any subtraction or addition.

And there is a further similarity. A number must be a thing-by-dint-of-being-which-it-is-a-unity, even though in our present ignorance we cannot give an account of just what it is by dint of which a number is a unity. (Unless it is not one after all: the choice is between (a) a number is not a unity by something like a heap or (b) a number is a unity and then it becomes necessary to give an account of what it is that makes it a single thing with many components.) And just so the definition is a unity and, again just so, this cannot at present be explained. And there is nothing odd about this result. The account of both number and substance is the same, and substance is a unity in the same way that number is. A substance is not, *pace* certain theorists, a unity as a kind of unit or point. Rather each substance is an actuality, a natural kind. (One other point: number does not tolerate the more/less, nor does formal substance. If any substance does, it is substance-with-matter.)

OK, we have covered:

(a) Commonly agreed, non-controversial substances get produced and destroyed – in what way is this possible and in what way not?
(b) Reduction of substance to number.

Enough definitions for now, I fancy.

ETA 4

This chapter is a fascinating investigation of various refinements of the notion of matter and of its application in explanation. Aristotle begins by making clear that the motion of matter is, as we might say, relative, with any given particular being derived from its proximate and also more remote and ultimately primary matter. For example, a box is derived from wood as its proximate matter, more remotely from earth, which is the proximate matter for wood, and more remotely still from the primary matter which underlies earth too. This hierarchy of matter makes it possible for the same entity to be realized in different matters and for different entities to be realized in the same matter. The main consequence of this for explanation is that, since explanation should always be in terms of the proximate cause, the characteristics of the proximate matter play a crucial part in material explanation. This has the consequence that there is a fundamental difference between the explanation of things with sensible, and that of things with non-sensible, matter.

A point now about material substance. Even if we assume that all things are produced from the same primary material, or from the same things as primary materials, and that it is the same matter that serves as principle for all products, it is still the case that each thing has its *proper matter*.

The proper matter, for example, of phlegm is sweet or fatty stuffs, the appropriate matter of bile bitter stuffs (or some other – though they may both come from the same stuff). And the same object will contain many matters when one material thing is itself the matter of another. To take our example, phlegm is materially composed of the fatty and, assuming that the sweet is derived from the fatty, from the sweet. But phlegm can also be produced even from bile, by the dissolution of the bile into its primary matter. You see there are two ways in which x can be produced/derived from y: either (a) y lies on the material route to x or (b) y has been dissolved into its material principle.

What makes possible the derivation of diverse products from what is a single material is the efficient cause. From wood, for instance, you can produce a box or a bed. There are, however, still some things whose diversity requires material diversity. For instance, that a saw cannot be produced from wood is not something to be laid at the door of any efficient cause. No efficient cause could make a saw out of wood or wool. If, conversely, it is possible for the same thing to be produced from different matter, obviously the skill/principle operating as the efficient cause is the same. Were both the matter and the efficient cause different, so too would be the product.

If, then, we are doing causal investigation, given this diversity of causal accounts, all admissible causes should be included in our account. What, we might ask, is the material cause of *man*? The sort of answer that we want is something like *menstrual fluid*. What is the efficient cause? Candidate answer – the *sperm*. What is the formal cause? The what-it-was-to-be-that-thing. What, finally, the final cause? The purpose of having *man* around. [**1044b**] (Of course, maybe the latter two are the same thing.) The point is that the proximate causes must figure in the account. In the material case, we can leave out fire and earth but must include the material peculiar to *man*.

With natural substances which get produced this is always the right method, assuming (a) that the causes are the ones we favour and that there are neither more nor fewer of them and (b) that it is the causes that interest the scientist. Not so, however, with those natural substances that are eternal. For it may well be that some of these lack matter, or that they have matter but matter unlike that of producible substances and characterized only by locomotion.

Also, anything that is natural but not a substance – say, an eclipse – will lack matter – there will be some substance that is their substrate. What, we ask, is the cause of an eclipse? (i) What is its matter? And here the answer is that the eclipse does not have matter but that the moon, which is a substance, is its substrate. (ii) What is the efficient cause – what extinguishes the light? The earth does. (iii) The final cause may well be an n/a. (iv) The formal cause is the account, which, however, illuminates nothing unless, as an account, it includes the efficient cause. (What does this mean? Well, take the question What is *eclipse*? and the answer *Privation of light*. This is the account minus efficient cause. Add *by the passage of the earth between moon and sun* and you have the account plus efficient cause.)

Sleep is another such natural non-substance, but here the primary substrate is moot. The animal, you will say. Of course, but in what respect – in what respect as a *primary* substrate? And here the sort of answer we want is the heart (or whatever). OK, what about the efficient cause? And when we have cleared that up, what exactly is it that happens to the animal in sleep? Happens, that is, to the primary substrate (whatever it turns out to be), not to the animal as a whole? Candidate answer – an ⟨. . .⟩ lack of motion. Sure, but by dint of what exactly happening to the primary substrate?

This chapter contributes three further supplementary points to the discussion of matter, most of them familiar from Aristotle's other discussions of matter. The first is that nothing can have matter unless it comes into, and passes out of, being by a process. Thus a point, for example, does not have matter. The second contribution is the explanation that matter is potentially both of a pair of contraries, being potentially the positive contrary by dint of having the form in question and being potentially the negative contrary by dint of privation of that form. This leads naturally to the final point, which is that the position reached does not commit us to saying that, for instance, wine is potentially vinegar or a body potentially a corpse. It is not the wine but its matter that is potentially vinegar (and similarly with the body), and that by privation of the form of wine (or of the soul).

Now some things have, or do not have, being without any process of production or destruction. Examples are points (if they have being) and forms in general. It is not, for instance, *white* that gets produced but white wood, assuming all production to be from something and of something. So it is not the case that all opposites are produced from one another. The derivation of a white man from a black man is quite different from that of *white* from *black*. Nor indeed does everything have matter. On the contrary, you only have matter if you get produced and are in mutual interchange with something else. Anything which either does, or does not, have being without any change does not have matter.

There is, however, a philosophical problem about the relation of the matter of each thing to its opposites. For example, the body is potentially healthy and disease is the opposite of health. Is, then, the body in potentiality diseased no less than healthy? Is water in potentiality no more wine than vinegar? If we balk at this, perhaps the thing to say is that water is the matter of wine by dint of being in a certain condition and having a form, whereas it is the matter of vinegar by dint of a privation and unnatural corruption.

And another question is why it is that wine is not the matter of vinegar, nor vinegar in potentiality. After all, vinegar is produced from it. Why, similarly, is a living thing not in potentiality a corpse? Perhaps processes of destruction are accidental, [1045a] so that it is the matter of the animal itself that is the potential and matter for the corpse in the event of destruction and mere water that is the potential and matter of vinegar. It is then only by a replacement on the night/day model that a corpse comes from an animal or vinegar from wine.

Any things, in fact, which in this way change into one another must do so by returning to their matter. If an animal comes from a corpse, what happens is that the corpse changes first into its matter and from this into an animal. Similarly, vinegar only gets to wine by going first through water.

ETA 6

The last chapter of Eta is devoted to a problem which became progressively important in the second half of Zeta and has been central to Eta, the problem of the unity of definition and thus of substance. In Zeta, Aristotle's assumption has been that definitions are purely form, in the sense that it is only form, and not the composite of form and matter, that is defined. In Eta Aristotle seems more sympathetic to the definition of the composite. This also leads to a modified approach to the problem of the unity of definition. In the account of formal definition in Zeta, unity was ensured by the fact that the genus is in a way contained in the differentia. In the account of composite definition in Eta, unity is secured by the fact that the material of the composite is in a similar way subsumed under the form. Matter is apt to be shaped by form, and form is apt to impose structure on matter. It is in this mutual adaptation that the unity of the composite and of its definition consists.

This notion of mutual aptitude points clearly towards the doctrine of potentiality and actuality, which has been in the background to the discussion of substance in Zeta and Eta. Potentiality and actuality are the central subjects of book Theta, after which the subject of unity is again considered in Iota.

To resume now the issue introduced above which applies both to definitions and to numbers, let us ask what is the cause, for these items, of their being a unity.

Now anything that has a plurality of parts but is not just the sum of these, like a heap, but exists as a whole beyond its parts invariably has a cause. In the case of bodies, for instance, it is contact that is the cause of being a unity for some of them, whereas for others it is viscosity or some other such affection. And with a definition what makes it a single account is not mere connection (as the *Iliad* is merely connected together) but the fact that it is a unity that it is the account of.

OK, but then the question is what makes *man*, say, a unity. Why is *man* a unity and not a plurality, of, as it may be, *animal* and *biped*? Especially if, as claimed in certain quarters, Animal Itself and Biped Itself exist. Why is *man* not the latter entities together? In which case it will not be by Participating in Man (or any other unity) that men exist but by Doing So in two things, Animal *and* Biped. And in every other way as well, *man* would not be a unity but a plurality, viz. *animal* and *biped*.

At any rate, it is plain as a pikestaff that the patrons of this method of definition and accounting (who do not shrink from offering definitions and accounts), cannot give a principled resolution of this difficulty. If, on the other hand, our account is adopted, so that we allow a matter component and a shape/form component, one existing potentially the other in actuality, the difficulty in which the question is held to be shrouded disappears. The present question, to wit, would be the same as would confront a definition of [*cloak*] as *round bronze*. Here the name would pick out the account, and then our question would be what the cause is of the fact that *round* and *bronze* are a unity. But then it is immediately clear that, if *this* is the difficulty, it has evaporated: the account is of a unity because one component is material, the other shape/form.

And then suppose we ask 'But what is the cause of the fact that what has potential being exists in actuality?' (Not, of course, asking for the productive cause in the case of the outputs of production.) But here the answer is just this: *there is no other cause* of the fact that what is potentially a sphere is in actuality a sphere. It is just being-a-sphere that is the what-it-was-to-be-that-thing for them both.

Let us, by all means, not forget that there is intelligible matter no less than there is perceptible matter. In all cases, however, there is a material and an actual component to the account. *Circle*, for instance, is *plane figure*. Anything, however, that has neither intelligible nor perceptible matter [**1045b**] (a possessor of thisness, a quality or a quantity) is straight off a unity of a kind (in each case), just as each is also straight off a being of a kind. (Hence the absence of both being and unity from definitions.) The what-it-was-to-be-that-thing too is a unity of a kind straight off, just as it is a being of a kind. And that is why none of these things has some other cause of their being a unity any more than they do of their being a being of a kind. Each is straight off both a being of a kind and a unity of a kind, nor is the cause of this their having being and unity as their genus nor their separability from particulars.

And it is because of this problem that some philosophers have espoused participation, though this plunges them into difficulties about what the cause of the participation is or indeed what participating is anyway. Another variation is to go for 'cohabitation'. Lycophron, for instance, has it that knowledge is the cohabitation of knowing and the soul. Yet another option is to say, say, that living is the synthesis or colligation of soul to body.

But the same argument ends up covering all the cases. For being well will just as well be the cohabitation/synthesis/colligation of soul and health; bronze being a triangle will be the synthesis of bronze and triangle, to be white to be the synthesis of surface and whiteness. And the cause of this is that both a unity-conferring account and a differentiation of potentiality and actuality are being sought; whereas, as here advertised, the last matter and the shape-form are the same thing and a unity, the one in potentiality the other in actuality. So what is being sought boils down to the question what the cause of unity and of something's being a unity is. For each thing is a unity, and the thing in potentiality is in a kind of way a unity with the thing in actuality.

There is, therefore, no cause here (except, boringly, whatever has caused the transition from potentiality to actuality). And, of course, with things that do not have matter, they are all unities of a kind *simpliciter*.

Book Theta

THETA I

The subject of book Theta is potentiality and actuality, which we have seen to be closely connected with the solution eventually given by book Eta to the problem of unity. The first chapter of Theta gives a kind of overview of the subject. Potentiality and actuality can be considered in regard to process or change and in regard to substance. The first five chapters of Theta are devoted to the former aspect and the next four to the latter. Within the kinds of potentiality that are connected with change, Aristotle now makes a variety of distinctions. The most important of these is that between active and passive potentiality. The agent of change has an active potentiality to change the object of change, and the object has a passive potentiality to be changed by the agent. Both these potentialities are realized when the change takes place, and in a way they can be considered the same potentiality. But from the point of view of the agent and the object separately, they are, of course, distinct.

The last section of the chapter deals with the subject of incapacity, the state in which some entity does not in fact have a potentiality which it would be natural for it to have. In discussing both potentiality and incapacity, Aristotle is in harmony with the account given in Delta XII (page 131).

We have, then, covered the bearer of primary being, that item relative to which all the other categories of what is are focused. This item is substance. (The accounts of the other bearers of being depend on the account of substance, those, that is, of quantity, quality and the other items with similar accounts. For, as our earlier discussions have made clear, all these will turn out to contain the account of substance.)

But, now, accounts of that which is are indeed distinguished as those of the *what*, quantity or quality, but they are also distinguished as those of potentiality and those of entelechy, and also by function. It is, then, time that we had a look at potentiality and entelechy.

And let us look first at potentiality as per the primary account, for all that it is not the most useful for our immediate project. For it is not the case that [**1046a**] potentiality and actuality are confined to those cases the account of which is in terms of process. With the account of primary potentiality behind us, however, we may deal with the other kinds of potentiality in the context of our treatment of actuality.

We have elsewhere indicated that there is a plurality of account of potentiality and of having a capacity. But we can weed out all those kinds of potentiality the account of which is by homonymy. In some cases, for instance, the account depends on some similarity, as in geometry, and ascriptions of potentiality and non-potentiality are sometimes based on a thing's being or not being in a certain way.

On the other hand, there are kinds of potentiality that are related to the same form, and these are all kinds of principle, their accounts relating to a single potentiality, which is a principle of change either (a) for something else or (b) for the thing that it is in *qua* something else. There is, for example, the potentiality for being affected, which is a principle, in the subject of change itself, of being changed by the action either of something else or by itself *qua* something else. And in contrast there is a condition of immunity to deterioration and destruction at the hands of an external agent or of the bearer of the condition itself *qua* something else through a principle of change. And in defining any potentiality of these kinds we must bring in the account of primary potentiality.

Another way of looking at it is that the account of potentialities of this stripe is in terms either of their having, or undergoing, an effect or of their doing either of these well. But this means that in accounts of the latter kind those of the former kinds of potentiality are somehow present.

An uncontentious point is that there is (a) a way in which the potentiality for action and affection are a single potentiality (something's potentiality may consist in its own capacity to be acted on and in something else's having the capacity to be acted on by it) and (b) a way in which they are different. They are different as follows:

(i) the one potentiality resides in the thing affected. For it is affected through containing a certain principle, and through its matter's containing a certain principle, such that different things are affected by different agents. For instance, an oily thing is inflammable and a thing with such-and-such a proclivity to subside is compressible and so on.

(ii) the other potentiality is in the agent. Examples are warmth and architecture, the one in the calorific agent, the other in the builder. (Corollary: to the extent that something is a natural product it is not affected by itself in any way. And this is because it is a single thing and not one thing and another.)

As for non-potentiality and incapacity, this is the corresponding privation to this kind of potentiality, and so every potentiality is of the same thing under the same aspect as the corresponding non-potentiality. There are, though, a plurality of accounts of privation, as follows:

(i) that which does not have F;
(ii) that whose nature is to have F, if it does not in fact have F (either at all or at a time when it would be natural for it to have F, and either in a particular way, as, say, completely or to some extent or other);
(iii) in some cases, things constituted to have F and lacking it through force, are said to be deprived.

THETA 2

In the second chapter, Aristotle introduces further refinements in the notion of a potentiality for change. He distinguishes between a rational and an irrational potentiality. Rational potentialities occur only in animate and rational beings, conspicuously in men, while irrational potentialities occur both in animate and in inanimate beings. The salient difference between them for Aristotle is that rational potentialities can produce either of their correlated pair of opposites, whereas irrational potentialities can produce only one. To take Aristotle's example, heating can produce only heat and not cold, whereas the rational potentiality of medicine can produce either health or disease. The arts and sciences in general are Aristotle's principal examples of rational potentialities.

In the last section of the chapter, Aristotle distinguishes between a mere potentiality to act and a potentiality to act well. The latter is always accompanied by the former, of course, but the former can easily occur without the latter. For many purposes, it is the latter potentiality to act in which we are interested.

Now there are principles of this kind in inanimate things and also others in the animates, in the soul and especially in the rational element of the soul. **[1046b]** So it is not a surprise that some of the potentialities too will be without, but others with, reason. Hence it is that all crafts and productive branches of sciences are potentialities, given that they are principles of change in something other than the bearer or in the bearer *qua* something else.

Now potentialities with reason are in every case the same as the potentiality of the opposite, whereas, with potentialities without reason, each potentiality is the potentiality of a single thing only. Thus heat is a potentiality only for warming, whereas medicine is a potentiality for both sickness and health. The explanation of this is that a science involves an account, and the same account elucidates both the object and the privation of it, though not, of course, in the same way. There is thus a way in which it is the account of both object and privation, but also a way in which it is rather the account just of the object. As a result, sciences of this kind must treat of opposites, though they are of the one *per se* and of the other not *per se*. This is because the account is of the object *per se* but of the privation in a way by accident, given that it is by negation and deletion that it elucidates the opposite. It is the opposite that is primary privation, which consists in the deletion of the correlate.

However, opposites are not to be found in the same entity and moreover science is a potentiality of that which has reason, and since the soul also contains a principle of process, we have the result that, whereas the salubrious produces only health, the calorific heat and the frigorific cold, the scientist is a potentiality for opposites, given that an account is of both opposites of a pair (though not in the same way) and in a soul containing a principle of process. For the soul will initiate both processes from the same principle, applying them to the same object. Hence it is that things whose potentiality is conditioned by reason produce the opposite outcome from those whose potentiality is not so conditioned, there being a single principle, the reasoned account, which embraces them.

What does not stand in need of defence is that a potentiality for mere action or affection is attendant on that for *good* action or affection, whereas the converse is not always the case. Patently, the man who does something well must also do it, whereas it is not, to be sure, necessary for the man who merely does something also to do it well.

THETA 3

Having now set out his conception of potentiality, Aristotle specifically defends it by attacking those who have most conspicuously rejected any distinction between potentiality and actuality. These are the School of Megara, whose position is that one is only potentially, say, building when one is actually building. Thus potentiality and actuality always coincide and should be identified.

Aristotle points out various absurd consequences which he holds to flow from any such identification. In the first place, it would mean that there could be no art or skill, possession of which just consists in having a potentiality which persists between its episodes of actualization. Secondly, no perceptible properties could exist except when perceived, and, more generally, there could be no coming into being at all and everything which did not exist would be impossible. This is a defence of the distinction by a reductio ad absurdum *of its denial.*

In the last section of the chapter, Aristotle offers a kind of etymology of actuality, stressing its primary connection with action and process. This fits better with the account of potentiality and actuality stressed in the first five chapters of Theta than with that defended in the next four.

Now there is a chestnut that enjoys quite widespread popularity, not least in Megara, to the effect that x is capable of being/doing the F only when it actually is/does the F. So the non-builder is no bearer of a potentiality for building – the only such bearer is the builder *when engaged in his building.* Etc., etc.

Exposing the idiocy of this buffoonery will not long detain us.

An immediate, and undeniable, upshot is that, if a man is not engaged in building, he is not even a builder!! (Assuming, as I take it that we may, that to be a builder is to have a potentiality for building.) And the case generalizes across the skills.

But, then, we assume that it is impossible to have such skills without having learned and acquired them at some time and that, thereafter, it

258

is impossible not to have them unless one has at some stage dis-acquired them (and the options here [**1047a**] are simple forgetting, physical or other impairment or mere lapse of time. One option that is not available is the destruction of the object of the skill – it is eternal!). So, the moment a man lays down his trowel, he will no longer have the skill. But, of course, he may very well start building again at any moment. But when (and how) will he have acquired the skill to do so?!

The argument carries over by parity of reasoning to the inanimates. There will be nothing cold or hot or pleasant or perceptible at all unless someone is currently observing it. So this Megarian wisdom turns out to boil down to rehashed Protagoras. And there is none. Nothing will have perception either unless it is actually engaged in perception. But then, if we take something to be blind if, though constituted to see, it does not, at times when it is natural for it to see and in ways in which it is natural for it to see, in fact have sight, the same individuals will go blind several times a day – and deaf to boot!

And that is still not the end of it. I take it that anything deprived of its potentiality lacks capacity. But then anything not currently happening will lack the capacity to happen, and anyone who says that what lacks the capacity to happen either does, or will, exist will be a liar (it was just this that the lack of capacity prevented them from doing). So our brilliant Megarian friends will now have done away with all process and generation! The standing will remain on their feet, and the seated on those places where the Megarians keep their brains, to eternity. After all, if anything is currently sitting, it is never going to arise – for it is not possible for anything that lacks the capacity to stand up to stand up.

I take it that we have qualms about taking a stand (or seat) on this. I take it that it is apparent that potentiality is one thing and actuality is another thing. The problem with Megarianism is that it collapses potentiality and actuality, and this is a fairly serious-scale chunk of common sense to be affronting.

OK, it is possible for something (a) to be capable of being something and yet (b) not be it, or indeed (a') to be capable of not being something and yet (b') to be it. And the point generalizes across the categories. It is possible that a potential walker not be walking and that a potential non-walker be ambulant.

The thing which is capable of doing/being the F is the thing such that there is no impossibility of its engaging in the actuality of which it is said to be the potentiality. So take sitting. If something has a capacity for sitting and if everything is set up in a way conducive to its sitting, then there will be no impossibility in sitting's actually coming about in that thing. Ditto with being moved or moving, with standing or sitting, with being or becoming or with not being and not becoming.

Important note on terminology: the name *actuality*. In our discussion it is assimilated to entelechy. This constitutes a shift away from processes towards other things as well. For an actuality is thought most normally to be a process, and it is normal to hesitate before ascribing being in a process to things that do not have being, for all that certain other predicates are ascribed, such as that these non-entities are the objects of thought and desire. It is just being in a process that is not ascribed to them and this is because actual being is a precondition of being in a [1047b] process, whereas such actual being is just what these things lack.

There are plenty of non-entities with potential being. Only, not being in entelechy, they are not.

THETA 4

Having rejected the identification of the potential with the actual, the error of the School of Megara, Aristotle now attacks the converse mistake, that of supposing that there is something which is possible but which will never be realized in actuality. To admit such a thing would be to deny the existence of the impossible. The impossible is precisely that which will never be realized, and it is a mistake to hold that it is still in some sense possible. What this shows is that anything that is possible must at some time be realized. The notion of a potentiality that is never realized is a contradiction in terms for Aristotle.

Now if what we have stated either is the possible or something attendant on the possible, there can, of course, be no question of its being a true thing to say that x is capable of being but will not be. But on these lines we seem to miss out badly on things that are incapable of being.

To see what I mean, take a man who says that the diagonal of a square is capable of being measured but will not be measured – such a person would lack a grasp of what it is to be incapable of being – on the grounds that there is nothing to prevent something that is capable of being or becoming from not being or being about to be. It is, after all, a necessary conclusion of our premises that there is nothing impossible in what is said, given that we might suppose that what is not but is capable of being either is or comes into being. And yet what is said is impossible – for it *is* impossible that the diagonal be measured. (We must distinguish carefully between the false and the impossible; it is false that you are standing up at this moment, but it is not impossible.)

Alongside this, we must take it as evident that if the being of b follows necessarily from that of a, then the possibility of b must follow from the possibility of a. For unless b be of necessity possible, what is to stop its being impossible for b to be possible?

Suppose, now, that a is possible. We would not get an impossible result if, with a being possible, a were supposed to be – but then b must needs be. But b was supposed to be impossible!

OK, let b be impossible. But then, if b is impossible, so must a be. But if the first of these two options is impossible, so must the second be.

So, then, if a is possible, so will b be (if it really is the case that the being of b be necessarily entailed by that of a). And if, given this relation between a and b, b were not in this way to be possible, then the ab relation will not be as supposed either. And if the necessity of b's being possible follows from a's being possible, then if a has being so must b. After all, the necessity of the possibility of b, given the possibility of a, amounts to b's also necessarily being at the time and in the manner if a is at the time at, and in the manner in, which it was supposed to be possible.

THETA 5

Aristotle now distinguishes between natural and acquired potentialities. This distinction coincides with that between irrational and rational potentialities, the subject of chapter 2. It is not possible to acquire an irrational potentiality, nor to have a rational potentiality inborn. The latter must be acquired by various kinds of training, habituation and education. Aristotle also stresses in this chapter something that has been implicit in the earlier discussion, that a potentiality must have a determinate objective. A potentiality is a potentiality for a determinate action in determinate circumstances. He also adds the point that rational potentialities are different from irrational ones in that they are not automatically triggered by the bringing together of the active and the passive potentiality. The possessor of a rational potentiality can decide not to use it even in circumstances in which it would be quite natural for him to do so. This is because rational choice is a condition for the deployment of a rational potentiality. Thus the appropriate conditions are both necessary and sufficient for the triggering of an irrational potentiality, but only necessary for that of a rational one.

Potentialities as a whole we can divide into the in-born, such as the senses, the acquired by practice, such as that for flute-playing, and the acquired by learning, such as that for skills. The last two of these groups are to be had on the basis of previous actualization, the potentialities, that is, that are conditioned by habituation and the grasp of an account. But such previous actualization is not required for those potentialities which, not of this kind, are conditioned merely by the bearer's undergoing a certain affection.

Furthermore, [1048a] the bearer of a potentiality has a potentiality *for x at time t and in manner m* (here insert all other qualifiers required by the definition). Also, some things are such that their process-potential is conditioned by a rational account and their potentialities are supported by reason, whereas other things, being themselves non-rational, have correspondingly non-rational potentialities. Given this, it is necessary that potentialities of the former kind reside in an animate bearer, whereas those of the latter kind are to be found in both animates and inanimates. There is also a further peculiarity of potentialities of the latter, non-rational kind, and it is this: whenever the potential active and the potentially affected items are associated in conditions propitious to the potentiality, the former must of necessity act and the latter must of necessity be affected. This is by no means the case with potentialities of the former kind.

The explanation of this is that non-rational potentialities are all such that there is a one-to-one correlation of potentiality and effect, whereas with the rational potentialities each potentiality is correlated with a pair of effects. So if the potentiality was, in the rational cases, automatically triggered, it would yield simultaneous contrary effects, which is clearly not possible.

And from this it follows that the triggering of such potentialities must be under the control of something else, and in saying this I have in mind desire or rational preference. The arrangement is that selection of the two possible contrary effects is under the control of desire and takes place when the context is propitious to the potentiality and the agent is associated with the item affected by the potentiality. And a necessary consequence of this is that, whenever a rational bearer of potentiality is, in propitious circumstances, moved by desire for the object of the potentiality, it acts on it. (The object affected by the potentiality must, of course, be in the appropriate condition. Its not being so will preclude the action of the agent. Hence the superfluity here of a *ceteris paribus* clause. The possession of a potentiality just is the possession of a potentiality to act, and such a potentiality is not unconditional but depends on the obtaining of propitious circumstances, which include the satisfaction of a *ceteris paribus* condition. The *cetera*, that is, are made *paria* by the very contents of the definition.)

Hence too not even the possession of a wish or desire for two simultaneous, or even contrary, actions makes their performance possible. Such a performance is excluded by the intrinsic character of the potentiality. The potentiality is not a potentiality for doing both things at the same time just because it is a potentiality for doing both the things of which it is the potentiality.

THETA 6

Aristotle now passes to the subject of potentiality in relation to substance and being. He begins by illustrating the notion of actual being by such examples as a statue which has been produced from wood rather than one that is still in the wood. A thing is actual when it has already become the thing that it is, having previously merely had a potentiality to be it. This sense of actuality is closer to such modern notions as actualization, as opposed to activity or enactment, which suit better the actuality of process.

Aristotle insists on the diversity of kinds of actuality and potentiality and illustrates these in some detail. A special case is that of the infinite (and the void), which has being only in potentiality and not in actuality (and thus seems to be an exception to the rule stipulated in chapter 3). The last part of the chapter draws an especially important distinction between incomplete and complete actions. The latter, but not the former, contain their purposes within themselves. To dance, for instance, is to engage in a complete action, whereas to fetch wood for a fire is to engage in an incomplete one. It is only the complete kind of action that constitutes the highest realization of the form of a being.

We have now covered that potentiality the account of which is conditioned by process. It is time to move on to actuality.

Here are two questions:

(i) What is actuality?
(ii) What *sort* of thing is actuality?

In fact, as we look into potentiality, a certain fact will become apparent. This is that we do not only give an account in terms of potentiality of things constituted to initiate processes in other things or to have processes initiated in themselves by others (and this either *simpliciter* or in some particular manner). There is also another way potentiality can be included in an account – and indeed it is for the sake of bringing this to light that we have studied the former cases so closely.

The fact is that the actuality of an object is its *obtaining*. And by this I do not have in mind its obtaining in that manner which we have accounted for in terms of potentiality. We say that something exists in potentiality if it is like a statue of Hermes existing in a block of wood or like a half-line existing in a whole line, given that the half-line could be detached. We say too that a man is a scientist in this way, even when he is not engaged in theorizing, providing that he is capable of theorizing. In the case when he is, we say that he is a scientist in actuality.

What we are getting at here will become clear inductively on a case by case basis. (It is not, in any event, right to seek a definition for everything – for some things an overview is to be had by analogy.) The point is that there is an analogous relation between the following pairs of items: [1048b] the engaged builder/the apt-to-build, the waking/ the sleeping, the engaged observer/the sighted animal with eyes closed, the thing carved from matter/the matter and the processed/the unprocessed. We then simply require that the former element of these pairs be the actuality by definition, and the latter the potentiality. (However, not all accounts of being in actuality are similar; rather there is an analogy between them. For instance, a is in b/relative to c::x is in y/ relative to z. Some cases of actuality stand as a process to a potentiality, others in the manner of the relation of a substance to a kind of matter.)

In addition, the account given of the being in potentiality and in actuality of the infinite, of the vacuum and of other such items is different from that of such being for many things that are, including such items as the thing seeing, the thing walking or the thing being seen. Ascriptions of potentiality and actuality to these latter items are, on occasion, straightforwardly veridical. Take the account of the seen item. The account is sometimes based on the fact that the item is currently being seen and sometimes on the fact that it is capable of being seen.

With the infinite, however, things are different. The infinite does not have being in potentiality in such a way that it will, at some time, have being in actuality and be separable. It is only cognitively separable. The absence of any end to division yields the result that the actuality of the infinite has being in potentiality, but not that it is separable.

Now, none of those actions characterized by some limit is a goal; they are all to be reckoned among the goal-related items. Consider thinning. Not only is the attenuation itself of this kind, but also its objects, when being thinned, are undergoing just such a process, being not yet in that state which is the purpose of the process. A carry-on of this sort is not an action, at any rate not a complete action, in as much as the mere procedure in itself is not a goal. By contrast, the proceedings that contain their own goal are an action.

Let us illustrate this contrast. When I am seeing, I also, and at the same time, have seen; when I am minded, I also, and at the same time, have been minded; when I am engaged in intuition, I also, and at the same time, have been so engaged. On the other hand, when I am learning, I am not also, and at the same time, in a state of having learned; when I am recovering my health, I am not also, and at the same time, in a state of having done so.

Prosperity and having prospered are simultaneous, as are happiness and having been happy. Were this not so, it would be necessary for the relevant carrying-on to cease at some point, as is the case with thinning. In fact, this is not the case. Rather, when one is living (in whatever manner), then one has already lived.

Given this discrimination of procedures, one lot are to be labelled processes, the other activities. All processes are incomplete, e.g. attenuation, learning, walking and building, which are both processes and incomplete procedures. For it is not that at the same time one is walking and one has walked, is building and has built, is coming into being and has come into being or is in process and has been in process. It is one thing that is initiating a process and another that has initiated one. By contrast, it is the same thing that has seen and that is seeing, that has, and that has had, intuition. And our word for procedures of this latter kind is activity, for those of the former kind process.

These and similar considerations give, we think, a clear answer to our original questions, both (i) and (ii).

THETA 7

This chapter addresses three problems. The first is that of specifying the circumstances in which one thing is potentially another. Aristotle distinguishes his two familiar cases, and says that in the case of the rational potentiality of an art, the potentiality is realized when it is both the case that the artist desires it and that there is no obstacle, whereas in the case of irrational potentialities all that is required is the second condition, that there should be no obstacle. He gives the example of earth which is potentially a man, but only after it has first become semen and then been deposited in a womb.

The second point that Aristotle makes in the chapter is that if one thing is made out of another, then the latter is always in a sense a potentiality for the former. Thus what is actual for one thing will be potential for another, and this continues down a hierarchy which leads ultimately to mere matter, which is not the actuality of anything but in a sense the potentiality for everything. It is a topic of traditional controversy whether Aristotle really accepts the existence of such matter.

The last issue concerns the relation of potentiality and actuality to the substrate/subject of a thing. Aristotle distinguishes two cases where one thing is a subject for another, the case where a substance is subject for its accidents and the case where matter is subject of a form. In the first case it is the accidents not the subject that is potential, whereas in the second case it is the subject, the matter, which is potential. Aristotle characteristically reinforces this point with an appeal to ordinary language. We do not use the nouns for the subject to describe the second case (which we do in the first case), but only adjectives derived from them. For instance, we say that a box is not wood, but wooden.

A question that we must confront is when a particular item has potential existence and when not – for it is not at just any time that it has it.

Consider: is earth potentially man? Well, no. **[1049a]** Earth is potentially man at those times at which it has already become seed. Indeed, perhaps not even just at those times. Similarly, not just anything would be made healthy by medicine or by chance. There is, rather, something that is susceptible of being made healthy, and it is this that is potentially healthy.

Now the definition of what comes into being-in-entelechy from being-in-potentiality through the operation of thinking is that it comes about whenever there is a wish for it (providing nothing extrinsic blocks it), whereas the definition of that which comes into being-in-entelechy in (here) what is made healthy is that it comes about just at those times at which there is nothing intrinsic to it to block this. In just the same way, a thing is potentially a house if (a) there is nothing in its contents and in its matter to prevent it from becoming a house, and (b) there is nothing that must be added to it, subtracted from it or changed in it. And the point can be generalized for all things the principle of whose production is external to them.

If, conversely, you take something the principle of whose production is intrinsic to it, such a thing is potentially all the things that it will be off its own bat, if nothing extrinsic prevents it. By this condition seed is *not* potentially a man. For to become such it needs to be in something else and to undergo a change. At such times, however, as it is already, through the principle intrinsic to it, of the appropriate kind, then is it already potentially a man. Before then it requires the other principle. And this is just as it is with earth too. Earth is not, as it is, potentially a statue. To be potentially a statue it must undergo a change and be bronze.

Now, the accounts of some things are framed not in terms of some x but in terms of being x-esque. We do not, for instance, account for a box as being wood but as being wood-esque. In turn, the wood is not said to be earth but to be earth-esque. (Perhaps, indeed, we can go on. Perhaps earth is to be said to be, not some other x, but some-other-x-esque.) About such things, we can make a generalization: in all cases such a thing is potentially the next item in the series *simpliciter*. So, for instance, the box is neither earth-esque nor earth, but rather wood-esque, and this is because it is wood that is potentially a box and it is this that is the matter of a box. (Wood *simpliciter* is matter for box *simpliciter,* and this bit of wood right here is the matter for this box right here.)

If, moreover, there is something primary accounting for which as x-esque in terms of some other x is no longer available, then this item is primary matter. If, for instance, earth is air-esque and earth is (not fire but) fire-esque, then it is fire that is primary matter. And such matter is not a *this-something.* (It is in this respect that the subject of predication and the substrate differ, in being or not being a *this-something.* The subject of affections is a man, say, a conjunction of body and soul, and its affections are such things as musicality and pallor. Hence, indeed, the subject, when music arises in it, is not called music but musical, and a man is not called pallor but pallid, not walk or movement but walking or moving. This is the same point as with the x-esque.)

Now, in all such cases, the last item in the series is a substance. In other cases, however, in which what gets predicated is some form and a *this-something,* the last item in the series is matter and substance–as–matter. And, in the end, it is right and proper that accounts in terms of being x-esque are applied to matter and to affections, **[1049b]** since it is both such items that are indeterminate.

Time to wrap up the discussion of when, and when not, to ascribe potential being to an item.

THETA 8

In this chapter Aristotle defends one of his most striking and characteristic theses, that of the priority of the actual over the potential. Aristotle most definitely holds that the chicken comes before the egg. It does so in three ways, in thought, in time and in substance. The priority of the actual in thought consists in the fact that one cannot have a conception of a potentiality without already having a conception of the actuality, while the reverse is not the case. The priority in time of the actual refers to the species rather than the individual. At the level of the individual, the potential, the egg, must indeed precede the actual, the chicken, but this is a relatively trivial fact. It is much more important that the species chicken must temporally precede the egg. The substantial priority of the actual is defended in terms of the equation of actuality with form and thus with the principle and cause of a thing's being and that of potentiality with matter. There is also an argument that the actual, being imperishable, must have priority over the potential, which is perishable.

On the basis of our elucidation of the variety of accounts of priority, there can be no question but that actuality is prior to potentiality.

The application of this remark is not restricted to potentiality as defined and whose account is that it is a principle of change either in some other thing or in itself *qua* other, but is extended, quite generally, to every principle of process or stasis. (The point is that a nature is something of the same kind as a potentiality. It is a processing principle, though it operates not in something other than what has it but in that very thing *qua* other.)

OK, so the actuality is prior to any potentiality of this kind. It is prior in account and in substance and both is, in one way, and is not, in another way, in time.

We need not linger over showing that it is prior in account. The primary potential, indeed, just is what is potential by dint of admitting of actualization. Our account, for instance, of *potential builder* is *possessing a potentiality to build*, that of *potential see-er* is *possessing a potentiality to see* and that of *potential visible* is *possessing a potentiality to be seen*. The account generalizes across the other cases, from which it follows of necessity that the account of the actuality is prior to that of the potentiality and that the knowledge of the former is prior to that of the latter.

With temporal priority, the situation is as follows. A species member in actuality has temporal priority over a member of the same species in potentiality, provided that it is not numerically the same species member. The point is this. Take a man already in being in actuality (or a crop or a see-er). Well, his matter (or the seed or visual capacity) have temporal priority – it is these things that are potentially man (or crop or see-er) but not yet so in actuality. But other things, which do have being in actuality, have temporal priority to these items, and it is from these other things that the items have been produced. In all cases, that which is in actuality is produced from that which is in potentiality by the agency of something that is in actuality, a man, say, coming from a man and a musician being produced by agency of a musician. In all cases, there is some primary initiator of the process, and this process-initiator already is in actuality. The point has already been made in the discussion of substance that every output of a production is produced from something, as something and by something and that the latter is conspecific with it.

A corollary of this is the general acceptance that if you have never built anything you cannot be a builder, that your never having picked up a guitar precludes your being a guitarist. It is, you see, *by playing the guitar* that, when one is learning to play the guitar, one learns to play the guitar. And this generalizes for all skill acquisition. This circumstance is the source of a celebrated piece of sophistry. The challenge goes: will it not then be the case that someone who lacks science x is doing the very thing which is the province of science x? (On the assumption that the learner is not a possessor of a science.)

This, however, is a mistake. Whenever something *is* being produced, some part of it must always *have been* produced. Quite generally, whenever something is undergoing some process, some part of it *must already have undergone* the process. (See our discussion of process.) So, by parity of reasoning, [1050a] the learner too must possess some part of the science he is learning.

This argument too, then, shows that in this aspect as well the actuality is prior to the potentiality in terms both of production and of time.

And – here we get to the crunch – the actuality also has *substantial* priority.

First reason: things posterior *in production* have formal and substantial priority. A man has formal/substantial priority over a boy, and a human being has formal/substantial priority over a sperm. And the reason for *this* is that the man/human being already has its form, whereas the boy/sperm does not.

Second reason: every output of a production *progresses* towards a principle, towards an end. A principle is something for whose sake something else is, and an end is something for whose sake a production occurs. But the end *is the actuality*, and it is for the sake of this actuality-end that the potentiality is brought in. It is not in order to possess sight that animals see, but in order to see that they possess sight. And similarly we bring in architects to build and are endowed with a capacity for theory in order that they may engage in theory. It is not, by contrast, to be endowed with a capacity for theory that we engage in theory – not, that is, unless we are acquiring theory by practice (and here we are only engaging in theory in a kind of a way or perhaps we do not need to engage in theory at all). Also, the point of matter's being in potential is that it may progress to the form. Whenever, by contrast, it has actual being, then it is (actually) in the form.

The same applies to other cases, especially those whose end is a process. Instructors, after all, think that they have demonstrated their end when they have displayed an actual up and running object of their instruction. And for these reasons nature does the same. This has to be the case, on pain of a rerun of Pauson's Hermes. You could not say whether the statue was in or out, and so would it be with knowledge of nature too. The fact is that a thing's active function is its end, and its actuality is its active function. Hence, indeed, the very name, actuality, has an account based on the active function, which is extended to the entelechy.

Now, it is true that there is a difference among actualities. For some, the use of the actuality is the last stage. Seeing is the last stage in the actualization of sight – no other active function over and above it is derived from sight. For others, though, there is some such product. The output of architecture is not just an act of building but also a house. Well, even so, the actuality, which is straightforwardly the end in the first type of case, is even in the latter kind of case at any rate more of an end than the potentiality. For the act of building resides in the object of building and has both its becoming and its being simultaneously with the house.

So, for all cases in which there is some other product over and above the mere employment of the potentiality, the actuality resides in what is made (with the act of building residing in the thing being built and the act of weaving in the thing being woven, etc., always the process residing in the thing being processed). And in cases in which there is no other function over and above the actuality the actuality resides in the subjects, seeing in the see-er, theorizing in the theorizer and life [**1050b**] (and so also well-being, a certain quality of life) in the soul.

I think that all this makes it pretty clear that the substance and the form are actuality. And the argument also suffices to show that actuality has substantial priority over potentiality and also, as we have said, one actuality always has temporal priority over another, going back to that which always, and in a primary way, initiates process.

There is, however, also a profounder aspect to the substantial priority of actuality. That is that (a) eternal things have substantial priority over perishables and (b) no eternal thing has potential being. And here's why:

Every potentiality is simultaneously the potentiality of the negation of what it is the potentiality of. It is indeed true that what could not pertain to something would not pertain to it in any circumstances, but that does not mean that it is not the case that anything that does have a potential for being might not be actualized. So something with a potentiality for being admits both of being and of not being, so that the same thing has a potentiality both for being and for not being. And conversely what has a potentiality for not being admits of not being. But whatever admits of not being is perishable either *simpliciter* or under the aspect relative to which it is said to admit of not being, whether in terms of place, of quantity or of quality.

But this means that nothing that is perishable *simpliciter* has being in potentiality *simpliciter* (it could, of course, have being in potentiality under some aspect, such as that of quality or that of place). So all such things have being in actuality.

And similarly nothing which has being of necessity has being in potentiality (and these, after all, are the primary things in as much as, if they did not have being, nothing would). Neither indeed does any process that may have eternal being have being in potentiality. And if there is any eternal mover, it is not in potentiality that it is in motion. (It can, however, be moving in potentiality relative to its point of departure and point of destination – there is no reason to prevent matter pertaining to it relative to these.)

Hence it is that the sun, the stars and the entirety of the heavens are eternally in actuality, and we can chuckle at the concern of the natural philosophers that they may one day come to a halt. Nor are they wearied in their task. For in their case movement has nothing to do, as with perishable things, with the potentiality of its negation, such that the continuity of movement would be laborious to them. Labour is an effect of substance as matter and potentiality, not of actuality.

But imperishables are also imitated by things immersed in change, such as earth and fire. They too are always in actuality, having their movement *per se* and in themselves. By contrast our earlier discussion has shown that the other potentialities are all potentialities for the negation (anything with a potentiality to initiate process in some particular way also has the potentiality not to initiate it in just that way, such potentialities being those accompanied by reason). On the other hand, the same potentialities not accompanied by reason will only be potentialities for the negation by their mere presence or absence.

A final thought: if there are any such natures or substances such as the purely logical thinkers claim the Forms to be, then there must be some thing that is very much more knowable than the Form of Knowledge and something very much more fully moved than the Form of

Movement. [1051a] It is these entities that will be rather the actualities, for which the Forms will be the mere potentialities.

I think we have made the point: actuality has priority not only over potentiality but over every principle of process.

THETA 9

This chapter draws a connection between the doctrine of actuality and potentiality and good and evil on the one hand and mathematics on the other.

With things that are good, the actuality is better than the potentiality. This is because the actuality rules out the actuality of the corresponding evil, whereas at the level of potential being it is possible for both the good and the evil to coexist. Evil itself is said by Aristotle to be posterior to the potentiality. This means that it does not have actual existence in itself, unlike the good, and is thus not one of the eternal and imperishable things.

The priority of actuality over potentiality is also evident in mathematics, especially geometry. A geometric proof consists in actualizing in thought the geometric relations potentially present, from the perspective of thought, in the figure.

Here's an argument to show that the serious in actuality is both better and more worthy of reference than the serious in potentiality. Anything that is accounted for in terms of its potentiality has also, and by the same token, a potentiality for opposites. Anything, for instance, which includes the potentiality for being healthy in its account is also something that includes in it that for being ill. And this at the same time. The potentialities, therefore, for the following are the same: being well/ being ill, being at rest/being in motion, building/demolishing and being built/being demolished.

The potentiality, then, for opposites pertains simultaneously to the subject. But, of course, opposites cannot simultaneously pertain, and the respective actualities (such as being well and being ill) cannot both pertain at the same time. It follows that one of the actualities must be the good. But the possession of the potentiality is both opposites in the same way or neither. So the actuality is better. And it is no less necessary with evils that the end–actuality is more evil than the potentiality. What merely has the potentiality for evil is just as much one opposite as the other.

Evil, then, is revealed by the argument not to be over and above matters of fact. This is because evil is naturally posterior to its potentiality. Hence too the circumstance that there is among the primordial and eternal things nothing that is evil, or defective or corrupt (for corruption is to be counted as an evil).

It is in actuality too that geometrical constructions are found. Discoveries happen when divisions are made. If the divisions had already been made, the constructions would not have needed to be found. In fact, before discovery, the divisions pertain to the figures, but only in potentiality.

Problem: why are the angles of a triangle equal to two right angles? Answer: the angles around a single point are equal to two right angles.

But, then, if the line parallel to the side had already been drawn, the proof would have been obvious at a glance.

Problem: why, quite generally, is the angle in a semicircle a right angle? Answer: if three lines, two base lines and a plumb line to the midpoint, are equal, then . . .

The conclusion is again clear at a glance, if you know that premise.

Clearly, then, discovery takes place by the bringing of the things that are in potentiality to actuality. And the cause consists in the fact that the thinking involved is the actuality. It follows that it is from the actuality that the potentiality is recognized and it is for this reason that it is by constructing that we gain knowledge. (The numerically single actuality is, of course, posterior in production.)

THETA 10

This chapter appears to digress from the central theme of Theta and return to a topic covered in Epsilon, namely being as truth and non-being as falsity. Aristotle examines the way in which statements can be true or false, which corresponds with the way in which things can have being or non-being. It draws an important distinction between the being of, and truth about, composite things and the being of, and truth about, simple things. Composite things are themselves of two kinds, their components being either necessarily or not necessarily combined in the way in which they are. In the case of things which are necessarily combined in the way they are, the same statement is always true or false, true if it combines the components in the way in which they are combined and false if it combines them in some other way. With composite things which need not be combined as they are, however, the same statement can at different times be now true and now false.

With non-composite, simple things, there is no possibility of combination of components in thinking about them. They can merely be intuited and spoken. There is thus no possibility of miscombination, so that falsity about such things is not possible. This also means that such things cannot have non-being, so that they are pure actualities and imperishable.

That which is and that which is not are accounted for both in terms of **[1051b]** the categories and in terms of the potentiality or actuality of these items or of their opposites. And further, and most fundamentally, that which is is the true and that which is not is the false. And these latter apply to things by their being put together or apart, and that in such a way that to think that what is put apart is put apart and that what is put together is put together is to hold a truth, whereas to have one's beliefs disposed oppositely to the facts is to have fallen into error.

Well, well, but when is that spoken of as true or as false on one hand and when is it not? We must ponder the account to be given of this.

It is not on account of our truly thinking that you are white that you are white; rather it is on account of your being white that we who assert as much are telling the truth.

Now some things are always put together and cannot be put apart, whereas others are always put apart and cannot be put together and still others admit of both being put together and being put apart. Against this background, to be is to have been put together and to be one and not to be is not to have been put together but rather to be several. Now in connection with things admitting of being either way, the same belief and the same account becomes on occasion both false and true, and it is possible for the holder of it at one time to hold a truth and at another a falsehood. In connection, however, with things not admitting of being otherwise, the same belief does not become now true, now false; rather the same beliefs are always true and always false.

But what about things not put together? What is being or not being and truth and falsity for them? Such a thing is not composed and thus such as to have being when it is put together and not to have being when it is divided, after the fashions either of the white log or the incommensurability of the diagonal. Nor will truth and falsity pertain to them in the same way as in the above cases.

Well, truth is not the same for these things and neither is being. And truth or falsity for such things are, in the case of truth, contact and assertion (mere assertion is not the same as affirmation) and in the case of falsity, ignorance is non-contact. There is no possibility, for such an item, of being illuded as to what it is, save only incidentally. (And just the same applies to non-composite substances, about which it is also impossible to be illuded.)

Moreover, all such items have being in actuality not in potentiality (else would they get produced and destroyed, whereas, in fact, that which is itself is neither produced nor destroyed – there would have to be something for it to be produced out of).

This shows that anything that is in such a way as to be a something and to have being in actuality is something about which it is not possible to be illuded – it is possible only either to intuit them or not. In asking a what-is-it? question about such a thing one is in fact asking whether or not it is of a certain quality.

As for being in the way of truth and not being in the way of falsity, for one of the two cases truth is a putting-together and falsity is a non-putting together, and for the other, if the thing has being, it has it in a certain way and, if it does not have being in a certain way, it does not have being at all. [1052a] Truth, then, for these things, is intuiting them, whereas falsity has no being in connection with them, nor illusion, but only non-acquaintance. (Such non-acquaintance, however, is unlike, say, blindness; blindness would be analogous here to a complete lack of the intuitive faculty.)

It need hardly be pointed out that with things that do not change there is no illusion with respect to time, given the assumption of their unchangeability. If I do not opine that the triangle changes, I shall not believe that on occasion its angles are equal to two right angles and on occasion not (that, I take it, would be a change). What I can believe is that some such thing is something and that some other such thing is not. I can, for instance, believe that no prime number is even or that some are and some are not. But not even this can be the case with something single in number. There is no possibility here of thinking that one of such things is something and that another of them is not. The truth or falsity of the belief, rather, will be in terms of something that is always this way not that.

Book Iota

Book four

IOTA I

The subject of unity has been important throughout the discussion both of substance and of actuality, and in book Iota Aristotle attempts to clarify this central concept. In this first chapter he proceeds in a fairly characteristic manner: he begins by setting out the accepted senses of unity or the one, and then gives his own definition of the essence of unity. This definition makes use of the notion of measure, which Aristotle feels to be itself in need of a definition. This is provided in the rest of the chapter.

The senses of unity that Aristotle countenances are (a) continuity, (b) being a whole, (c) being a specific unity and (d) being a numerical unity. All these senses are to be examined in the discussion that makes up the bulk of Iota.

Aristotle's own definition of the essence of unity is being indivisible by dint of something determinate and particular or by being an indivisible whole. The clearest case of this is that of a primary measure, especially with regard to quantity.

We are thus owed some account of the notion of measure, which is, at the least, closely connected with that of unity. Aristotle ascribes six characteristics to measure, saying that it is what we know quantity by, that it is the primary unit, that it cannot be altered without this being noticed, that there can be a multiplicity of units of measurement for the same object of measurement, that a unit of measurement must be homogeneous with its object and that scientific knowledge and perception are not the measure of things in the world, but rather are themselves measured by them.

That there is a plurality of accounts of unity will be a point familiar to those who have followed our discussion of the pluralities of accounts.

This plurality is indeed extensive, but, summarizing, we can isolate four styles of giving primary and *per se* (non-accidental) accounts of unity:

(a) The continuous. And this either *simpliciter* or, more especially, the naturally (i.e. not by contact or connection) continuous. And among things naturally simple those have unity and priority more fully whose processes are relatively indivisible and simple.

(b) Also like this, indeed more so, is whatever is a whole with a certain shape and form, especially when something is like this by nature and not by the application of force (i.e. when you make something a unified whole by gluing it, banging nails into it or tying it up), when, that is, it contains in itself the cause of its being continuous.

Something counts as being like this if its movement is single and locally and temporally indivisible. A clear corollary of this is that if something has by nature a primary principle of primary movement (by which is meant a rotatory orbit) then it is a primary unified magnitude.

OK, this is the way in which some things are unities – by being continuous or a whole. Other things, however, get to be unities by dint of the fact that the account of them is a single account. This latter group comprises those things a thought about which is a single thought, and such things are those a thought about which is an indivisible thought. And a thought is an indivisible thought if it is a thought about a formally or numerically indivisible object.

(c) The numerically indivisible, the particular.

(d) The formally indivisible, something cognitively and scientifically indivisible. Hence what causes substances to be single things should be thought of as the primary unity.

Such, then, is the diversity of accounts of unity: the continuous-by-nature, the whole, the particular and the universal. The reason why all these things are unities is indivisibility. In some, it is indivisibility with regard to movement, in others with regard to thought and the account.

An important distinction. [1052b] Giving a list of what sort of things are said to be single unities is not to be thought to be the same as trying to state the what-it-was-to-be-that-thing for a unity, to identify the account of unity. It is, indeed, the case that the accounts of unities are as diverse as we have shown and that each particular of the things that fall under some one of these modes of unity will be a single thing.

However, the what-it-was-to-be-that-thing for unity will on some occasions be the what-it-was-to-be-that-thing for one of these modes but on other occasions will be the what-it-was-to-be-that-thing for something else. And this something else will in fact be closer to the name of unity (with the others being closer to its effect).

We would find the same with element and cause if we had to give an account of them based both on discriminating the objects to which they applied and on demonstrating the definition of the name. Fire, you see, is in a way an element (and no doubt the infinite or something like it is a *per se* element) and in a way not. The what-it-was-to-be-that-thing of fire and the what-it-was-to-be-that-thing of element are not the same. Rather, fire, as a certain kind of thing and a nature, *is* an element, whereas the name *refers to* the pertaining to something of such a characteristic, to the fact that something is a primarily present constituent of something else. This applies, then, to cause and unity and all such items.

Hence the what-it-was-to-be-that-thing for unity is the what-it-was-to-be-that-thing for indivisibility, by dint of having thisness and of being specially separable either spatially or formally or cognitively. Alternatively, it is the what-it-was-to-be-that-thing of wholeness and indivisibility. Most of all, however, it is the what-it-was-to-be-that-thing of the primary measure for each kind, and most fundamentally the primary measure of quantity (from quantity indeed it has been extended to the other categories). For it is the measure by which quantity is known, the knowledge of quantity *qua* quantity arising either through one or through some number and the knowledge of number arising through one. Hence all quantity *qua* quantity is known through one, and One Itself is that through which quantities are primarily known. Hence one is the principle of number *qua* number.

By extension from this case that item is said to be the measure for the others through which each of them is primarily known, and for each the measure is a one, in length, in breadth, in depth, in weight or in speed. Weight, in fact, and speed are common to a pair of opposites, and this is because both are doubles. Weight, for instance, is both what has any amount at all of displacement and that which has an excess of displacement, while speed is both what has any amount at all of motion and that which has motion in excess. There is, after all, some speed of the slow, some weight of the relatively light.

In all these cases the measurement and starting-point is something single and indivisible. (Even in the geometry of lines there is an atomic unit, the one-foot line.) In all cases what is required as a measure is something single and indivisible, and this then counts as single, be it in quality or in quantity. And in cases where it is not possible either to subtract or to add, the measure for such things is exact. And so it is in the case of number that the measure is most exact, given that the unit is stipulated to be indivisible in every respect. [1053a] Other cases approximate to this.

Of course, an addition to, or subtraction from, a stade and a talent and any relatively large item would be less easily detected than with something relatively small. The result is that when something is the first from/to which a subtraction/addition would not be noticed by our senses it is universally accepted as a measure both of wet and of dry goods, both of weight and of volume. And it is when they know a quantity through this measure that people are confident that they know it.

Movement too is known by the simple movement and by the most rapid movement (which takes up least time). Hence in astrology too a one of this sort is the principle and measure: the movement of the entire heaven is taken as uniform and as the most rapid movement, and other movements are calibrated against it. Hence too in music the quarter-tone (smallest interval) is the measure and in speech the letter. And it is in the way that we have described that all these things are a single unity. It is not that the one is something common to them all.

The measure, however, is not always numerically single. There is sometimes a plurality of measures. Quarter-tones, for instance, are two, as established not by hearing but through their ratios, and there are several sounds by which speech is measured. The diagonal, too, and the side of the square are measured by two things, and ditto all magnitudes. It is in the following way, then, that the one is the measure of all things: we come to know the things of which the substance is composed by dividing it either quantitatively or formally. And the indivisibility of the one can be ascribed to the indivisibility of the first of each class of entities. (However, not every case is indivisible in the same way. Take a foot and a unit. The unit is indivisible in every respect, but the foot should be allocated to things indivisible relative to the senses (see above). Presumably, everything that is continuous is in fact divisible.)

The measure has a certain affinity, too, in each case with its object of measurement. A magnitude is thus the measure of magnitudes, more particularly a length being the measure of length, a width being the measure of width, a voice being the measure of voice, a weight being the measure of weight and a unit being the measure of units. This is in fact the way to put the point. It would be wrong to say that a number is the measure of number. Of course, parallelism of the account would suggest it, but the plausibility is by no means parallel. To insist on parallelism would be like saying that units, not a unit, are the measure of units, given that number is a multiplicity of units.

It also gets said, of course, that knowledge (and the senses) is the measure of things. This is for the same reason, that we know something through them. But they are the things that get measured rather than those that do the measuring. The position that we are in is comparable to one in which someone else is measuring us up and we learn how large we are by the cubit's being applied x number of times.

When Protagoras quipped that man is the measure of all things, he had in mind, of course, the knowing or perceiving man. [**1053b**] The grounds are that they have perception/knowledge and that these are said to be the measures of objects. Nonsense on stilts!

Conclusions: the what-it-was-to-be-that-thing of one, going along with the name to the full, is a kind of measure, fundamentally of quantity, derivatively of quality, some things being of this kind by being quantitatively, others by being qualitatively, indivisible.

The one, then, is indivisible either *simpliciter* or *qua* one.

IOTA 2

Aristotle deals first with an issue which has already appeared in book Beta. This is the controversy between the Pythagoreans and Platonists on the one hand and the natural philosophers on the other, as to whether the one is a substance or an attribute.

Aristotle directs his fire against the Platonists, arguing that the one cannot be a substance on two grounds. First, one is a universal entity and no universal can be a substance, as was painstakingly shown in the second half of Zeta. Secondly, and more obscurely, unity or the one must always be determinate, which suggests that it must be a determinate property of some substance and not a substance in itself.

As to the substance of unity and its nature, the question is in which of two states it is. In fact in the Philosophical Puzzles we addressed the question what the one is and how we could frame our conceivings of it. Is the One Itself a kind of substance, as first the Pythagoreans and now latterly Plato have held? Or is it rather that there is an underlying nature here and that a more familiar style of account is required of unity, more in the manner of the natural philosophers? One such thinker, for instance, accounts for unity as Love, another as Air and another as the Indefinite.

Now one of the conclusions we reached on substance and being was that none of the universals can be a substance. And, presumably, being cannot itself be a substance as a single thing set apart from the many – it must surely be something common to them, must therefore be no more than something that is predicated of them. Ergo, ditto unity. After all it is being and unity that are universally predicated more than anything else. So a double conclusion: (a) genera are not kinds of nature and substances separable from other entities, and (b) unity cannot be a genus, and for the same reasons that being and substance cannot be either.

The application of all this, moreover, must be to all cases of unity. The accounts of being are equal in number to those of unity. And just as unity is a something among qualities and a kind of nature, so is it too among quantities. So clearly we have to ask our question (What is unity?) across the board, as also with the question what being is. We cannot rest content with the observation that its nature is to be this very thing.

If, then, we take the case of colours, unity will be a colour, say white. And then, obviously, the others will be products of this and of black (black is the privation of white, as darkness is of light). Accordingly, if the things that are were colours, then the things that are would be some number. Fine, but the question is what would they be a number of. Well, of colours, stupid. And unity would be some one in particular, say white. *Beziehungsweise*, if the things that are were melodies, they would still have been a number, only now of quarter-tones, but that does not mean that their *substance* would be a number. And unity would then be a something whose substance would not be unity but the quarter-tone. **[1054a]** Or suppose that all the things that are were spoken sounds, then they would be a number of letters, and unity a vowel. Suppose they were rectilinear figures – they would be a number of figures, and unity the triangle.

The same account goes for the other genera too. There are numbers some unity both in affections, in qualities, in quantities and in movement, and for all of them number is number of some things and unity is some unity. But our argument shows that nevertheless its substance is not just that – and the same must go for substances too. The condition is uniform across the cases.

Conclusions, conclusions: (a) in every genus unity is some nature, and (b) for no such item is its nature this very thing, unity. In colours, after all, the answer a single colour is the answer to the question 'What are we looking for as the One Itself?' So for substances it follows that the One Itself is a single substance.

In a way, too, being and unity pick out the same thing. As witness the one-to-one correlation of it with the categories and its not being *in* any one of them. It is, for instance, neither in the what-is-it category nor in the category of quality. Things with it are just as they are with being. As witness the absence of any further predication in *one man* relative to *man*: being too is nothing over and above substance, quality or quantity. As witness the fact that the what-it-was-to-be-that-thing for a single thing is what-it-was-to-be-that-thing for a particular. .

IOTA 3

In this chapter Aristotle develops the contrast between unity and multiplicity, which takes a variety of forms, notably that of the opposition between indivisibility and divisibility, and then moves on to associate unity with three other important concepts, identity, similarity and equality, the different senses of which are explored.

Identity has three main senses: numerical identity, formal and numerical identity and purely formal identity. Similarity has four main senses: the possession of the same form with differences of individual substance, the possession of the same affection to the same extent, the possession of the same affection to differing extents and the possession of more equal than diverse attributes. Aristotle also distinguishes three senses of dissimilarity: opposition to the identical, lack of numerical and/or formal identity and mathematical dissimilarity. He distinguishes dissimilarity or diversity from difference in that the latter is restricted in application to differences of genus or species.

Now there are several ways in which the one and the many are in opposition. One of these lies in the fact that the one and the many are opposed as indivisible and divisible. What is either divided or divisible is accounted for as a kind of plurality, whereas what is indivisible or not divided is said to be a unity.

Now there are four modes of opposition. And in this case, the account of the other term is not based on privation, nor does it stand as a contradiction or as things whose account is focused on something else. They must, then, be contraries. Indeed, the account and elucidation of unity is derived from its contrary, as that of the indivisible from the divisible in as much as plurality and the divisible are more patent to the senses than the indivisible and this perceptibility entails the definitional priority of plurality over the indivisible.

Recall the diagram schematically setting out the contraries. Here unity comprised the same, the like and the equal, whereas plurality comprised the other, the unlike and the unequal. Now there are several accounts of sameness. (1) Sometimes – in one way – the account of sameness is numerical, but also (2) a thing is said to be the same if it is one both in account and in number (as you are one with yourself both in form and in matter). [**1054b**] Again, a thing is said to be the same if (3) the account of its primary substance is one, so that, for instance, equal straight lines are the same and ditto equal and isogonous quadrangles (there are, to be sure, a great many isogonous triangles, but among them equality is unity).

As for being alike, things are alike if they are not just the same *simpliciter*, exhibiting differences in their substrate substance but being formally the same. Examples are larger and smaller quadrangles and unequal straight lines; these are alike but not the same *simpliciter*. Another case of being alike is that in which things have the same form and are things admitting of gradation but do not in fact have any gradation. Other cases are those in which things have the same affection (it is formally one), say whiteness, in different gradations. Such things are said to be alike in virtue of their formal unity. Other things said to be alike are those with more of the same than of different affections (either *simpliciter* or with regard to their most striking characteristics). Tin, for instance, is like silver by dint of being white, or fire is like gold by dint of being yellow and ruddy.

From this it should be clear that there is also a plethora of accounts of the other and the unlike. And under one account, otherness stands as a contrary to sameness, which is why everything is, in relation to everything else, either the same or other. Under another account, things are other unless their substance and their form are one (which is why you are other than the next fellow). And on the third account, otherness is as in mathematics.

And this is why everything is said to be either-other-or-the-same with regard to everything – everything, that is, which is a unity and has being (for otherness is not a contradiction of sameness – hence, unlike not-the-same, this is not said of things that do not have being, though it is said of everything that does have being). After all, anything that has being by nature and is a unity will be either one or not one with anything.

Such, then, is the opposition between otherness and sameness. Difference, however, is not the same as otherness. For there is no need for the other and that than which it is the other to be other under a particular aspect (given that everything that has being is either other or the same). Whereas that which is different is different from something under some aspect, so that there must be something the same in respect of which they differ. And this something the same is genus or species, since everything that is different differs either in genus or in species (they differ in genus if their matter is not common and there is no production-relation between them – such as things falling under different schemas of predication – and in species if they have the same genus, the account of this latter being that by dint of which both differing items are said to be the same in point of substance).

Contraries, then, are different and contrariety a sort of difference, a supposition whose justice can be inductively established. For all contraries too are clearly different, being not just other but, in some cases, other in respect of genus and, in others, in the same column of predication and thus in the same genus and the same in genus. [1055a] (Elsewhere we have discriminated the quality of things that have sameness or otherness in genus.)

IOTA 4

In this chapter Aristotle moves to a topic that arises out of the discussion in the previous chapter of the concepts connected with unity and which effectively comes to dominate the whole of the rest of Iota. This is the topic of contrariety, which arises immediately out of the discussion of difference with which the previous chapter ends, since Aristotle here characterizes contrariety as maximum difference. From this it follows that contrariety is complete or perfect difference and so can only obtain between two extremes. Contraries, therefore, must come in pairs. Aristotle, as usual, analyses the received senses of contrariety and finds that they are in conformity with his claim.

In the second half of the chapter, Aristotle distinguishes contrariety from contradiction, in that the former but not the latter necessarily involves intermediaries, and from privation in that contrariety is complete privation. Thus there can be privation without contrariety, but there cannot be contrariety without privation.

Now the difference of differing things admits of gradation. So there must be some maximum difference, and this I dub contrariety. And it is by induction that we show that it is indeed the maximum difference.

After all, things generically different from one another have no *route* to one another – they are too greatly removed for that and there is no comparison between them. And with things differing in species generation occurs from the contraries as extremes. And of course the difference between extremes is the greatest. So the distance between the contraries must be so too.

This at least is certain: the greatest item in each genus is a complete item. For the greatest item is that which admits of no excess, and something is complete if it is not possible to find anything lying beyond it. The completing *differentia* contains an end point. (Just, indeed, as the account of the completion of other things is based on their containing an end point.) And nothing lies beyond an end point. The end point is the extreme in all cases and comprises everything else. So there is nothing beyond the end point, nor does that which is complete stand in need of any addition.

So much by way of proof that contrariety is complete difference. And given the plurality of accounts of contraries, they will be complete in a way determined by the way in which they are contraries.

OK. Given all this, it is evident that there cannot be several contraries to a single thing (there cannot be anything more extreme than the extreme, and there cannot be more than two extremes in a single range) quite generally evident, in fact, if contrariety is a difference, and if difference, and so also complete difference, is of two things.

Moreover, the other standing definitions of contrariety must also be true.

First of all, the complete difference is the maximum difference (given that it is impossible to find items further apart among things differing generically or indeed among things differing in species – recall the inductive argument to the effect that you cannot have difference with regard to things outside your genus and that the complete difference is the maximum difference of things falling in the same genus). And secondly, whatever differ the most in the same genus are contraries (the complete difference between these items is the maximum difference), and, thirdly, whatever differ the most in the same recipient matter are contraries (the contraries will have the same matter after all), and, fourthly, those differing most of things subject to the same capacity will be contraries (what with a single genus forming the domain of a single science). In these, then, the complete difference will be the maximum difference.

Now primary contrariety obtains between a state and its privation. This does not, however, apply to every privation (NB plurality of accounts of privation), only to whatever privation may be complete. And it is by reference to such contrariety that the accounts of the other contraries are framed: for some in that they comprise it, for others in that they produce it or are, at any rate, productive of it and for still others in that they are acquisitions or surrenders of such or of other contraries.

But, then, if opposition breaks down into contradiction, privation, contrariety and focal relation, [1055b] it is contradiction that is primary among them. And with contradiction there is no intermediate state, whereas with contrariety there can be. So clearly contradiction and contrariety are not the same.

And privation is a kind of contradiction. For it is that which quite generally cannot be in a state, or which, having the natural capacity to be in it, still is not which is in privation either generally or in some delimited respect. (Here there are already accounts in play, which we have isolated elsewhere.) So privation is indeed a kind of contradiction or incapacity either specified by a definition or connected with the recipient matter in question. Hence, whereas contradiction does not have an intermediate state, privation in some cases does. Whereas everything is indeed either equal or not equal, not everything is either equal or unequal, or, if so, only within the recipient of equality.

And indeed if productions come to matter from contraries, arising either from the form and the possession of the form or from some privation of the form and shape, then it is clear that every case of contrariety would be a case of privation, whereas perhaps not every case of privation is a case of contrariety (this because whatever is in privation can be in privation in a plurality of ways). Contraries, after all, are extremes out of which changes arise.

There is also an inductive argument for this:

Every case of contrariety involves the privation of one of the contraries, but not all do so in the same way. So inequality is the privation of equality, dissimilarity the privation of similarity and wickedness the privation of virtue, but they differ as has been said. In the one case, there is privation if the thing has merely undergone privation, whereas in another this is only so if it has undergone privation at some time or in some part (e.g. in its maturity or in its principal organ) or overall.

Hence for the former cases there is an intermediate state – there is, for instance, a man who is neither good nor bad – whereas for the latter there is not (a number, for instance, *must* be either odd or even). Another aspect is that for some contraries the substrate is delimited, for others not.

It is clear, then, that the account of one of a pair of contraries is always in terms of privation. In fact, this need only be the case for primary contraries, generic contraries (e.g. unity and plurality), given the reducibility to them of the others.

IOTA 5

In this and the next chapter Aristotle examines and rejects two possible objections to his claim that contraries must come in pairs. The objections are similar in that they suppose that the claim would rule out two otherwise plausible contrarieties. The first concerns the opposition between the equal and the large and the small and is dealt with in the present chapter, and the second concerns the opposition of the one and the many and is dealt with in chapter 6.

The argument in the present chapter defuses the objection by accepting that the opposition between the equal and the large and small cannot be a case of contrariety and giving it a different characterization. It cannot be a case of contrariety, because (a) the equal cannot be contrary either just to the large or just to the small, (b) it cannot, by the claim Aristotle is making, be the contrary of both and (c) the equal must be an intermediary between the large and the small and no intermediary can be a contrary. Thus the opposition between the equal and the large and the small is indeed not a case of contrariety. Aristotle characterizes it as follows: equality is a privative negation of the large and the small. The rest of the chapter is devoted to exploring and clarifying what this means.

On the assumption that a single thing has a single contrary, a possible question might be *in what way* unity and plurality are opposites, and *in what way* equality is opposite to greatness and smallness.

A clue is the use of the interrogative 'whether'. It is, after all, only in cases of opposition that we use this term. We ask 'whether' something is white or black and 'whether' it is white or not white, but not 'whether' something is a man or white. An exception is for cases in which there is some previous restriction, so that our question amounts to 'whether' it was the Cleon or Socrates that came. Obviously, this sort of opposition is not a necessary feature of any genus, but it is derived from the case of necessary opposition. For it is only opposing things that cannot be simultaneously present, and it is this impossibility that is being derivatively exploited in the question 'whether' it was A or B that came. [1056a] The question is ill-formed if they might both have come. (In fact, even in this case, there can be a similar opposition, that between either one of them coming and both of them coming; the question would then be 'whether' both came or (opposedly) one of them.)

OK. So the 'whether' question always involves opposites. And, conspicuously, we can ask 'whether' a thing is greater-or-lesser or equal. So what kind of opposition is there between the former and equal? After all, equality is not a contrary to either of them alone, nor to both. What possible reason could there be for its being contrary to greater rather than to lesser?

Another point is that equality is contrary to inequality, so that there is already more than one item to which it is contrary.

Well, if *inequality* picks out simultaneously-the-same-as-both-greater-and-lesser, then *equality* would be the contrary of both-greater-and-lesser. (The point in fact shores up those who want to claim that inequality is a duality.) However, this will not work, because *per impossibile* we will have one thing contrary to two.

Clearly, too, the equal is an intermediate between the great and the small. But with contraries there is neither evidence of any intermediate contrary, nor is such possible by the definition. For, being intermediate to some range, it would fail to be complete and indeed would rather always have something intermediate to itself.

The possibilities left, then, are that the opposition is contradiction or privation. However, it cannot be either the contradiction or the privation of some one of the two items (again, what reason could there be for its being more so of, say, greater than of lesser?). So what it is is the contradiction by privation of both.

And this is also why 'whether' is asked with regard to them both, not to some one (we do *not* ask 'whether' it is greater or equal or 'whether' it is equal or lesser). There are, after all, always three questions to be asked here.

The privation, however, is not a necessary one. It is not the case that everything that is not greater or lesser is equal, but only such things as are naturally constituted to admit of such an opposition.

The equal, therefore, is what is neither great nor small but is naturally constituted to be great or small. It is opposed to both these two as a contradiction by privation. And this also accounts for the fact that it is intermediate. What is neither good nor bad, too, is opposed to both good and bad. It, however, has no name. For with these cases, each of the two has several accounts and the recipient is not single. What is neither white nor black is more a case in point, though this too does not have a single account. However, the cases are in a way defined in terms of which an account by privation can be given of this contradiction. They must be either grey or yellow or something else similar.

We should not, then, accept the criticism which suggests that the account of all such cases is similar, with the result that anything which is neither a shoe nor a hand is an intermediate between a shoe and a hand, by parallel reasoning from the fact that what is neither good nor bad is an intermediate of good and bad – the key assumption being that there is some intermediate in all cases.

In fact, the result can be avoided. For the one case involves a joint contradiction of opposites, between which there is an intermediate and which have a natural range, whereas in the other case there is no such *difference*. [**1056b**] Things which are jointly contradicted are in different genera, so that there is no single substrate.

IOTA 6

In this chapter Aristotle deals with the second of the two objections raised against his view that contraries must come in pairs. The objection concerns the one–many opposition, which is plausibly regarded as a case of contrariety which does not conform with Aristotle's claim.

Aristotle begins by insisting that this opposition cannot be considered to be absolute and univocal on pain of absurd consequences. It is necessary to distinguish two senses of multiplicity: (a) that of an absolute or relative excess and (b) that of a number. The objection fails when it is realized that the one is only opposed to the second sense of multiplicity. Furthermore, that opposition is itself of a special kind, being a sort of relational opposition, such that the one is the measure for the many. Thus Aristotle's tactics in dealing with both these objections are the same, to deny the tacit premise that each opposition can only be plausibly taken as a more or less straightforward case of contrariety.

A similar line of questioning could be opened up with regard to unity and plurality. The supposition that unity is opposite to plurality *simpliciter* produces absurd consequences.

For a start, unity will then be *a* few (or few), given the opposition of plurality and paucity.

Also, two will turn out to be many, assuming that the double is manifold and that the account of it is based on two. And from this it follows that one is few. After all, relative to what, except one (and few), is two many? There is, to be sure, nothing fewer.

Also, if much and few are to plurality what long and short are to length, and if whatever is much is also many and whatever many also much (unless there be a difference to be found in the case of a well-defined continuum), then few will be a kind of plurality. But this means that one, assuming it is few, will be a kind of plurality. But it must be few, if two are many.

Well, perhaps there is a difference. In a way the account of many is also an account of much, but perhaps there is the sort of difference we see in the fact that water is much but not many. Many, then, will be applied to things that are divisible, in one way, if there is a plurality containing an excess, either *simpliciter* or relative to something (and few if there is a plurality similarly containing a deficiency), and, in another way, as a number, being only in this way opposite to one.

After all, to speak of one or many is similar to speaking of one and ones or a white thing and white things and to setting the objects of measurement against the measure. And it is in this way too that we speak of things being manifold. The reason for saying of each number that it is many is just that it is ones and that each number is measured by the one. And it is many as opposite to one, not to few.

In this way, indeed, two too are many, whereas two are not many as a plurality containing an excess either relative to something or *simpliciter*. Two are a primary plurality. And two are few *simpliciter*. Two are primary plurality containing deficiency. (Anaxagoras got it wrong with his peremptory conclusion that 'all were together, unlimited both in plurality and in smallness'. Instead of 'and in smallness', he should have said 'and in paucity', but then they could not have been boundless in paucity.) And this is because paucity arises, *pace* certain opinions, not through unity but through duality.

Thus the opposition between one and the many in numbers is like that between the measure and the thing measured. And the opposition between the latter is like that between correlatives which are not *per se* correlatives. The two accounts to be given of correlatives have been discriminated by us elsewhere, such that in the one they are as contraries and that in the other they are in the relation that knowledge is in to the thing known, by dint of the fact that the account of something else is based on it.

[1057a] There is, however, nothing to stop one being fewer than something, perhaps to two, say – for its being fewer does not entail its being also few.

Plurality is as the genus of number. For number is plurality as measured by unity. And in a way unity and number are opposites, not as contraries but in the way in which some of the correlatives have been said to be opposites. The opposition consists in the fact that one is the measure and the other thing measured. Hence is it not the case that whatever is one is number – for instance, anything indivisible will not be a number?

The account of knowledge is indeed similarly related to the object of knowledge, though the demonstration is not in a similar manner. Knowledge might be held to be the measure and the object of knowledge the object of measurement, but whereas all knowledge is an object of knowledge it is not the case that every object of knowledge is knowledge. Thus there is a way in which the knowledge is measured by the object of knowledge.

In any case, plurality is neither contrary to paucity (it is muchness that is contrary to paucity as an excessive plurality is contrary to the plurality that it exceeds) nor, in every way, to unity. There is, however, a way in which they are contraries, as has been said, in that plurality is divisible and unity indivisible, and there is a way in which they are related as correlatives, in the way that knowledge is related to the object of knowledge, in the case that plurality is number and unity is its measure.

IOTA 7

Considerable emphasis has been laid on the concept of contrariety, and this in turn depends upon the notion of an intermediary state between extremes. The present chapter is devoted to clarifying the notion of such an intermediary state. Aristotle makes three main points. First, intermediaries must be of the same genus as the extremes. This is because change consists of a transition from one extreme to another, this transition must pass through the intermediary state and all transition must be within the same genus. Secondly, intermediaries must stand between contraries. There can be no intermediaries between the poles of contradictions or the terms of relations. Thus there can also be no change except between contraries.

The third point that Aristotle makes in this chapter is more elaborate and obscure. His claim is that intermediaries must be composed of contraries. The argument seems to rest on the three following considerations. Contrary species must be marked by contrary differentiae. Intermediary species must be composed of intermediary differentiae and the genus. But the intermediary differentiae (and thus the intermediary species) must themselves be composed of contrary differentiae. It is difficult to assess this argument, but the point is perhaps best taken as an attempt to underwrite the other two claims about intermediaries advanced in this chapter.

Now contraries admit of an intermediate, and indeed there is an intermediate in some cases. And from this it follows of necessity that the intermediates must be composed of the contraries.

After all, all the intermediates are in the same genus as the items to which they are intermediate. For intermediates are said to be those items to which the subject of change must first change. For example, if we move through the smallest intervals from the highest to the lowest string, we will come before to the intermediate notes. And, with colours, if we are passing from white to black, we will come before black to scarlet and grey, and so also in the other cases. But it is not possible to have change from one genus to another genus, except accidentally, as in a change from a colour to a figure. So, of necessity, intermediates must be in the same genus both as each other and as the items to which they are intermediate.

But anyway all intermediates are intermediates to opposites of a sort. For from these alone can there be *per se* change (that is why it is impossible to be intermediate to things that are not opposites – there would be change, but not from opposites).

Now, among oppositions, there is no intermediate of contradiction. After all, contradiction is just this: opposition such that one of the two opposite elements is present in anything at all and that it has no intermediate. The other oppositions break down into correlatives, privation and contraries. As to correlatives, all those that are not contraries lack an intermediate, and this is just because they are not in the same genus. What, after all, is the intermediate between knowledge and the object of knowledge? **[1057b]** On the other hand, there is an intermediate between great and small.

If, however, as has been made clear, the intermediates lie in the same genus, and if it is contraries that they are intermediate to, then they must of necessity be composed of these contraries.

Either there will be a genus of them or there will be no genus. If, then, there is a genus, such that it is a prior thing to the contraries, the differentiae which produce the contrary species of the genus will be prior contraries. The species are, after all, composed of the genus and the differentiae.

For example, suppose black and white are contraries, and suppose that one is a piercing, the other a coercing, colour. Then these differentiae, piercing and coercing, will be prior, so that they are prior as mutual contraries.

Moreover, contrarily differentiated species are the more fully contrary species. And the others, the intermediates, are composed of the genus and the differentiae. (Such are the colours that are intermediate to white and black – they are to be accounted for from the genus, in this case colour, and certain differentiae, and these differentiae will not themselves be the prior contraries, on pain of each colour being either white or

307

black. They will, then, be other than those differentiae. They will, then, be intermediate to the primary contraries, and the primary differentiae will be piercing and coercing.)

We must, then, investigate these primary contraries which are not contraries in a genus and ask what their intermediates are composed of. (With things that are in the same genus, they must either be composed of items not composed of the genus or be non-composite.)

Well, contraries are not composed of one another, so that they are principles. Intermediates, on the other hand, must either all be non-composite or none be non-composite.

There is, however, something produced from the contraries, such that there will be change to this before there is change to either of the contraries themselves, since it will be both less and more x than either contrary. So this too will lie intermediate to the contraries.

But, then, all the other intermediates must be composite; for anything that is more x than a and less x than b will in a way be a composite of those items of which it is said to be more x than one and less x than the other. And since there are no other items of the same genus prior to the contraries, all intermediates must be composed of the contraries. So too, then, all the sub-ordinates, both contraries and intermediates, will be composed of the primary contraries.

Clear upshot: intermediates are all in the same genus, are intermediate to contraries and are all composed out of the contraries.

IOTA 8

In this chapter Aristotle examines a topic which is closely connected with that of contrariety. This is the topic of the diversity or difference of species. There are restrictions on what can make one species different from another. Aristotle here gives a summary of these. The first restriction is that species difference must consist in some difference with regard to a common factor shared by both species, and this common factor must be the genus to which they both belong. The second restriction is that this difference within the genus must be a contrariety. All opposition within a genus is in fact a case of contrariety, given that we have already seen that contrariety is complete or perfect opposition. Thirdly, Aristotle argues that the diversity of species implies the indivisibility of species. Finally, he makes a point which seems to follow from the first restriction, namely that no species can be identical with its genus (although Aristotle does not explicitly rule out the possibility of a genus with only one species in it), and no species can have a specific difference from a species in some other genus.

The other in species is something other than something else in some respect, and this must be present to them both.

If, for instance, there is an animal other in species, then both it and that to which it is other are animals. So things other in species must necessarily be in the same genus. And for genus, in this context, I am speaking of that by which both are said to be one and the same, comprising a non-accidental differentiation, [**1058a**] having its being either as matter or in some other way.

Not only, though, must the commonality be present, such that they are both animals, but this very commonality, being an animal, must be different for both, such that the one is a horse, the other a man. Thus the commonality is other in species of each of the two items. Indeed, the one will be *per se* an x animal, the other *per se* a y animal, say one a horse and the other a man. Necessarily, then, the differentia here is an otherness of the genus. For in speaking of a differentia of genus I have in mind an otherness which makes other the genus itself.

And this (as can be shown inductively) will accordingly be a case of contrariety. For it is by opposites that all things are divided, and we have established that contraries are in the same genus. We have shown, that is, that contrariety is a complete differentia, and that the differentia in a species is always from something in some respect, so that this last is both the same thing and the genus for them both (hence in the same column fall all those contraries of predication that are different in species and not in genus, and these are most fully other than one another – for the differentia is complete – and cannot be mutually co-present). This shows that the differentia is a contrariety.

This, then, is the what-it-was-to-be-that-thing for things other in species, namely being in the same genus and having a contrariety while being atomic (and things the same in species are those which, being atomic, do not have a contrariety). For it is in division that contrarieties are produced even among the intermediates, before we reach the atomic items.

And this shows that with regard to what is called the genus none of the species as of the genus is either the same as, or other than, it in species, appropriately enough, given that it is through negation that matter is elucidated and the genus is the matter of that of which it is said to be the genus – and this not, indeed, in the way of the genus of the Heraclidae but in the way in which a genus is in the nature of something, nor relative to things not in the same genus, though it will be different generically from them and specifically from things in the same genus. For a differentia by which something is different in species must, of necessity, be a contrariety, and such is only present for things which are in the same genus.

IOTA 9

Aristotle has told us that every case of species difference is a case of contrariety, but he cannot allow that the reverse is the case, because there are clearly many more instances of contrariety than there are of species difference. But on what grounds can he explain the fact that not all cases of contrariety create a difference of species? For instance, to take Aristotle's own example, masculine and feminine are clearly contraries, and clearly things belonging to the same genus can differ in that one is masculine and the other feminine. For example, a man and a woman both belong to the genus animal and differ in this respect. Why, then, should we not say that man is one species of animal and woman another?

Aristotle's answer is ingenious and, within the terms of his distinctions, convincing. The reason why the contrast between having or not having wings, say, produces a difference of species, while that between being masculine and being feminine does not, is that the former has to do with the form of the animals in question, whereas the latter only has to do with their matter. Thus formal contrarieties produce species difference, whereas material contrarieties merely produce diversity within a species.

A possible question is this: why is woman not specifically different from man? After all, female and male are contraries and their differentia is a contrariety. Why, further, are a female and male animal not specifically different? After all, this difference is *per se* for the animal and not like whiteness or blackness; female and male belong, rather, to the animal *qua* animal.

This query is in fact more or less the same as the following: why does one contrariety produce things specifically other and another not? Footed, for instance, and winged produce things specifically other, but whiteness and blackness do not. The answer here, no doubt, is that the former are proper affections of the genus, whereas the others are so to a lesser extent. And a possible additional answer is that, given that there is both the account of the thing and its matter, [**1058b**] all the contrarieties that are in the account produce a specific difference, whereas those in the thing taken along with its matter do not.

Thus whiteness or blackness in a man does not produce a specific difference, nor is there a specific difference in a white man as against a black man. Nor would there be even if a single name was introduced for each. For it is as matter that man is here introduced, and matter does not produce a differentia. Nor are men species of men because of matter, even though the flesh and bones from which A and B are composed are other. The composite is, of course, other, but not specifically other, because the contrariety is not in the account.

This, indeed, is the ultimate, the indivisible. Callias is the account with the matter; so too, then, must the white man be, given that Callias is white. But this means that *man* is only accidentally white.

Nor is there, then, a specific difference between a bronze and a wooden circle. Nor is there one between a bronze triangle and a wooden circle because of their matter, but because there is a contrariety in their accounts.

But perhaps matter does produce things specifically other, when it is in a way itself other, or it is as though it produces them. Why, after all, is horse x specifically other than man y, even though their accounts are associated with matter?

Perhaps there is here a contrariety in the account. For there is indeed a contrariety between white man and black horse, and a specific contrariety at that, but not by dint of the one's being white and the other black, since even had they both been white they would still have been specifically other.

But with male and female we have indeed proper affections of *animal* but not in regard to substance but in the matter, the body, and so it is that the same sperm becomes female or male by being affected by a particular affection.

What you now know: (i) what it is to be specifically other and (ii) why some things are specifically different and others not.

In this chapter Aristotle makes a further point in connection with the relation between contrariety and species diversity and uses it to highlight a further difficulty with the doctrine of Platonic Forms. The point he makes is that things that are perishable and things that are imperishable must be not only specifically but also generically different. It might be supposed that, of two items in the same species, one could be perishable and one imperishable, just as one could be black and the other white (which, as we have just seen, would not produce a difference of species, being merely a material contrariety). However, the difference between being perishable and being imperishable is of quite a different order from that between being black and being white. The latter is a merely accidental contrariety, which therefore does indeed not produce a species difference, but the former is not accidental but necessary, and it thus constitutes a contrariety in a substantial predication, a predication which affects the substance of the thing. Such a contrariety will produce not only a difference of species, but a difference even of genus.

Clear realization of this point provides another ground for attacking the Theory of Forms. The Theory of Forms holds that the species of man, for instance, must comprise both an imperishable member, Man Himself, and perishable ones, particular individual men, such as Socrates and Callias. But the argument we have just seen shows that there cannot be a species which comprises two things which thus differ in a contrariety regarding a substantial predication.

But now, if contraries are specifically other, and the perishable and imperishable are contraries (privation being a circumscribed lack of potentiality), the perishable and imperishable must be generically other.

The discussion hitherto has been conducted using the universal names themselves. And this might make it appear that it is not necessary for each and every perishable and imperishable thing to be specifically other, any more than each and every white and black thing must be specifically other. For the same thing can be both and even at the same time, if it is one of the universals. *Man*, for instance, could be both white and black. And the point holds even at the individual level, for the same man might be white and black, only not at the same time. Yet white is contrary to black.

Well, some things have certain of the contraries accidentally. There are the examples just given and many others. Other contraries, however, cannot be so had, **[1059a]** and they include perishable and imperishable.

This is because nothing is accidentally perishable. For what is accidental admits to not applying, whereas if anything has the property of being perishable it has it of necessity, on pain of one and the same thing being perishable and imperishable, if it were indeed possible for perishability not to apply to it.

So for anything perishable perishability must either be its substance or be present in its substance.

And the same account can be given of the imperishable – they are both things applying of necessity. So an opposition is involved in that by which and according primarily to which one thing is perishable and another imperishable, so that they must of necessity be generically other.

This, by the way, also makes it clear that there cannot be Forms of the kind that some suppose. For then there would also be perishable man and imperishable Man. But Forms are supposed to be specifically the same as particulars and not merely homonymous and there is an even wider gap between the generically, than between the specifically, other.

Book Kappa

KAPPA I

Book Kappa is composed of recapitulations of earlier material from the Metaphysics *and also sections from the* Physics. *There has been much debate about the origin and purpose of the book and about the connection between it and books Beta, Gamma and Epsilon, which are the sections of the* Metaphysics *which it mainly recapitulates. In my chapter introductions, I confine myself to indicating the main points of difference between the text of Kappa and the source text.*

Chapter 1 recalls the doctrine of book Alpha, that wisdom is concerned with causes and principles, and then reviews puzzles 1−7 of Beta (pages 51−3). It makes two additions, between puzzles 4 and 5, where the issue whether wisdom should study final causes is moved from its inclusion in the discussion of puzzle 1 in Beta, and between puzzles 5 and 6, where a new problem is inserted as to whether wisdom should study the matter of mathematical entities.

It is clear from our first sections that philosophy is a kind of science that deals with principles. For it was in those sections that we engaged in controversy with the claims advanced by others in regard to principles. But this still leaves open the question whether philosophy is to be taken as a single science or as several. An objection to its being taken as a single science is that the domain of a single science is always sets of contraries, whereas principles are not contraries. On the other hand, if it is not a single science, of what kind are those various sciences of which it must be supposed to consist?

Here are some other queries:

(i) Are the principles of demonstrative reason the domain of a single science or of several? If they belong to a single science, why this science and not any other arbitrarily selected science? If to several sciences, what should the common characteristic of these sciences be supposed to be?

(ii) Does philosophy concern itself with all substances or not? On the latter supposition, there is a problem about ring-fencing those with which it is concerned. On the former, there is a problem about how a single science can have to do with a plurality of domains.

(iii) Does philosophy concern itself solely with substances or also with their accidents? After all, whereas demonstration is available for accidents, it is not for substances. But then, if the sciences are different, of what kind are they each and which is philosophy? If philosophy is taken as demonstrative, then it must be the science of accidents, whereas if it deals with primary entities, then it must be the science of substances.

It is also to be noted that we must not suppose that the science that we are investigating has to do with the causes set out in the *Physics*. Philosophy is not concerned with the final cause (for this is the good, which pertains to questions of action and to things subject to process – and it is also the primary source of process, being as it is the end, whereas with things not subject to process there is no primary source of process). In any case, more generally, there is a puzzle as to whether the science that we are currently investigating ever has to do with perceptible substances or is rather concerned not with them [1059b] but with certain others.

If it does have to do with other substances, then these would be either the Forms or the mathematicals. But, first off, it is patently the case that there are no Forms.

(Digression: OK, suppose we say that there are Forms. Why is the situation for non-mathematical things-for-which-there-are-Forms not parallel to that for the mathematicals? The point is this: they blithely posit the mathematicals between the Forms and perceptibles, as being Third Entities between the Forms and the things round here. But there is no Third Man or Third Horse between Man/Horse Itself and particular men/horses. But then if we throw out mathematicals, with what sort of items are we to suppose that the mathematician is engaged? He is not, to be sure, concerned with the things round here, none of which is remotely like the sort of things investigated by mathematics. End of Digression.)

318

And secondly the science we are after is not about mathematicals either (none of them, you see, is separable).

But also philosophy is not about perceptible substances (they, you see, are prone to destruction).

More questions:

What is the science that deals with problems of the matter of the mathematicals?

Well, it is not physics. The entire preoccupation of the physicist is with things that contain within themselves a principle of movement and rest. And it is not the science of demonstration, the science of science. The subject of this science is, well, demonstration and science.

So it is left to philosophy, our present concern, to be the science of the mathematicals.

Is the science we are after to be supposed to be concerned with principles, that is with those items that are called by some elements. It is generally acknowledged that such things are present in composites. But there is a strong converse inclination to suppose that the science we are after is concerned with universals. Every account, indeed, and every science has to do with universals and not with *lowest types*, so that from this point of view philosophy would be concerned with the highest kinds.

And these highest kinds would be being and unity. For it is these that would be most plausibly supposed to comprise all entities and, given their natural primacy, to be closest to principles, in that if they are eliminated then everything goes with them – everything has being and unity. On the other hand, if we suppose that being and unity are kinds, the differentiae must of necessity participate in them. But no differentia participates in the genus. So on this line of reasoning, we arrive at the view that they must be treated neither as kinds nor even as principles.

On the assumption, again, that the relatively simple is more of a principle than the relatively less simple, and that if the lowest kinds of the genus are simpler than the genera (after all, the former are indivisible, whereas the genera divide into several different species), there would seem in this to be grounds for supposing that the species more than the genera are the principle. On the other hand, the fact that species are conjoined in the elimination of genera makes the latter seem more like principles, on the basis that a principle is that whose elimination entails that of something else.

[**1060a**] Such is our budget of queries, by no means exhaustive.

KAPPA 2

This chapter continues and completes the review of the puzzles presented in Beta. The order of presentation, however, is changed, and puzzle 8 (page 54), concerning the existence of supra-sensible entities, is given a more extensive treatment.

Back to questions:

(iv) Should we, or should we not, suppose there to be something over and above particulars, and, if not, is philosophy about particulars?

Objection: there is an infinity of particulars. Counter-objection: OK, but the things over and above particulars are genera or species, and philosophy is not about either of these, as we have just seen.

In fact, it is a question, quite generally, whether a philosopher is to suppose that there is separable substance, over and above perceptible substances, things round here, or that there is not and that it is the latter that are the things that are and that it is with them that philosophy is concerned. It is indeed some other sort of substance that we seem to be after, and this is why we encounter this problem, viz. that of seeing whether there is something separable in itself and not pertaining to any of the perceptibles.

(v) If, in addition to perceptible substances, there is some other substance, over against which of the perceptible substances is this other substance set? Why, in fact, is it to be supposed that this substance is to be set over against men rather than horses, or the other animals, or indeed even inanimate things quite generally? But then the introduction of other, eternal substances one for each of the perceptible, perishable substances would seem to fall outside the pale of common sense.

If, on the other hand, the principle for which we are now seeking is not separable from bodies, then what might one more plausibly suppose to be this principle than matter? Well, one response might be that matter does not exist actually, but only potentially. And thus form/shape would seem rather to be a principle and to be more fundamental than matter. Form/shape, however, is taken to be perishable, and on this basis there is no eternal, separable, *per se* substance at all. And yet this is odd: after all, has not a principle and substance of this kind been taken to exist and investigated by the brightest luminaries of philosophy? How, indeed, is there to be an arrangement of the world at all, in the absence of something eternal, separable and permanent?

(vi) Suppose, then, that there is some substance and principle of a nature such as we are currently examining. Suppose that it is a single substance for all things, the same both for eternal and for perishable items. There is now a real difficulty as to why, with the principle being the same, some items falling under the principle are eternal and some, absurdly, are not. If, however, there is one principle for perishables and another for eternals, and if even that for perishables will itself be eternal, our difficulty will not have been much alleviated. Why, the question now is, if the principle is eternal, are the things that fall under the principle not also eternal? If, however, the principle of perishables is perishable, then there is some other principle for this and another again for that one and so on *ad infinitum*.

(vii) Suppose, alternatively, that we posit those principles that are most plausibly thought to be immune from process, to wit being and unity. [**1060b**] First off, if we do this, assuming that each of these does not pick out a this-something and a substance, how are they to have separable and *per se* being? Yet such must be the eternal primary principles that we are after. If, conversely, both being and unity do display a this-something/substance, then all the things that are will be substances, given the predication of being of all things (and the predication of unity of several). But it is just plain false that all the things that are are substance.

(viii) How can there be a shred of truth in the assertion that unity is the primary principle and that this is a substance, with number being generated first from unity and matter and this being claimed for a substance? How is one to think of duality and each of the other compound numbers as one? They have no answer to this and it is not easy to see how they could have.

Suppose, alternatively, that we posit lines and the entities next to them (primary surfaces) as principles. Well, in any event, these are not separable substances, but sections and divisions, some of surfaces, some of bodies and some (points) of lines, and by the same token limits of the same. All these items pertain to other things, none of them being separable. Anyway, how are we to suppose that there is a substance of unity and point? With every substance there is production, but not so with point, given that a point is a division.

(ix) Every science has to do with universals and the *such*. But substance is not to be found among the universals, but is rather a this-something and separable. And science is also about principles. So how are we to suppose that the principle is substance?

(x) Is there something over and above the thing-as-a-whole (meaning by this the matter and that which is with matter) or not? If, on the one hand, there is not, then what about the fact that all things in matter are perishable? But if, on the other hand, there is, then this must be form/shape. As for form/shape, it is problematic to say in which cases it is something over and above and in which it is not. There are at any rate some cases, such as that of a house, in which it is clear that the form is not separable.

(xi) Are the principles the same in (a) form, (b) number? (If (b), everything will be the same.)

KAPPA 3

This chapter recapitulates book Gamma 1–2, which sets out the various ways in which things can have being while insisting that these all form the domain of a single science, which also studies the main contrarieties of being, and contrasts the metaphysical study of being qua *being with the mathematical study of being and quantity, the physical study of being and change and the dialectical study of the accidental properties of being.*

Being *qua* being, taken universally and not in regard to some part of it, is the domain of the science of philosophy.

But the accounts of being are several and not after a single fashion. And if these accounts are merely homonymous, lacking any common feature, then being does not form the domain of a single science. For things like that do not constitute a single genus. If, on the other hand, the accounts are based on a common feature, then being would form the domain of a single science.

In fact, the accounts of being seem in a way like those of medical and healthy, for each of which there are several accounts. Now there are accounts of this kind for all things which are as follows: the account of medical makes reference in some way to medical science, and that of healthy in some way to health, and in other cases the reference is to something else, but always to the same thing in each case. So a discourse, say, or a knife is said to be medical, **[1061a]** by dint of the one's being based on medical science and the other's being useful to it. And it is the same with healthy. One thing is called healthy because it is a symptom of health, another because it is productive of it. And this carries over to other cases.

And so it is too with the account of all being. For the account of each of the things that are is based on being an affection of being *qua* being or a state of it, or an arrangement, process or other such. And since there is a reference to a single common thing for everything that is, each of the contraries will also be referred to the primary differentiae and contraries of being, whether these primary differentiae of being are plurality and unity or similarity and dissimilarity or yet others (let's not go into that now). Nothing hangs on the reference of that which is being to being or to unity, given that even if they are not the same but different they are interchangeable – what is one is in a way also being and what is being is in a way also one.

Now since it is for one and the same science to examine each pair of contraries and in each case the account of the one is derived from the privation of the other (in fact with some contraries there is a puzzle as to how the account can be thus derived from privation, with those namely for which there is an intermediary, as injustice and justice), it is in all these cases appropriate that the privation not be posited of the whole account, but of the lowest type. For instance, if the just man is *observing of the laws by dint of a certain settled disposition*, the unjust man will not in all cases be the man deprived of the whole account. Rather he may be *in some way deficient in law observance*, it being in this way that the privation applies to him. And the same goes for the other cases.

And just as the mathematician is conducting a study into things in abstraction (for his study commences after the removal of all perceptible features, such as weight and lightness and hardness and the contrary of hardness, as also heat and cold and the other perceptible contrarieties, leaving only quantity and continuity, in one, two or three dimensions, and the affections of things *qua* quantitative and continuous, not contemplating them relative to anything else, and examines, on the one hand, the mutual relations of some and the features of those relations, and, on the other, [**1061b**] the commensurabilities and incommensurabilities of others, and of yet others the proportions – but for all that we suppose geometry to be one and the same science for all these), so do things also stand with being.

It is for philosophy, and for philosophy alone, to study the accidents of being in so far as it is being, the contrarieties of being *qua* being. To physics is ascribed the study of things not *qua* things that are but *qua* participants in process. And dialectics and sophistics have, indeed, to do with the accidents of things that are, but not *qua* things that are, nor about that which is just in so far as it is that which is. It is left, then, to the philosopher to study the items we have mentioned, to the extent that they are as we have said.

And since, despite the plurality of accounts, everything that is is said to be by virtue of one common feature, and the contraries in the same fashion (they are referred to as the primary contrarieties and differentiae of being), and since it is possible for these to fall under a single science, the puzzle originally cited is resolved, that namely of how there is to be a single science of a plurality of things differing in kind.

KAPPA 4

The text here recapitulated is Gamma 3, which explains that the fundamental axioms of logic fall within the domain of metaphysics, being peculiarly suitable to the generality of the interest in being which is distinctive of metaphysics.

Also, since the mathematician himself applies common axioms, but does so in a special way, it would seem to fall first to philosophy to examine the principles of these too.

For instance, that when equals are subtracted from equals equals remain is common to all quantities, but mathematics discriminates and conducts a study into a certain part of its proper matter, i.e. into lines, or angles, or numbers or some one of the other quantities, not *qua* things that are but just *qua* each as a continuity in one, two or three dimensions. Philosophy, by contrast, does not examine some portion of what is, in respect of the accidents of each such group of things, but contemplates being, as the being of each of such things.

And physics is in the same boat as mathematics. It studies the accidents and principles of entities, *qua* participating in process and not *qua* being. And in contrast we have said that primary science is the science of these things in so far as they, its subjects, are things that are, and not in regard to any other feature.

Hence both physics and mathematics are to be considered mere parts of total understanding.

KAPPA 5

This chapter recapitulates chapters 4, 3 and 8 of book Gamma, which contain the remarkable defence of the principle of non-contradiction.

Now there is a principle in things that are for which illusion is impossible and whose truth, rather, we cannot fail to acknowledge, the principle that it is not possible for the same thing both to be and not to be at one and the same time, [**1062a**] or indeed harbour any other such pair of contraries.

There can be no demonstration of these things *simpliciter*, but there can be *ad hominem*. It is not, that is, possible to draw this principle as a conclusion from some more certain principle than it, but that is what it would take for it to be demonstrable *simpliciter*. However, if you have on your hands a guy who is making opposite assertions and you want to show him the falsity of his ways, you are going to have to get out of him some concession which amounts to the principle that it is not possible for the same thing both to be and not to be at one and the same time, even though it may not be thought to be the same.

Only in this way can the principle be demonstrated in the face of one who says that it is possible for opposite statements to be true in respect of the same thing. In any case, if any two people are going to have a debate, there has to be some common ground. Without it what joint basis for discussion will there be? What, then, is needed is that each of the words used must be familiar and indicate something, not several things but only one. (Or if it does indicate a plurality of things, it must be made clear to which of these things the word is being applied in the context.)

Given these ground rules, anyone who says that a given thing both is and is not is denying what he is asserting, so that he is denying that the word indicates what it indicates, which is impossible. If, then, something is indicated by saying that a given thing is, it is impossible for the denial of it to be true in respect of the same thing.

On top of that, if the word indicates something and is asserted truly, this must be of necessity. And what is of necessity does not admit of ever not being. Thus it is not possible for opposite statements to be true in respect of the same thing. And also, if the statement is no more true than the denial, there will be no more truth in saying *man* than in saying *not-man*. And indeed it is supposed that if one asserts that a man is not a horse one is saying something that is either more, or at any rate not less, true than that he is not a man, so that it will also be right to say that the same man is a horse. (Our assumption was that opposite statements could be equally truly made.) So it turns out that the same man is also a horse or any other animal you like.

Well, there is no demonstration of these things *simpliciter*, but demonstration is possible to anyone making these suppositions. No doubt, had one questioned Heraclitus himself in this way, we would have forced him to agree that it is never possible for opposite statements to be true with regard to the same things. In fact, he took up this view without understanding what his own position amounted to. Anyway, if his claim is true, then even the following principle will not be true, namely [**1062b**] that it is possible for the same thing at one and the same time both to be and not to be. This is because, just as, when the statements are discriminated, neither the denial nor the assertion is said more truly, in the same way – what with the combined and conjoined statement being like a single assertion – the denial will not be any the more true than the whole considered as an assertion.

Finally, if nothing can be truly asserted, even the following claim would be false, the claim that there is no true assertion. And if there is a true assertion, this is a refutation of what is pretended by the raisers of these objections, being as they are the comprehensive eliminators of all debate.

KAPPA 6

This chapter recapitulates chapters 5–8 of book Gamma and continues and completes the recapitulation of the defence of the principle of non-contradiction.

There is a certain affinity between what we have just been discussing and the dictum of Protagoras. He remarked that man is the measure of all things, and in saying this his point was just that whatever is thought by each individual to be the case most assuredly also is the case for him. But if this is so, it will turn out that the same thing both is and is not, both is evil, say, and is good, and all the other things that can be said of it by means of opposite assertions. After all, very often a certain thing seems beautiful to one group of people and the opposite to another. And it is what each man takes to be the case that is the measure.

We can, however, dispose of this riddle, if we consider what is the root of this position. In some aspects, it would seem to derive from teaching of the Philosophers of Nature, in others merely from the circumstance that it is not the case that all men hold the same opinions on all subjects, but rather one group will take a given thing to be pleasant, another the contrary.

Now, the claim that nothing is produced from what is not and everything from what is is one up to which pretty nearly all of those who have concerned themselves with nature have signed. But then nothing white can be produced from what is completely white and in no respect not-white. So the white thing produced is produced from what is not white. So (the argument goes) it is produced from something that is not, unless there was originally one and the same thing that was both white and not-white.

No need to linger long over this. The *Physics* has already dealt with the way in which things are produced from that which is not and the way in which they are produced from that which is.

It is, in any event, the policy of the simpleton to attend with equal relish to the opinions and whimsies of those locked in mutual controversy. It is patently the case that one or other of them must be in error. This is clear even from sensory occurrences; for it is never the case that the same thing appears pleasant to one group [**1063a**] and the contrary to another, unless one group or the other is corrupted and impaired with respect to the discriminating *sensorium* for the flavours in question. But if this is the case, then we should embrace the other group as our measure, while rejecting the victims of impairment. And the point carries over to good and evil, beautiful and ugly, etc., etc.

In fact, there is no difference between Protagoreanism and saying this: if you stick your finger under your eye and make single things seem to be two, then they are two, just because they seem to be two, and also one, because if you do not thus distort your vision then what is one you see as one.

The objection to be made here, in fact, is more radical still. It is that you cannot take the fact that things round here appear to change and never to stay in the same condition and use it as the basis for assaying an evaluation of the way things are in truth. If it is the way things are in truth that you are after, you must start with things that are always in the same condition and which never undergo change, of which kind are the contents of the heavens. They do not appear like so and so at one point and like such and such at another, but are ever the same and have no part in any change.

Also this. If there is a process, there is something undergoing the process and everything proceeds *from* something *to* something else. So what undergoes the process must at first be in that from which it proceeds and later not in that from which it proceeds, must proceed to something else and be produced in that. But this means that the contents of the contradictions do not simultaneously truly apply to it (*pace* our friends).

If, too, the things round here undergo continuous flux and process in respect of quantity (which let us suppose, though it is not strictly the case), why should they not enjoy permanence in respect of quality? You see, the claim that contradictory predications can be made of the same thing would seem not least to be derived from the assumption that bodies have no permanence with respect to quantity. This is taken to justify the remark that the same thing both is and is not four cubits long.

However, substance is relative to quality, and this of a defined nature, whereas quantity is of an undefined nature.

What about when a medic orders this particular food to be served to the patients? Why do the patients accept it? Why, we might ask, is it any more the case that this food is, say, bread than that it is not? So it would not make any difference whether they ate it or not.

In practice, of course, the patients do indeed accept the prescribed food, and in so doing betray their belief that they have the truth on the issue and that it is, as a matter of fact, the prescribed food. But this would be a ludicrous procedure, if there really were no permanency in the nature of perceptibles and all natures were at all times the playthings of process and flux.

And anyway if we are always changing and never remaining the same, it is hardly surprising if we are like sick people and things never seem the same to us. [**1063b**] Sick people, to be sure, by dint of the fact that they are not in the same dispositional condition and when they are well, do not feel that perceptible things are the same. But this does not mean that the objects of perception themselves need have a share in change, for all that they produce other sensations in sick people and not the same ones. So things must be like this, it would seem, for us too, if the constant change alleged in fact occurs.

If, on the other hand, we do not change but continue to be the same people, then there would be something in us that persists.

There are, of course, also those who reach these exotic conclusions *a priori*. Now their position is hard to rebut. What you need is that they should accept some statement for which they no longer require a reason. Such must be the basis of any argument and demonstration. It is the policy of assuming nothing that destroys discussion and indeed rationality in general. Against anyone who adopts this stance reason is consequently not a weapon.

But if someone is in a bit of a muddle because of the received riddles, it is easy to give him an answer, to remove the sources of his confusion, as has already been made clear.

It is, then, quite clear from the discussion that contradictory assertions about the same thing cannot both be true at a single time, nor indeed can contraries, given that all contrariety is based on privation, as a reduction to principle of the accounts of contraries makes clear. In the same spirit, no intermediate state could be predicated of one and the same thing as a contrary. If something is white, it would be wrong to say that it is neither-black-nor-white, since then it would both be and not be white, since the second conjunct, which is the contradiction of white, truly applies to it.

It cannot then be right to adopt the position either of Heraclitus or indeed even of Anaxagoras. If it were, contraries would turn out to be predicable of the same thing. You see, when Anaxagoras says that there is a share of everything in everything, he is denying that anything is any more sweet, say, than bitter and so for all the other contraries, if everything is indeed present in everything not just potentially but actually and in a discriminable manner.

By the same token, it is not possible that all assertions could be false or that all assertions could be true. This is shown both by the many other embarrassments that arise out of this position and in particular because if, on the one hand, they are all false it would not be true to say even that they are all false and, on the other, if they are all true it would not be false to say that all are false.

KAPPA 7

This chapter recapitulates chapter 1 of book Epsilon. It is one of the closest recapitulations in Kappa.

Every science is on the hunt for certain principles and causes for each of the items that fall in its domain. Consider medicine and P.E. Consider, in fact, [**1064a**] any of the other sciences, whether productive or mathematical.

Each of these sciences circumscribes some kind of thing as its domain and endeavours to get to grips with it. It assumes that things of this kind exist and have being, but it does not study them *qua* things that are. There is another science that does this, and it is different from any of these.

Each of the sciences to which we have referred, assumes in some way the what-it-is for each kind and then tries to show what follows from this, with the appropriate degree of precision. The assumption of the what-it-is takes place in some cases through perception, in others by hypothesis. So from an inductive argument on these lines it can be shown that there is no demonstration of substance and the what-it-is.

Now there is a science that deals with nature, and clearly it will be different from either a practical or a productive science. For with productive science the principle of process, be it a skill or some other capacity, is in the producer not the product, and similarly with practical science the process is rather in the subjects than in the objects of action. In contrast to both, the science of the student of nature is concerned with those things that have within themselves the principle of their processes, and this shows us that physical science must be neither practical nor productive but theoretical (assuming this trichotomy to be exhaustive).

Now it is a requirement on each of the sciences that in some way or other it cognize the what-it-is and take this as its principle. And so. we must not overlook the way in which the student of nature is to provide a definition and how he is to take the account of substance, whether on the *snub* or on the *concave* model. Of these two, the account of *snub* is given with the matter of the thing, whereas that of *concave* is given without matter. For snubness is produced in a nose, so that the account of it is studied with the nose, and *snub* is *concave nose*. And this shows that the account of flesh and eye and the other bodily parts is in all cases to be given with the matter.

But there is also a science of that which has being *qua* possessed of being and separable. So we must decide whether this science is to be considered the same as the science of nature or rather different. Well, the science of nature has to do with those things that have a principle of process within themselves, whereas mathematics is a theoretical science and is indeed a science of permanent things, but not of separable things. So there is some science, different from either of these, which is about what has separable being free from process, if indeed there be any such substance, a substance, that is, which is separable and unprocessed. And that there is we shall endeavour to show.

But just suppose that among the things that are there is some nature of this kind. In this, if anywhere, would we find divinity. This would be the primary and fundamental principle. [**1064b**] And this shows that there are three kinds of theoretical science, physics, mathematics and theology. And the highest kind of science is the theoretical kind, and of theoretical sciences the highest is the last in our list. It has to do with the most valuable of the things that are, and it is the proper object of a science that determines its relative excellence.

A question that remains is whether or not we should consider that the science of being *qua* being is a science of the universal. After all, whereas each of the mathematical sciences is concerned with some one delimited kind, universal mathematics is concerned with all kinds. So if natural substances are primary among the things that are, then so too would the science of nature be primary among the sciences. But if there is some other nature and substance, separable and immune to process, then the science of it must both be different and also prior to physics and, by dint of being prior, universal.

KAPPA 8

This chapter recapitulates the remainder of book Epsilon. It adds some remarks from the Physics *on the subject of chance, which have a clear relevance to the treatment of accidental being.*

Given that there is a plurality of styles of account of being *simpliciter*, and that one of these is the account of being in terms of an accident, we ought first to have a look at what is in this manner.

Well, it is at least clear that none of the received sciences takes the accidental as its domain. It is not the business of architecture, for instance, to worry about what is destined to befall those who make use of a house, pondering, as it might be, whether their life in it will turn out hard or the reverse. Nor indeed are such concerns any business of weaving, cobbling or the concoction of sauces. No, each of these sciences considers what is special to it in each case, its own proprietary objective.

Or consider the following pearl: when a man is musical and becomes grammatical, that man will be both those two things *at the same time*, not having been them before; but then whatever is, without having always been, must have become, so that our friend must have become both musical and grammatical *at the same time*. I take it that among those activities which are generally taken to be sciences there is not one that seriously looks into this sort of thing, oh except, of course, sophistics. Sophistry has taken out an exclusive franchise on the accidental, and maybe Plato was not so way off line when he made out that the sophist devotes his life's work to the Non-Entity.

In fact, it is not even possible for there to be a science of the accidental. Something that you get to understand when you try to sort out what on earth the accidental after all is. Now it is our settled position that everything either (i) is always and of necessity (and the necessity here

336

is not that of any force but that, rather, which we employ in the business of demonstration), or (ii) is for the most part, or (iii) is neither for the most part nor always but rather as it so happens. An example of the last case would be the occurrence of chilly weather in high summer. This is not, I take it, something that occurs either always and of necessity or for the most part, and yet it could happen from time to time. [1065a] Now it is precisely the accidental that occurs, but neither always nor of necessity nor for the most part.

There's a statement for you of what the accidental is, and there should be little obscurity as to why there is no science of such a beast. The field of any science is what is either always or for the most part, and the accidental falls under neither of these two heads.

It is also clear that there are no causes and principles of the accidental such as there are for what is *per se*. Were there such, everything would be of necessity. For if x is if y is and y is if z is, and the occurrence of z is a matter not of chance but of necessity, then that of which z was the cause will also be of necessity, right down to the so-called ultimate effect (which, however, was in this case *ex hypothesi* accidental). So everything will be of necessity, with a thing's being whichever of two ways it happens and the possibility of something's being or not being being deleted wholesale from the totality of things that happen.

Even if the cause be supposed not indeed to be, but to be becoming, the same consequences will follow. Everything will still happen of necessity. Tomorrow's eclipse, say, will occur if x occurs and x will occur if y occurs and y if z. And in this way if we count back over the finite time between now and tomorrow, we will eventually get to the present state of affairs, so that, given the existence of this, everything after it will occur of necessity, and so everything happens of necessity.

Now a thing can be by dint of being true and accidental. Here the first feature derives from a conjunction of thinking and is indeed an affection of thought – hence the absence of an inquiry into the principles of what is in this way, whereas principles are sought for what is externally and separably – whereas the other (accidentality) is not necessary but indefinite, its causes chaotic and without limit.

As for one thing's being *for* another, this is something to be found among things produced by nature or by thought. And when one of such things occurs by accident, it is deemed to be luck. In fact, just as that which is can be either *per se* or accidental, the same applies to a cause. Luck, then, is an accidental cause among things occurring for something else in which rational choice is involved, with the consequence that luck and thought are in the same line of business. After all, there can be no choosing without thought. Even so, the causes of the outcomes of luck are indefinite, which is why luck is inscrutable to human reason, causation by accident and of nothing *simpliciter*. Luck, be it also noted, is good when the outcome is good and bad when the outcome is bad, [**1065b**] amounting, when the outcome is on the grand scale, to downright good or bad fortune.

Of course, nothing accidental is prior to something which is *per se*, and so no accidental cause has priority either. So even if luck or *the automatic* are the cause of the world, mind and nature are prior causes still.

KAPPA 9

Chapters 9–12 of Kappa are not recapitulations of the Metaphysics *but excerpts from the* Physics. *They mainly have to do with the principal subject of that work, process and change. Their relevance to the central issues of the* Metaphysics *is far from clear. The present chapter discusses process in connection with the notions of potentiality and actuality. The excerpts are taken from* Physics *III: 1–3.*

There are things, now, that have being only in actuality, things that have being in potentiality and things that have being in potentiality and actuality. The first of these are this-somethings, the second quantities, the third from the others. And apart from objects there is no process, given that change always takes place through the categories of being and that there is no common thing above them and not in any single category.

And there are two ways in which each category belongs to every entity. Take the category of thisness. Thisness comes either as shape/form or as privation of the form. And with quality, we have, on the one hand, white, say, and, on the other, black, with quantity the complete and the incomplete, with movement upwards and downwards (and we also have light and heavy). Thus there are as many species of process and change as there are of being.

And if we discriminate, for each kind of thing, between what is in potentiality and what is in entelechy, then I am calling the actualization of what is in potential, *qua* a thing just of that kind, a process. And that this is on the right lines can be shown as follows.

When something potentially constructed, *qua* being just what we say to be potentially constructed, is in actualization, what is happening is that it is being constructed, and this is the construction process. Ditto: learning, curing, walking, hopping, growing old and maturing. The process is undergone when the entelechy as such is, neither sooner nor

339

later. It is therefore the entelechy of the potential being, just when, being in entelechy, is actualized, and not as itself but as a subject of process, that is process.

Let me say a word or two about *qua* here. The bronze, I take it, is potentially a statue. But this does not mean that the entelechy of bronze *qua* bronze is a process. For the what-it-was-to-be-that-thing is not the same for bronze and a particular potentiality, since if they were the same *simpliciter*, in terms of its account, then the entelechy of bronze would be a sort of process. In fact they are not the same, as can be shown by considering contraries. A potentiality for health and a potentiality for sickness are not the same – were they the same, so too would being healthy and being sick be – but rather the subject, which is both healthy and sick, be it moisture or be it blood, is what is one and the same. So given that these are not the same, any more than colour is the same as the visible, it is the entelechy of the potential *qua* potential that is a process.

We have shown, I fancy, that this is so, and that process occurs when the entelechy as such is present, neither sooner nor later. After all, [**1066a**] everything is capable of sometimes being actualized and sometimes not – cf. our potential construct *qua* potential construct. And it is the actualization of the potential construct *qua* potential construct that is the process of construction.

Surely, the actualization is either just this, the process, or the house. However, when the house is, the potential construct is not, and it is the potential construct that undergoes the process of construction. There is no way round it,' then. The actualization is the process of construction, and the process of construction is a process. Ditto all processes.

There are at least two reasons for accepting all this, the *consensus sapientium* on the subject and the sheer difficulty of framing any other definition of process. For a start, it would not be possible to subsume it under any other class of things. This much is shown by the consensus. Process has been variously dubbed otherness, inequality and non-being, but process is not a necessary feature of any of these. Also it is no more the case that change occurs to these things or from them than that it occurs to/from their opposites.

Now the reason for subsuming process under these things is that it is thought to be something indefinite, the principles in the second of the two columns of contraries being privative and therefore indefinite – none of them is either a this or a such or an item in any other of the categories. And the reason why it is thought to be indefinite is that it cannot be subsumed under either the potentiality or the actuality of entities. Neither what is potentially a certain amount nor what is actually a certain amount undergoes process of necessity. On the other hand, process is thought to be a kind of actualization, though an incomplete one. And the reason for this is that the potentiality of which it is the actualization is incomplete. This is what makes it so hard to understand what process is – it must be subsumed either under privation, or under potentiality or under actualization *simpliciter*, but it appears that none of these subsumptions is possible. So all that is left is the account that we have given, the actualization/non-actualization we have set out. This may be hard to discern but there is no reason why it should not have being.

It is also clear that process is in the thing processed, since it is the entelechy of the process induced by the processing agent. And the actualization of the processing agent is none other than that of the thing processed. It has to be the entelechy of both agent and object, for the following reasons: a thing is an agent of processing by dint of being capable of processing and a processor by dint of actualization, but it is the object of processing that it is capable of actualizing, and so the actualization of both is one in the same way as there is the same gap from one to two and from two to one, or as an incline is the same as a decline, and yet being is not one for them. That is the way in which also the actualization of the processor and of the thing processed is one.

KAPPA 10

This chapter consists of excerpts from Physics *III: 4–7. Their topic is the impossibility of the actual existence of the infinite, to which reference has already been made in book Theta.*

Now the infinite is either something that cannot be crossed because it does not lie in its nature to be crossed, just as it does not lie in the nature of the voice to be visible, or something that permits only incomplete crossing, or something which hardly permits crossing at all, or something which, although it lies in its nature, does not in fact permit crossing or contain a limit. Further something may be infinite **[1066b]** either by addition or by subtraction or by both.

Now it is not possible for the infinite to be separable from perceptibles and a *per se* something. Assume that it is neither a magnitude nor a plurality and that infinity itself is its substance, not an accidental feature. In that case it will be indivisible, given that the divisible is either magnitude or plurality. But if it is indivisible, then it is not infinite, except in the way that voice is invisible. But that is not the account usually given of infinity, nor is it an infinity like that that we are studying. We are studying the infinite as that which cannot be crossed.

Moreover, how can the infinite be *per se*, unless number and magnitude also, of which the infinite is an affection, are *per se*? Also, if the infinite has being as an accidental feature, then it would not *qua* infinite be an element of the things that are, just as the invisible is no element of spoken language, for all that the voice is invisible.

It is also clear that the infinite cannot have being in actuality. If it could, any part taken from it would be infinite. After all, if the infinite is indeed a substance and not a predicable, the what-it-was-to-be-that-thing for the infinite and the infinite are the same. So either the infinite is indivisible or, if you can have parts of it, it must be divisible into infinites! But it is, I take it, not on for the same thing to consist of a plurality of infinites. And the infinite will be a part of the infinite just as much as air is a part of air, if it is a substance and principle. This shows us two things: you cannot have parts of the infinite and the infinite is indivisible.

But the infinite with being in entelechy cannot be like this, since it must be some quantity. So the infinite must be present as an accidental feature. But if this is the way in which it is present, then it has already been said that it cannot be a principle. It will be whatever is an accidental feature of what is the principle, whether this be air or an even number.

Now our investigation of the infinite is universal in character, but it can also be shown as follows that the infinite is not to be found among perceptibles. Let the account of body be *bounded by planes*. But then there can be no infinite body, either perceptible or intuitable. Nor indeed can there be a number which is separable and infinite, given that it is either number or the possessor of number that is denumerable.

Now this can be shown by the following considerations, which are naturalistic in character. The infinite cannot be either a compound body or simple.

I. The infinite cannot be a compound body.
Reason: the elements are limited in plurality. The contraries must be equal and there cannot be some one among them which is infinite. If the potentiality of one of the two contrary bodies falls even the slightest bit below that of the other, then that which is limited will be destroyed by the infinite. And it is not possible for each of them to be infinite, given that body is what has extension in every direction and the infinite is the limitlessly extended, so that if the infinite is a body it will be infinite in every direction.

II. The infinite cannot be a single and simple body.
Reason: it cannot be, as claimed by some, a thing over and above the elements (from which they produce these), nor can it have being *simpliciter*. There is no such body over and above the elements. Everything can be dissolved back into that of which it is composed, and there is no evidence of any such ultimate component beyond the simple bodies. [**1067a**] Nor can the infinite be fire or any other of the elements.

For leaving aside any one of them's being infinite, it is not possible for the entire universe, even if it were to be limited, either to be or to become some one of them (recall Heraclitus' claim that from time to time everything becomes fire). In fact, the same reasoning applies to the infinite as to the One introduced over and above the elements by the philosophers of nature. After all, everything changes from one contrary to another, from hot, say, to cold.

Also a perceptible body has some location, and both whole and part are in the same place, as with the whole and a part of the earth. So if the supposed infinite body is of the same kind as its parts, it will be either immune from, or constantly subject to, process-motion. And this is impossible, because there is no reason for it to move either up or down or anywhere any more than anywhere else. Suppose, for instance, that there was this sod which was part of any infinite body. Where is this to have either process-motion or stasis? For the place of the body that is of common kind with it is infinite. But is this sod then to occupy the entire place? And how, pray, is this to happen? And what are stasis and process-motion to be for the sod? Perhaps it is in a state of stasis everywhere? But then how is it to undergo process-motion? Maybe it is in a state of process-motion everywhere? But then how is it ever to be in a state of stasis?

But, then, suppose that the universe is dissimilar from its parts. In that case, the places of whole and part are also dissimilar. So the body of the universe (a) will not be a unity except by contact, and (b) will be either limited or infinite in type. Now it is not possible for them to be limited in type, because then those of some types would be infinite and those of others not (assuming an infinite universe). So fire, say, or water would be infinite, but any such infinite element would spell the destruction of its contraries. If, on the other hand, the universal parts are infinite and simple, then so too are their places infinite and there will be an infinity of elements. If, conversely, this is impossible, and places are limited, then the universe too must be limited.

Still more generally, it is not possible for an infinite body to have being and for there to be a place for bodies, if every perceptible body has either weight or lightness. For such a body will be borne either towards the middle or upwards and neither of these can happen to either the whole or a half of the infinite. After all, how is it to be divided? For that matter, how is half of the infinite to be down and half up, or half at the edge and half in the middle?

Also, every perceptible body is in a place, and the types of place are six, none of which can be in an infinite body. Basically, if it is impossible for there to be infinite place, then there cannot be infinite body either, because what is in place is somewhere, and this indicates either up or down or one of the other directions. And each such direction is a limitation.

The infinite is not the same as a single nature in magnitude, process-motion and time, but the posterior is said to be infinite relative to the prior. Process-motion, for instance, is said to be infinite relative to the magnitude through which the process of motion, alteration or increase occurs, and time is said to be infinite because of the process-motion that occurs in it.

KAPPA 11

This chapter is an excerpt from Physics v: 1. *Its subject is the different kinds of change.*

[1067b] When something undergoes a change, this can either be accidental to it – as, for instance, it is accidental if the musical thing goes through the change of walking – or it is said to change *simpliciter* by dint of a change to something in it. Examples of the latter are things that change relative to their parts, the body, for instance, becoming healthy because the eye does.

There is, however, also something which is in itself the primary undergoer of process. This is what is susceptible of process *per se*.

And the same trichotomy applies also to the processor – its processing can be either accidental or part-relative or *per se*. And there is also something which is the primary processor, as well as the undergoer of process and the period and initial and end states of the process.

By contrast, the types, affections and place, into which the processing of the processed occurs, do not themselves undergo processing. Examples are knowledge and heat. And of course it is not heat, say, which is a process but heating. In any case, non-accidental change is not to be found in all things, but only among contraries and the intermediate state and in connection with contradiction, as can be shown by induction.

Now what undergoes change changes either from something positive to something positive, or from something negative to something negative, or from something positive to something negative, or from something negative to something positive. (And here something positive is to be taken as what is revealed by an affirmative assertion.) It follows that there must be three changes, since a move from negative to negative is not a change, there being no opposition given that there is neither contrariety nor contradiction.

Now change from negative to positive (involving contradiction) is production, production *simpliciter* from change *simpliciter*, particular production from particular change. But, of course, there is a plurality of accounts of non-being, and neither non-being involving composition nor non-being involving division can undergo process, nor can non-being involving potentiality, which is the opposite of that which is *simpliciter*. (Well, there is accidental processing of the not-white or not-good, since a man, say, could be not-white, but there is no way in which a non-this *simpliciter* could undergo a process.) So the non-being cannot undergo process. But then it is also impossible for production to be a process – it is, after all, the non-being that gets produced. We can go on saying till we are blue in the face that the non-being is produced accidentally. It is still the case that non-being is present in what is produced *simpliciter*. By the same token, what is not cannot be in a state of stasis either.

So we are already in trouble here, but there is another problem, assuming that everything that undergoes process is in place and that the non-being is not in place (if it were, it would have to have a location!).

And it also turns out that destruction is not a process. The contrary of a process is either process or stasis, but the contrary of destruction is production. [1068a] And since every process is a kind of change, and the three changes are those that we have specified, and of these those involving production and destruction are not processes, and since processes involve contradiction, the inevitable upshot is that only positive-positive change is process. Further, positives are either contrary or intermediate (let us take even privation to be a contrary) and are revealed by an affirmative assertion, such as asserting something to be naked, or toothless or black.

KAPPA 12

This chapter is an excerpt from Physics *v: 1–3. Its subject is the connection between movement and the categories.*

If the categories are distributed into substance, quality, place, action and affection, relation and quantity, there must be three processes, those of quality, of quantity and of place. There will not, on the other hand, be any process relative to substance, since nothing is contrary to substance. And there will be no process relative to relation, in as much as, when one of two relational items changes, it is possible that the relation can no longer be truly asserted of the other, even though it has not changed a whit, so that the processing of such things is accidental. And there will be no process relative to what acts or is acted on, nor to the processor and thing processed, because there is no process of process, nor production of production, nor, more generally, change of change.

If there were to be process of process it would have to be in one of the following two ways: (a) the process might underlie a process. For instance, just as a man, say, can undergo a process in changing from white to black, so too the process might undergo heating, say, or cooling or might change in place or increase. But this is clearly impossible – process is not the sort of thing that can underlie. Or (b) something else, which does underlie, might change from change into some other type of thing, just as a man can change from a state of illness to a state of health. This too, however, is impossible, except accidentally. For every process is change from one thing to another. So too are production and destruction, except that these are changes into things opposed in one way and process is change into things opposed in another. So at one and the same time something both changes from health to illness and changes from this very change to another. So clearly, if something

348

has become ill, it will have changed into whatever change is relevant (OK, it could also be in stasis), changing too, on each occasion, not into an arbitrary change. And the new change will also be from something particular into something else. So it will in fact be the opposite change, normal development.

However, this is clearly accidental. It is like a change from remembering to forgetting by dint of the fact that that to which these states pertain undergoes a change, at one point towards knowledge and at another towards ignorance.

There will also be an infinite regress if we are to allow change of change and production of production. So if something is the case with the posterior change, it must also be with the prior. For instance, if production *simpliciter* was once produced, then so will what is being produced have been produced. [**1068b**] So what is produced *simpliciter* was not yet in being, but what was being produced as what is being produced was! And indeed this was at some point in a state of being produced, so that at that point it was not yet getting produced as something else!

In any case, there is no primary item of an infinite sequence, so that in this case there will be no primary item and thus no subsequent one either. So nothing could get produced, undergo process or change in any way.

Again, this same thing must have the opposite process available and also stasis, as well as production and destruction. So what is produced, once it has been produced as what is produced, will be destroyed. After all, it cannot be destroyed just as soon as it is being produced nor later, given that what is destroyed must have being.

In any case, anything that gets produced and changed must have underlying matter. So what will this be in this case, in the way that the altered body or soul is, what will be what is produced as process or production? What, too, is the end state of the process? For the processing or production of a thing from one thing to another should be something. But how is this to come about? For learning will not be the production of learning, and so nothing will be the production of production either.

There is, as we said, no process of substance, relation or action and affection, so it remains that process is relative to quality, quantity and location, for each of which there is contrariety. And quality here is not intended as quality-in-substance (after all, the differentia is a quality) but rather quality as affection, in terms of which something is said to be affected or immune to affection.

And what is immune to process is either what is quite generally incapable of undergoing process or what can only undergo it with difficulty and over a long period of time or what commences slowly to be processed or what is naturally constituted to undergo process and is capable of being processed but is not being processed in the time, place and manner for which it is constituted to be processed. It is only this among the things immune to process that I call the thing in stasis. For stasis is contrary to process, so that it must be a privation in the recipient of process.

Things are together in place if they are in a single primary place and apart if they are in different primary places. And things whose extremities are together are in contact. And the intermediate is that into which it is natural for what undergoes change to arrive before changing to the other extreme, assuming continuous natural change. Contrary in place is something most distant in a straight line, and something is sequential if it is after the beginning, as defined in terms of position or type or in some other way, with none of the things of the same kind between it and that to which it is sequential, such as lines for a line, points for a point and houses for a house (there is nothing to stop something of a different kind being between them). For the sequential is sequential to something and a posterior thing. [1069a] One is not sequential to two, nor is the first day of the month sequential to the second.

And if something is both sequential and in contact, it is contiguous. And since all change occurs among opposites, and since opposites are contraries and contradiction, and since there is no midpoint of a contradiction, it is clear that the intermediate occurs among contraries.

And the continuous is as a kind of contiguity. I say that things are continuous when the boundary of each of them, by which they are in contact and held together, is one and the same, so that clearly continuity occurs in those things from which it is natural for some unity to arise by virtue of their contact.

It is clear that the primary here is the sequential. The sequential does not have to be in contact, but anything that is in contact is sequential.

And if something is continuous, then it is in contact, but it can easily be in contact without being continuous. And for things for which contact is impossible there can be no conjunction of natures. That is why a point is not the same as a unit. For points, but not units, are capable of contact. Units have only sequentiality. And there can be something between two points, but not between two units.

Book Lambda

LAMBDA I

*Book Lambda constitutes a complete and independent course in general philo-
sophy, which gives a central emphasis to theology. Its relation to the bulk of the
Metaphysics is a subject of intense debate. It certainly offers perspectives on the
doctrine of substance which are not found elsewhere in the work. Lambda divides
into two halves: the first six chapters, which are a comprehensive course in
natural philosophy, and the last four chapters, which present Aristotle's mature
theology.*

*Chapter 1 launches the general course in natural philosophy. It broaches the
topic of substance and echoes Zeta 1 in stressing that philosophy investigates the
principles and causes of substance. It stresses the priority of substance and sketches
the dispute between naturalists and idealists about the nature of substance.*

*Aristotle himself proposes three fundamental kinds of substance, substance
which is perceptible and perishable, substance which is perceptible and imperishable
and substance which is immune to change of any kind. The first two of these
fall in the domain of natural science, the latter in that of logic and mathematics.
If there is some common source of all substance then it is the business of theology
to investigate this. The rest of this first chapter is devoted to a presentation of
the general doctrine of change found in* Physics *1.*

1. Our whole investigation is into substance. For what we are really
   seeking is the principles and causes of the substances. Because:
   (a) if
      (i) the universe is physically a kind of whole, then substance is its
         primary constituent, and if
      (ii) it conforms to the ontology of the *Categories*, then on
         this approach also substance will be primary, then quality, then
         quantity.
   (b) at the same time such things as qualities and movements are not
      even beings in the simple way of speaking. If we did count them as

beings, we would also have to admit the not-white and the not-straight – for, to be sure, we assert being of these things too, cf. '. . . is not-white'.

(c) again, none of the other categories is separable.

(d) the Presocratics in effect bear this out. For their inquiry was really into the principles, elements and causes of substance. (There is a contemporary tendency to posit universals as substances (for the kinds are universals, which modern thinkers are inclined to assert to be principles and substances, given their dialectical approach), whereas in antiquity particular things, such as fire and earth, were taken as substances, not the general thing, body.)

2. Now there are three substances, of which:

(a) one sort is sensible, of which:

   (i) the one is eternal and

   (ii) the other destructible (This substance, that of plants and animals, is universally acknowledged, and we must grasp its elements and decide whether they are one or many.), and

(b) the other is unmoved. (This substance is sometimes asserted to be separable; some philosophers divide it into two, while others assign both Forms and mathematicals to the same nature, and still others only admit mathematicals from this group.)

3. Now 2(a)(i) and (ii) belong to the study of nature (for they are associated with movement), [**1069b**] while (b) belongs to another study, assuming that they have no principle in common.

4. At any rate, sensible substance is susceptible of change. Now:

   (i) change is from opposites or the intermediate, and

   (ii) not from all opposites (for there cannot be change from the colour white to a voice, say, although white is indeed an opposite of voice) but from contraries, so

   (iii) there must necessarily be some underlying thing changing into the contrary state, since the contraries themselves do not change.

LAMBDA 2

This chapter continues the exposition of the doctrine of change found in the Physics. *The doctrine stresses that there must be something which persists through change and this chapter associates this persistent with matter. It proceeds to enumerate the four kinds of change and connects the doctrine of change with that of potentiality and actuality. Matter is presented as the source of diversity and variety in the world. The general conclusion is that there are three causes and fundamental principles of perceptible substance, form, privation and matter.*

The teaching of the first two chapters of Lambda is close to that of the Physics, *though it is distinctive both for its compression and for the greater role that it assigns to the notions of potentiality and actuality. It forms the basis for the further observations on natural philosophy which make up the rest of the first half of Lambda.*

5. There is then, in change, a continuant, while the first of the two contrary states involved does not persist. There is then a third thing in addition to the contraries, namely matter.

6. There are, of course, four kinds of change, corresponding to the four kinds of question 'What is x?', 'What is x like?', 'How great is x?' and 'Where is x?' Now:

   (i) the first kind, change involving a 'this', is generation or destruction *simpliciter*,

   (ii) quantitative change is increase and diminution,

   (iii) qualitative change is alteration and

   (iv) locational change is travel.

   A change, then, is made what it is by the pair of contraries that it involves.

7. Now it is surely necessary that the changing matter should potentially be both contraries. What-is being twofold, all change is from what-is potentially to what-is actually, from potentially white, say, to actually

357

white (similarly with increase and diminution and the others). This is the reason why not only is there coming-to-be from what-is-not accidentally, but every case of coming-to-be is also from what-is. It is from what-is potentially but not actually.

8. This is, in effect, a refinement of Anaxagoras' doctrine of the One. It is, surely, an improvement on his 'All things were together' – as also the mixing of Empedocles and Anaximander, and indeed the position of Democritus – to adopt the view that all things originally were in potentiality but not in actuality. In any case, it would seem on this construal that these thinkers were feeling their way towards the notion of matter.

9. However, although everything that changes has matter, the kinds differ. For those of the eternal things that are not generated but do change by locomotion also have matter, but their matter is ungenerated, though it is susceptible of change as travel.

10. (There is perhaps this further problem: what sort of what-is-not is the starting point for generation. This arises because what-is-not is threefold.)

11. A thing, then, may potentially be, but what it potentially is is not contingent; rather, different actualities realize different potentialities. Nor is it a sufficient explanation of the world to say just that all things were originally together. For things differ in matter. Indeed, why otherwise did an infinity of things come-to-be and not just one? Mind, after all, is single, so that if matter too were single, the only thing that would have actually come-to-be would be what matter was, potentially, a single thing.

12. To sum up, there are three causes and three principles. Two of the principles are contraries, of which one is the form and account and the other the privation, and the third is matter.

LAMBDA 3

The subject of chapter 3 shifts away from change towards substance. There are a variety of points in the chapter, which coheres rather loosely. Aristotle begins by stating that, whereas it is only primary matter and primary form that are in fact exempt from generation, in explanation the components of a composite entity should be treated as primary in definition. This is followed by some remarks on accidental and spontaneous generation in sympathy with the account given in Zeta 7. The problem with accidental generation is that the formal cause does not seem to be appropriately operative. Aristotle's solution is to characterize such generation as generation by formal privation.

The next question addressed is that of the existence of immaterial form. Aristotle softens his normal hostility to the extent of admitting that, whereas immaterial form is not possible for artefacts, it may be possible for natural entities. Finally the traditional argument from causation for the existence of the Forms is refuted by the insistence that the formal cause is not temporally prior to the composite. The efficient cause is thus prior, but this gives no reason to infer the existence of separable Forms, and in any case both efficient and formal cause are non-separable. The efficient cause of a man is a man, and the formal cause is his soul not Man Himself.

Supplementary note 1: in the claim that neither matter nor form are generated, it is ultimate matter and form that is intended.

Our model of change is that in all cases there is (a) a thing that undergoes change, [**1070a**] (b) something by which it is changed and (c) something into which it changes. We further claim that the role of (b) is played by the primary mover, that of (a) by the thing's matter, and that of (c) by its form.

On this model, however, there will be an infinite regress of explanation if it is not merely the case that bronze becomes spherical but also that sphericality and bronze also come into being. In practice, there must be some stopping point.

Supplementary note 2: each substance is generated from a synonym, whether it is a natural existent or something else.

There are four modes of substantial generation: artificial, natural, fortuitous and spontaneous. Artifice, then, is a principle in something different from, nature a principle in something the same as, the thing generated (e.g. man produces man), and the other modes are privations of these.

Supplementary note 3: there are three kinds of substance. There is (a) matter, which is a 'this such' to the senses (for everything that is apprehended just by touch and not as a whole organism is underlying material), and there is also (b) a thing's nature, which is both a 'this such' and a certain condition into which it develops. Finally, the third kind of substance is (c) the composite particular, such as Socrates or Callias.

Now, in some cases there is no 'this suchness' apart from the composite substance. The form of a house is an example. It can only have separate existence if the art of architecture is itself a separate existent. Nor is there any generation and destruction of these artificial forms. The existence or non-existence of an immaterial house is of quite a different kind, and also that of health and of every other product of art. So if there is in fact any separate existence of non-composites, then it occurs in the case of natural things. So Plato was not wrong to make his Forms coextensive with natural existents, if indeed there are Forms. But that does not mean that he should have allowed such Forms as Fire, Flesh and Head; for these are all material, and it is the last that is the material of what is most clearly a substance.

Supplementary note 4: motive causes are causes as pre-existent entities, while formal causes are simultaneous. For when a man is healthy, it is then too that health exists, and the shape of the bronze sphere exists simultaneously with the bronze sphere.

It is, however, an open question whether any component survives the dissolution of the composite. After all, in some cases nothing prevents this from being so, as for instance if the soul is such a component – not all of it, just the intellect (it is perhaps impossible that it should all be). A positive answer, however, would provide absolutely no grounds to suppose that there must be Forms; it is a man that generates a man, a particular that generates a thing of its kind, and particular generation also occurs with artefacts. The form of health just is the doctor's competence.

LAMBDA 4

Chapter 4 is again a rather loose structure, but it is unified by its anti-idealist thrust. Aristotle begins by arguing against the supposition that there can be some more fundamental constituent (he has in mind numbers, defended in this role by the Pythagoreans and their allies, notably Speusippus), which underlies the categories of being. To accept any such constituent is to erode the crucial distinction between substance and the non-substantial categories. Aristotle is equally trench-ant in rejecting universal causal agents. With the exception of form, privation and matter, which we have seen to be universal causes, all other causal agents are restricted to their appropriate genera. Causal generalization across genera is unfruitful.

The chapter also adds the efficient cause as a principle in addition to the elements of the composite, form, privation and matter, and the discussion of the kinds of cause is completed by the identification of the ultimate final cause with the prime mover, to be described in detail in the theological chapters of Lambda.

A. Now there is a way in which the causes and the principles of different things are themselves different, but there is another – if one is speaking at the level of universals, where analogy arises – in which the causes and the principles are the same for all things.

There is, now, a possible controversy over the following point. Are the principles and the elements of substances the same as or different from those of relational entities, and similarly, indeed, with each of the categories?

(1) In fact, it would be absurd if they were the same for all; for in that case relational entities and substances would be produced from the same things. [**1070b**] What then will they be? Apart from substance and the other categories, there is no common entity,

and yet an element must be prior to the things of which it is an element. Very obviously, substance cannot be an element of relational entities, nor any of these an element of substance.

(2) Furthermore, how is it even possible for there to be the same elements for all things? No element can be identical to a compound of elements; for instance, neither B nor A can be identical to BA. It is a rider to this that none of the intelligible entities, such as existence or unity, can be an element. For these also apply to all composites.

No element, then, will be either a substance or a relational entity. And yet this would have to be the case, if substances and relational entities were to share principles and elements. So it follows that there are not the same elements for all things.

B. Or perhaps, as we said, in a way there are, and in a way there are not. For instance, perhaps heat is a formal element of sensible bodies and also, in another way, its privation, cold, while the material element is whatever has a primary and intrinsic potentiality to be these. These elements themselves will be substances, and so will be their compounds (of which they will also be the principles), that is, whatever becomes one thing from heat and cold, such as flesh and bone, given the necessary substantial difference between element and compound.

Such entities, then, will indeed share elements and principles (and other things will share others), but, in this way of speaking, there will be no universal elements. They will be said to be only by analogy, as in the claim that there are just three principles, form, privation and material. But each such principle will be different in connection with a different genus. For instance, in the case of the colours, they will be white, black and the surface respectively, and another threesome would be light, darkness and air, from which are derived day and night.

C. Not only intrinsic elements are causes, however, but also some external factors, conspicuously the motive cause. This makes it clear that principle and element are different things, and that both are causes (and that principles divide into elements and non-elements), and that the source of motion or rest is a kind of principle. Thus, at the level of analogy, the number of elements is indeed three, but that of the causes and principles is four.

But both elements and the primary motive cause differ in different cases. Consider the threesome health, disease, body; in this case, the motive cause is medicine. Consider form F, disorder as seen, bricks: here the motive cause is architecture. Such are the subdivisions of the motive principle.

D. Now in the case of natural objects the motive cause is something of the same species, such as a man causing a man. In the case of the products of calculation, however, the motive cause is the form or the opposite. There is, thus, a way in which there are three causes, but in the way which we are considering there are four. For in a way health is indeed the same thing as medicine and architecture as the form of a house, and man does indeed breed man, but then, in addition to these, there is that which moves all as the first thing of all.

LAMBDA 5

This chapter is a close continuation of chapter 4 and begins with a reassertion of the fundamental importance of substance, which was one of the main themes of the earlier chapter. To the universal principles allowed in chapter 4 actuality and potentiality are now added with certain restrictions, but it is insisted that the use of actuality and potentiality in explanation must be in compliance with the characteristics of each genus and species. The chapter also points out that explanation in terms of actuality and potentiality is not really supplementary to explanation in terms of the earlier principles, since the actual is to be identified with form, the composite and privation and the potential is to be identified with matter.

The second main business of chapter 5, and of chapter 4, is to stress that material potentiality on its own is insufficient to explain the production of the composite. An external efficient cause with actual being is required to initiate the process of production, although this is indeed conditioned by the material cause. Together with the previous chapter, this chapter offers a clear statement of Aristotle's substance-based metaphysics, in distinction to the idealism of the Pythagoreans and the Academy and the materialism of those who reject the diversity of causation.

A. Given that there are some things that are separate and some that are not separate, it is the latter that are substances. [**1071a**] Hence there are the same causes for them all, in as much as without substances there are no qualities and movements. Now, further, these causes will in a given case be, say, soul and body, or, alternatively, intellect and appetite and body.

B. There is, however, also another way in which, at the level of analogy, principles are the same, and this is that of activation and potential. These too, though, both differ for different things and also apply in different ways.

365

There are certainly things that exist at one time actually and at another time potentially. Wine is an example, or flesh, or a man. (For such things there is also a good fit between their activation and potential and the causes that have been outlined. Activation is the form's mode of existence, assuming its separation, and also the composite's, the privation is comparable to darkness or something diseased, and the potential is matter's mode of existence, given that it is the matter that has the potential to become both the others.)

In another way, however, there are things for which the activated and potential existence is different. I have in mind things that do not share the same matter, and of which there is not the same form but a different one. This is the way, for instance, in which his elements are a cause of man. Now his elements are, materially, fire and earth and, formally, his peculiar form. There is, however, also a further, external factor, on the one hand in the role of the father, but also, in addition, in that of the sun and its oblique rotation. These external factors are not material, nor are they a form nor a privation nor a member of the same species. What are they? They are motive causes.

C. Let me show you on the board just how one column of causes and principles can be said universally and the other cannot. On the one hand, then, the first principles of all things are (a) whatever has, in activation, the primary 'thisness' and (b) whatever is potentially F for the appropriate F. Now these causes and principles, which we have been discussing, are logical, not real, entities. For a principle of particular things must itself be a particular thing. It is true that man is a principle of man at the universal level, but there is no universal man in reality. Rather it is Peleus that is the motive cause of Achilles and your father that is yours. A particular B is the motive cause of a particular BA, even though at the unqualified level it is indeed the universal B that is the cause of the universal BA.

Furthermore, the causes and elements of substances (albeit different causes of different ones) are also, as has been said, the causes and elements of things not in different categories, of colours, sounds, substances, quality alike, but they are only so by analogy. But also even things in the same species have different causes, differing not, evidently, by species but in as much as particular things have different causes. For instance, your matter, form and motive cause are all different from mine. But for all that, at the universal level of description, they are the same.

To the questions, then, what are the principles and elements of substances, relational entities and qualities, and whether they are the same or different, the answer is clear. When many different ways of speaking are run together, the principles are indeed the same, but, when the ways are distinguished, they are not the same but different, except, of course, in the way at which I am now pointing. In this way, i.e. at the level of analogy, they are the same for all things, in that they are matter, form, privation and motive cause. And it is in this way that the causes of the substances are the causes of all things, in that when substances are removed so is everything else. And the primary-in-activation also belongs in this column. In the other column, on the other hand, the primary causes are not the same for all. These are all opposites that do not define genera and are not spoken of in a multiplicity of ways. And similarly with the varieties of matter.

OK. [1071b] We have now set out what are the principles of sensibles and how many of them there are, and in what way they are the same and in what way different.

LAMBDA 6

Chapter 6 has a pivotal role within the structure of Lambda, being both the conclusion to the general philosophy of nature which is the content of the first half of the book and the first stage of the theological exposition which occupies the last four chapters. The chapter contains a proof of the necessary existence of an eternal substance which is immune to change. The argument runs as follows. There must be some eternal and unchanged substance because otherwise all substance would be perishable and that would mean that everything in the world was perishable. However, the world itself and time are clearly not perishable. But they could only be imperishable if there is something immanent which is itself imperishable. Therefore there must be an eternal and imperishable substance. This argument has already been used by Aristotle in Physics VIII, and it is usually objected that it commits the fallacy of distribution. Because the whole world is imperishable (if it is), it does not follow that anything in it is imperishable.

However, Aristotle makes an addition to the argument in the present chapter which is perhaps intended to meet the force of this objection. He identifies the eternal substance with pure actuality. The eternal substance can never have merely potential being, since, in that case, the continuity of its existence would not be guaranteed. But if there is an eternal substance which is never potential and always actual, then the eternity of the world is guaranteed in a way that would not be the case if there were no such substance. It is possible for the world to be eternal, without anything in it being eternal, but it is not possible for it to be necessarily eternal, Aristotle is arguing, unless there is something in it which is necessarily eternal. Such a thing would have to be a substance having being in pure actuality. Such a substance would also explain the production of the world, in contrast to a Platonic form, which would be inert as an efficient cause.

1. Now since there were three substances, two of them natural and the third unmoved, we should say about this last that there must be a kind of eternal unmoved substance.

2. To begin with, substances have priority among things that are. So, if they are all destructible, then all things are destructible. It is, however, impossible that movement should either come-to-be or be destroyed. It must always have been in existence, and the same can be said for time itself, since it is not even possible for there to be an earlier and a later if time does not exist. Movement, then, is also continuous in the way in which time is – indeed time is either identical to movement or is some affection of it. (There is, however, only one continuous movement, namely spatial movement, and of this only circular rotation.)

3. Suppose, now, that there is indeed something that is such as to move and affect other things but that it is not active. In such circumstances, there may still be no movement, since it is quite possible for something that has a capacity not to be active. In that case, there would be no advantage at all from the admission of eternal substances, as in the Theory of Forms, unless there is among them a principle capable of moving something else. Not even this, however, is sufficient, nor any other substance in addition to the Forms. Unless the further factor is active, there will still be no movement.

4. Nor will it be enough even for it to be active, if its substance is potentiality. Then there will be movement, but not eternal movement, since for anything that is potentially its not-being might obtain.

5. There must then be a principle of such a kind that its substance is activity. Ergo, these substances must be without matter. For their eternity is a condition on that of anything else. They, then, must be actuality.

6. And yet there is a problem: for it is generally accepted that, while everything that is active is also potential, not everything that is potential is active. Potentiality, accordingly, will be the prior thing. But yet if so, there might perhaps have been none of the things-that-are; for it is possible for them to be capable of being but not yet to be.

7. Alternatively, suppose we were to accept the mythical genesis of the world from night or the natural philosophers' claim that 'all things were originally together'. We are still left with the same impossible consequence. How is everything to be set in motion, unless there is

actually to be some cause of movement? Matter is not going to set itself in motion – its movement depends on a motive cause, such as carpentry. (Similarly, menstrual fluids need to be set in motion by sperm, and the earth by seed.)

8. Such considerations have led some (e.g. Leucippus and Plato) to posit eternal actuality, on the assumption that there must always have been movement. But they neither explain their reasoning, nor specify the kind of actuality, nor indeed give the reason for the resultant movement's being any one way rather than another. (Nothing, in fact, will be moved by chance, but some causal factor must always be present. In our world, something will undergo natural movement in one way and enforced movement (either by mind or by something else) in another.) We are also owed an answer to the question which kind of movement is primary. For this makes a great deal of difference.

9. Plato, indeed, for his part, cannot even name what he from time to time supposes to be the principles, the self-mover. [1072a] After all, on his story, the Soul is later to, and/or at the same time as, the heavens. On the one hand, then, to suppose that potentiality is prior to actuality is to speak correctly, and in another way it is not, and we have explained which these ways are.

10. The priority of actuality is also attested by Anaxagoras (his Mind is actuality), by the Empedoclean doctrine of love and strife, and by those who, with Leucippus, insist that there is always movement.

11. Accordingly, there was no eternity of chaos and night, but there have always been the same things, either in periodic exchange or in some other way, given that actuality is prior to potentiality. (If they have been always the same in periodic cycles, there must still always have been something that is permanently actual.)

12. But if there is to be generation and destruction, there must always be a different thing active in one way or another. For it is necessary that this must in one way act *per se* and in another way in virtue of something else, either something further or what is primary. In fact, it must be the latter. For otherwise this will be cause for the former and for the original thing. But the primary must surely be superior,

and better, clearly, than that which is always in a different way. Surely it is thus, then, with movements. Why then should we seek for other principles?

LAMBDA 7

In this famous chapter, Aristotle gives his statement of the nature of the Deity as part of his system. His theology builds directly on the physical conclusions presented in chapter 6.

We begin with the claim that the eternal actual substance must also be the prime mover, the source of all process and change in the universe. But, although it is the ultimate source of all process, it cannot itself be subject to process of any kind. Aristotle must therefore explain how it is possible for the initiator of a physical process (let alone all physical processes) to be immune from process itself. His solution is that the prime mover must cause process by being an object of desire, what modern philosophers call an intentional object. He digresses to establish that the movement of the heavens could not be spontaneous (since in that case it might change) and then proceeds to show how the prime mover acts as an intentional object for the heavens.

It would only be possible for the prime mover to be the Supreme object of desire in this way if its existence was supremely desirable or enviable. The prime mover must therefore enjoy the best possible life, and this is a characteristic traditionally ascribed to the divine. Thus the prime mover is to be equated with God. But an explanation is still required of what the highest form of life is. Aristotle draws on his ethical theory to argue that the highest form of life is contemplative thought. The prime mover must enjoy this life of necessity, and this can only be secured if his contemplation is of a special, reflexive kind. He must be permanently engaged in contemplation of contemplation, thought about thought. It is much disputed what precisely this can mean, but it is perhaps the case that Aristotle wishes to suggest that the prime mover is conscious of his contemplation in a way that exceeds the capacity of ordinary, including human, thinkers.

The rest of the chapter is devoted to attacks on rival theories of the divine and to showing that his account is in line with popular opinions.

(a) The account that we have offered is a coherent one. If it is incorrect, then there is no alternative to the world's generation being from night and from everything being together and from that which is not. I take it that this confirms our solution: there is something which is always moved through an uninterrupted motion, and this motion is circular (as is evident not merely by argument but as a matter of fact), and consequently the primary heaven will be eternal.

But there will then also be something that moves them. And since that which is moved and which also moves is an intermediate, it follows that there must be something that moves without being moved. This will be eternal, it will be a substance and it will be activation.

(b) Now it is in just this way that the object of desire and the object of thought produce movement – they move without being moved. And indeed the primary objects of both are the same. The object of appetite is what seems good, and the primary object of wish is what really is good. (This is because it is rather the case that we desire something because we believe it to be good than that we believe a thing to be good because we desire it. It is the thought that starts things off.)

(c) Now the source of movement for the thought is the object of thought, and, of the two systoecheiae, one is intrinsically the object of thought. On this side, then, substance is primary and, within substance, that which is simple and is in activation. (By the way, single and simple are not the same. The former indicates a certain measure, while simplicity indicates a thing's state.)

But, look, the good and the intrinsically desirable are on the same side of the list. And obviously whatever is primary is also the best of any group or analogous to it. [1072b] Furthermore, the end of anything must always be among those things that are not moved. To show this, we must draw a distinction. An end is either a beneficiary or an objective, but it is only one of these that is unmoved. Now the end in the latter sense produces movement by dint of being the object of desire, and it does so primarily in the heavens and, through them, in everything else.

(d) Now whatever is itself moved admits of being in a different state.

Hence the primary circuit of the heavens, even if it exists in activation, could be in a different state from that in which it is in fact moved. But there is in fact something that moves without being itself moved, existing in activation, and this does not admit of being in any way in another state. For spatial movement is the first of the changes, and of spatial movements rotation is the first. And it is this movement that the first mover produces. Its existence, then, is necessary, and in that it is necessary it is good, and it is in this way that it is a principle. For there is necessity as in the following ways: (i) what is enforced, in that it is contrary to its tendency, (ii) that on which well-being is conditional, and (iii) whatever does not admit of being in any other way than absolutely.

(e) On such a principle, then, does the heaven and the natural world depend, and its continuous life is like ours at its very best for short moments. Such is its eternal state, which for us would be impossible, since its activation is also its pleasure. (At any rate, this explains why waking, perception and thought give us so much pleasure, and why they in turn sweeten hopes and recollections.)

(f)(i) The intrinsic object of thought is what is intrinsically best, and the intrinsic object of absolute thought is the absolutely best. And in apprehending its object thought thinks itself. For it too becomes an object for itself by its contact with, and thinking of, its object, so that the thought and its object are one and the same.

(ii) For thought is whatever is receptive of the object of thought, the intelligible substance, and it is activated by the possession of its object. It is accordingly the object, rather than the thought, that is the divine element that thinking is believed to possess. Hence too the supreme pleasure and excellence of contemplation. If then God's well-being is forever what ours is at moments, then it is a fit object of wonder, and all the more so if it is even greater. And this last is in fact the truth.

(iii) And God also has life; for the activation of thought is a life, and He is that activation. His intrinsic activation is supreme, eternal life. Accordingly we assert that God is a supreme and eternal living being, so that to God belong life and continuous and eternal duration. For that is what God is.

(g) As for those who suppose, with the Pythagoreans and Speusippus, that the highest excellence and goodness are not at the beginning, on the grounds that both for plants and for animals their causes are indeed their first principles, but excellence and perfection arise in what comes from them, they err. For source of the seed is other, formerly complete specimens, and the primary thing is not the seed but the complete specimen. [1073a] Of course, one would say that a man is prior to his seed, meaning not the man to come from that seed but the other man, from whom comes the seed.

(h) Our discussion has, In fancy, established that there exists a kind of eternal, unmoved substance that is separate from sensible things. It has further been shown that it is impossible for it to have any magnitude but that it is without parts and indivisible. The reason is that it is a source of movement for infinite time, and nothing that is finite has an infinite capacity. Hence, given that every magnitude is either finite or infinite, it could not have a finite magnitude. But neither could it have an infinite one, since there is quite generally no such thing as an infinite magnitude. It has also been shown that it is without affection or alteration, since all the other motions are posterior to those in space. It should be quite clear, then, why the first mover is as we have said.

LAMBDA 8

It might be said that in moving from chapter 7 to chapter 8 of Lambda we pass from the sublime to the ridiculous. Whereas the whole thrust of chapter 7 had been to show that there could only be a single prime mover, who is to be equated with God, chapter 8 raises the question whether there is a plurality of such movers and indeed how many there are. It provides the extraordinary answer that there are either 47 or 55 such movers.

The chapter begins by insisting that the issue about the number of prime movers can only be posed if substances rather than numbers are taken to be fundamental. It then gives an argument for a plurality of prime movers based on an astronomical argument about the number of eternal movements in the heavens. This argument is complex and its conclusion is obscure. Aristotle seems to hesitate between 47 and 55 as the number of prime movers, and the arguments in favour of 47 seem better to justify 49. The astronomical arguments are followed by logical arguments to show that there must be the same number of prime movers as there are eternal movements. This argument itself, however, is immediately followed by a logical argument to show that there can only be a single prime mover! The chapter ends with a reconciliation of the doctrine of multiple prime movers with traditional religious belief.

The chapter is on any account vexed. Although attempts have been made to show its compatibility with the rest of Lambda, the consensus of opinion is that it is a somewhat confused interpolation.

(a) We must now consider two questions. Should we admit one such substance or several, and, if several, how many? We should also give notice that the assertions of our rivals in answer to the latter question do not even admit of clear statement.

The Theory of Forms has no proprietary answer here. The theory holds that the Forms are numbers, but, as for numbers themselves, some versions take them to be unlimited and some to be circumscribed by the decad. But as to a reason why the multiplicity of numbers should be just so great, nothing sufficiently serious is offered to be considered a demonstration. So let us address the question on the basis of our own suppositions and distinctions.

(b) Our principle, the primary being, is unmovable both intrinsically and accidentally and yet is the source of the primary movement, which is eternal and single. However:

[1] necessarily, what is moved is moved by something,

[2] necessarily, the prime mover must be intrinsically unmoved,

[3] necessarily, (a) eternal movement must be produced by something eternal, and (b) single movement must be produced by something single,

[4] we observe, in addition to the simple course of the whole universe (which we are asserting to be produced by the primary, unmoved substance), other eternal courses, to wit those of the planets,

[5] the *Physics* has demonstrated that the rotatory body is eternal and unresting,

[6] it follows of necessity that each of the planetary courses is also the product of an intrinsically unmoved and eternal substance.

Further:

[7] the nature of the stars is a kind of substance and therefore eternal,

[8] the source of movement is eternal and prior to what gets moved,

[9] necessarily, whatever is prior to a substance is a substance, so

[10] it is clearly necessary that the number of substances eternal in their nature and intrinsically unmovable (and without magnitude, for the reason given above) should equal that of the movements of the stars.

The upshot of this is that the movers are substances, **[1073b]** and it is also clear that the order of priority among them corresponds to the order of the stellar courses. But how many such courses are there? To answer this, we must turn to that one of the mathematical sciences that has the profoundest affinity to philosophy, namely astronomy. The preoccupation of astronomy is with substance that is, on the one hand, sensible but, on the other, eternal, while the other branches of mathematics, such as arithmetic and geometry, are concerned with no kind of substance.

Now, even the most cursory consideration will reveal that the number of courses exceeds that of the bodies – after all – each of the wandering stars travels in more than a single course. But what is this number in fact? Let us begin, to get a feel for the issue, with the proposals of a few mathematicians. This will give us, at least, a definite number to play with. Thereafter, we must combine our own researches with a scrutiny of the results of others. Should it be that any of the specialists have suggestions at variance with what we have so far supposed, then we should 'befriend both sides but run with those who hit the spot'.

The system of Eudoxus. The courses of the sun and the moon each occur in three spheres. The first is that of the fixed stars, the second rotates through the middle of the zodiac and the third at an inclination to the width of the zodiac. The difference is that the angle of inclination of this third sphere is greater for the moon than for the sun. The courses of the planets each occur in four spheres. The first two are the same as with the sun and moon. (The sphere of the fixed stars is the one that carries all the others, and the second sphere, immediately beneath it and rotating through the middle of the zodiac, is also common to all bodies.) For all the planets, the poles of the third sphere lie in the circle that bisects the zodiac, and the course of the fourth sphere is in the circle that is inclined at an angle to the equator of the third sphere. And the poles of the third sphere are particular for all the planets, except for those of Venus and Mercury, which coincide.

The system of Callippus. The position of the spheres is as with Eudoxus. As for their number, it is the same for the spheres of Jupiter and Saturn. To those of the sun and moon, however, two extra spheres have to be added, to comply with observation, and one to each of the other planets.

However, [1074a] this is still not enough to comply with observation.

In fact, each of the planets must have other spheres, one less than the Callippan ones in each case, which counteract the Eudoxan-Callippan ones. These will return to its position the first sphere of the star in each case immediately below. This is the only way in which the universe as a whole can produce the courses of the planets.

Thus:

[1] spheres of the planetary courses   8 + 25 = 33
[2] (given that only those by which the lowest situated planet is moved need not be counteracted) spheres counteracting the first two planets   6
[3] spheres counteracting the next four planets   16
[4] total number of spheres, carrying and counteracting   55.

If one does not assign the additional movements that have been mentioned to the sun and moon, then the total will come to 47.

OK. This is our estimate of the number of spheres. The point is that it is plausible to assume that the number of substances and unmovable principles is the same. (We leave to more rigorous thinkers than ourselves the proof of all this!)

(c) On the other hand:

[1] If there can be no course that does not contribute to the course of a star, and
[2] every nature and every substance that is unaffected and has intrinsically achieved the best state must be held to be a purpose,
[3] then there could not be any other nature besides these, and the number of substances must be what we have given.

For consider:

[4] if there were others, then they would, as purposes, produce courses, but
[5] it is impossible that there be other courses beyond those mentioned.

It is plausible to suppose this from the bodies in circuit, as follows:

[6] if every carrier exists for the sake of what is carried and every course is for the sake of something carried,

[7] then no course would exist either for its own sake or for that of any other course, but rather for the sake of the stars.

For:

[8] suppose there were a course for some course's sake. Then

[9] the latter would in turn have to exist for the sake of something else, so that, to avoid an infinite regress,

[10] the purpose of every course will be some one of the divine bodies travelling through the heaven.

(d) That the heaven itself is single is, at least, clear. For:

(e) [1] if there were many heavens, as there are many men, then

    [2] the principles for each heaven will be one in form but many in number.

    [3] But everything that is numerically plural has matter. (One and the same form, such as that of man, applies to many things. Yet an individual, such as Socrates, is numerically single.)

    [4] But the primary essence does not have matter, since it is an entelechy. So

    [5] the unmovable first mover must be both formally and numerically single. So

    [6] the permanent and continuous object of movement must also be single. So

    [7] there is one single heaven only.

(f) We should also consider tradition. From old – and indeed extremely ancient – times [**1074b**] there has been handed down to our later age intimations of a mythical character to the effect that the stars are gods and that the divine embraces the whole of nature. The further details were subsequently added in the manner of myth. Their purpose was the persuasion of the masses and general legislative and political expediency. For instance, the myths tell us that these gods are anthropomorphic or resemble some of the other animals and give us other, comparable extrapolations of the basic picture. If, then, we discard these accretions and consider the central feature, that they held the primary substances to be gods, we might well believe the claim to have been directly inspired. We might also conclude that, while it is highly probable that all possible arts and doctrines have been many times discovered and lost, these ancient cosmologies have been preserved, like holy relics, right up to the present day. It is these, and these alone, that we can know clearly of the ancestral – indeed primordial – beliefs.

LAMBDA 9

After the interruption of chapter 8, the argument returns in chapter 9 to a central topic of chapter 7, the notion of thought about thought. Unfortunately, chapter 9 by no means fully clarifies this obscure notion, but it does give arguments to show that the object of thought must be reflexive in this way, and they may throw some light on Aristotle's conception.

The requirement that thought be about itself for the prime mover is intended to eliminate various possibilities that would undermine the dignity of his thought. His thought might not have any object at some point, a danger which is avoided by its being permanently actual. But it might also depend on the operation of some other agency, in which case it would be dependent and thus not supremely desirable, or it might be directed at something higher than itself, in which case that latter thing, not the thought of it, would be the supreme object of desire. Alternatively, thought might be about some unworthy object. All these unattractive possibilities are avoided in Aristotle's view if the object of thought is thought itself. This will guarantee both the continuity of thought and that its object will always be worthy of it without exceeding it in dignity and thus desirability.

There are, however, certain difficulties with our account of divine thought.

(a) On the one hand, it is readily agreed that thinking is the most godlike of things in our experience, but there are some problems involved in showing exactly what state it must be in to be of this kind. Suppose that it is empty of content. Where then would be its grandeur? It is in that state that it would be in if it were asleep. Alternatively, suppose that it thinks, but that its doing so is under the control of some other factor, so that what is its substance is not, now, the activation of thought but merely the potential for it. In that case, its substance would fall short of supreme excellence, since it is thinking that confers its merit on it.

(b) And again: either potential thought or actual thinking is its substance, but in either case what does it think? Obviously, it either thinks of itself or some other thing, and either of the same objects always or of different objects. Does it then make any difference, or none at all, whether it thinks of the good or of any arbitrary object whatever?

(c) Also, are there not some objects about which it is absurd that it should ratiocinate?

Well, clearly, its object is the most divine and worthy thing there is, and it is also not subject to change (for any change would be a deterioration, and such a thing is already a kind of movement). And, if we suppose that it is not activated thinking but the potential thereof, then, first, it is plausible that the continuity of its thinking would be rather arduous for it, and, secondly, there would clearly then be something else of higher merit than the thinking, to wit the object of thought.

Now indeed thinking and thought will belong even to one who thinks the worst thought. How do we get round this? (Remember that there are things it is not even better to see than not to see.) We deny that it is mere, unqualified thinking that is the best thing. That is just why it must think itself, if it is to retain supremacy, and absolute thinking is the thinking of thinking.

But:

(d) It certainly seems that knowledge and perception and opinion and thought are always of something else, and of themselves only incidentally, and

(e) if to think and to be thought are different, from which of these does thinking derive its excellence? For it is not indeed the same thing to be thinking and to be being thought.

Let us look at it this way. [1075a] In some cases, knowledge just is the object. In the case of the productive sciences, without matter, the substance and essence is the object, while in the case of the theoretical studies it is the account and the thinking itself that is the object. It follows that, since the object and subject of thought do not differ for

BOOK LAMBDA

all things that do not have matter, they will be the same in these cases, and the thinking will be one with its object.

But there still remains a problem as to whether the object of thought is composite. If so, the thinking would change between parts of the whole. However, everything that does not have matter is indivisible. As the thinking of man, and indeed of any composite entities, is for a certain period of time (for it does not have its excellence at one time or another, but rather its best performance requires a certain whole period, since it is a different thing from the thinking itself), so will the thinking of thinking be for all eternity.

LAMBDA 10

This last chapter provides a conclusion to both the theological and the physical sections of Lambda, though in reverse order. The first section defends the claims that the universe as a whole is good and that its goodness derives from the prime mover. Aristotle uses a metaphor to explain the derivation of the goodness of the world from the prime mover. The universe is compared to an army, and just as the excellence of an army stems from its general, so does that of the universe stem from the source of process and change in it. The goodness of the universe is also defended against the objection that it contains chance processes. These no more undermine the goodness of the universe as a whole than the presence of slaves in a household undermines the law-abiding nature of the household as a whole. These metaphorical arguments are strikingly different in character from the arguments used in chapters 7 and 9.

The second part of the chapter reasserts and defends some of the doctrine of the natural philosophy presented in the first six chapters. The notion of a substrate persisting through change is defended against the explanation of change merely in terms of contraries, and the existence of both perishable and imperishable things is argued to be explicable only on the basis of the doctrine of the diversity of substances. Finally, Aristotle argues that the unity of the composite can only be secured by the identification of the efficient with the final cause.

1. (a) Now for another inquiry. In which of the two possible ways does the nature of the universe possess goodness and excellence? Is it as something separated and by itself, or is it by dint of its arrangement? But why should it not be in both ways? This is the case with an army, for instance. In an army, goodness resides both in the organization and in the general. But more in the general. After all, he does not exist because of the organization, but it because of him.

(b) Now a problem. In a way, to be sure, all things are in a certain arrangement. But many things, such as fish, fowl and flower, are not arranged in the same way. Nor is the condition of the universe such that these two groups are not connected one with another. There is a connection, in that all things are indeed arranged around a single purpose.

The arrangement of the universe is in fact like that of a household. In a household, it is the free members that have the least liberty to do whatever they please. Most, if not all, of their actions are prescribed. The slaves, on the other hand, and the livestock have little to contribute and for the most part act as they please. (The nature of each of these groups is given by some such principle as this.) I mean by the parallel that all objects in the universe share the need to come to a dissolution, and there are other features which, in a similar way, all things share with the universe as a whole.

II. (a) Let us, however, not overlook the wide range of impossible or absurd consequences of the rival accounts. Let us, indeed, survey the more sophisticated theories, to see which are the least problematic.

(i) All theories hold that all things are composed of opposites. But this is wrong in two respects, both in applying to all things and in deriving them from opposites. Above all they do not explain how those things in which the opposites arise can themselves be composed of opposites. (Remember that there can be no mutual affection of opposites.) Now in our theory this difficulty receives a plausible solution in our postulation of a tertium quid. The other theories assign the role of our matter to one or other of the opposites; for instance, some make the unequal the substrate of the equal, others the many substrate of the one. But the same objection applies to this, that matter, as we conceive it, is not the opposite of anything.

(ii) Again, on this mere-opposites theory, everything except the one will be a participant in evil. Evil itself will be one of its two elements. The alternative is to admit neither evil nor good as principles. But evidently the good is a principle for all things and is so in the very highest degree.

(iii) Now the first approach rightly insists that the good is a principle. Its fault is that it does not explain in what way it is a principle, whether as a purpose, [**1075b**] as a source of movement or as a form.

(iv) This absurdity occurs in the position of Empedocles. His Love is what corresponds to the good. But this is a principle both as the source of movement (it produces the contraction) and as matter (it is a part of the mixture). Now it might be an accidental property of something that it is a principle both as matter and as a source of movement, but it could not be essential to it to be both. In which way, then, we demand, is Love a principle? Another absurdity is that he is committed to the indestructibility of Strife, for this is his equivalent to the nature of the bad.

(v) Anaxagoras, at least, is clear about this. For him, the good is a principle as the source of movement. His Mind is a motive factor. However, it produces movement for the sake of something, and this must be something else on any theory other than ours. (We are able to say that the motive medicine is in a certain way the final health.) Another absurdity is that he allows no opposite to the good, i.e. Mind. In fact, all theories that postulate opposites make no use of them, unless they take on our further constraints.

(vi) Moreover, none of these theories can account for the fact that some things are destructible and others are not, given that they compose all things from the same principles. Also, some have things that are made from what is not, and it is precisely to avoid this that others assert that all things are one. Also, none of these theories explains why there will always be generation, nor what is the cause of generation.

(vii) Again, if you posit two principles, you most posit also a third more powerful one. Equally, if you accept the Theory of Forms, you must allow that there is also another more powerful principle. Only thus can you answer the question why something has come to participate, or is participating. Also, the other theories are committed to the existence of an opposite to wisdom and the highest state of knowledge, but ours is not. For there can be no opposite to our primary, since all opposites have matter and also potential existence. The opposite of wisdom is ignorance and this would be what would yield an opposite object, but in fact there is no opposite to a primary.

(b) Further, if there are no other entities besides sensibles, then we lose principle, order, generation and even the heavenly bodies. We will be left with an infinite regress of principles, as with theological accounts and, for that matter, all the natural philosophical ones. And if we allow Forms or numbers, they will not be the cause of anything, or, if that is too strong, they will at any rate not be the cause of any movement. How, too, are magnitude and continuity to come from things without magnitude? Neither as a source of movement nor as a form could number produce continuity. And it certainly will not be possible for one of the opposites to act as what produces and moves. It is perfectly possible for an opposite not to exist. At the very least, its action would be posterior to its potential. But this would not guarantee the eternity of the world. Yet the world is eternal. So one assumption must be abandoned, and we have already indicated how this should be done.

(c) Another complaint is that there is absolutely no explanation from any quarter of the respect in which numbers, or soul and body, or in general form and thing are a unity. And this is not surprising. It cannot be explained, unless, as in our theory, it is the source of movement that produces the unity. Also, those who assert that the mathematical entity number is the primary, and in this way posit a continuing sequence of substances, with different principles in each case, [1076a] render the substance of the universe utterly episodic. For on this view one substance makes no contribution to any other either by existing or by not existing. They also require a multiplicity of principles. The universe, however, has no use for so bad a constitution –

'Too many kings are bad – let there be one!'

Book Mu

MU I

Aristotle's investigation has so far been into the general nature of substance and related concepts and problems, but in book Lambda especially he has stressed the thought that a coherent doctrine of substance must allow for a certain diversity of substance and thus leave open the question whether all substances are perceptible or, rather, that there are some substances that are not perceptible and, if so, what role, if any, such substances play in the world. Books Mu and Nu are devoted to this issue.

In the first chapter of Mu, Aristotle sets out the agenda. He will consider two candidates for being imperceptible substance, mathematical objects and Forms. Both of these had, of course, been defended in various ways by the Platonists, and so Aristotle's discussion of them is to some extent a discussion of Platonism in general. But, as we have seen, he is interested not only in the arguments for and against the acceptance of mathematical objects and Forms but also in the assessment of the claim that such entities play a fundamental constitutive role in the metaphysics of the objects of our experience. This first chapter therefore announces that the discussion of mathematical objects and Forms as principles and causes will be the third section of the inquiry.

This agenda is broadly followed in books Mu and Nu, though there are also various interpolations. Chapters 2 and 3 of Mu consider mathematical objects, and chapters 4 and 5 of Mu (which are transferred from chapters 6 and 9 of book Alpha) consider Forms. There follows a discussion of particular Platonist theories in chapters 6, 7, 8 and the first section of 9 of Mu, after which the third subject of inquiry is announced in the middle of Mu 9 and, after a methodological note in chapter 10 of Mu, pursued in detail, though with very substantial interruptions, in the course of Nu.

As, then, to the substance of perceptible things, we have explained what it is, first, in the *Physics*, as to matter and now latterly as to actualized substance. But since we also need to know whether or not there is some other substance beyond the perceptible ones, which is unchanging and eternal, and, if there is, what it is, let's first consider the things that have been come up with by others, so that if they have said anything incorrect, we may not be guilty of the same mistake, and if there is any opinion that is shared by us and them, then we may spurn taking esoteric umbrage. No, no, we should be glad if someone else puts things either better or at any rate no worse.

Now there are two opinions here: some claim that the objects of mathematics, such as numbers and lines and their cognates, are substances while others hold that Forms are. And given that some posit two such kinds, the Forms and mathematical numbers, while others opine that there is a single nature for them both, and yet others pronounce that there are only mathematical substances, we must first consider the objects of mathematics, not assuming any other nature for them, such as whether they turn out to be Forms or not, but just as objects of mathematics, whether they have being or not, and if they have being how they do. And then after this we must have a separate discussion of the Forms. The treatment can be summary, though, and is really only not to leave a gap. There has been considerable discussion of them even in the popular works, and in any case the wider discussion will have to confront this inquiry, when we ponder whether the substances and the principles of entities are numbers and Forms. For after the investigation of the Forms this is to be our third topic.

One caveat. It is necessary, if the objects of mathematics have being, that they are either in perceptible things as some say or separate from perceptible things (for there are also those who think that); and if they have being in neither way, then either they just don't have being or they have being in some other way. Our controversy, then, turns not on whether they have being but on the mode of their having being.

MU 2

This chapter begins the attack on mathematical objects, which have always seemed the most probable sort of entities posited by Platonists. The intuition behind the introduction of mathematical objects is the attractive one that geometry, for instance, cannot be about physical representations of geometrical figures in the sand, say, on a blackboard or on paper (or perhaps on a computer screen), so it must be about some other ideal entities to which the representations are mere crude approximations. This view is clearly present in Plato's dialogues and was no doubt developed further in the Academy. The Platonism which Aristotle attacks in this chapter claims that mathematics concerns objects which are totally separate from the objects of the world of our sensory experience, but which are nevertheless not merely products of our own minds. A modified version of the theory claims that these objects are somehow involved in the objects of the world, though still distinct from them.

Aristotle mounts three kinds of argument against such objects. The first line of attack is that these objects are a mere repetition of the objects in the world which have no explanatory value. He also suggests that the number of such objects will be indefinite. His second approach is to attack the basis for postulating such objects, the argument that for us to think of such things at all they must have being, which is indeed suspect. Finally, he asserts his own view that the metaphysical foundation of the world must be substance and repeats that this is incompatible with the acceptance of separately existing mathematical objects.

As to the fact, then, that it is impossible that they should be included in the perceptible things and that to claim that they are is to indulge in fantasy, the point has been established in the *Problematics* that it is impossible that [**1076b**] there can be two solids occupying a single space at the same time, and also that it follows from the same argument that the other potentialities and natures are inherent in perceptible things and none of them is separate.

393

These points, then, have been made before, but it is clear quite apart from them that under the account we are looking at it is impossible that any body be divided. For such a body will be divided with respect to a plane, and this by a line and this by a point, so that, if it is impossible to divide the point, then so also the line and the plane and all the others. And what difference does it make if perceptible things are taken to be such natures or that, while perceptible things are not so taken, there are supposed to be such natures in perceptible things? The same result will occur. For when the perceptible things are divided they will be divided, or alternatively not even the perceptible things will be.

But no more could such natures have being in separation. For if there are solids beyond the perceptible ones, then they must be separate and different from these and prior to them, and it is clear that with planes too there must also be other, prior ones in separation, and so too with points and lines (for the same argument applies). And if these things are the case, then in addition to the mathematical solids there must be planes and lines and points which are separated (for the non-composite are prior to the composite; and if there are bodies prior to perceptible things they must be imperceptible, and, by parity of reasoning, prior to planes in unchanging solids will be those with being in themselves, so that these other planes and lines will be prior to those that go with the separate solids. For some will accompany the mathematical solids and some will be prior to the mathematical solids.)

So again, there will be lines of these planes, to which it will be necessary by the same reasoning that other lines and points have priority. But to the points in the prior lines there must also be other points that have priority, to which others will not in turn be prior. And the extension becomes absurd (for there turn out to be single solids in addition to the perceptible ones, and there are three planes in addition to perceptible planes – those additional to the perceptible ones, those in the mathematical solids and those additional to those therein – and lines will be fourfold, and points fivefold). So with which of these will the mathematical sciences deal? For they will surely not be about the planes, lines and points of the unchanging solids – for science is always about what is prior.

And the same argument will apply to numbers. For in addition to each collection of points there will be different collections of units, and so too in addition to each collection of entities, whether perceptible or intelligible, so that there will be infinite kinds of mathematical numbers.

And again how will it be possible to resolve [**1077a**] the difficulties that we raised in the *Problematics*? Take for example the subject matter of astronomy; there will be items additional to the perceptible objects no less than with the subject matter of geometry. But how is it to be possible for some additional heaven and its parts to exist, or for an additional anything else which undergoes a process? And the same will go for optics and harmonics. There will be a voice and sight additional to the perceptible ones, the particulars, and of course this will also go for the other senses and the other sensory objects. For why should it go for one rather than for the others? And then if this is so there will also be additional animals, if there are to be additional sensory states.

Some universal pronouncements are made by the mathematicians, however, which are additional even to these supposed substances. It follows that there must also be some further additional substance, between the Forms and the intermediaries and separate from both, a substance which will be neither number nor point nor magnitude nor time. But assuming this is impossible, it is clear that it is also impossible for these themselves to have being in separation from perceptible things.

And indeed this result, arising from the assumption that the objects of mathematics exist in this way as certain separate natures, is precisely the reverse of what it is normal, and right, to suppose. For it would be necessary, because of their existing in this way, that the objects of mathematics be prior to perceptible magnitudes, whereas in fact they are posterior. The unbounded magnitude, though prior no doubt in creation, is posterior in substance, just as the inanimate is posterior in substance to the animate.

In any case, in what respect and when will the mathematical magnitudes be a unity? For it is reasonable that things of our acquaintance should be unified in the soul or in part of the soul or in some other item (if not then there will be a plurality and the 'thing' will be broken up). But for the putative mathematical entities, being as they are divisible quantities, what will be the cause of their being a unity and remaining together?

The circumstances of their generation also highlight this point. First of all it is in terms of length, then in terms of breadth, and finally of depth that things are generated, at which point we have the complete object. If, then, what is posterior in origin is prior in substance, body should be prior to plane and length.

And here is another way in which body turns out rather to be complete and whole, namely that it is body that becomes animate. How could there be an animate line or plane? The very idea is beyond our comprehension.

And again the body is a kind of substance (for in a way it has completeness straight off), but how are lines to be substances? For they cannot be so by dint of being form or shape, the way in which the soul, if it is a substance, is a substance, nor as matter, the way in which body is. It is evident that nothing can be composed of lines, planes and points, whereas if they were indeed a material substance, they would clearly be able to have this happen to them.

In account, however, let us suppose them be prior. Even then, though, [**1077b**] not all things that are prior in account are prior in substance. For those things are prior in substance which, in separation, have the greater capacity for existence, whereas things are prior in account to other things the accounts of which are derived from the accounts of them. And these do not automatically coincide. For if there are no affections additional to substances, such as *in-movement* or *white*, then in account white will be prior to the white man, but not so in substance. For it is not possible for it to exist in separation but it must always be together with the whole thing (meaning the white man), and this shows that neither is the thing-in-abstraction prior nor is the thing-by-addition posterior (it is by an addition to white that we speak of a white man).

To the effect, then, that the objects of mathematics are not substances to a greater degree than bodies nor prior in being to perceptible things but only in account, and that it is not possible for them to have being in separation, enough has been said. But since it is also not possible for them to have being in perceptible things, it is clear either that they do not have being at all or that they have being in some particular way (there are, after all, many ways in which we speak of having being) and hence do not have being *simpliciter*.

MU 3

In chapter 3, Aristotle presents his own view, which is that what is distinctive about mathematics is not that it deals with a special kind of object but that it deals with ordinary objects in a special way. He has two ways of making this point. The first is to say that the mathematician considers physical objects but not as ('qua') physical objects, and the second is to say that the mathematician considers physical objects but ignores those features of such objects which are merely accidental from his point of view. It is clear that Aristotle regards these two formulations as pretty much coinciding. His purpose is to show that even mathematics, like metaphysics more generally, can be made sense of without extravagantly postulating separate entities.

Universal assertions in mathematics are not about separable entities which are beyond and apart from magnitudes and numbers. They are about these very things, only not *qua* such things as have magnitude and are divisible. So clearly there can be both assertions and demonstrations in connection with perceptible magnitudes, not, however, *qua* perceptible but *qua* their being of a certain sort. There are, to be sure, many assertions to be made about things just *qua* their being moved, assertions separable from the questions what each such thing is and what accidental features it has. (And we should not, for this reason, rush to conclude that there is either some thing-in-motion separable from perceptible things or some demarcated nature within them.) And conversely, if you take the class of things which are moving, there will be assertions and scientific studies which deal with them not *qua* things which are moving but just *qua* bodies, and indeed those that deal with them just *qua* planes or *qua* lengths, or *qua* divisible or *qua* indivisible but having order or *qua* indivisible exclusively. So since it is true to say *simpliciter* not only that there are separable things but also that there are inseparable things (by, for instance, asserting that there are things which are moving), it is also true to say *simpliciter* that the objects of mathematics have being and that they are of such a sort as is claimed.

Now it can truly be said of the other sciences *simpliciter* that they do not deal with the accidental. So even if we have a science of the healthy, and the healthy happens to be white, the science of the healthy does not deal with white. Rather, each science deals with its own domain, so that the science of the healthy is what studies something *qua* healthy and the science of man is what studies something *qua* man. [1078a] And the same goes for geometry. The sciences of mathematics are not going to take perceptible entities as their domain just because the things they are about have the accidental feature of being perceptible (though, of course, they are not studied *qua* perceptible). But, on the other hand, neither will they take as their domain some other entities separable from the perceptible ones. There are many things that are *per se* features of objects *qua* the fact that each such object is of a certain sort. For instance, there are features that are peculiar to animals *qua* female or *qua* male, and yet we do not have *male* or *female* separable from animals. And in the same vein things have features just *qua* lengths or *qua* planes.

Now a scientific subject will possess more accuracy (i.e. simplicity) the more that it is about conceptually prior and simpler things, and so it will be more accurate without than with magnitude being involved and above all without movement being involved or, if movement is involved, if this movement is primary and therefore simplest and, of such movement, above all uniform movement.

This same assertion can also be made of harmonics and optics. Optics does not study its object *qua* sight, nor harmonics its object *qua* voice. Rather both study their objects *qua* lines and numbers, which, of course, are proprietary affections of sight and voice. And mechanics does the same. Accordingly, if one supposes there to be things separable from their accidental features and then investigates some aspect of them *qua* such, one will not in so doing be perpetrating a falsehood, any more, indeed, than if one were to draw a foot in the dust and say that it was a foot long when it was not a foot long. The falsehood does not lie in the setting up of the assertion.

In fact the best way to conduct the study into each thing is as follows. Do what the arithmetician and the geometer in fact do. Suppose what is not separable to be separable. A man, for instance, *qua* man is an indivisible unity, and so the arithmetician supposes a man to be an indivisible unity and then investigates whatever accidental features a man has *qua* indivisible. And the geometer will investigate a man neither *qua* a man nor *qua* indivisible, but *qua* a solid. For those features that he would have even if he were not indivisible at all he can clearly have even without the features that he has by being indivisible. And that is why the assertions of geometers are correct, and also why, when they discuss things as having being, they do indeed have being (for what has being is twofold, what has being in entelechy and what has being materially).

Now the good is one thing and the beautiful is another (the good is always in some action, whereas the beautiful can also be in things without movement). So those that claim that the sciences of mathematics have nothing to say concerning the beautiful and good are claiming what is false. In fact, mathematics has much both to state and to show about them. Just because they do not name them in showing their functions and proportions, it is not the case that they are not talking about them. And the major Forms of the beautiful are order, symmetry and delimitation, and these are very much objects of the proofs of the mathematical sciences. And since these Forms of the beautiful (I am thinking, for example, of order and delimitation) [1078b] are clearly the causes of many things, it is obvious that mathematics is also treating of causation of this kind, viz. the fact that the beautiful is in a way a cause. We will, however, have rather more details to give about this elsewhere.

MU 4

For the discussion of Platonic Forms, Aristotle gives a reworked version in this and the next chapter of the contents of chapters 6 and 9 of book Alpha. In that book, Aristotle was giving a historical summary of the earlier metaphysics and was therefore concerned to locate Plato's thought against the background of the Pythagoreans and of Socrates. The unifying theme of the discussion in the book as a whole is the evolution of the concept of the principles or fundamental causes of natural things. In Mu and Nu the issue about principles and causes is the third section of the subject matter, reserved for Nu, and there is in general less interest in historical doxography. These considerations explain the manner in which the material from book Alpha is reworked in the present chapter and its successor.

On the subject, then, of the objects of mathematics, let this much suffice as to the fact that they are entities and as to how they are entities, and also as to the way in which they are, and the way in which they are not, prior. Passing to the subject of the Forms, we must first focus on the Theory of Forms quite generally, prescinding from any connection with the nature of numbers and considering instead what grounded the original supposition of the Forms by those who first posited them.

Now the starting point for those who came up with the Theory of Forms was a conviction of the truth of the Heraclitean considerations to the effect that all perceptible objects are in a permanent state of flux, so that a condition on the very possibility of knowledge and understanding was the existence in addition to the perceptible ones of certain other natural entities which are not in a state of flux, on the assumption that entities in flux were not possible objects of knowledge. Socrates, for his part, was concerned with the moral virtues and sought, for the first time, to provide general definitions of them. (Among the natural philosophers Democritus alone had toyed with this approach and only very superficially. There is a sense in which he can be said to have defined the hot and the cold. The Pythagoreans, it is true, had already offered definitions of a limited range of things, giving accounts based on numbers; examples are timeliness, justice and marriage.) It is, however, not surprising that Socrates sought essences. His project was to establish formal logic, of whose syllogisms essences are the foundations. Obviously, dialectical sophistication was not yet such at that time as to permit the scrutiny of opposites independently of an essence, nor even to consider whether it is the same science that deals with opposites. It is in fact Socrates who can fairly be credited with two innovations, inductive arguments and also general definitions, which are both concerned with the foundations of science.

Crucially, however, whereas Socrates never made his universals (or definitions) *separable*, that is precisely what his followers did, and it is just such entities that they called Forms. This committed them, effectively by the same reasoning, to postulate Forms for every universal term. It was as though one wanted to have counting but felt that this would be impossible if there were too few things to count and so introduced more entities and thus admitted counting! (For there is a sense in which the Forms outnumber perceptible particulars, even though [**1079a**] it was perceptible particulars that the Forms were postulated to explain. This is because the particular is homonymous generally for things to which one-over-many applies even apart from the substances, and this goes for entities environmental to us and for eternal entities.)

In any case, all methods employed by them to demonstrate the Forms fail. There are some which can be given no valid logical form. Others produce Forms even for those things for which they do not suppose there to be Forms. Take the Argument from the Sciences. It will yield a Form for every possible object of a science! One-over-many arguments produce Forms for negations, and the Argument from the Thought of a Perished Object gives Forms for things that have been destroyed – they can still feature in the imagination, after all. Take the most rigorous of their arguments. Some give Forms for relational entities, for which an intrinsic *genus* is officially denied, and the rest run straight into the

Third Man. Across the board, the arguments for the Forms rule out just those entities to which the Form theorists are more committed than to the existence of Forms. It must follow from them, for instance, that it is not number but duality that is primary, and the relational entity will in turn be prior to this and also prior to the *per se* existent. And then there are all the contradictions with the principles that have bedevilled all attempts to *develop* the Theory of Forms.

Another objection is that acceptance of their grounds for advancing the Forms will lead to Forms not just for substances but for many other things as well. This is because conceptual unity does not apply only to substances but also to non-substantial entities, nor are the sciences confined to substances. There are endless further such cases. And yet of necessity (and by the Theory) if the Forms are to be objects of participation they must be confined to substances. (Participation in them cannot be accidental, and a thing must be the object of participation in the same way in which it cannot be an object of predication. To clarify, suppose something participates in Duality as such. Then it will also participate in the eternal, but *this* participation will be accidental, since the eternal is an accidental feature of Duality.) Forms, then, must be substances. And the same term must denote substance in our world and in the Form world (otherwise what is the content of claiming that something exists beyond the objects environmental to us (one-over-many arguments)?).

Also, if the Forms and the participants share some form, then there will be some form common to them. (Otherwise, why should it be any more the case that duality is one and the same thing for perishable dyads and for the several (but eternal) dyads than it is for Duality as such and the particular two?) Of course, if they do not have a common form, then they are mere homonyms. [**1079b**] To deny this would be like saying that both Callias and a block of wood were 'man' on the basis of no perceived commonality whatever.

One way out would be to say that *in other respects* general terms correspond to Forms, e.g. *plane figure* and the other parts of the definition in the case of the Circle as such, but that an essence must be added. But this, it seems, would be completely empty. What, pray, are we to add to it? To *centre*? To *plane*? To all of them? All the entities in the substance are Forms (remember *animal* and *biped*). It is also patently obvious that there must be some Thing as such and some nature that will be present in all the Forms as their genus.

MU 5

This chapter continues the reworking of Alpha 9. It concentrates on the problem of the relation of the separate Forms to the particular individuals of the perceptible world. It is true that discussion of this issue really belongs with the examination of Forms as possible principles of natural things, but Aristotle clearly feels that the impossibility of establishing any coherent connection between separate Forms and natural individuals is so profound and central an objection to the whole Theory of Forms that it belongs here in the general consideration of that theory.

There remains, however, a yet profounder objection. What possible *contribution* can the Forms make to perceptible entities, whether they be eternal or subject to generation and destruction? They cannot be the causes of *movement* for them, nor indeed of any other *change*. What about a contribution to the *knowledge* of other entities? This too is impossible, given that the Forms cannot be the substances of other entities, on pain of being constituents of them. And a contribution to their *being* is ruled out by the fact that they are not present to their participant entities.

Perhaps it is intended that they should be causes for other entities in something like the way that *the white* is sometimes said to be a cause by immixture with the white thing. This account was first proposed by Anaxagoras and later taken up in the investigations of Eudoxus and a few others. It is, however, trivially dismissible. It is a simple matter to assemble a whole range of difficulties and absurdities against any version of this view.

It is, moreover, patently impossible that other entities should 'be from' the Forms, in any of the accepted uses of that locution. The claim, for instance, that the Forms are paradigms and that other entities participate in them accordingly is quite empty of content, amounting to no more than poetic metaphors. There would surely have to be some agency, on this story, that produces objects on the model of the Forms. But what could this be? And in any case there can be no objection to an entity's both being and becoming *even without bearing a similarity to anything else*. It would be perfectly possible for a person resembling Socrates to exist, quite independently of whether Socrates did in fact exist or did not. Nor, obviously, would matters be different if Socrates were an eternal entity. Another problem is that there will be several paradigms for the same object (and so several Forms). *Animal* and *biped* will be paradigms of man, no less than Man as such. Finally, the Forms would have to function as paradigms not just for other entities *but also for themselves*. For instance, Genus would have to be the Form for anything existing as a genus. But this produces an absurd fusion of the paradigm and the copy.

A quite different line of objection is that it is impossible for a substance to have being separately from that of which it is the substance. But if [1080a] this is right, how can the Forms, while being the substances of things, have being separately from them? Now the *Phaedo* formulation holds that Forms are causes both of being and of generation. But even if we grant the Forms, still nothing is going to be generated unless there is *something to be the source of the movement*. Anyway, many other things are going to be generated, houses, rings and so forth, for which there are officially no Forms. But then it is obvious that the entities for which there officially are Forms can also have both being and generation by the same sort of causes as the entities just mentioned and not by dint of the Forms.

These are just some of the many, many objections that can be raised against the general Theory of Forms both in the informal style of the present discussion and with recourse to greater formality and rigour.

MU 6

Aristotle has now dismissed the Platonist account of mathematical objects and Forms, and according to the agenda of chapter 1 he should now turn to consider the claim that Forms and/or numbers are the principles of the natural world. However, before doing so he looks in detail at particular Platonic theories of number in chapters 6, 7 and 8. This is reasonable, given the role that number is to play in the discussion of principles and causes. The discussion in these chapters covers the theories of Aristotle's contemporaries Speusippus and Xenocrates, but the emphasis seems to be on the theory held by Plato himself. Although the concentration is on numbers, Aristotle does connect the discussion with geometry at various points.

In the present chapter, Aristotle introduces the discussion by giving a kind of taxonomy of the theoretical notions of number that have been advanced. Unfortunately, this is neither completely clear in itself nor very perspicuously connected with the subsequent discussion.

We have, then, got clear about the Theory of Forms. We are now ready to have a look at what happens with the numbers for those who hold that they are separate substances and the primary causes of entities.

Well, assuming that number is some kind of nature and that there is not some other substance of it but just number itself (not a view without supporters), then there are necessarily two possible ways in which the argument can go.

First position:
Basic assumption: there is in number a primary and a subsequent, each being different in form.

First construal:
This difference in form applies to all units without exception.

So no unit of any kind can be associated with any unit of any kind.

Second construal:
All units are in succession, and association is unrestrictedly possible between kinds of units (this is what mathematical number is said to be like – in mathematical number no unit is different in any way from any other).

Third construal:
Some units are associable and some not.

Illustration:
Suppose that *two* comes first after *one* and then *three* and then the other numbers and also that the units *within each number* are mutually associable (so the units in *two* are associable with one another and the units in *three* are associable with one another and so on, but the units in *two* are not associable with the units in *three* and so on for the whole number series). This means that, whereas in mathematical number two is counted after one *by the addition of another unit to the original unit* and three is counted after two *by the addition of another unit to the original two* and so on, our number is counted *one* then *two*, with the *two* being quite distinct and not containing the original *one* and the *three* not containing the *two* and so on with the rest.

Second position:
There are various kinds of number, one like that which was mentioned first, one like the so-called 'mathematical number' and the third like that mentioned last.

A further classification of numbers is into those separated from things and those not separated but in perceptible things. [1080b] The latter, however, is not meant in the way which we first considered but in the sense that perceptible entities arise from the numbers, which are present in them. And it is possible to hold that some number is separated and some not, or that all number is.

We have given what must necessarily be an exhaustive classification of the possible modes of being for numbers. It is a reasonable generalization to say that almost all those who have held that the one is a principle, substance and element of all things and that it is from this and something else that number arises have held that number exists in one of these ways (with the exception that it has not yet been claimed that all units whatsoever are inassociable). This, in fact, is hardly surprising. There *could* be no other way for them to be beyond those we have mentioned. Thereafter, however, opinions diverge: some hold that both kinds of numbers exist, number with before and after, Form number, and also mathematical number, not to be identified with either the Forms or perceptible objects, and that both are separable from perceptible objects, while others hold that there is only mathematical number, the first of the things that exist, separated from perceptible entities. The Pythagoreans share the belief that there is one number, the mathematical, but they deny that it is separable and assert rather that perceptible substances are composed from it. For them the entire universe is constructed from numbers, not, however, unitary numbers, since they suppose conversely that the units have magnitude. There appears, however, to be no explanation in their theory of how the first one comes to have magnitude. There is a certain other thinker who holds that the first number, that of the Forms, alone exists, while others again identify mathematical number with this latter.

The same situation prevails with lines, planes and solids. Some insist on the distinction between the figures of mathematics and the Form figures, and of those who deny this some admit mathematical figures and handle them mathematically (those who refuse to make the Forms numbers and in general deny the Forms), while others allow mathematical figures but do not give them a mathematical treatment, denying as they do that every magnitude can be divided into magnitudes and that any two units of whatever kind compose a two. All those who assert that the one is the element and principle of the entities (with the exception of the Pythagoreans, who take numbers to have magnitude (see above)) assume that the numbers are unitary.

We can be satisfied that this is a comprehensive survey of the ways in which the numbers can be described. On the other hand, they are one and all impossible, save that some are perhaps more so than others.

MU 7

This chapter introduces and commences to attack the main theory of number which Aristotle is opposing and which seems to have been the theory that Plato himself held. The theory is that the subject of arithmetic is the totality of unique Form numbers, each one quite different from any other number. These numbers are made up of units which are said to be combinable in some ways but not in others. It is by no means clear exactly what this theory is, and in any case Aristotle seems to attack three distinct versions of it. The last version is probably the one closest to what Plato himself actually held, and it therefore receives the greatest amount of attention. The discussion of it runs over into the next chapter.

The first question now is accordingly whether the units are associable or inassociable, and the next is whether, if they are inassociable, in which of the two ways distinguished they are so. [1081a] The two possibilities are (a) that any kind of unit is inassociable with any kind of unit and (b) that the units in the *two* as such are inassociable with the units in the *three* as such and that in this way the units in each of the primary numbers are inassociable with those in any other.

If, then, we take it that all units are associable and undifferentiated, we have mathematical number as the only kind of number that there is, and it is impossible for the Forms to be the numbers. To see this, ask what kind of number Man as such will be or Animal or any other of the Forms. For there must be one Form for each of these (e.g. one for Man as such and another one for Animal as such), whereas, since things that are of the same kind and undifferentiated are without limit, there will be no reason why any particular *three* will be Man as such rather than any other. But, further, if the Forms are not numbers, then they cannot exist at all. For from what principles are these Forms to arise? For it is number that arises from one and the indefinite dyad, and the principles themselves and the elements are said to be of number, and so the Forms can neither be classed as prior nor as posterior to numbers.

If, on the other hand, the units are inassociable, and this in the way that any unit is inassociable with any other, then the number that we get cannot even be mathematical number. For mathematical number is based on undifferentiated units, and all demonstrations in terms of mathematical number presuppose this. But neither can it be Form number. For the primary dyad cannot be composed from the one and the indefinite dyad (and then the rest of the number series, the so-called 'dyad, triad and tetrad'), because the units in the primary dyad are generated simultaneously either from unequals (as the original holder of the theory claimed – he held that units came about when the unequals were equalized) or in some other way. The reason for this is that if one unit were to be prior to another, then it will also be prior to the dyad composed of the latter on the basis of the general rule that wherever there is prior and posterior their product is prior to the one and posterior to the latter. Look at it another way. If the One as such is first and of the other ones there is some one that is first and thus second only to the One as such, and indeed a third one, second after the second one and third after the first One, this will have the nasty consequence that the units will be prior to the numbers from which they are labelled: e.g. there will be a third unit in the dyad before the triad exists and a fourth (and fifth) unit in the triad before those numbers exist.

Well, no Form theorist has actually claimed that the units are inassociable in this way, and yet it is perfectly reasonable that they should be by their principles, though, of course, quite incompatible with the truth. [1081b] It is perfectly reasonable that there should be prior and posterior units, given that there is a primary unit and a primary one, and similarly with the dyads, given that there is a primary dyad. For after the primary it is reasonable, indeed necessary, that there should be some secondary and, if a secondary, a third, and so on with the rest of the series. What you cannot, however, do is have it both ways, saying both that a unit is the first after the One as such as the second altogether and that the dyad is the first after it. The inconsistency in the Theory, however, is not this but in having a primary unit and One, but not a second and a third, and a primary dyad but also no second and third.

It is also patently impossible to postulate a Two in itself and a Three in itself and so on and *also* say that all units are inassociable. For whether the units are undifferentiated or do differ each from each, number must be *counted* by addition, e.g. two by adding another one to the one and three by adding another one to the two and similarly four. But if this is right, there is no possibility that numbers can be produced in the way that they produce them from the two and the one. For, on our model, two is part of three and three of four, and the same applies to the rest of the series. But they produce four from the primary two and the indefinite two, two twos, then, different from the two in itself. (On the rival view, the two in itself will be a part of four and some one other two will be added. And, in the same spirit, two will come from the one in itself and some other one. But if this is right, then the other element cannot be the indefinite dyad, since this other element produces a single element and not a definite two.)

And how will it be possible for there to be *other* threes and twos over and above the three in itself and the two in itself? And in what way are they to be composed from prior and posterior units? All these suggestions are pure fiction – there just cannot be a primary two *and also* a three in itself. But that is just what there has to be if the one and the indefinite dyad are to be elements. And, as always, if the consequences are impossible, then so too must the principles be.

If, then, the units are all different from one another, we necessarily get these and other similar consequences. If, on the other hand, the units in different numbers are different from each other, but the units in the same number are undifferentiated, we still get into just as much trouble. [1082a] For instance, in the Ten itself there will, on the one hand, be ten units, but also, on the other, the Ten will be composed of two fives. But since the Ten in itself is not an arbitrary number, nor composed of arbitrary fives, nor, for that matter, of arbitrary units, the units in this Ten must necessarily be differentiated. For unless they are differentiated, the fives from which the Ten is composed will not differ either. The fact, conversely, that they do differ shows that the units also differ. But, on the assumption that they differ, will there be no other fives in the Ten besides these two or will there be others? To say that there will be no others is absurd, but, if there are others, of what kind will the Ten be that they compose? For there is no other ten in the Ten except the Ten itself. And it is actually necessary, for them, that the four cannot be composed of arbitrary twos. For the indefinite dyads, it is claimed, by taking on the definite dyad produced two dyads, being duplicatory of what it takes on.

What about the claim that, in addition to the two units, the two is a certain nature and so is the three, in addition to the three units? How plausible is this? Well, either one will participate in the other, as the white man exists in addition to *white* and *man* (for he participates in these), or it will be the case when one is a differentia of the other, as man exists in addition to *animal* and *biped*.

Then there is the point that some things are one by contact, some by mixture and some by position. But none of these can apply to the units of which the two and the three are composed. Rather, just as a pair of men do make some one thing in addition to themselves, so is it of necessity also with the units. And they will not differ merely in virtue of the fact that they are indivisible. After all, points are indivisible, and yet a couple of them is not some other thing in addition to the two points.

A further consequence that we must not let through is that there will turn out to be prior and posterior units, and so too with the other numbers. Suppose the twos in the four are simultaneous to one another. Nevertheless, they will be prior to those in the eight, and, just as the two generated these, so did they generate the fours in the Eight itself. So if the primary two is a Form, these latter will be Forms of a kind too. And the same reasoning applies to the units. The units in the primary two generated the four units in the four, with the result that all the units become Forms and we get Forms composed of Forms. Obviously, then, the things of which these latter happen to be the Forms will be composite; for instance, if there are Forms of animals, it would be possible to say that animals are composed out of animals.

[1082b] Any version of the view that the units are differentiated is absurd and as good as fiction (by which I mean anything that one has to say merely to be consistent). For in respect neither of quantity nor

of quality do we observe unit differing from unit, and a number must be either equal or unequal (this applies to all, but obviously it applies especially to the unit), so that if a number is neither larger nor smaller it must be equal, and yet in the case of numbers we assume the equal and the completely undifferentiated to be the same. If this is wrong, then not even the two in the Ten will be undifferentiated, given that they are equal. After all, what grounds could be given by anyone who insisted that they were undifferentiated? Also if any unit and any other unit make two, the unit from the two itself and the two from the three itself will be composed of different units, and the question will then arise whether they are prior to the three or posterior. For it would seem that it must necessarily be prior. For one of the units is simultaneous with the three and one with the two. Thus, while we can say that quite generally one and one, whether they be equal or unequal, are two (e.g. the good and the bad and man and horse), the advocates of the theory cannot even say this much of two units.

And it would be very odd if it turned out that the number of the three itself is not greater than the number of the two itself. But if it is greater, then it must obviously contain a number equal to the two, so that this will be undifferentiated from the two itself. This, however, cannot be on the assumption of primary and secondary number.

Finally, the Forms will not be numbers. This very point is rightly stressed by those who claim that the units must differ if they are indeed Forms (see above). For there can only be one kind, so that if the units are undifferentiated then so must the twos and the threes be. So, on this theory, counting 'one, two . . .' cannot be a matter of addition to what is already there. The reason for this denial is that neither will there be generation from the indefinite dyad nor will it be possible for a number to be a Form, on pain of one Form's being present in another and all Forms turning out to be parts of some one. So their position is consistent with their starting point, but inconsistent with the facts. For there is a huge cost, given that they acknowledge that it is a vexed question whether, when we count and say 'one, two, three . . .', we are doing so by an addition or by separate modules. We are, of course, doing both, and it is consequently ridiculous to get out of this difficulty at the cost of introducing so vast a metaphysical distinction.

MU 8

This chapter continues and concludes the argument against the main version of the Platonic theory of Form number. The argument is followed by a brisk dismissal of the number theories of Speusippus and Xenocrates. The result of the whole discussion is that there is no coherent theory of separately existing number.

The second half of the chapter consists of a string of arguments, loosely related to the various subjects of Mu and Nu, which runs over into chapter 9. It is not possible to establish any clear thematic connection between this string of arguments and the previous or subsequent sections of Mu, and it must therefore be accepted as an interpolation. It is no doubt plausible to suppose that the editors of Mu found the subject matter difficult and were therefore less offended by the incongruity of the present arrangement than they might have been.

[1083a] In any case, the first thing that we ought to get clear about is what is the differentia of number, and what of the unit, if there is any. Evidently, it must be either by quantity or by quality that they differ, but it seems that neither of these is possible. Now number *qua* number must differ in quantity, but if the units also were to differ in quantity, then even numbers that were equal would differ by virtue of the size of their units! And then the question seems to arise whether the primary units are greater or smaller and whether subsequent ones make an addition or the reverse. All such questions are, of course, absurd.

But equally it is not possible for them to differ in quality. They can undergo no affection, since even for numbers it is assumed that quality is posterior to quantity. Nor could they derive their quality either from the one or from the dyad, since the former has no quality and the latter is productive of quality, this nature being the cause of the plurality of entities. If, on the other hand, all this is wrong, then this should be said right at the start and the differentia of the unit should be clarified in general and particularly as to why it must pertain. If they will not do this, what is the content of the differentia claim?

The upshot of our whole discussion is that, *if* the Forms are numbers, it is possible neither (a) that all units are associable, nor (b) that they are inassociable with each other in either of the possible ways.

On the other hand, there is no greater merit in the way that certain other thinkers discuss numbers. I refer to the school who do not think that there are Forms, either in general or as a kind of number, but who hold that there are objects of mathematics and that the numbers are the first of the entities and that their principle is the one itself. Now one absurdity of this is that they have a primary one of ones, but not a primary two of twos or a primary three of threes, although there can be no principled difference between the cases. And in any case, if this is the way it is with number and one posits only mathematical number, then the one is not a principle. The argument for this goes as follows. Necessarily, such a one must differ from the other units, but, if so, then so must any primary two from the twos, and so on with the rest of the number series. If, on the other hand, the one is a principle, then the situation with numbers must be rather as Plato said and there must be a primary two and a primary three, with the numbers not being mutually associable. But, again, if this is supposed, we have already seen that many, many impossible consequences follow. And yet the situation must be one way or the other, so that, if it cannot be either, we can reject the underlying assumption – that number is separable.

[1083b] All this makes it radiantly clear that the third way of handling numbers is worst of all (this is the view that identifies Form number and mathematical number). This single account inherits two flaws. For (a) it is impossible for mathematical number to be in this way and the advancer of this view is constrained to put up a smoke screen of his own *ad hoc* assumptions, and (b) the theory encounters every one of the difficulties of identifying the Forms with number.

Passing on to the Pythagoreans, we see that in a way it has fewer difficulties than those we have gone through but in another way it has perplexities of its own. On the one hand, by not making number separable they avoid many impossible consequences, but, on the other, it is not on to have bodies composed of numbers and this number be mathematical. It is, in the first place, false to introduce atomic magnitudes and anyway, even if we could have such magnitudes, still units would not have magnitude. And how can magnitude possibly be composed of indivisibles? But obviously arithmetical number is unitary. The Pythagoreans, however, say that number *is* the entities (or at least in applying their theorems they *treat* bodies as composed of those numbers).

OK, this is the conclusion. Assume that number is a thing in its own right and a full-blooded member of the things that are. Then it must be so in one of the ways that we have been looking at. But none of these ways is possible. Ergo, there is no such nature of number as is contrived by those who suppose number to be separable. QED.

Here are some further questions:

(a) Does each unit come from the equalization of the great and the small, or one from the small and one from the great? On the latter assumption, we lose both the composition of each thing from all elements and non-differentiation of the units (since there will be the great in one unit and the small, contrary in nature to the great, in another). How, further, is it to be with the units in the three itself? The problem is that one of the units is odd. (And perhaps this is the reason that they make the one itself middle to the odd.) If, alternatively, each of the units is from the equalization of both kinds, how will the two come about, being as it is a single nature from the great and the small? How, indeed, will it differ from the unit? Also, the unit is prior to the two (if it is removed then so is the two). It follows that it must be a Form of a Form, being prior to the Form and produced earlier. But produced from what? The whole point of the indefinite dyad was that it made things *two*.

(b) It is necessary that the number be either unlimited or limited. They, after all, are assuming number to be separable, [1084a] so that it cannot but be one or other of these. But (1) it is clearly impossible that it should be unlimited (the unlimited is neither odd nor even and numbers are in all cases produced as odd or even number: one means of production is that an odd number arises when one is added to an even number, another is when a number coming from the doubling of one is produced by adding two, and another when the other even numbers are produced by the addition of the odd numbers (also if every Form is a Form of something and the numbers are Forms, then unlimited number will have to be a Form of something, either of one of the perceptible things or of something else – but both options are impossible either on the general assumption or on the particular argument of those who structure the Forms in this way)) and (2), if it is limited, then we ask to what quantity is it limited. And we await an answer that gives not just the fact but the reason for it. Suppose that number is limited to ten, as some philosophers have held. For a start we will soon run out of Forms – if, say, three is Man as such, what number is going to be Horse as such? Remember that the number series is limited to ten, so it has to be one of the numbers in this group (these are the substances and Forms). But clearly there are not going to be enough such numbers (there are not going to be as many as there are kinds of animals!).

(c) It is also clear that if the three is Man as such in this way, then so will the other threes (for things in the same numbers share properties), which means that there will be an unlimited number of men: either every three is a Form, in which case every three will be Man as such, or, if not, then in any case every three will be a man. And if the lesser is a part of the greater (for number produced by the associable units in the same number), and if, *ex hypothesi*, the four as such is the Form of something, e.g. of *horse* or *white*, it will turn out, if Man as such is two, that Man is a part of Horse! There is also something absurd in there being a Form for ten but not a Form for eleven or the numbers thereafter. Also certain things which do not have Forms have both existence and generation, but why then do they not have Forms? This shows that the Forms cannot be causes. Absurd too, if number up to ten is more of a definite existent and Form than ten itself and yet there is no production of the number series as a single thing, whereas there is of ten. They try to get away with making the number series to ten complete. It is, at any rate, on the basis of ten that they produce the things that come next, the void, proportion, the odd and so forth. For while they ascribe some to the principles, such as movement and stasis, good and bad, they ascribe others to the numbers. Thus, one is the odd (for if oddness was a property of three, how could five be odd?). Also magnitudes and all such things can be explained within a limited number, [**1084b**] e.g. the primary, and indivisible line, then the two and then all these other things up to ten.

(d) If number *is* separable, one might well raise the puzzle whether the one is prior or the three and the two. On the assumption that number is composite, the one must be prior, but on the assumption that the universal and Form has priority, number must be prior. For each of the units is a part of number as its matter, whereas number is a part as its form. And there is a clear sense in which the right angle is prior to the acute angle (the sense in which it is definable and given by an account), but there is also a perfectly good sense in which the acute angle has priority (the sense in which it is a part of the right angle and the right angle can be reduced to it). In the manner, then, of matter, we can say that both the acute angle and the element *and the unit* are prior, but in the manner of form and definable substance the right angle is prior and so is the whole composite of matter and form. For the composite is nearer to the form and the subject of definition, though later in production. In what way, then, is the one a principle? Official answer of you-know-who: in that it is not divisible. But mere indivisibility is a property of universal, particular and element alike (admittedly, they are so in different ways, the universal conceptually, the particular and element temporally). In which, then, of these two ways is the one a principle? Remember that there is a sense in which we can say that the right angle is prior to the acute angle and there is a sense in which we can say that the acute angle is prior to the right angle (and each one is a single thing). What they are doing amounts to making the one a principle *in both ways*. But this is just not on: for it is as form and substance that the universal is a principle, while it is as part and as matter that the particular is. And each of them is in a way one. Each unit is indeed potentially one (if indeed a number is a single existent and not merely like a heap but rather, as they claim, with each number being composed from different units), but it is not one in entelechy. The reason why they went wrong was that they tried to settle the question both mathematically and logically at the same time. Mathematically, they made the one the principle in the way the point is (the unit is a positionless point). They followed the precedent of various other philosophers in composing the entities from their smallest elements. In this way the unit becomes the matter of numbers and at the same time both prior to the two and posterior to it, given that the two is a kind of whole and unity and form. And from the logical quest for the universal they treated the predicable unity as in this way too a part. But it is impossible that the same thing should be both at the same time. Finally, if the one as such must be a single positionless thing (for it differs from the other ones in no other respect except that it is a principle), and the two is divisible but the unit not, then the unit would rather be like the one itself. But if the unit is more like the one, then the one must be more like the unit than like the two. But this is not what they say – at any rate not what they do, since they produce the two first. [1085a] And, finally finally, if the two itself is a kind of unity and so is the three itself, then they both amount to a two – and from what is *this* two produced?

*The first half of the chapter continues the string of assorted arguments which
began in chapter 8.*

*The second half of the chapter, which begins suspiciously abruptly, announces
the start of the advertised third section of the inquiry, the investigation of the
claim that numbers and/or Forms are the principles and causes of the world.
However, the discussion does not in fact begin until Nu. The rest of the present
chapter consists of a digression containing yet another attack on the Theory of
Forms, this time concentrating on the impossible requirement that the Forms be
both particular and universal.*

(e) With numbers there is sequence, but not contiguity, of those units
   between which there is nothing (e.g. between the units in two and
   the units in three). Are then the units in sequence to the one itself
   or not? And is two prior, or one or other of the units of two, prior
   to those that are in sequence from *it*?

The difficulties crop up in much the same way in connection with the
genera posterior to number, with line, plane and solid.

(a) Some philosophers construct them from the kinds of the great and
   small, constructing lines, for instance, from the long and short, planes
   from the broad and narrow and solids from the deep and shallow,
   all of which are kinds of the great and small. And from among these
   different thinkers posit the principle corresponding to one in different
   ways. Now these approaches exhibit a myriad impossibilities, fantasies
   and inconcinnities with sound reasoning. One upshot is that the
   various genera are completely detached from one another, unless the
   principles are logically connected in the sense that the broad and
   narrow *is also* the long and the short. But (i) the point will then be
   the same thing as the plane and the plane the same thing as the solid,

and (ii) how are we to demonstrate angles, figures and so forth on this basis?

(b) We get the same consequences as with number. They are affections of magnitude, not the source of magnitude, and in the same way the line is not composed of the straight and the bent nor solids of the smooth and rough.

(c) A common difficulty for all these claims is a query one can raise about Forms as of a genus, if universals are admitted. The query is whether the Animal as such or some other animal is in the particular animal. Now if the universal is not separable, there is no puzzle here, but if the one and the numbers are separable, as this theory holds, it is not an easy problem to crack (if we can take 'not easy' to be a reasonable synonym for 'impossible'). Whenever one apprehends the one in the two and in number in general, is it the one itself that one apprehends or some other one?

(d) It is, then, from matter like this that some philosophers produce magnitudes. Others, however, produce them from points (and they take a point to be not a one, but something like a one) and of other matter of the same kind as plurality, only not plurality. But these moves do not avert the difficulty. For if the matter is one, then line, plane and solid are the same thing (anything coming from the same things is the same thing and a single thing), but if the matter is diverse, one kind for the line, one kind for the plane [**1085b**] and one kind for the solid, either they will be logically connected or not, so that the upshot will be the same even after this move: either the plane will not have line or it will be line.

(e) As to how it is even possible for number to come from the one and plurality – no attempt is even made to answer this. On any version, the same difficulties occur as with saying that number comes from the one and the indefinite dyad. One philosopher may produce number from the predicated universal and not from a particular plurality, another from a particular plurality, but the primary plurality (on the assumption that the dyad is a kind of primary plurality), so that there is in practice no difference and the same confusions follow – mixture or position, blending or generation and all the others. And a further question that one might well raise, if each unit is one, is what it is from. For obviously it cannot be that each unit is the one itself. Well, the obvious answer is that it must come from the one itself and plurality or a part of plurality. It is certainly impossible to hold that the unit is a kind of plurality, since it is indivisible. On the other hand, to hold that it is from a part of plurality involves many other difficulties, since it is both necessary that each of the parts is indivisible (or they must be a plurality and the unit divisible) and then the one and plurality will not be an element (since each unit is not from plurality and the one). And anyway anyone saying this is simply producing *another* number, since the plurality of indivisibles *is* number. And another puzzle about this version of the theory is whether the number is unlimited or limited. For there is also, it would seem, a limited plurality, from which and from the one the limited units are derived. But there is also the other plurality in itself and unlimited plurality. So which kind of plurality is the element and the one? And one might ask exactly the same question about the point and the element from which they produce magnitudes, since no more is this point the only one that there is. From what then is each of the other points derived? It will certainly not be from a kind of distance and the point itself. Indeed it is not possible for there to be indivisible parts of the distance, as there can be of the plurality from which the units come. For number is, but magnitudes are not, composed from indivisibles.

(f) All these arguments and other similar ones make it clear that it is impossible for number and the magnitudes to be separable. The disharmony among these ways of dealing with number is a symptom of the factual error from which all the confusion arises. [**1086a**] For all who suppose that, in addition to perceptible things, there are only the objects of mathematics, observing the difficulties and consequent resort to fiction attendant on the Theory of Forms, abandoned Form number and constructed mathematical number. Those, on the other hand, who wanted to introduce both Forms and numbers at the same time, not seeing, if one is to make these principles, in what way it will be possible for mathematical number to exist in addition to Form number, identified Form number and mathematical number in their account (in practice they quietly dropped mathematical number) and ended up with assumptions that are quite peculiar to them and have nothing in common with mathematics. In fact, the original founder of the theory that there are Forms and that the Forms are numbers and that there are objects of mathematics, did well to separate them. The general picture is that they all got it right in some one respect, but their general picture was quite wrong. And they effectively acknowledge this by their mutual disagreement. The diagnosis is that the fundamental assumptions and principles are false, and, as Epicharmus so aptly put it, it is hard to say good things on the basis of not good things – and they only have to be spoken out to be seen to be not good things.

Enough puzzles and positions about number. If you are already per-suaded, you could only be more persuaded by further cases, and if you are not yet persuaded no amount of further points will do any good!

We turn now to the subject of first principles, primary causes and elements. The account given by perceptible-substance-only theorists is to some extent presented in the *Physics* and to some extent outside the scope of the present inquiry. The examination, however, of the account given by those who insist that there are other substances in addition to perceptible things follows on directly from what we have just been discussing. Some philosophers claim that the Forms and numbers are just such substances and that their elements are the elements and principles of the things that there are. So let us examine what this amounts to and exactly how it is to be taken. Subsequently, we will have to consider also those who claim that (mathematical) numbers are the only separable substances.

As to the Theory of Forms, we can at one and the same time consider its content and its folly. Their root problem is that they posit Forms that are universal and *at the same time* Forms that are separable and therefore particular. We have surely already established that this is not possible. Why did those who asserted that substances were universals ever confuse these two positions? Because they did not confine substances to the perceptible substances. Their intuition was that perceptible particulars were in radical flux and that none of them was a stable entity, [**1086b**] but that the universal existed in addition to them and was something else. This whole approach (see above *ubique*) was initiated by Socrates with his definitions, but *he* did not go so far as to separate universals from particulars. He rightly understood that they cannot be separated. This is demonstrable from plain fact: the acquisition of scientific knowledge is impossible without universals, and it was their separation that was responsible for all the problems with the Forms. The Theorists, however, assuming that, if there were any substances in addition to perceptible things in their radical flux, then these would have to be separable, and having no other substances to hand, were pleased to expel the universally predicated substances and thus in effect made the nature of universals and that of particulars the same. This in itself amounts to a profound difficulty for the Theory.

MU 10

The final chapter of Mu prepares the way for the discussion of principles in Nu by confronting an objection which might be raised against the very project of attempting to establish principles. This objection has already appeared in puzzles 9 and 12 of book Beta (pages 54–5). The objection is that the principles or elements of the world must be either particular or universal, but if they are universal then they cannot be substances (and Aristotle is assuming that this guarantees that they cannot be principles) and if they are particular then they cannot be intelligible and thus explanatory. It is the second assumption that Aristotle attacks. This assumption is based on the idea that to be intelligible the principles must themselves have elements and these elements must be universal. Aristotle defuses the assumption by conceding that in some sense the principles must themselves have elements to be intelligible but denying that these elements need be in any sense universal. Thus it is a coherent project to seek for principles of the natural world, and book Nu can examine whether there is any case for supposing that such principles are either numbers or Platonic Forms.

There is, however, a problem which is common to those who accept and those who reject the Theory of Forms. It has already been discussed towards the beginning of the *Problematics*, but a word is appropriate here.

Suppose, then, that substances are not separate (i.e. separate in the way in which particular entities are thought to be). You have, the problem claims, eliminated just that substance that we want to discuss. All right, suppose that substances are separable. How, then, says the problem, will you introduce their elements and principles?!

Dilemma:
1. Substances are particulars and not universals. But then the entities will be as numerous as the elements and also the elements will not be possible objects of knowledge.

426

Analogy with first horn:

Let the syllables in speech be substances and let their elements be the elements of substances. Then, on this horn, BA must be one and each of the other syllables must be one. After all, they are not universal and the same in form, but rather each is one in number and a particular thing (and that not by homonymy). (It is, in fact, an assumption that that which really exists is in each case a single thing.) And if this goes for the syllables, then it also goes for the things from which they are composed. So there will be no more than one alpha, nor more than one of any of the other elements on the same grounds as there cannot be more than one of each of the syllables. But if all this is the case, then there will be nothing else existing in addition to the elements, but only the elements.

Corollary:

The elements will not be possible objects of knowledge, because they will not be universal, while knowledge is of the universal. And this is clear both from the demonstrations and from the definitions – you do not have formal syllogisms to the effect that *this particular triangle* is equal to the sum of two right angles, except that every triangle is equal to the sum of two right angles, nor to the effect that *this particular man* is an animal, except that every man is an animal.

II. The principles are universals. But then either the substances coming from them will also be universals, [**1087a**] or a non-substance will be prior to a substance.

(The universal is not a substance, but the element and principle is universal, and the element and principle is prior to that of which it is the element and principle.)

There is no way that this problem can be avoided if you allow elementary composition of the Forms and also hold that, in addition to the substances that have the same form, there must be some single separated substance. On the other hand, there is nothing to stop the situation being just as with the elements of speech. There are many alphas and betas and no alpha in itself or beta in itself in addition to them. That is why there can be an unlimited number of similar syllables.

As for the fact that all knowledge is of the universal, so that it is necessary that the principles of the things that are are also universal and not separated substances, this contains the profoundest problem of all that we have mentioned. Even so, there is a way in which it is true and a way in which it is not. For knowledge is, like indeed knowing, a double thing, being both potential and actual. Now potentiality is like matter. It is universal and indefinite and it is the potentiality of something that is universal and indefinite. But actuality is definite and of something definite, being the *this such* of a *this such*. Accidentally, to be sure, sight sees universal, in that the particular colour that it sees *is colour*, and similarly the object of the grammarian's perusal, this alpha, *is alpha*. If, then, the principles must be universal, then the things from them must also be universal, as with demonstrative reasoning. But if this is right, then *there will not be any separate thing nor any substance*.

Perhaps all we can say is this: in a way knowledge is universal, in a way it is not.

Book Nu

NU I

Book Nu is to discuss the third item announced in the agenda given in Mu 1. However, the discussion is held up until at least the second half of chapter 2 and does not really get under way until towards the end of chapter 5. The official topic is the role of numbers (and/or Forms) as the causes and principles of the natural world, but this issue is entangled with the issue of whether numbers themselves can have principles or elements. It is to this latter issue that the first two chapters of Nu are devoted.

The first chapter is directed against the Platonic view that the elements of number must be opposite or contrary principles. Aristotle argues both against the opposition supposed to obtain between the principles and to the characterization of the principles themselves given by the Platonists.

Enough said, then, about separable substance. Let's move on to principles.

All philosophers say that principles are contraries, just as much for substances that undergo no process as for natural things. And yet to the universal principle of all things there can be nothing prior. So *this* principle cannot be a principle *by dint of being something else*. Suppose that one said that *the white* is a principle not *qua* something else but *qua* white, but also said that, being white, it was a predicable entity and existed as something else. The point is that that 'something else' must be prior to *the white*. But surely, if everything comes from contraries, the latter must be contrary properties *of some subject*. So the problem we propose applies to contraries head on, given that contraries are in all cases *of* some subject and never separable things, [**1087b**] whereas to a substance there can be no contrary (see common sense and the well-known argument). So the universal principle *proprement dit* is not from among the contraries. It is something else.

On the other hand, our friends want *matter* to be one of the contraries. There are two ways of doing this. You can assume that the unequal is the nature of plurality and make it the matter of the one, the equal. Or you can, as one of them does, just make plurality the matter of the one. In both styles, you produce the numbers using the one as substance, in the first version from the unequal two, the great and small, and in the other from plurality. However, to say that the elements are the unequal and the one (with the unequal being the two from great and small) is to identify the unequal with the great and small. This amounts to a failure to distinguish between definitional and numerical identification.

Even the principles which they call elements, though, are poorly explained. Opinions are divided as between (a) the great and small together with the one, these three, being the elements of number, the first two as matter and the one as form, (b) the 'many and few' (and the one), on the point that the great and small belong more by nature to magnitudes, and (c) the universal, rather, over and above these, the exceeding and the exceeded. Anyway, it makes no difference for the consequences, as far as I can see, which you take. It is merely a matter of logical hygiene, which is important for them since they are trying to mount formal arguments. Except that it is part of the same reasoning to hold that the exceeding and exceeded are principles and not the great and small and that number is prior to the two from the elements, in that both the e. and e. and number are closer to being universals. They, however, accept the former but not the latter priority. Another option is to oppose the different and the other to the one, and yet another to make plurality and the one the contraries. If, however, as they want, entities do come from contraries, and either nothing is contrary to the one or, if you insist, plurality (and the unequal is contrary to the equal, the different to the same and the other to the identical), then it surely makes most sense to make the one the contrary of plurality, though even this is not enough, since the one will turn out to be a kind of few (plurality is contrary to paucity, the many to the few).

It is also clear that the one means *a measure*. Now in all cases of measurement there is some other thing that is the subject. For example, in harmony there is a quarter-tone, in magnitude inch, foot and so forth, in prosody a beat or syllable and in just the same way in weight there is some standard defined weight. And this applies in the same way in all cases, [1088a] a kind of quality being the subject in the measurement of qualities and a kind of quantity in that of quantities. And in both cases the measure is indivisible, in kind for qualities and to perception for quantities. And all this is because the one does not exist as a *per se* substance. Nor is it surprising that this is so. For the one means that it is the measure of a kind of plurality, while number is measured plurality and a plurality of measures. This is why it is right to deny that one is a number; after all, the measure is not measures and both of these, the one and the measure, are principles. In all cases, the measure must be the same as the things measured, so that, if horse is the measure, then it is horses that are measured and, if man is the measure, then it is men that are measured. And if man, horse and god are the measure, then it is, I suppose, animal that is measured, and animals will be the number of them. And if the measure is man, white and walking, then there will not be a number for them, given that they all pertain to the same thing, which is numerically one. And yet there will be a number of the kinds here, or whatever you want to call the sorts.

What is out of the question is positing the unequal as some single thing and also bringing in the indefinite dyad. For these are affections and accidents, rather than subjects, for numbers and magnitudes, the many and few for number, the large and small for magnitude, just as the odd and even are, the smooth and rough and the straight and curved. This, then, is one blunder, and another is that the great and small and all other such must be relational entities. But relational entities are the last things of all to be natures and substances and are posterior even to qualities and quantities. So the relational entity is, as has been said, an affection of quantity and not matter, on the assumption that there is some other subject both to relational items quite generally and to their parts and kinds. For there is no great and small, nor many and few, nor quite generally any relational item, but that something else, being the subject, is many/few or great/small or whatever relational item. The claim that a relational item is the last of things to be a substance and a kind of entity is borne out by the fact that for them alone there is no generation and destruction nor are they subject to any process, as there is increase and diminution with regard to quantity, alteration with regard to quality, locomotion with regard to place and generation and destruction *tout simples* with regard to substance.

Relational items are unique in this respect. For something can be now greater now lesser without undergoing a change, if some other object undergoes a change in respect of its quantity. And, of course, it is necessary that the matter of each thing [**1088b**] be potentially of the same kind as that thing and thus potentially be of its substance, but a relational item cannot be a substance either potentially or in actuality. So it is absurd, nay rather it is impossible, to make a non-substance an element in, and prior to, a substance. On the contrary, all other categories are posterior to substance. Yet again, no element is *predicated* of that of which it is an element, whereas the many and few are predicated of number both severally and jointly, and the long and the short of line, and it is a plane which is broad and narrow. But, finally, suppose that there is a kind of plurality (say, two) of which paucity is always a feature (two is a good choice, because, if it were many, then the one would have to be few). It would follow that there would also be a many *simpliciter*. (Perhaps it would be ten or, if that seems a bit niggardly, ten thousand!)

How, in sum, can number be from the few and many? Either both would have to be predicable of it or neither, but in fact only one of the two is so predicated.

NU 2

The first half of this chapter continues the attack on the Platonic doctrine of opposite principles of number, but adopts a broader perspective. The objection here raised is to allowing principles or elements for any eternal entity (such as the Platonists are, of course, supposing number to be). The argument is that anything that has elements must have matter and that nothing that has matter can be eternal.

The second half of the chapter begins the third section of the original agenda by launching a series of diverse attacks on the claim that numbers exist and that they play a causal role.

Let's now take a quite general look at the following question: *is it possible for eternal things to be composed of elements?*

Well, if they are, they will have matter (reason: everything that has elements is a compound of matter and form).

But now:
It is necessary that anything, be it an eternal existent or the sort of thing that would have had generation, comes to be from that of which it is composed.

And everything comes to be from that which is potentially that which comes to be (for it would never have come to be from, nor could it ever be, that which could not potentially be it).

And that which is potentially can either be actualized or not.

Ergo, ergo, it makes no difference how much number *does in fact exist for ever* (or anything else that has matter). IT WOULD BE POSSIBLE FOR IT NOT TO EXIST. No less so than for something having either one day behind it or as many years as you please. The point is that if the entities of the last sentence *could fail to exist*, then so could an entity having behind it so long a time that there is no limit to it.

So these putatively eternal entities would not be eternal, on the plausible assumption (which we have defended elsewhere) that whatever admits of the possibility of non-existence is not eternal.

So the account currently under the microscope contains an inconsistency. If (a) it holds universally that there is no eternal substance except any substance that just exists as actuality and (b) elements of substance would be matter of substance, then no eternal substance would have elements in the sense of items internal to it from which it comes.

(Some of these philosophers make the indefinite dyad the element that complements the one, ejecting the unequal. Rightly, given the impossible consequences. But this only gets round the difficulties inevitably attendant on making the unequal and the relational item an element. They still confront all the problems that arise independently of this dogma, whether it is the Form number that they construct from these elements or mathematical number.)

There are many explanations of the side-track into postulating this sort of cause, [**1089a**] but the fundamental one is that their setting up of the problem is archaic. Their *Grundprinzip* was that 'all things would Be One, the Existent Itself', unless somebody crack and/or face down Parmenides' Exocet:

'Ne'er shal thys dicte be fast: what is not is.'

They thought it imperative to show that the non-being is. In this way, assuming pluralism, entities were to have their being from the being and something else.

1ST Objection: 'the being' is a multiple, not a single, item. In one way, 'the being' picks out a substance, in another way it picks out a quality, in another a quantity and ditto for the rest of the categories. So what kind of a One would All Things Be unless Not Being Is? Would it be the substances, or the affections or the others in the same style, or all of them? Or is it that the this and the such and the so much and all the other indicators of some one thing Are One? It is just crazy, just impossible that *some single nature* could, by coming to be, be the cause of its being the case that one thing was a this, one thing a such, one thing a so much, one thing an over there!

2ND Objection: from a combination of which kind of not being and which kind of being do the things that are come? 'The not being' is, every bit as much as 'the being', multiple. Not being a man means not being a this-here, not being straight means not being of this-here kind and not being three cubits means not being of this-here quantity. So I repeat, from what kind of being and not being come the plurality of entities?

Well, Plato's answer is that it is falsity and its nature that is not being. From this and from being come the plural entities. Hence the dictum that there must be a false assumption (in something like the way in which geometers assume a line to be, say, one foot long, when in fact it is not). But this cannot possibly be right, and anyway geometers do not really make any false assumptions − it is not as though they are introducing a premise to a formal argument. Nor indeed is it from this sort of not being that the entities are generated nor into this that they are destroyed. In fact, not being is, by the declension of cases, said in as many ways as there are categories, and on top of these there is the not being that is said as false and the not being that is said as in potentiality. And it is from this last that generation occurs, man coming from what is not man but is man potentially, white coming from what is not white but is white potentially, and so on just as much if it is many as if it is one thing that is coming into being.

Evidently, their inquiry into how what is is many is in fact concerned with being said of substance. For numbers, lines and solids are what are produced. But it cannot be right to investigate the plurality of being in the sense of what a thing is but to neglect it in the sense of what a thing is like or how many things there are. It surely cannot be that the indefinite dyad or the great and small are causes of there being two *white* things or of a plurality of colours or flavours or shapes. [**1089b**] For in that case these too would just have been numbers and units. Had they, however, considered the ontogenesis of qualities and quantities, they would have perceived what is in fact also the cause of being for substances, which must either be the same or the corresponding factor.

The same root error lies behind (or beneath) the fact that those who investigate the contraries to the thing that is and to one (with the things that are arising from these pairs of contraries) have suggested the relational entity and the unequal. But this latter is not the contrary, or a negation, of the former. It is simply one nature of the things that are, like substance and quality.

And a further indispensable side to this investigation is that into relational entities. In what way are they many, not one? But current practice is to investigate in what way there can be many units after the primary one, but to neglect the question how there can be many unequals besides *the* unequal. Of course, this does not stop them making explanatory use of the varieties of inequality. They invoke the great and small, the many and few (basis of numbers), the long and short (basis of length), the broad and narrow (basis of the plane) and the deep and shallow (basis of the masses). And there are many more varieties of relational entity that they cheerfully cite. But what pray, is the reason for the plurality of *these*?

Well, as we have claimed, for each thing we must give what is potentially that thing. Now the original advocate of the theory that we are presently discussing did attempt to do this, at least for the case of the *this*, for substance. (It, presumably, is something that does not exist in itself.) The potentiality of substance, in his view, is the relational entity. (By this, I think that what he was really trying to say was that the potentiality of substance is quality.) The relational entity/quality, however, is *not* the potentiality of the one or of the thing that is, nor is it a negation of the one or of the thing that is. It is merely *one of* the things that are. In any case, just to bang the table a little, if the question is in what way the things that are are plural, then this question is not just about the entities in some one category – so, how are there many substances? or how are there many qualities? – but is just the question how are there many things that are? Although, of course, they will all be substances or properties or relational entities.

Now, in the case of the non-substantial categories, there is a certain other stumbling-block to understanding in what way they are many. Qualities and quantities are not separable items. This means that they get their plurality from the fact that their subject (a) comes into being and (b) is many things. In a way, it would make more sense if there were a special kind of matter for each kind of thing that there is. But there cannot be matter in separation from substances. In the case of substances, however, there is no parallel problem about how they can be plural. (Assuming we exclude the possibility of something that is both a substance and an item in some other category.) The problem with substances, on the other hand, is rather this: how can there be many substances *in actuality*, and not just one?

OK. Say we agree that substance and quantity are not the same thing. Then no account has been given of how and why the things that are are plural, only how quantities are plural. For all number picks out a kind of quantity, as does the unit (unless it is a unit of measurement, as a quantitatively indivisible extension). So there is a dilemma: either quantity and substance are different things, in which case no account has been given either of the origin of substance [**1090a**] or of the manner of its plurality, or they are the same thing, in which case the most salient plurality is that of the problems confronting any holder of this whole view!

Let's move on. A completely different line of inquiry that one might adopt about numbers is that of what grounds our confidence that they exist. Now, if you buy the Theory of Forms, then at least numbers explain your entities (after a fashion). The idea is that each of the numbers is a Form and that the Form is the cause of being for the other entities. As to how this can possibly be supposed to happen, we will make no cavil at the moment. But suppose that you do not buy the Theory of Forms (you see all the difficulties in it about what the Forms are and so on). So that cannot be your reason for supposing numbers to exist. But you still suppose that mathematical number does exist. Why should we believe your claim that this sort of number exists? And what use can it be for explaining the other entities? Indeed, even advocates of mathematical number do not claim that it explains any entity. It is just a particular kind of *per se* nature. And it is hardly *just obvious* that mathematical number is causal. Arithmetical theorems, at any rate, apply, as we have said, equally easily to perceptible entities.

NU 3

This chapter continues the discussion of the existence and causal role of numbers which was begun at the end of the previous chapter and which continues into the first section of the subsequent chapter.

The section can be considered as the first treatment of the third item on the agenda of Mu, but to do so is to be at least generous to the structural clarity of the discussion. The whole argument in both Mu and Nu, and this section in particular, runs together three officially distinct questions, whether numbers exist, whether they have principles or elements and, if so, what these are and whether numbers (and/or Forms) play a role as principles and causes for things in the world, as alleged by the Pythagoreans and some Platonists.

So adherents of the Theory of Forms who hold that the Forms are numbers assume that each is a single thing by dint of its being one over many. This amounts, it cannot be denied, to giving a kind of reason why number exists. But of course, far from being necessary, these assumptions are not even possible. So this cannot possibly be a basis for asserting the existence of number.

The Pythagoreans, for their part, took the fact that they saw many properties of numbers being-in perceptible bodies to show that the things that are are numbers. They did not, indeed, admit separable numbers, rather they derived the things that are from numbers. But why did they do that? Well, the properties of numbers are-in the scale, the heavens and many other things that there are.

Anyone, on the other hand, who admits only mathematical number cannot, on his own assumptions, give number anything like this sort of role. Hence the once popular claim that the subjects of the sciences cannot be perceptible objects. (A claim we deny (see above).) It is also quite clear that mathematical entities are not separable – for how could the properties of separable things be-in bodies?

Well, the Pythagoreans get through on the point about separation. But as for their claim that physical bodies are derived from numbers, that things having weight and lightness come from things not having weight and lightness, it would seem to be some other heaven and other bodies that they are on about, not the perceptible ones. Those, on the other hand, who hold number to be separable base their supposition that it exists and is separable on the fact that its axioms do not apply to perceptibles and that the theorems of mathematics are true and speak directly to the mind [**1090b**] (the same goes for mathematical magnitudes). Obviously, the opposite view will say the opposite to this, and the problem raised recently will have to be dealt with by those who take this view. The problem was this: why is it, if numbers are never in perceptible things, that their properties are–in the perceptibles?

Some philosophers hold that the existence of natures of this kind follows of necessity from the fact that the point is the boundary and outer point of the line, the line of the plane and the plane of the solid. So we should have a look at this claim too, to see if it is not too flimsy to sustain its burden. Well, outer points are not substances but are rather, all of them, boundaries. Consider walking and, in fact, any kind of movement. This has a boundary, so that *this* boundary would, on this argument, turn out to be a substance and a this!!! But even if we allow, for the sake of argument, that, yes, boundaries are substances, they will all be substances *of the given perceptibles* (it was in connection with such entities that the whole argument got going). So how are they going to be separable?

In any case, if you want a strenuous life, there are many more questions you can ask about number in general and the mathematicals. In particular, you could ask why there is no contribution between them, from those that come first to those that come later. After all, even if number does not exist, there will still nevertheless be the magnitudes for those who allow existence only to the mathematicals. And if these do not exist, there will still be the soul and the perceptible bodies. Nature, however, from the observations that we are able to make is not a hack play. She is not just a string of disconnected episodes.

We are not looking at something that is a problem for the Theory of Forms. It is, after all, from matter *and* number that they derive the magnitudes, from the dyad that they derive lengths, from three (perhaps) planes and the solids from four – or maybe the numbers are different, it does not really matter. But will all these entities, then, be Forms? Or, if not, what will be their mode of existence? And what contribution will they make to the things that are? They will make no contribution, any more than the mathematicals do. They do not even have any theorem to show for themselves, unless the whole study of mathematics is to be turned upside down and idiosyncratic new assumptions introduced. (It is, of course, no labour of Heracles to dream up some whacky assumption and then spell out the consequences *ad nauseam*.) So this attempt to conflate Forms and mathematicals founders. The original theory, by contrast, was that there were two kinds of number, Form number and mathematical number. The problem that they never wrapped up, and indeed which cannot be wrapped up, is how, and on what basis, is mathematical number to exist? It is suspended between Form number and perceptible number. If it is derived from the great and small, then it will turn out to be the same as Form number (and then some other great and small is needed for the derivation of the magnitudes!), [1091a] and if some other component is given, then the number of components here is troublingly high. And also one is supposed to be the principle of both kinds of number. So the one will have to be something that they have in common. But how, we then ask, can the one be so many things, given that number cannot be derived, on this Theory, but from one and the indefinite dyad?

What a mess! Internal inconsistency spiced with contempt for common sense. Simonides' 'long story' springs to mind (see whether your slaves tell you as good a one next time they have something to hide). Can I hear the protestations of the very elements themselves, the great and small, at this molestation? There is no way in which they, after all, can produce number (except numbers doubled from one).

It is also mildly odd, better it is a paradigmatic impossibility, to bring production into an account of eternal entities. The Pythagoreans at least put their cards on the table. Do they bring in production or do they not bring in production? Yes, they very clearly do. Their story is that *when* the One was Composed (Either From Plane Or Surface Or From Seed, Or From We Know Not What) then verily was the nearest of the boundless straight drawn in and by the boundary bound. Please make allowances – they are doing a cosmogony and being Natural Scientists. But, to be fair, we should take their account of nature seriously enough to question it a bit and at any rate to let them off the present hook. What we are after is the principles in the things that do not change, so it is only the production of numbers of this kind that lies within our remit.

NU 4

This chapter first concludes the discussion of the existence and causal role of numbers commenced in chapter 2 and continued throughout chapter 3. It then proceeds to a digression on the connection between the doctrine of principles and the concept of the Good. This continues into chapter 5.

The Good is, of course, a central conception for Plato and the Academy, but Aristotle is usually reluctant to admit that there can be such a Form of Good over and above the inherent purposes of particular things. Here, however, he accepts the Good for the sake of argument and criticizes two attempts to accommodate it to the notion of principles. Speusippus denies that the Good is a principle, while Plato argues that the Good is to be equated with the One. Aristotle mounts objections to both these accounts, and the suggestion of his argument is that you cannot have both the Good and principles, as the Platonists wish to do.

Now production of the odd they do not allow, on the assumption, we must assume, that there is production of the even. The even itself is produced in some cases as the primary derivative from unequals, by the equalization of the great and the small. So there must have been some previous time, before equalization, in which inequality was-in them. If they were always equalized, then there would not have been such a previous period of inequality (nothing is previous to always). From this it follows that it is not just for theoretical economy that they bring in number production.

A scandal for philosophy. The connection between the elements and principles and the good and fine is deeply problematic. And has been blithely overlooked. The problem is this: is some one of the elements the sort of thing that we would be disposed to label the good in itself and the best thing? Or is this not the case, since the latter are derived later?

Now the theological tradition would appear to be in harmony with that strand of contemporary philosophy which denies such an identification. Traditionally, the evolution of entities must be advanced before either the good or the fine make their entry. And there is very real difficulty that they thus escape but which conflicts head on with the view, not without adherents, that the one is a principle. [1091b] This difficulty, let us be clear, does not arise from the ascription, as an in-being component, of the good to the principle, but from the insistence that the one is a principle and a principle, at that, as an element and that number is derived from the one. This whole view permeates the poetry of antiquity. Sovereign power does not, in their *oeuvre*, rest with that which is primary – Night, Heaven, Chaos, Ocean – but rather with that Johnny-come-lately Zeus. (Actually, this is an oversimplification. In this poetry the rulers of the things that are are in the habit of changing, so that they do sometimes get to allow sovereignty to the primary. Primary sovereignty ascription is found in all such writers who blend the non-mythical with the mythical (Pherecydes et al.), in the Magi and in certain more recent philosophers such as Empedocles (Love) and Anaxagoras (Mind).) Moreover, the school that asserts the existence of unmoved substances contains a strand which identifies the good itself with the one itself, but they held that its substantiality resided primarily in its oneness.

That, then, is the dilemma, primary sovereignty or not? Now what would be a surprising result would be if in that which is primary and eternal and the most completely self-sufficient this very primacy, its self-sufficiency and self-preservation, were not to be-in it as a good. Surely its indestructibility and its self-sufficiency can belong to it for no other reason than that it is good. So what could be more natural than that it be right to insist that the principle is, in this way, good? What, however, would not be natural, or even possible, would be to claim that such a principle is the one or, failing that, an element and an element of numbers to boot. The name of the ensuing problems is legion – so much so that some have given up the theory altogether rather than face them, agreeing that the one is a primary principle and element, but of mathematical number only. One awkward consequence is that every unit becomes a kind of good, which rather floods the market in goods.

Look at it another way. If Forms are numbers, then, on this view, every Form is a kind of good. But suppose we extend the range of Forms to cover any object whatsoever. Then either (a) if there are Forms only of goods, then Forms will not be substances, or (b) if there are also Forms of substances, then every single animal, every single plant, anything at all, in short, which participates in a Form will be a good. Pfaw!

As though this were not enough, it will also turn out that the opposite component, be it plurality, the unequal or the great and small, would be Evil itself. There was indeed a Certain Philosopher who for this very reason declined to ascribe the good to the one as a necessary feature on the grounds that, what with production being derived from opposites, Evil would be the nature of plurality. (Others simply say that the unequal is the nature of Evil.) A consequence of this position is that all the things that there are participate in Evil except the one itself alone and that numbers participate in more unmitigated Evil than do magnitudes. And there is more. [1092a] Evil turns out to be the domain of good, so that it participates in, and yearns for, its destructive agent (opposites destructive of opposites). Last and worst, if matter is the potential particular (see above), so the matter of actual fire is potential fire, then Evil itself will be the potentiality of good!!

Diagnosis:

(a) every principle is taken to be an *element*,
(b) opposites are taken to be principles,
(c) one is taken to be a principle, and
(d) numbers are taken to be primary substances, *separabilia* and Forms.

NU 5

The chapter first concludes the discussion of the Good and then reverts to the attack launched in Mu 1–2 on the Platonic conception of the principles of number.

Finally, towards the end of this chapter, the subject of numbers as principles and causes is at last directly addressed. The discussion is continued into chapter 6 and forms the concluding section of Mu and Nu.

So we can rule out either simply not including the good among the principles or including it in the way that we have just been examining. So they must be wrong both about principles and about primary substances. And it would also be quite wrong-headed to see a parallel between cosmological principles and those in zoology and botany. (The thinking would be that in all cases what is more designed comes from what is more indefinite and less designed. In fact he applies this assumption to the primary entities themselves, with the result that the one itself is not even a thing that is.) For even the special sciences have design-rich principles from which their entities are derived. It is man that produces man. We do not have primacy of the sperm.

Now another objection is that place is produced *at the same time* as mathematical solids. In fact, place is peculiar to particulars (whence their spatial separation), whereas 'Where is it?' is not a question to ask about mathematical entities. They also end up saying that mathematical entities *are somewhere*, but not what place is.

Now anyone that says that the things that are derived from elements and that numbers are the primaries of the things that are is obliged to distinguish the ways in which one thing is derived from another and to say in which of these ways it is that number is derived from its principles. By mixture perhaps? But not everything can be mixed, and the thing produced must be different from the producer, and, crucially,

447

the one will not turn out to be separable and a different nature, as they want it to. By assembly, then, like a syllable? But then position will have to be-in the elements, and it is by separate apprehensions that the mind apprehends the one and plurality, so that number will turn out to be the unit *plus* plurality or the one *plus* the unequal.

Another problem. If you are derived from certain things, then, in one way, those things are-still-in you and, in another way, they are not. How does it stand with number? The former option is only available for things that are produced. So could number be derived like *this*, like coming from sperm? But, of course, nothing can emerge from the indivisible. Well, is the derivation that from the non-persistent contrary? But anything so derived is also derived from something else which is persistent. Now one philosopher posits the one as the contrary of plurality, [**1092b**] another takes it as the contrary of the unequal (treating the one as being equal). So on this view number is indeed derived from contraries. But this means that the existence or production of number is from one thing that persists and one that does not.

We are also owed an explanation of how it is that, whereas all other things that are derived from contraries or that have contraries get destroyed (even if it is derived from the whole of its contrary), this is not the case with number. Deafening silence. However, whether being-in or not being-in, contrary always destroys contrary, as Strife destroys Mixture. (Come to think of it, this is not a very good example. Strife and Mixture are not contraries.)

We now broach a topic basking in an explanatory vacuum. In which of the two possible ways are numbers *causes* of substances and of being?

First possible way of being a cause: be a boundary. E.g. points are boundaries of magnitudes. An interesting illustration of this approach is the contribution of Eurytus. This philosopher had a way of assigning numbers to things. So he could say things like 'Here we have the number of Man' or 'Here we have the number of Horse'. He achieved this by taking some humble pebbles and using them to create likenesses of the shapes of living things. (This is a bit like taking the numbers and arranging them in the figures triangle and square.)

Second possible way of being a cause: harmony is a ratio of numbers.

448

(So, in fact, is man and everything else.) But how can *properties*, white, sweet, hot and the rest, be numbers? In any case, it is surely clear that it is not numbers that are a thing's substance and responsible for its shape. It is the ratio that is the substance and the number belongs to the matter. Do you mean that number is the matter of flesh and bone? It is in that the substance of these is three parts fire and two parts earth. Anyway, in all cases, a number, whatever it may be, is always a number of some things, whether of fire, of earth or of units. But the substance of a thing just is there *being* a certain amount to a certain amount in its mixture. And *this* is not just a number. It is a ratio of the mixture of numbers, be they numbers of body or of anything else.

So number is not causal by productivity. Neither number in general, nor unitary number. Nor is it either a material cause or a rational/eidetic cause of things. (I assume that I do not have to show that it is not a final cause.)

NU 6

This chapter concludes the discussion of number as cause. Given that we have waited so long for it, it is somewhat disappointing in profundity and scope. It is no doubt true that Aristotle found the claim that number is the cause of the world too absurd to be a normal philosophical target. Perhaps the most interesting conclusion that emerges from this section is that the root of the error of supposing that number can be a cause is a naïve conception of the nature of causation. This is a central topic in the Physics, *to which reference is made in various parts of the* Metaphysics. *It sits very well with the central doctrine of the* Metaphysics, *that the foundation of the world is natural substance and not some separate and ideal entity, whether mathematical or other.*

One might, though, ask what the helpful contribution made by numbers is to the fact that a mixture is given in a number (either easily calculated or odd). Take honey water. Mix it in three times the proportions and it does not become any healthier. On the contrary, there is more point to mixing it in no proportions and simply diluting it than to having it undiluted though mixed in the right numerical proportions.

Anyway, you get ratios of mixtures by adding numbers, not just by numbers themselves, e.g. 'three *to* two' not 'three times two'. For multiplicands have to be of the same kind, so that it is by *a* that the product of *abc* is to be measured and by *d* that that of *def* is. So all products must be measurable by their factors. It follows that it cannot be that the number of fire is *becg*, while that of water is 2×3.

[1093a] If, furthermore, it is necessary for everything to have a commonality of number, it must turn out that many things are the same, with the same number belonging to each of them.

So is it, then, number that is a cause and is it because of this that a thing exists, or is it still unclear? There is a number of the movements of the sun, as there is, in turn, of those of the moon, and there is a number for the life and for the age of each of the animals. Why should it not be that some of these are squares and some are cubes, some equal, some double? Far from there being anything to prevent this, they would in fact have to be distributed among these kinds, if everything is indeed to have a commonality of number.

There is also a danger, on this approach, that different things will fall under the same number. So if there were certain things of which the same number was an accidental property, then all members of this group would be the same as one another, by dint of having the same form of number as an accidental property. So, for instance, the sun and the moon would be the same thing.

But why should we accept such things as causes? Seven is the number of the vowels, *and* of notes of the scale, *and* of the Pleiades, *and* of the point at which animals (some, in fact, but not all) lose their teeth, *and* of the Champions against Thebes. Is it because of the characteristic nature of the number seven either that those Champions numbered seven or that the Pleiades is a constellation of seven stars? Is it not perhaps more likely that there were seven Champions because there were seven gates to the city (or some other similar reason), while it is a Greek convention to number the Pleiads as seven and the Bear as twelve, but in other systems they have more stars.

It is indeed sometimes argued that xi, psi and zeta are concords and that it is because there are three concords there are three double consonants. What this overlooks is that there could be ten thousand such consonants (I create one by stipulating that gamma and rho could be put together, and so on). If, on the other hand, the argument is that each of these consonants is equal to a double of the others, but that any other consonants would not be, and that the reason for this is that in each of the three oral regions a single letter is applied to the sigma, then the point would be that it is for this reason, and not because there are three concords, that these consonants number but three. And in fact there are more than three concords, whereas there cannot be more than three double consonants.

Adherents of this view resemble those quondam Homerists who fastened on pedantically nit-picking similarities while totally neglecting the major ones.

There are those who make a specialism of citing many such examples. The middle notes are 9 and 8 and the hexameter has 17 (= 9 + 8) syllables, with 9 after the caesura and 8 before it. **[1093b]** The distance in terms of letters between A and Ω is equal to that in terms of the notes of the flute between the bombyx and the highest, the number of which is in turn equal to the concert of the universe. There is, however, a suspicion that it is not really hard to find and set out such correlations among eternal things, given that they are present even in perishables.

The natures among the numbers are endlessly praised, as are the contraries of them and, in general, the subject matter of mathematics, at least as they are habitually described by those who make them the causes of nature. And yet, under the present examination, they seem to evaporate. For not one of them is a cause in any of the ways that we have distinguished in connection with principles.

And yet, on their way of arguing, it transpires that the good is-in number and that under the column of the fine are to be found odd, straight, equal by equal and the powers of certain numbers. For the seasons sit with a kind of number; and this is also the thrust of all the other cases that they harvest from mathematical theorems. They have, therefore, a curious air of coincidence. They are accidental properties and yet all proper to one another and one in analogy. For there is analogy in every category of what is, straight in length being analogous to level in surface and perhaps to odd in number and to white in colour.

And anyway it cannot be among the Form numbers that we find the causes of harmonic intervals and suchlike. For numbers of this sort are different that are equal to one another in Form, and this is because their units are different. So *this* cannot be a reason for resorting to Forms.

OK. OK. Enough examples of what happens on this theory. Many more could be marshalled, but enough. The endless, endless difficulties about production, the total non-obtaining of any mode of schematizing, which afflict Form numbers are surely plausibly construed as a sign. They are a sign that MATHEMATICAL ENTITIES DO NOT EXIST IN SEPARATION FROM PERCEPTIBLE OBJECTS (as widely advertised) and that PRINCIPLES OF THIS KIND GIBT ES NICHT.

BIBLIOGRAPHY

Any bibliographer of Aristotle is confronted with a maze of extraordinary complexity and bewildering proliferation. A prudent policy is to eschew the ambition of producing a comprehensive plan and to content oneself with indicating the most promising points of entry. This bibliography, like this volume, is aimed at the introductory reader, with a certain degree of philosophical confidence, who wants to avoid blind alleys and circuitous detours at a relatively early stage of his or her exploration of, for a change of metaphor, the intriguing but daunting continent of Aristotle.

One further constraint that I have imposed is that of confining the survey, with a very few exceptions, to works written in, or translated into, English. Given the very strong continental tradition of the study of Aristotle, this restriction eliminates a rather larger proportion of the literature than would be the case in some other areas of philosophy, and it is fair to say that the serious student of Aristotle would ideally be equipped with the ability fluently to read French and German, with, if possible, the addition of Italian and Latin.

1. *General Works on Aristotle*

J. L. Ackrill, *Aristotle the Philosopher*, Oxford, 1981.

D. J. Allan, *The Philosophy of Aristotle*, Oxford, 1970.

J. Barnes, *Aristotle*, Oxford, 1982.

J. Barnes, M. Schofield and R. Sorabji (eds.), *Articles on Aristotle*, vols. 1–4, London, 1979.

D. W. Graham, *Aristotle's Two Systems*, Oxford, 1987.

M. Grene, *A Portrait of Aristotle*, London, 1963.

T. H. Irwin, *Aristotle's First Principles*, Oxford, 1988.

J. Lear, *Aristotle: the Desire to Understand*, Cambridge, 1988.

G. E. R. Lloyd, *Aristotle: the Growth and Structure of His Thought*, Cambridge, 1968.

J. M. E. Moravcsik (ed.), *Aristotle*, London, 1968.

2. *Editions and Commentaries on the* Metaphysics

J. Annas, *Aristotle's Metaphysics Books Mu and Nu*, Oxford, 1976.

D. Bostock, *Aristotle's Metaphysics Books Zeta and Eta*, Oxford, 1994.

M. Frede and G. Patzig, *Aristoteles, Metaphysik Z*, Munich, 1988.

M. Furth, *Aristotle, Metaphysics Books Zeta, Eta, Theta and Iota*, Indianapolis, 1985.

C. Kirwan, *Aristotle's Metaphysics Books Gamma, Delta and Epsilon*, Oxford, 1971.

W. D. Ross, *Aristotle's Metaphysics*, Oxford, 1924.

3. *General Works on the* Metaphysics

M. Furth, *Substance, Form and Psyche: an Aristotelian Metaphysics*, Cambridge, 1988.

M. L. Gill, *Aristotle on Substance: the Paradox of Unity*, Princeton, N.J., 1989.

A. C. Lloyd, *Form and Universal in Aristotle*, Liverpool, 1981.

J. Owens, *The Doctrine of Being in the Aristotelian Metaphysics*, Toronto, 1963.

C. Witt, *Substance and Essence in Aristotle*, Ithaca, N.Y., 1989.

4. *Books and Articles on Individual Sections of the* Metaphysics

ALPHA AND ALPHA THE LESSER

J. Annas, 'Forms and first principles', *Phronesis*, 1974.

H. Cherniss, *Aristotle's Criticism of Presocratic Philosophy*, Baltimore, Md, 1935.

H. Cherniss, *Aristotle's Criticism of Plato and the Academy*, Baltimore, Md, 1944.

H. Cherniss, *The Riddle of the Academy*, Berkeley, Calif., 1945.

W. K. C. Guthrie, 'Aristotle as a historian of philosophy', *Journal of Hellenic Studies*, 1957.

J. G. Stevenson, 'Aristotle as historian of philosophy', *Journal of Hellenic Studies*, 1974.

BETA

S. Mansion, 'Les apories de la métaphysique aristotélicienne', *Autour d'Aristote*, Louvain, 1955.

GAMMA

J. Barnes, 'The law of contradiction', *Philosophical Quarterly*, 1969.

P. Butchvarov, *Being qua Being: a Study of Identity, Existence and Predication*, Bloomington, Ill., 1979.

J. D. G. Evans, *Aristotle's Concept of Dialectic*, Cambridge, 1977.

J. D. G. Evans, 'Aristotle on relativism', *Philosophical Quarterly*, 1974.

I. Husik, 'Aristotle on the law of contradiction and the basis of the syllogism', in *Philosophical Essays*, Oxford, 1952.

A. J. P. Kenny, 'The argument from illusion in Aristotle's *Metaphysics*', *Mind*, 1967.

C. Kirwan, *Aristotle's Metaphysics Books Gamma, Delta, Epsilon*, Oxford, 1971.

J. Lukasiewicz, 'Aristotle on the law of contradiction', in Barnes, Schofield and Sorabji (eds.), *Articles on Aristotle*, vol. 3.

F. C. T. Moore, 'Evans off target', *Philosophical Quarterly*, 1975.

G. E. L. Owen, 'Logic and metaphysics in some earlier works of Aristotle', in *Aristotle and Plato in the Mid-Fourth Century*, Göteborg, 1960; also in Barnes, Schofield and Sorabji (eds.), *Articles on Aristotle*, vol. 3.

G. Patzig, 'Theology and ontology in Aristotle's *Metaphysics*', in Barnes, Schofield and Sorabji (eds.), *Articles on Aristotle*, vol. 3.

M. C. Scholar, 'Aristotle *Metaphysics* IV 1010b1–3', *Mind*, 1971.

DELTA

K. T. Barnes, 'Aristotle on identity and its problems', *Phronesis*, 1977.

R. A. Cobb, 'The present progressive periphrasis and the *Metaphysics* of Aristotle', *Phronesis*, 1973.

F. D. Miller, 'Did Aristotle have the concept of identity?', *Philosophical Review*, 1973.

R. Polansky, 'Aristotle's treatment of *ousia* in *Metaphysics*, v, 8', *Southern Journal of Philosophy*, 1983.

R. K. Sprague, 'Aristotelian periphrasis: a reply to Mr Cobb', *Phronesis*, 1975.

J. W. Thorp, 'Aristotle's use of categories', *Phronesis*, 1974.

N. P. White, 'Aristotle on sameness and oneness', *Philosophical Review*, 1971.

EPSILON

F. Brentano, *The True and the Evident*, London, 1966.

J. Hintikka, 'Time, truth and knowledge in ancient Greek philosophy', *American Philosophical Quarterly*, 1967.

ZETA AND ETA

R. Albritton, 'Forms of particular substances in Aristotle's *Metaphysics*', *Journal of Philosophy*, 1957.

G. E. M. Anscombe, 'The principle of individuation', in Barnes, Schofield and Sorabji (eds.), *Articles on Aristotle*, vol. 3.

R. Bolton, 'Essentialism and semantic theory in Aristotle', *Philosophical Review*, 1976.

D. Bostock, *Aristotle's Metaphysics Books Zeta and Eta*, Oxford, 1994.

E. Buchanan, *Aristotle's Theory of Being*, Cambridge, Mass., 1962.

M. Burnyeat et al., *Notes on Book Zeta of Aristotle's Metaphysics*, Oxford, 1979.

M. Burnyeat et al., *Notes on Books Eta and Theta of Aristotle's Metaphysics*, Oxford, 1984.

V. Chappell, 'Aristotle's conception of matter', *Journal of Philosophy*, 1973.

W. Charlton, 'Aristotle and the principle of individuation', *Phronesis*, 1972.

W. Charlton, 'Prime matter – a rejoinder', *Phronesis*, 1983.

A. Code, 'The persistence of Aristotelian matter', *Philosophical Studies*, 1978.

S. Cohen, 'Aristotle and individuation', *Canadian Journal of Philosophy*, supp. vol. 10, 1984.

S. Cohen, 'Aristotle's doctrine of the material substrate', *Philosophical Review*, 1984.

I. M. Copi, 'Essence and accident', *Journal of Philosophy*, 1954.

M. J. Cresswell, 'Essence and existence in Plato and Aristotle', *Theoria*, 1971.

R. M. Dancy, 'On some of Aristotle's first thoughts about substances', *Philosophical Review*, 1975.

R. M. Dancy, 'On some of Aristotle's second thoughts about substances: matter', *Philosophical Review*, 1978.

M. Ferejohn, 'Aristotle on focal meaning and the unity of science', *Phronesis*, 1980.

G. Fine, 'Separation', *Oxford Studies in Ancient Philosophy*, 1984.

M. Frede, *Essays in Ancient Philosophy*, Oxford, 1987.

M. Frede and G. Patzig, *Aristoteles, Metaphysik Z*, Munich, 1988.

M. Furth, 'Transtemporal stability in Aristotelean substances', *Journal of Philosophy*, 1978.

D. W. Graham, 'The paradox of prime matter', *Journal of the History of Philosophy*, 1987.

M. Grene, 'Is genus to species as matter to form?', *Synthese*, 1974.

J. E. Hare, 'Aristotle and the definition of natural things', *Phronesis*, 1979.

E. S. Haring, 'Substantial form in Aristotle's *Metaphysics* Z1', *Review of Metaphysics*, 1956–7.

E. D. Harter, 'Aristotle on primary *ousia*', *Ancient Philosophy*, 1975.

E. Hartman, 'On the identity of substance and essence', *Philosophical Review*, 1976.

E. Hartman, *Substance, Body and Soul*, Princeton, N.J., 1977.

R. Heinaman, 'An argument in Aristotle's *Metaphysics* Z13', *Classical Quarterly*, 1980.

G. J. Hughes, 'Universals as potential substances: the interpretation of *Metaphysics* Z13', in Burnyeat et al., *Notes on Book Zeta of Aristotle's Metaphysics*.

B. Jones, 'Aristotle's introduction of matter', *Philosophical Review*, 1974.

H. R. King, 'Aristotle without *materia prima*', *Journal of the History of Ideas*, 1956.

C. A. Kirwan, 'How strong are the objections to essence?', *Proceedings of the Aristotelian Society*, 1970–71.

J. Kung, 'Can substance be predicated of matter?', *Ancient Philosophy*, 1978.

A. R. Lacey, '*Ousia* and form in Aristotle', *Phronesis*, 1965.

J. M. LeBlond, 'Aristotle on definition', in Barnes, Schofield and Sorabji (eds.), *Articles on Aristotle*, vol. 3.

J. H. Lesher, 'Aristotle on form, substance and universals: a dilemma', *Phronesis*, 1971.

W. Leszl, 'Knowledge of the universal and knowledge of the particular in Aristotle', *Review of Metaphysics*, 1972–3.

A. C. Lloyd, 'Genus, species and ordered series in Aristotle', *Phronesis*, 1962.

A. C. Lloyd, 'Aristotle's principle of individuation', *Mind*, 1970.

M. J. Loux, 'Form, species and predication in *Metaphysics* Zeta, Eta and Theta', *Mind*, 1979.

S. Mansion, 'The ontological composition of sensible substances in Aristotle (*Metaphysics* VII 7–9)', in Barnes, Schofield and Sorabji (eds.), *Articles on Aristotle*, vol. 3.

D. K. Modrak, 'Forms, types and tokens in Aristotle's *Metaphysics*', *Journal of the History of Philosophy*, 1979.

D. R. Morrison, 'Separation in Aristotle's *Metaphysics*', *Oxford Studies in Ancient Philosophy*, 1985.

G. E. L. Owen, *Logic, Science and Dialectic*, London, 1986.

R. Robinson, *Definition*, Oxford, 1950.

R. Rorty, 'Genus as matter: a reading of *Metaphysics* Z–H', *Phronesis*, supp. vol., 1973.

T. Scaltsas, 'Substratum, subject and substance', *Ancient Philosophy*, 1985.

M. Schofield, '*Metaph.* Z3: some suggestions', *Phronesis*, 1972.

W. Sellars, 'Substance and form in Aristotle', *Journal of Philosophy*, 1957.

J. A. Smith, '*Tode ti* in Aristotle', *Classical Review*, 1921.

F. Solmsen, 'Aristotle and prime matter', *Journal of the History of Ideas*, 1958.

R. R. K. Sorabji, 'Aristotle and Oxford philosophy', *American Philosophical Quarterly*, 1969.

D. Stahl, 'Stripped away', *Phronesis*, 1981.

R. D. Sykes, 'Form in Aristotle', *Philosophy*, 1975.

N. P. White, 'Origins of Aristotle's essentialism', *Review of Metaphysics*, 1972–3.

D. C. Williams, 'Form and matter', *Philosophical Review*, 1958.

M. J. Woods, 'Problems in *Metaphysics* Z, chapter 13', in Moravcsik (ed.), *Aristotle*.

M. J. Woods, 'Substance and essence in Aristotle', *Proceedings of the Aristotelian Society*, 1974–5.

M. J. Woods, 'Universals and particular forms in Aristotle's *Metaphysics*', *Oxford Studies in Ancient Philosophy*, supp. vol., 1991.

THETA

J. L. Ackrill, 'Aristotle's distinction between *energeia* and *kinesis*', in R. Bambrough (ed.), *New Essays on Plato and Aristotle*, London, 1965.

J. Hintikka, 'Necessity, universality and time in Aristotle', in Barnes, Schofield and Sorabji (eds.), *Articles on Aristotle*, vol. 3.

A. J. P. Kenny, *Action, Emotion and Will*, London, 1963, chap. 8.

A. P. D. Mourelatos, 'Aristotle's "powers" and modern empiricism', *Ratio*, 1967.

T. C. Potts, 'States, activities and performances', *Proceedings of the Aristotelian Society*, 1965.

C. C. W. Taylor, 'States, activities and performances', *Proceedings of the Aristotelian Society*, 1965.

IOTA

N. Goodman, 'Seven strictures on similarity', in *Problems and Projects*, New York, 1972.

D. Wiggins, *Sameness and Substance*, Oxford, 1980.

KAPPA

G. Reale, *Il concetto di filosofia prima*, Milan, 1961, pp. 215–57.

LAMBDA

A. P. Bos, *On the Elements of Aristotle's Early Cosmology*, Assen, 1973.

D. R. Dicks, *Early Greek Astronomy to Aristotle*, Ithaca, N.Y., 1970.

H. J. Easterling, 'The unmoved mover in early Aristotle', *Phronesis*, 1976.

W. K. C. Guthrie, 'The development of Aristotle's theology', *Classical Quarterly*, 1933.

P. Merlan, 'Aristotle's unmoved movers', *Traditio*, 1946.

R. Norman, 'Aristotle's philosopher-god', *Phronesis*, 1969; also in Barnes, Schofield and Sorabji (eds.), *Articles on Aristotle*, vol. 4.

E. E. Ryan, 'Pure form in Aristotle', *Phronesis*, 1973.

MU AND NU

R. E. Allen, 'The generation of numbers in Plato's *Parmenides*', *Classical Philology*, 1970.

J. Annas, *Aristotle's Metaphysics Books Mu and Nu*, Oxford, 1976.

H. G. Apostle, *Aristotle's Philosophy of Mathematics*, Chicago, 1952.

P. Benacerraf, 'What numbers could not be', *Philosophical Review*, 1965.

J. Findlay, *Plato: the Written and Unwritten Doctrines*, London, 1974.

T. L. Heath, *Mathematics in Aristotle*, Oxford, 1949.

J. Kung, 'Aristotle on thises, suches and the Third Man Argument', *Phronesis*, 1981.

F. Lasserre, *The Birth of Mathematics in the Age of Plato*, London, 1964.

E. A. Maziarz and T. Greenwood, *Greek Mathematical Philosophy*, New York, 1968.

G. E. L. Owen, 'The Platonism of Aristotle', in P. Strawson (ed.), *Studies in the Philosophy of Thought and Action*, Oxford, 1968.

R. Sorabji, 'Aristotle, mathematics and colour', *Classical Quarterly*, 1972.

A. E. Taylor, 'Forms and numbers', *Mind*, 1926–7.

A. Wedberg, *Plato's Philosophy of Mathematics*, Stockholm, 1955.

READ MORE IN PENGUIN

In every corner of the world, on every subject under the sun, Penguin represents quality and variety – the very best in publishing today.

For complete information about books available from Penguin – including Puffins, Penguin Classics and Arkana – and how to order them, write to us at the appropriate address below. Please note that for copyright reasons the selection of books varies from country to country.

In the United Kingdom: Please write to *Dept. EP, Penguin Books Ltd, Bath Road, Harmondsworth, West Drayton, Middlesex UB7 ODA*

In the United States: Please write to *Consumer Sales, Penguin Putnam Inc., P.O. Box 12289 Dept. B, Newark, New Jersey 07101-5289.* VISA and MasterCard holders call 1-800-788-6262 to order Penguin titles

In Canada: Please write to *Penguin Books Canada Ltd, 10 Alcorn Avenue, Suite 300, Toronto, Ontario M4V 3B2*

In Australia: Please write to *Penguin Books Australia Ltd, P.O. Box 257, Ringwood, Victoria 3134*

In New Zealand: Please write to *Penguin Books (NZ) Ltd, Private Bag 102902, North Shore Mail Centre, Auckland 10*

In India: Please write to *Penguin Books India Pvt Ltd, 11 Community Centre, Panchsheel Park, New Delhi 110017*

In the Netherlands: Please write to *Penguin Books Netherlands bv, Postbus 3507, NL-1001 AH Amsterdam*

In Germany: Please write to *Penguin Books Deutschland GmbH, Metzlerstrasse 26, 60594 Frankfurt am Main*

In Spain: Please write to *Penguin Books S. A., Bravo Murillo 19, 1° B, 28015 Madrid*

In Italy: Please write to *Penguin Italia s.r.l., Via Benedetto Croce 2, 20094 Corsico, Milano*

In France: Please write to *Penguin France, Le Carré Wilson, 62 rue Benjamin Baillaud, 31500 Toulouse*

In Japan: Please write to *Penguin Books Japan Ltd, Kaneko Building, 2-3-25 Koraku, Bunkyo-Ku, Tokyo 112*

In South Africa: Please write to *Penguin Books South Africa (Pty) Ltd, Private Bag X14, Parkview, 2122 Johannesburg*

PENGUIN AUDIOBOOKS

A Quality of Writing That Speaks for Itself

Penguin Books has always led the field in quality publishing. Now you can listen at leisure to your favourite books, read to you by familiar voices from radio, stage and screen. Penguin Audiobooks are produced to an excellent standard, and abridgements are always faithful to the original texts. From thrillers to classic literature, biography to humour, with a wealth of titles in between, Penguin Audiobooks offer you quality, entertainment and the chance to rediscover the pleasure of listening.

You can order Penguin Audiobooks through Penguin Direct by telephoning (0181) 899 4036. The lines are open 24 hours every day. Ask for Penguin Direct, quoting your credit card details.

A selection of Penguin Audiobooks, published or forthcoming:

Little Women by Louisa May Alcott, read by Kate Harper

Emma by Jane Austen, read by Fiona Shaw

Pride and Prejudice by Jane Austen, read by Geraldine McEwan

Beowulf translated by Michael Alexander, read by David Rintoul

Agnes Grey by Anne Brontë, read by Juliet Stevenson

Jane Eyre by Charlotte Brontë, read by Juliet Stevenson

The Professor by Charlotte Brontë, read by Juliet Stevenson

Wuthering Heights by Emily Brontë, read by Juliet Stevenson

The Woman in White by Wilkie Collins, read by Nigel Anthony and Susan Jameson

Nostromo by Joseph Conrad, read by Michael Pennington

Tales from the Thousand and One Nights, read by Souad Faress and Raad Rawi

Robinson Crusoe by Daniel Defoe, read by Tom Baker

David Copperfield by Charles Dickens, read by Nathaniel Parker

The Pickwick Papers by Charles Dickens, read by Dinsdale Landen

Bleak House by Charles Dickens, read by Beatie Edney and Ronald Pickup

PENGUIN AUDIOBOOKS

The Hound of the Baskervilles by Sir Arthur Conan Doyle, read by Freddie Jones

Middlemarch by George Eliot, read by Harriet Walter

Tom Jones by Henry Fielding, read by Robert Lindsay

The Great Gatsby by F. Scott Fitzgerald, read by Marcus D'Amico

Madame Bovary by Gustave Flaubert, read by Claire Bloom

Mary Barton by Elizabeth Gaskell, read by Clare Higgins

Jude the Obscure by Thomas Hardy, read by Samuel West

Far from the Madding Crowd by Thomas Hardy, read by Julie Christie

The Scarlet Letter by Nathaniel Hawthorne, read by Bob Sessions

Les Misérables by Victor Hugo, read by Nigel Anthony

A Passage to India by E. M. Forster, read by Tim Pigott-Smith

The Iliad by Homer, read by Derek Jacobi

The Dead and Other Stories by James Joyce, read by Gerard McSorley

On the Road by Jack Kerouac, read by David Carradine

Sons and Lovers by D. H. Lawrence, read by Paul Copley

The Prince by Niccolò Machiavelli, read by Fritz Weaver

Animal Farm by George Orwell, read by Timothy West

Rob Roy by Sir Walter Scott, read by Robbie Coltrane

Frankenstein by Mary Shelley, read by Richard Pasco

Of Mice and Men by John Steinbeck, read by Gary Sinise

Kidnapped by Robert Louis Stevenson, read by Robbie Coltrane

Dracula by Bram Stoker, read by Richard E. Grant

Gulliver's Travels by Jonathan Swift, read by Hugh Laurie

Vanity Fair by William Makepeace Thackeray, read by Robert Hardy

Lark Rise to Candleford by Flora Thompson, read by Judi Dench

The Invisible Man by H. G. Wells, read by Paul Shelley

Ethan Frome by Edith Wharton, read by Nathan Osgood

The Picture of Dorian Gray by Oscar Wilde, read by John Moffatt

Orlando by Virginia Woolf, read by Tilda Swinton

READ MORE IN PENGUIN

A CHOICE OF CLASSICS

Plautus	**The Pot of Gold and Other Plays**
	The Rope and Other Plays
Pliny	**The Letters of the Younger Pliny**
Pliny the Elder	**Natural History**
Plotinus	**The Enneads**
Plutarch	**The Age of Alexander** (Nine Greek Lives)
	The Fall of the Roman Republic (Six Lives)
	The Makers of Rome (Nine Lives)
	Plutarch on Sparta
	The Rise and Fall of Athens (Nine Greek Lives)
Polybius	**The Rise of the Roman Empire**
Procopius	**The Secret History**
Propertius	**The Poems**
Quintus Curtius Rufus	**The History of Alexander**
Sallust	**The Jugurthine War/The Conspiracy of Cataline**
Seneca	**Four Tragedies/Octavia**
	Letters from a Stoic
Sophocles	**Electra/Women of Trachis/Philoctetes/Ajax**
	The Theban Plays
Suetonius	**The Twelve Caesars**
Tacitus	**The Agricola/The Germania**
	The Annals of Imperial Rome
	The Histories
Terence	**The Comedies (The Girl from Andros/The Self-Tormentor/The Eunuch/Phormio/The Mother-in-Law/The Brothers)**
Thucydides	**History of the Peloponnesian War**
Virgil	**The Aeneid**
	The Eclogues
	The Georgics
Xenophon	**Conversations of Socrates**
	A History of My Times
	The Persian Expedition

READ MORE IN PENGUIN

A CHOICE OF CLASSICS

Hesiod/Theognis	**Theogony/Works and Days/Elegies**
Hippocrates	**Hippocratic Writings**
Homer	**The Iliad**
	The Odyssey
Horace	**Complete Odes and Epodes**
Horace/Persius	**Satires and Epistles**
Juvenal	**The Sixteen Satires**
Livy	**The Early History of Rome**
	Rome and Italy
	Rome and the Mediterranean
	The War with Hannibal
Lucretius	**On the Nature of the Universe**
Martial	**Epigrams**
Ovid	**The Erotic Poems**
	Heroides
	Metamorphoses
	The Poems of Exile
Pausanias	**Guide to Greece** (in two volumes)
Petronius/Seneca	**The Satyricon/The Apocolocyntosis**
Pindar	**The Odes**
Plato	**Early Socratic Dialogues**
	Gorgias
	The Last Days of Socrates (Euthyphro/ The Apology/Crito/Phaedo)
	The Laws
	Phaedrus and **Letters VII and VIII**
	Philebus
	Protagoras/Meno
	The Republic
	The Symposium
	Theaetetus
	Timaeus/Critias

READ MORE IN PENGUIN

A CHOICE OF CLASSICS

Armadale Wilkie Collins

Victorian critics were horrified by Lydia Gwilt, the bigamist, husband-poisoner and laudanum addict whose intrigues spur the plot of this most sensational of melodramas.

Aurora Leigh and Other Poems Elizabeth Barrett Browning

Aurora Leigh (1856), Elizabeth Barrett Browning's epic novel in blank verse, tells the story of the making of a woman poet, exploring 'the woman question', art and its relation to politics and social oppression.

Personal Narrative of a Journey to the Equinoctial Regions of the New Continent Alexander von Humboldt

Alexander von Humboldt became a wholly new kind of nineteenth-century hero – the scientist–explorer – and in *Personal Narrative* he invented a new literary genre: the travelogue.

The Pañćatantra Visnu Sarma

The Pañćatantra is one of the earliest books of fables and its influence can be seen in the *Arabian Nights*, the *Decameron*, the *Canterbury Tales* and most notably in the *Fables* of La Fontaine.

A Laodicean Thomas Hardy

The Laodicean of Hardy's title is Paula Power, a thoroughly modern young woman who, despite her wealth and independence, cannot make up her mind.

Brand Henrik Ibsen

The unsparing vision of a priest driven by faith to risk and witness the deaths of his wife and child gives *Brand* its icy ferocity. It was Ibsen's first masterpiece, a poetic drama composed in 1865 and published to tremendous critical and popular acclaim.

READ MORE IN PENGUIN

A CHOICE OF CLASSICS

Sylvia's Lovers Elizabeth Gaskell

In an atmosphere of unease the rivalries of two men, the sober tradesman Philip Hepburn, who has been devoted to his cousin Sylvia since her childhood, and the gallant, charming whaleship harpooner Charley Kinraid, are played out.

The Republic Plato

The best-known of Plato's dialogues, *The Republic* is also one of the supreme masterpieces of Western philosophy, whose influence cannot be overestimated.

Ethics Benedict de Spinoza

'Spinoza (1632–77),' wrote Bertrand Russell, 'is the noblest and most lovable of the great philosophers. Intellectually, some others have surpassed him, but ethically he is supreme.'

Virgil in English

From Chaucer to Auden, Virgil is a defining presence in English poetry. Penguin Classics' new series, Poets in Translation, offers the best translations in English, through the centuries, of the major Classical and European poets.

What is Art? Leo Tolstoy

Tolstoy wrote prolifically in a series of essays and polemics on issues of morality, social justice and religion. These culminated in *What is Art?*, published in 1898, in which he rejects the idea that art reveals and reinvents through beauty.

An Autobiography Anthony Trollope

A fascinating insight into a writer's life, in which Trollope also recorded his unhappy youth and his progress to prosperity and social recognition.

READ MORE IN PENGUIN

A CHOICE OF CLASSICS

Aeschylus	**The Oresteian Trilogy**
	Prometheus Bound/The Suppliants/Seven against Thebes/The Persians
Aesop	**Fables**
Ammianus Marcellinus	**The Later Roman Empire (AD 354–378)**
Apollonius of Rhodes	**The Voyage of Argo**
Apuleius	**The Golden Ass**
Aristophanes	**The Knights/Peace/The Birds/The Assemblywomen/Wealth**
	Lysistrata/The Acharnians/The Clouds
	The Wasps/The Poet and the Women/ The Frogs
Aristotle	**The Art of Rhetoric**
	The Athenian Constitution
	De Anima
	Ethics
	Poetics
Arrian	**The Campaigns of Alexander**
Marcus Aurelius	**Meditations**
Boethius	**The Consolation of Philosophy**
Caesar	**The Civil War**
	The Conquest of Gaul
Catullus	**Poems**
Cicero	**Murder Trials**
	The Nature of the Gods
	On the Good Life
	Selected Letters
	Selected Political Speeches
	Selected Works
Euripides	**Alcestis/Iphigenia in Tauris/Hippolytus**
	The Bacchae/Ion/The Women of Troy/ Helen
	Medea/Hecabe/Electra/Heracles
	Orestes and Other Plays